JN448704

BERNARD MALAMUD

THE ASSISTANT

WITH ESSAYS IN CRITICISM

Annotated with
Critical Introduction
by

Kwang-sik Hyon

SHINASA

Bernard Malamud

CONTENTS

CRITICAL INTRODUCTION

1. Bernard Malamud의 생애와 작품

Malamud는 1914년 아버지 Max Malamud와 어머니 Bertha Fidelman Malamud의 차남으로, New York의 Brooklyn구에서 태어났다. 그의 부모는 Russia로부터 이주해 온 유태인이었으며 Brooklyn구의 Flatbush에서 작은 식료품점을 경영하면서 가난한 생계를 이어 갔다. 그들은 빈곤하여 정규교육을 받지 못했지만, 아이들의 교육에는 열심이었고, 작가가 되려는 Malamud의 포부를 이해하고 격려를 아끼지 않았다. 어렸을 때의 Brooklyn구에서의 경험, 부모에 대한 깊은 애정, 이웃에 사는 유태인들에 대한 관찰 등은 후일 그의 창작생활에 많은 영향을 미쳤다.

1928년에서 1932년까지 그는 Erasmus Hall High School에 다녔으며 그 학교의 문예지에 수편의 단편소설을 발표하기도 했다. 1936년에 New City College를 졸업, 1942년에 Columbia University에서 Hardy의 *Dynasts*에 관한 논문으로 석사학위를 받았다. 졸업 후 New York에서 교사 자리를 찾았으나 그때는 대공황 후기라 일자리를 얻지 못하고, Washington, D.C.의 인구조사국에서 근무한 일도 있었고, 틈틈이 단편을 써서 발표하기도 했다.

1940년에서 1948년까지 그는 New York에 있는 모교 Erasmus Hall High School에서 야간에 영어를 가르치고 낮에는 창작에 열중하였다. 1945년에 이탈리아계의 여성 Ann de Chiara와 결혼했고 2년 후에 장남 Paul이 탄생했다. 1948년에서 1949년까지 Harlem High School에서 야간에 영어를 가르쳤으며, 사실적인 단편 "Black Is My Favorite Color"와 환상적인 단편 "Angel Levine" 등에는 흑인, 폴란드인, 기타 인종들과 접촉했던 그 당시의 경험이 나타나 있다.

1949년, 35세 때 Oregon 주립대학의 영문과 전임강사로 부임하여 1961년까지 12년간 근무했으며, 대부분 1학년 작문을 맡았고 때때로 문학개론, 단편소설론 등을 맡기도 했다. 전통을 중시하는, 기술, 농업계통의 대학에서 박사학위도 없는 작가지망의 교수 Malamud는, 상당히 고된 생활을 보낸 듯하며, 이 대학에서의 경험이 세번째 장편 *A New Life*의 소재가 되어 있다. 그는 이곳에서 창작활동에 열중하여 세 개의 장편을 완성했고 단편을 여러 편 발표했다.

1952년에 발표한 첫 장편 *The Natural*로서, 그는 미국문단의 주목을 끌게 되었으며, 1956년에 Partizan Review Fiction Fellowship을 받아 유럽에 여행하고 또 Rome에 체재할 기회를 얻게 되었다. 단편 "The Maid's Shoes", "The Lady of the Lake", "The Last Mohican", "Behold the Key" 등은 이탈리아에서의 견문과 경험이 그 소재로 되어 있다.

1957년에 출판된 두번째 장편 *The Assistant*로서 그는 미국문단의 주요작가가 되었고, 미국문예협회의 Rosenthal 상과 미국유태도서 협의회의 Daroff Fiction 상을 받았다.

그의 첫번째 단편집 *The Magic Barrel*은 1958년에 발표되어 문단의 호평을 받고 미국도서상을 수상했다.

1961년, 47세의 Malamud는 비유태적 환경에서 일하는 유태인 교사의 이야기 *A New Life*를 발표하고 Oregon 주립대학을 떠나 Vermont주의 Bennington College로 옮겨 어문학부 교수로서 소설과 문학강좌를 담당하게 되었다. 두번째 단편집 *Idiots First*는 1963년에 출간되었고 그 다음 해에 그는 미국문예 도서상 위원회의 위원이 되었다. 1965년에 France, Spain, Soviet Union 등을 여행하고 돌아와 그 다음 해에 네번째 장편 *The Fixer*를 발표했으며 이 작품으로 미국도서상과 Pulitzer 상을 받았다. 1969년, 여섯 편의 단편으로 이루어진 세번째 단편집 *Pictures of Fidelman: An Exhibition*이

출판되었고 1971년에는 다섯번째 장편 *The Tenants*를 발표했고 네번째 단편집 *Rembrandt's Hat*는 1973년에 나왔다. 자전소설(自傳小說) *Dubin's Lives*는 1979년에 발표되어 호평을 받았고 일곱번째 장편 *God's Grace*는 1982년에 출판되었다.

그는 1986년 3월, 향년 71세로 아직도 창작활동을 계속할 수 있는 아까운 나이에 세상을 떠났다.

2. 주인공 Frank의 변화와 성장
—— 강도가 유태교 신자로 ——

*The Assistant*의 줄거리를 훑어보면서 주인공이 고난의 과정을 통해 정신적으로 변화하고 성장해 가는 모습을 살펴보고자 한다.

이 작품의 주인공 Frank의 생애는 어려서부터 시련의 연속이었다. Frank가 태어난 지 1주일 후에 어머니는 사망했고 다섯 살 때에 아버지는 자취를 감춰 버려 그는 고아원에서 자라나게 된다. 이것은 *The Natural*의 Roy, *A New Life*의 Levin, *The Fixer*의 Yakov과 똑 같은 운명이다. 여덟 살 때에 양자로서 딴 집에 나가 살게 되었지만, 그 집 사람들에게 정이 들지 않아 거기서 뛰쳐나와 유랑생활을 하게 된다.

그러던 어느날 갑자기 기이한 생각이 머리에 떠오른다. 나쁜 짓을 하고 모험을 함으로써 돈을 벌어 왕자처럼 살아 보자는 생각이다. 그는 처음으로 인생의 목표를 정하고 직업을 결정할 단계에 이르렀는데, 그 목표란 범죄를 저질러 일확천금하겠다는 허황된 망상이었다. 남이야 희생이 되든 말든 돈만 벌면 된다는 무서운 탐욕과 이기주의에 사로잡힌 것이다. 자신이 능력있는 인물이고 남다른 무언가를 지녔다고 확신하는 자는, 그런 확신을 못 가진 못난 놈들에 비해 훨씬 나은 기회와 가능성이 있다고 믿게 된 것이다. 그러나 깡패인 Ward와 함께 유태인 가게를 털기로 한 그날밤 가게 안으로 들어가

입을 손수건으로 가렸을 때, 그는 이제껏 품은 생각이 어리석은 것이었음을 깨닫는다. 머리를 얻어 맞아 피투성이가 된 유태인 Morris를 보고, 그는 가장 크고 또 가장 씻기 어려운 죄를 범했음을 깨닫는다. 나쁜 짓을 해서라도 팔자를 고쳐 보겠다고 생각한 때부터 큰 잘못을 저질렀다고 깨달을 때까지 긴 시간이 경과된 것도 아니고 무슨 엄청난 경험이나 신비로운 계시를 받은 것도 아니다. 경솔하고 이기적인 생각에서 큰 잘못을 저질렀을 뿐이다. 가난한 유태인 Morris가 자기 때문에 중상을 입었다고 생각하게 되자 양심의 가책을 받아 줄곧 괴로와하는 것이다.

자기가 강도질한 사실을 감추고 Morris의 가게에서 점원으로 일하게 된 지 얼마 후에, 그는 강도질할 때 사용한 권총을 찾아 없애려고 Ward와 만난다. Ward는 그를 보자 다시 유태인 술장수 Karp의 가게를 털자고 유혹하지만 죄를 뉘우친 Frank는 깨끗이 거절한다. 그는 자기의 과오를 씻고 부상당한 Morris를 돕기 위해 가게에서 일하고 있으며, 훔쳐서 둘이 나눈 7불 50센트는 금전등록기에 반환했다고 말한다. 그러자 Ward는 조롱하는 말투로 "I never thought I would meet up with a goddam Salvation Army Soldier."라고 빈정댄다. Ward는 다시 "It's something else. I hear those Jew girls make nice ripe lays."라고 말한다. 그가 가게에서 일하는 것은 속죄할 목적에서가 아니라, Morris의 딸에게 접근할 음흉한 동기 때문이라고 Ward는 단정한다. Ward의 마음을 Evil Urge가 완전히 점령한 결과, 참회한 Frank의 마음과 속죄하려는 그의 동기를 이해할 수 없다. 참회할 줄 모르는 강도 Ward는 점점 악해지고 그의 말로는 비참해 질 수밖에 없다. 그는 후일 Morris의 가게 2층에 있는 Frank의 방에 들어와 술을 마시게 돈을 내놓으라고 강요하고, 응하지 않는다면 Morris에게 편지로 그가 강도였음을 폭로하겠다고 위협한다. Helen이 Frank와 데이트하기로 약속한 날 밤, 밤 늦게 혼자 공원에서 Frank를 기다리고 있을 때, Ward는 rape하려고 그녀에게 야수처럼 덤벼들지만 Frank에게 얻어 맞고 달아난다. 쌓이고 쌓인 죄의 보응(報應)을 받아 그는 당뇨병에 걸린다. 그 결과 술을 마시면 구역질이 나는데 그래도 술을 마시고 싶어 견딜 수 없다. 밤중에 그는 몰래 Karp의 술가게에 들어가 gin을 마시다가 담배에 불을 붙이고 아직 다 꺼지지 않은 성냥개비를 알콜 위에 던진다. 화재가 일어나자 그는 유리창으로 빠져나가려 했으나 철창에 걸려 타 죽고 만다.

Frank는 Ward와 달라 나쁜 짓을 한 후에 참회할 줄 아는 사람이며 특히 St. Francis의 이야기를 읽을 때마다 감명을 받아 울음이 터져 나온다고 말한다. Frank와 그가 사모하는 St. Francis는 유사한 점이 있다. 두 사람은 이름부터 Frank와 Francis로서 비슷하며, Frank가 수염이 많이 난 것처럼 St. Francis도 마찬가지다. St. Francis는 자기의 소유물을 다 남에게 주었으므로 그가 입은 'brown garment'는 그의 단벌 옷일 것이며, Frank가 입은 외투도 입고 잔 것같아 보이므로 그의 단벌 옷임에 틀림없다. St. Francis가 새들을 사랑하고 새들에게 전도한 것처럼 Frank도 새들을 사랑하고 먹을 것을 준다. 또 Frank가 돈을 탐하는 것도 사실이지만 한편 St. Francis의 청빈(淸貧)을 높이 평가하는 것으로 보아 돈 이외의 가치—신앙, 자선, 정직 등—도 중시하고 있음을 알 수 있다.

St. Francis를 존경하는 Frank는 Ward와 달라 마음속에 Good Urge가 살아 있어 참회할 줄 알기 때문에 정신적으로 성장할 가능성이 있다. Malamud는 Frank와 Ward라는 두 젊은이를 등장시켜 함께 강도질하게 만들지만, 그 후 죄책감으로 참회하느냐의 여부에 의해 완전히 다른 인생행로를 걷게 한다. 그는 전자를 정신적으로 변화시켜 진정한 유태인이 되게 하고, 후자를 타락을 거듭하여 멸망하고 마는 심승이 되게 한다. Judaism의 영향을 받은 Malamud는 이처럼 참회를 중시하고 있는 것이다.

Frank는 Ward와 함께 범한 자기의 강도죄를 회개하고 또 그 죄를 씻기 위해 Morris를 돕고 있지만, 한 번의 참회로 인하여 못된 습성을 완전히 버린 것은 아니다. Freedman의 말처럼 불의한 '옛생활'(old life)을 버리고 새 사람으로 재생하는 것은 하루 이틀로 되는 일이 아니다. 그는 Ida가 없는 틈을 타 상품을 판 돈에서 1불이나 1불 50센트를 자기 주머니에 몰래 집어 넣는 도둑질을 반복한다. 그는 과거에도 종종 느껴 본 일이지만 해서는 안 될 불의한 짓을 저지를 때마다, 비참한 느낌이 들면서도 동시에 '기묘한 즐거움'을 느끼는 것이다. 그는 Morris가 가게에 있어도 슬쩍 1불 정도를 훔치고, 자기의 능숙한 도둑 솜씨에 자신도 놀라 웃음을 금치 못하는 것이다. 그는 또 dumb-waiter를 타고 올라가 목욕하는 Helen의 나체를 훔쳐 보기도 하고, 그녀에게 말을 걸고 싶어 거짓말로 전화가 왔다고 속여 그녀를 불러낸다. Frank는 이런 못된 짓을 한 후 양심의 가책을 받아 괴로와하지만, 과단성 있게 자기의 악습을 끊어 버리지 못한다.

Helen과 Frank는 한 집에서 지내게 되자 점차 가까운 사이가 된다. 그들은 도서관과 공원에서 자주 만나, 과거의 경험담을 들려 주고 대학진학의 문제를 상의한다. 그러는 사이에 그들은 사랑하는 사이가 되었고 Frank는 그녀의 육체를 수차 요구하지만, Helen은 자기의 진정한 사랑을 확신할 때까지 결코 관계를 맺을 수 없다고 거절한다. 그녀는 Frank에게 정욕을 억제하는 힘, 즉 자제력을 기르라고 충고한다. Helen은 지난 여름 처음으로 Columbia 대학 대학원생 Net와 육체관계를 맺은 일이 있지만, 진정한 사랑도 없이 그런 관계를 맺었음을 뼈저리게 후회했던 것이다.

그 후 Frank는 자제하라는 그녀의 말을 자주 회상하지만 왜 그 말이 자기에게 깊은 감명을 주는지 그 이유를 깨닫지 못한다. 그러나 북을 두드리는 스틱처럼 그 말은 Frank의 머리 속에 계속 울려 오는 것이다. 그는 점차 자제력이라는 말이 지닌 의미와 미를 인식하게 되고 자기의 성격을 반성하기 시작하여 자제력 없이 가게에서 훔쳐 온 140여불을 몽땅 갚을 생각을 하게 된다. Frank는 우선 주머니에 있는 6불부터 금전등록기에 반환해 버린다. 그는 정신적으로 훌륭하게 자라나고 있는 것이다. 6불을 갚고 나니 마음속 Good Urge의 승리로 인해 기쁨이 파도처럼 그의 가슴에 밀려온다.

그런데 공교롭게도 바로 그 날, Helen으로부터 밤에 데이트를 하자고 전화가 온다. 주머니에 있던 6불을 금전등록기에 반환했기 때문에 데이트 비용이 없다. 하는 수 없이 1불을 다시 훔치다 Morris에게 발각되어 나가라는 명령을 받게 된다. 그동안 훔친 돈을 다 갚기로 결심하고 그대로 실천하기 시작했고 또 Helen과의 사랑도 무르익어 가는 마당에, 얄궂은 운명은 그를 또 다시 시련 속에 던져 버린 것이다.

그가 약속한 데이트장소에 가 보니 Ward가 Helen을 rape하려는 위험한 찰나였다. Ward를 때려 쫓아 버린 다음, 그녀를 가슴에 안았을 때, 앞으로 그녀를 만날 수 없으리라는 절망감이 엄습해 온다. 그는 Helen을 잃기 전에 육체관계를 맺어야겠다고 결심하고 그녀의 완강한 저항에도 불구하고 강제로 욕심을 채우고 만다. 그의 짐승 같은 행동은 그녀의 사랑을 그에 대한 증오와 저주로 바꾸어 놓는다. Helen의 사랑을 상실하고 Morris에게 추방된 Frank는 이제 아무도 의지할 사람이 없음을 절감한다.

"Morris의 세계에서는 모든 의지할 대상이 다 제거된 후 비로소 완전한 자기인식과 반성이 나타난다."고 William Freedman은 강조한 적이 있다. 인간은 막다른 골목에 이르렀을 때 비로소 참된 자아를 발견하고 진정한 참회를 한다는 뜻이다. 가게에서 추방된 후 Morris가 죽어 가게로 다시 돌아올 때까지의 기간은 고독과 번민 가운데 모든 잘못을 참회하는 기간이며, 또 참회에 의해 그가 정신적으로 자라나는 기간이다.

Frank를 변화시키는 또 다른 요인은, 자기의 강도죄를 Morris와 Helen에게 고백하려는 양심의 충동이다. 가게에서 일하게 된 후, Frank는 줄곧 자기의 강도죄를 Morris에게 고백하려 한다. 자기의 숨김없는 'true self'를 그에게 알려 주고 깨끗한 양심으로 새 출발을 하고 싶어 하지만 쫓겨날지 모른다는 불안 때문에 몇 번인가 고백하려다 못 하고 만다. 고백하려는 의욕을 더욱 자극한 것은 Helen에 대한 그의 사랑이다. Frank는 자기의 사랑이 순결하게 지속되기를 갈망하기 때문에 자신부터 정결한 사람이 되어야 겠다고 생각한다. 그러나 또 한편 이 고백을 듣고 Morris와 Helen이 어떻게 생각할지 몰라 감히 입 밖에 내놓지 못한다. Frank는 미루고 미루다가, 드디어 Morris의 두번째 추방명령을 받았을 때 이 고백을 하고 만다. 그러나 Frank가 강도였다는 사실을 자기는 이미 알고 있었다는 Morris의 말을 듣고 그는 깜짝 놀라고 만다. 그가 강도인 줄 알면서도, 당장 가게에서 내쫓지 아니한 Morris의 자비심에 Frank는 깊은 감명을 받는 것이다.

그의 정신적 변화와 성장을 촉구하는 요인으로서 참회, Helen의 충고, 고백 등 여러 가지가 있지만, 무었보다도 중요한 것은 Morris의 교육과 감화라고 할 수 있다. 물론 Frank도 Morris를 처음부터 자기의 spiritual teacher로 여기고 그의 가르침을 받으려 한 것은 아니다. 그는 가게에서 일하면서 Morris와 다른 유태인들을 관찰하고, 처음에는 그들이 태어날 때부터 고통받기로 운명지워진 특별한 종족일 거라고 경멸했던 것이다. '자학증' (masochism)에 걸린 사람들이 아닐까 하고 의심도 했다. Frank의 눈에는 유태인 Morris, Al Marcus, Breitbart들은 모두 다 Job처럼 고난의 운명을 지고 있는 것으로 비친다. 더러운 손가락으로 싸구려 상품을 고르는 손님들을 접대하며 오랜 세월을 보낸 Morris를 생각하면 Frank는 구역질이 나올 것 같다. 치명적인 병에 걸렸지만 그래도 살겠다고 버둥대는 안색이 창백한 종이장수 Al Marcus, 그리고 아내가 동생과 함께 가출한 후, 전구행상으로 전락된 옴장이 Bartbreit 등은, 모두 고난받기 위해 사는 존재로 Frank에겐 느껴지는 것이다.

하루는 Frank가 Morris에게 유태인과 유태인의 신앙에 대하여 질문한다. Morris는 유태인이 되기 위해 필요한 것은 'a good heart'뿐이라고 대답하고, 중요한 것은 율법인데 유태인은 반드시 이 율법을 지켜야 한다고 강조한다. Frank가 다시 유태인들은 어찌하여 그토록 심한 고통을 받느냐고 질문하자, Morris는 ". . . if a Jew don't suffer for the Law, he wil' suffer for nothing."이라고 답변한다. 불

의하고 부조리한 사회에서 성실하게 율법을 지키며 살아가려면 실패할 수밖에 없고 고난을 받을 수밖에 없다는 뜻이다. 유태인들은 자학증에 걸렸기 때문에, 즉 고통받는 것이 즐거워서 고난받는 것이 아니라 율법을 지키기 위해 고난을 받는다는 것이다. 따라서 실패하고 고난받는다는 것은 율법을 지키고 자기의 'moral integrity'를 보존하고 있다는 증거가 되는 셈이다. 하루는 Frank가 식료품 장사는 이문이 박하니 속임수를 써서 이윤을 더 남기는 게 좋겠다고 부추기자, Morris는 "Why should I steal from my customers ? "라고 정색을 하며 되묻는다. 남을 속여 돈을 벌고 부자가 되는 것보다 율법을 지키며 가난하게 사는 편이 훨씬 나은 생활이라고 Morris는 Frank에게 강조한다.

Morris는 율법에 따른 착한 행위를 Frank뿐 아니라 모든 사람에게 베푼다. 겨우 3센트의 빵 때문에 새벽잠을 깨워 놓는 Poland계 할머니에게도 언제나 불평 없이 가게를 열고 빵을 판다. 주정뱅이 어머니의 딸인 10세의 소녀가 가게에 들어와 외상을 달라고 하자 불경기인데다 외상값을 못 받을 것을 뻔히 알면서도 그는 버터, 빵, 식초 등을 준다. 불쌍한 전구행상 Breitbart가 가게에 들리면 그 피곤한 모습에 동정하여 레몬차 대접을 잊지 않았으며 아무리 심한 불경기에도 Al Marcus를 위해 약간의 종이 주문을 한다. Morris가 죽은 후 어떤 사람이 가게에 들어와 자기에게 외상을 준 상점주인은 Morris밖에 없었다고 말하고 Frank에게 11불을 갚는다.

Morris가 죽은 후 Frank가 가게를 떠맡게 되자 그도 스승의 본을 실천한다. 아침에 일찍 일어나 Poland계 할머니에게 3센트어치 빵을 판다. 전구행상 Breitbart가 무거운 전구 상자를 끌며 가게에 들어오자, 레몬차를 대접한다. 한번은 Morris에게 70불 이상 외상을 진 칠장이 Carl에게 외상값을 받으러 갔는데 그 집 아이들의 굶주린 모습을 보고 다시 돌아와, 자기 돈 3불을 꺼내어 그의 아내에게 주려고 달려간다. Morris가 죽은 후 두 모녀를 위해 쉬지 않고 일하는 것도 스승인 Morris에게 배운 율법과 Morris의 신세를 갚겠다는 결심 때문이다. 그는 Morris의 생전의 소원이던 Helen의 대학교육을 위해 전력을 기울인다. 낮에는 손님을 더 끌려고 새로운 요리를 만들어 팔고, 밤에는 coffee shop의 counterman으로 일하여 매주 35불을 번다. 그는 야간대학에 다니는 Helen의 학비를 대려고 매월 90불이라는 엄청난 가게세를 Ida에게 꼬박꼬박 지불한다. 자신을 위해서는 최소한의 필요한 경비만 지불할 뿐 돈을 아끼려고 겨울에도 내복 없이 지낸다. 그는 아직 젊지만 밤낮으로 일이 고되어 극심한 피로를 느낀다. 그래도 Frank는 Morris의 생애에 의미를 주기 위해 Helen이 계속 대학에 다니도록 끈질기게 일한다. 그는 남을 위해 희생하는 종교적인 '새생활'을 영위하고 있는 것이다.

그런데 Frank가 진심으로 사랑하는 Helen은 공원에서 그가 rape한 이래 줄곧 그를 증오하고 멸시한다. 그녀는 대학원에 다니는 Nat와 다시 친숙해져 자주 데이트 하고 야간 드라이브를 즐기며 가게의 hall에서 포옹하고 키스한다. Frank의 마음은 질투심으로 찢어지는 듯하다. "Jesus," he said, "why am I killing myself so ?" 희생하고 봉사하려는 정신보다 질투심이 더 강해지자, 그는 절대로 하지 않겠다고 결심한 나쁜 짓을 다시 하기 시작한다. Helen의 나체를 또 몰래 훔쳐 보고 손님이 저울을 지켜보지 않을 때 그들을 속이고 거스름돈을 덜 주기도 한다.

그러나 Frank는 이내 마음을 고쳐 모든 나쁜 짓을 하지 않기로 결심하고 그대로 실천한다.

약 2년 반 못된 짓을 하고 다시 뉘우치는 과정을 반복하다 드디어 그는 이 악습을 완전히 버림으로써 정신적으로 바람직한 변화를 이룩한 것이다. 4월 어느 날 Frank는 Morris와 같은 유태교 신자가 되려고 병원에 가서 할례를 받는다. 할례는 믿음의 조상 Abraham으로부터 시작된 의식으로서 '육의 더러움을 벗는 성결의 표적'이다. Freedman은 할례를 율법의 구속에 따를 것을 다짐하기 위해 유태인이 신과 맺은 계약의 표시라고 본다.

Frank는 'uncircumcised dog', 또는 'undisciplined beast'로부터

할례받은 진짜 유태인으로 변한 것이다. 인생의 목표도 종교도 없는 부랑자이자 강도가, Morris의 곁에서 1년 반을 배우고 또 홀로 1년간 가게를 경영하면서 성숙한 사람이 되어 진짜 유태교 신자로 재생한 것이다.

이상으로서 *The Assistant*의 줄거리를 훑어보고 주인공이 고난의 과정을 거쳐 정신적으로 성장해 가는 모습을 살펴보았다.

이 작품 안에는 여러 가지 주제가 들어 있지만 그 중에도 가장 중요한 주제는 인간은 변화할 수 있다는 것이다. Ward처럼 악하게 변할 수도 있고 Frank처럼 나쁜 짓을 반복하면서 점차 선하게 변할 수도 있다는 것이다. 악하게 변하느냐 선하게 변하느냐의 갈림길은 결국 Judaism에서 말하는 두 Urge, 즉 마음속의 Good Urge와 Evil Urge의 투쟁에 달려있으며 Good Urge가 Evil Urge를 극복할 때 선이 승리하게 되는 것이다. Sandy Cohen은 Malamud가 인간의 '선천적 선'(the inherent goodness)과 완전가능성을 믿고 있다고 말했는데, 결국 이 말은 인간은 자신의 노력에 의해 Evil Urge를 극복하고 신이 만든 본래의 상태로 변하여 신과 같은 경지로 발전할 수 있다는 뜻이며, 이 사상도 Judaism에서 연유된 것이다. Malamud는 유태인이긴 하나 Judaism의 신자가 아닌 secular Jew에 불과하다. 그러나 Malamud는 어려서부터 유태인들의 사회에서 자라나 Judaism의 영향을 받았고, 구약성경 특히 Job기에 의해 깊은 감명을 받았기 때문에 그의 작품에는 Judaism의 사상이 깊숙이 배여 있다.

부랑생활, 강도질, 좀도둑질, 강간 등 온갖 나쁜 짓을 범해 온 Frank도 유태인 Morris의 교육과 Helen의 충고를 받아들이고, 고난 중에도 착해 지려고 노력한 결과 마침내 Morris 같은 진짜 유태인으로 변한 것이다. 이 작품에는, 인간은 원래 신의 형상대로 만들어졌고 인간에게는 Good Urge와 율법이 주어졌기 때문에, 자신의 노력에 의해 착하게 변하고 무한히 성장할 수 있다는 Judaism의 사상이 충실히 반영되어 있는 것이다.

THE TEXT

1

The early November street was dark though night had ended, but the wind, to the grocer's surprise, already clawed.* It flung his apron into his face as he bent for the two milk cases at the curb.* Morris Bober dragged the heavy boxes to the door, panting.* A large brown bag of hard rolls stood in the doorway along with the sour-faced, gray-haired Poilisheh* huddled there, who wanted one.

"What's the matter so late?"

"Ten after six," said the grocer.

"Is cold," she complained.

Turning the key in the lock he let her in. Usually he lugged in* the milk and lit the gas radiators, but the Polish woman was impatient. Morris poured the bag of rolls into a wire basket on the counter and found an unseeded one* for her. Slicing it in halves,* he wrapped it in white store paper. She tucked the roll into* her cord market bag and left three

---

***the wind . . . already clawed**:「바람은 벌써 살을 에는 듯했다」

***curb**=kerb:「길가의 연석(緣石), 차도와 인도(人道)의 사이를 구분하여 놓아둔 돌」

***dragged the heavy boxes to the door, panting**:「헐떡이며 무거운 상자를 문간까지 날고 갔다」

***the sour-faced, gray-haired Poilisheh**:「상을 찡그린 백발의 폴란드계 할머니」

***lug in**:「끌어들이다」 lug=draw, pull

***an unseeded one**:「씨앗이 들어 있지 않은 빵」

***Slicing it in halves**:「두 조각이 나게 벤 다음」

***tucked the roll into ~**:「빵을 ~안에 밀어 넣었다」 tuck into=thrust into

pennies on the counter. He rang up the sale on an old noisy cash register,* smoothed and put away the bag the rolls had come in,* finished pulling in the milk, and stored the bottles at the bottom of the refrigerator. He lit the gas radiator at the front of the store and went into the back to light the one there.*

He boiled up coffee in a blackened enamel pot* and sipped* it, chewing on a roll, not tasting what he was eating.* After he had cleaned up he waited; he waited for Nick Fuso, the upstairs tenant, a young mechanic who worked in a garage in the neighborhood. Nick came in every morning around seven for twenty cents' worth of ham and a loaf of bread.

But the front door opened and a girl of ten entered, her face pinched and eyes excited.* His heart held no welcome for her.*

"My mother says," she said quickly, "can you trust her till tomorrow for* a pound of butter, loaf of rye bread and a small bottle of cider vinegar?"

He knew the mother. "No more trust."

The girl burst into tears.

Morris gave her a quarter-pound of butter, the bread and

***He rang up the sale on an old noisy cash register**:「그는 판 돈을 소리가 요란한 구식 금전등록기에 넣었다」

***smoothed and put away the bag the rolls had come in**:「빵이 들어간 봉지를 펴서 치우고」

***light the one there**:「거기에 있는 가스 난로에 점화했다」 the one=the gas radiator

***a blackened enamel pot**:「시커멓게 그을린 에나멜 남비」

***sip**=drink little by little

***not tasting what he was eating**:「먹는 것을 맛보지도 않고」

***a girl of ten entered, her face pinched and eyes excited**:「얼굴은 마르고 눈엔 흥분한 빛을 띄고, 10세 가량의 소녀가 들어왔다」 her face 이하는 독립분사구문임.

***His heart held no welcome for her**:「그 소녀가 들어오는 것이 반갑지 않았다」

***trust her till tomorrow for ~**:「내일까지 그녀에게 ~을 외상으로 주다」

vinegar. He found a penciled spot on the worn counter,* near the cash register, and wrote a sum under "Drunk Woman."* The total now came to $2.03, which he never hoped to see.* But Ida would nag if she noticed a new figure, so he reduced the amount to $1.61. His peace—the little he lived with—was worth forty-two cents.*

He sat in a chair at the round wooden table in the rear of the store and scanned, with raised brows, yesterday's Jewish paper that he had already thoroughly read. From time to time he looked absently through the square windowless window cut through the wall,* to see if anybody had by chance come into the store. Sometimes when he looked up from his newspaper, he was startled to see a customer standing silently at the counter.

Now the store looked like a long dark tunnel.

The grocer sighed and waited. Waiting he thought he did poorly.* When times were bad time was bad.* It died as he waited, stinking in his nose.

A workman came in for a fifteen-cent can of King Oscar Norwegian sardines.

Morris went back to waiting. In twenty-one years the store

***a penciled spot on the worn counter**:「낡은 카운터 위의 연필로 써 놓은 곳」

***wrote a sum under "Drunk Woman"**:「"주정뱅이 여자"라고 기록된 밑에다 그 금액을 써 넣었다」

***which he never hoped to see**:「(그 금액을) 지불받으리라고는 전혀 기대하지 않았다」

***His peace—the little he lived with—was worth forty-two cents**:「그의 마음의 평화는 비록 작은 것이기는 하나—42센트의 가치는 있었다.」

***the square windowless window cut through the wall**:「벽에 뚫린 창문 아닌 네모난 창구멍」 *e.g.* a small windowless anteroo「작은 창문 없는 곁방」

***Waiting he thought he did poorly**:「기다리면서, 그는 자기가 장사를 제대로 못한다고 생각했다」

***When times were bad time was bad**:「불경기일 때는 매기(買氣)가 없다」 hard (bad) times「불경기」 good times「호경기」

had changed little. Twice he had painted all over, once added new shelving. The old-fashioned double windows at the front a carpenter had made into a large single one. Ten years ago the sign hanging outside fell to the ground but he had never replaced it. Once, when business hit a long good spell, he had had the wooden icebox ripped out and a new white refrigerated showcase put in.* The showcase stood at the front in line with* the old counter and he often leaned against it as he stared out of the window. Otherwise the store was the same. Years ago it was more a delicatessen; now, though he still sold a little delicatessen, it was more a poor grocery.

A half-hour passed. When Nick Fuso failed to appear, Morris got up and stationed himself at the front window, behind a large cardboard display sign the beer people had rigged up in an otherwise empty window.* After a while the hall door opened, and Nick came out in a thick, hand-knitted green sweater. He trotted around the corner and soon returned carrying a bag of groceries. Morris was now visible at the window. Nick saw the look on his face but didn't look long. He ran into the house, trying to make it seem it was the wind that was chasing him.* The door slammed behind him, a loud door.

***when business . . . put in**:「오래동안 경기가 좋았을 때 그는 나무로 된 아이스박스를 치우고 새 흰 색 냉장고 진열함을 들여놓았다」

※ he (s) had had (v)···ice-box (o) ripped (oc) out and···showcase (o) put (oc) in : 사역의 구문임.

***in line with ~**:「~와 일직선으로」

***a large cardboard display sign . . . empty window**:「(그것이 없다면) 빈 창문에 불과한 곳에 맥주회사 사람들이 임시변통으로 달아 준 큰 판지광고판」 rig up=construct as a makeshift:「임시변통으로 만들다」

***trying to make it seem it was the wind that was chasing him**:「그를 몰아치는 것이 바로 바람인 것처럼 보이게 하면서」 make 다음의 it는 it was . . . him의 명사절임. seem 다음에 that가 생략됨.

The grocer gazed into the street. He wished fleetingly that he could once more be out in the open, as when he was a boy —never in the house, but the sound of the blustery wind frightened him. He thought again of selling the store but who would buy? Ida still hoped to sell. Every day she hoped. The thought caused him grimly to smile, although he did not feel like smiling.* It was an impossible idea so he tried to put it out of his mind. Still, there were times when he went into the back, poured himself a spout of coffee and pleasantly thought of selling.* Yet if he miraculously did, where would he go, where? He had a moment of uneasiness as he pictured himself without a roof over his head. There he stood in all kinds of weather, drenched in rain, and the snow froze on his head. No, not for an age* had he lived a whole day in the open. As a boy, always running in the muddy, rutted streets* of the village, or across the fields, or bathing with the other boys in the river; but as a man, in America, he rarely saw the sky. In the early days when he drove a horse and wagon, yes, but not since his first store. In a store you were entombed.*

The milkman drove up to the door in his truck and hurried in, a bull, for his empties.* He lugged out* a caseful and

---

***The thought caused him grimly to smile, although he did not feel like smiling**:「그는 미소하고 싶은 마음은 없었지만 그 생각을 하니 저절로 쓴 미소가 떠올랐다」

***Still, there were times . . . selling**:「그래도 이따금 뒷방에 들어가서 커피 한 잔을 분수처럼 쏟으며 팔 생각을 즐겁게 생각해 볼 때도 있었다」 spout=분류, 분수

***an age**=long time「오래동안」

***As a boy, always running in the muddy, rutted streets**:「소년시절에는 바퀴 자국이 난 진흙 길을 항상 뛰어다니며」

***In a store you were entombed**:「일단 가게에서 일하게 되면, 무덤 속에 묻히는 신세가 되는 것이다」

***hurried in, a bull, for his empties**:「빈 병을 가지러 황소처럼 힘차게 들어왔다」

***lug out**=drag out「끌어내다」

returned with two half-pints of light cream.* Then Otto Vogel, the meat provisions man, entered, a bushy-mustached German carrying a smoked liverwurst* and string of wieners* in his oily meat basket. Morris paid cash for the liverwurst; from a German he wanted no favors.* Otto left with the wieners. The bread driver, new on the route,* exchanged three fresh loaves for three stale and walked out without a word. Leo, the cake man, glanced hastily at the package cake on top of the refrigerator and called, "See you Monday, Morris."

Morris didn't answer.

Leo hesitated. "Bad all over, Morris."*

"Here is the worst."

"See you Monday."

A young housewife from close by bought sixty-three cents' worth; another came in for forty-one cents'. He had earned his first cash dollar for the day.

Breitbart, the bulb peddler,* laid down his two enormous cartons of light bulbs and diffidently entered the back.

"Go in," Morris urged. He boiled up some tea and served it in a thick glass, with a slice of lemon. The peddler eased himself into a chair,* derby hat and coat on,* and gulped the

---

***two half-pints of light cream**:「반 파인트짜리 크림 두 병」 pint=0.47 liter
***a smoked liverwurst**:「훈제한 간(肝)소시지」
***string of wieners**:「위너 소시지 한 줄」
***from a German he wanted no favors**:「독일인으로부터 외상으로 물건을 들여놓고 싶지 않았다」
***new on the route**:「처음 이곳으로 오는 길에」 on the route=en route「도중에」
***Bad all over, Morris**:「모리스, 어디나 다 불경기죠」
***the bulb peddler**:「전구행상인(電球行商人)」
***eased himself into a chair**:「의자에 편히 앉았다」
***derby hat and coat on**:「중산모자를 쓰고 코트를 입고」 derby 앞에 with를 보충할 것.

hot tea, his Adam's apple bobbing.

"So how goes now?" asked the grocer.

"Slow,"* shrugged Breitbart.

Morris sighed. "How is your boy?"

Breitbart nodded absently, then picked up the Jewish paper and read. After ten minutes he got up, scratched all over, lifted across his thin shoulders the two large cartons tied together with clothesline* and left.

Morris watched him go.

The world suffers. *He* felt every schmerz.*

At lunchtime Ida came down. She had cleaned the whole house.

Morris was standing before the faded couch, looking out of the rear window at the back yards. He had been thinking of Ephraim.

His wife saw his wet eyes.

"So stop sometime, please."* Her own grew wet.*

He went to the sink, caught cold water in his cupped palms and dipped his face into it.*

"The Italyener," he said, drying himself, "bought this morning across the street."

She was irritated. "Give him for twenty-nine dollars five

***Slow**:「형편 없어」 불경기라는 뜻.

***lifted across his thin shoulders . . . with clotheslines**:「빨랫줄로 함께 묶은 큰 종이 상자 두 개를 여윈 어깨에 메었다」

****He* felt every schmerz**:「그는 온갖 괴로움을 자기 한 몸에 느꼈다」 der Schmerz「고통, 슬픔, 상심」

***So stop sometime, please**:「이제 좀 울지 마시구려」

***Her own grew wet**:「그녀의 눈도 눈물이 나오고 있었다」

***caught cold water in his cupped palms and dipped his face into it**:「손바닥을 오목하게 하여 찬 물을 받아 그 안에 얼굴을 적시었다」

rooms so he should spit in your face."*

"A cold water flat,"* he reminded her.

"You put in gas radiators."

"Who says he spits? This I didn't say."

"You said something to him not nice?"

"Me?"

"Then why he went across the street?"

"Why? Go ask him," he said angrily.

"How much you took in till now?"*

"Dirt."*

She turned away.

He absent-mindedly scratched a match and lit a cigarette.

"Stop with the smoking," she nagged.

He took a quick drag, clipped the butt with his thumb nail* and quickly thrust it under his apron into his pants pocket. The smoke made him cough. He coughed harshly, his face lit like a tomato. Ida held her hands over her ears. Finally he brought up a gob of phlegm* and wiped his mouth with his handkerchief, then his eyes.

"Cigarettes," she said bitterly. "Why don't you listen what the doctor tells you?"

"Doctors," he remarked.

***Give him for twenty-nine dollars five rooms so he should spit in your face**:「29 달러의 방세로 방을 다섯 개나 주었더니 이제 그는 당신 얼굴에 침을 뱉는구려」

***A cold water flat**:「찬물밖에 나오지 않는 방이니까」

***How much you took in till now?**:「지금까지 얼마나 벌었수?」

***Dirt**:「형편 없어」

***He took a quick drag, clipped the butt with his thumb nail**:「그는 한 모금 급히 빨더니 엄지손톱으로 담배꽁초를 끊고」

***he brought up a gob of phlegm**:「그는 가래침을 뱉았다」 bring up=vomit「내뱉다」 gob「(가래침 따위의) 덩어리(lump)」

Afterward he noticed the dress she was wearing. "What is the picnic?"*

Ida said, embarrassed, "I thought to myself maybe will come today the buyer."

She was fifty-one, nine years younger than he, her thick hair still almost all black. But her face was lined, and her legs hurt when she stood too long on them, although she now wore shoes with arch supports.* She had waked that morning resenting the grocer for having dragged her, so many years ago, out of a Jewish neighborhood into this. She missed to this day their old friends and landsleit*—lost for parnusseh unrealized. That was bad enough, but on top of their isolation, the endless worry about money embittered her.* She shared unwillingly the grocer's fate though she did not show it and her dissatisfaction went no farther than nagging*—her guilt that* she had talked him into* a grocery store when he was in the first year of evening high school, preparing, he had said, for pharmacy.* He was, through the years, a hard man to move.* In the past she could sometimes resist him, but the

---

***What is the picnic?**:「뭔가 좋은 일이 있어？」 picnic=something specially agreeable

***shoes with arch supports**:「발바닥의 오목한 곳에 보첨을 댄 구두」

***landsleit**=landsman (동향인)의 복수.

***the endless worry about money embittered her**:「돈에 대한 끊임없는 걱정이 그녀를 짜증나게 했다」

***her dissatisfaction went no farther than nagging**:「그녀는 불만을 디뜨러 봤자 성가신 잔소리 정도였다」

***her guilt that**=her guilt was that

***talk～into**:「설득하여 ～하게 하다」

***when he was . . . for pharmacy**:「그의 말에 의하면 약학공부를 한다고 야간고등학교 1학년에 다니고 있을 때」

***He was, through the years, a hard man to move**:「여러 해를 지내면서도 그의 마음은 좀처럼 동요하지 않았다」

weight of his endurance was too much for her now.*

"A buyer," Morris grunted, "will come next Purim."*

"Don't be so smart.* Karp telephoned him."

"Karp," he said in disgust. "Where he telephoned—the cheapskate?"*

"Here."

"When?"

"Yesterday. You were sleeping."

"What did he told him?"

"For sale a store—yours, cheap."

"What do you mean cheap?"

"The key is worth now nothing.* For the stock and the fixtures that they are worth also nothing,* maybe three thousand, maybe less."

"I paid four."

"Twenty-one years ago," she said irritably. "So don't sell, go in auction."*

"He wants the house too?"

"Karp don't know. Maybe."

"Big mouth.* Imagine a man that they held him up four times in the last three years and he still don't take in a

---

***the weight of his endurance was too much for her now**:「그의 인내심 때문에 그녀의 반항도 쓸모가 없었다」

***Purim**: 옛날 Persia왕의 신하 Haman의 유태인 학살계획이 수포로 돌아간 유태인의 축제일, 유태력으로 6월 14일 (구약성서 에스더 9:21).

***Don't be so smart**:「너무 똑똑한 체하지 마세요」

***the cheapskate**=the stingy fellow「구두쇠」

***The key is worth now nothing**:「권리금은 이제 없는 거나 마찬가지죠」

***For the stock and the fixtures that they are worth also nothing**:「재고품과 내부설비 등 다 합쳐도 얼마 되지 않아요」

***So don't sell, go in auction**:「그러니 팔지 말고 경매에 붙이세요」

***Big mouth**:「허풍쟁이」

telephone.* What he says ain't worth a cent. He promised me he wouldn't put in a grocery around the corner, but what did he put?—a grocery. Why does he bring me buyers? Why didn't he keep out the German around the corner?"*

She sighed. "He tries to help you now because he feels sorry for you."

"Who needs his sorrow?" Morris said. "Who needs him?"

"So why *you* didn't have the sense to make out of your grocery a wine and liquor store when came out the licenses?"*

"Who had cash for stock?"

"So if you don't have, don't talk."

"A business for drunken bums."*

"A business is a business. What Julius Karp takes in* next door in a day we don't take in in two weeks."

But Ida saw he was annoyed and changed the subject.

"I told you to oil the floor."

"I forgot."

"I asked you special. By now would be dry."*

"I will do later."

"Later the customers will walk in the oil and make everything dirty."

"What customers?" he shouted. "Who customers? Who

***Imagine a man . . . telephone**:「지난 3년 동안 강도를 세 번이나 만나고서도 전화를 놓지 않는 등신을 생각해 봐」

***Why didn't he keep out the German around the corner?**:「왜 그는 길 모퉁이에 독일인이 못 들어오게 막지 못했어?」 keep out=prevent from coming in, shut out

***So why . . . licenses?**:「그럼 왜 당신은 영업허가가 나왔을 때, 식료품점을 주류판매점으로 바꿀 만한 센스가 없었소?」

***A business for drunken bums**:「주정뱅이 상대의 장사에 불과해」

***take in**:「벌다」

***I asked you special. By now would be dry**:「당신에게 특별히 부탁드렸죠. (기름 칠했었으면) 지금쯤 말랐을 거에요」

comes in here?"

"Go," she said quietly. "Go upstairs and sleep. I will oil myself."

But he got out the oil can and mop and oiled the floor until the wood shone darkly. No one had come in.

She had prepared his soup. "Helen left this morning without breakfast."

"She wasn't hungry."

"Something worries her."*

He said with sarcasm,* "What worries her?" Meaning: the store, his health, that most of her meager wages went to keep up payments on the house;* that she had wanted a college education but had got instead a job she disliked. Her father's daughter, no wonder she didn't feel like eating.*

"If she will only get married," Ida murmured.

"She will get."

"Soon." She was on the verge of tears.*

He grunted.

"I don't understand why she don't see Nat Pearl anymore. All summer they went together like lovers."

"A showoff."*

"He'll be someday a rich lawyer."

"I don't like him."

***Something worries her**:「무언가 고민거리가 있는 모양이죠」

***with sarcasm**:「비꼬아서」

***went to keep up payments on the house**:「집 값의 월부금을 지불하는 데 사용되었다」 *e.g.* monthly payments on a television set「텔레비전의 월부지불액」

***Her father's daughter, no wonder she didn't feel like eating**:「그런 아비의 딸이니 밥맛이 없는 것도 당연한 일이었다」

***She was on the verge of tears**:「그녀는 곧 울음을 터뜨릴 것만 같았다」 of 다음에 bursting into가 생략되어 있음.

***A showoff**:「뽐내기 좋아하는 놈」

"Louis Karp also likes her. I wish she will give him a chance."*

"A stupe," Morris said, "like the father."

"Everybody is a stupe but not Morris Bober."

He was staring out at the back yards.

"Eat already and go to sleep," she said impatiently.

He finished the soup and went upstairs. The going up was easier than coming down. In the bedroom, sighing, he drew down the black window shades. He was half asleep, so pleasant was the anticipation.* Sleep was his one true refreshment; it excited him to go to sleep. Morris took off his apron, tie and trousers, and laid them on a chair. Sitting at the edge of the sagging wide bed, he unlaced his misshapen shoes and slid under the cold covers in shirt, long underwear and white socks.* He nudged his eye into the pillow* and waited to grow warm. He crawled toward sleep. But upstairs Tessie Fuso was running the vacuum cleaner, and though the grocer tried to blot the incident out* of his mind, he remembered Nick's visit to the German and on the verge of sleep felt bad.

He recalled the bad times he had lived through, but now times were worse than in the past; now they were impossible. His store was always a marginal one, up today, down tomorrow—as the wind blew.* Overnight business could go down

---

***I wish she will give him a chance**:「Louis Karp가 접근할 수 있도록 그 애가 기회를 주었으면 좋겠는데」

***He was half asleep, so pleasant was the anticipation**:「그는 벌써 반쯤 잠이 든 상태였다. 잠 잘 기대는 이처럼 즐거운 것이었다」

***slid under the cold covers in shirt, long underwear and white socks**:「셔츠와 긴 내의를 입고 흰 양말을 신은 채로 싸늘한 이불 속으로 들어갔다」

***He nudged his eye into the pillow**:「그는 눈을 베개에 살짝 대었다」

***blot ~ out**=wipe ~ out「지워 버리다」

***His store was always a marginal one . . . the wind blew**:「그의 상점의 형편은 항상

enough to hurt; yet as a rule it slowly recovered—sometimes it seemed to take forever—went up, not high enough to be really *up,* only not down. When he had first bought the grocery it was all right for the neighborhood; it had got worse as the neighborhood had.* Yet even a year ago, staying open seven days a week, sixteen hours a day, he could still eke out* a living. What kind of living?—a living; you lived. Now, though he toiled the same hard hours, he was close to bankruptcy, his patience torn.* In the past when bad times came he had somehow lived through them, and when good times returned, they more or less returned to him. But now, since the appearance of H. Schmitz across the street ten months ago, all times were bad.

Last year a broken tailor, a poor man with a sick wife, had locked up his shop and gone away, and from the minute of the store's emptiness Morris had felt a gnawing anxiety.* He went with hesitation to Karp, who owned the building, and asked him to please keep out another grocery.* In this kind of neighborhood one was more than enough. If another squeezed in they would both starve. Karp answered that the neighborhood was better than Morris gave it credit* (for schnapps, thought the grocer), but he promised he would look for

---

한계선에 놓여 있었고 바람 부는 대로 오늘은 좀 올랐다가 내일이면 또 떨어졌다」

***it had got worse as the neighborhood had**:「인근 일대에 매기가 없어져 그 가게의 형편도 악화되어 갔다」 had 다음에 got worse를 넣어서 해석할 것.

***eke out**=spin out「(생계를) 근근히 이어가다」

***his patience torn**:「인내력도 사라지고 말았다」 patience 다음에 was가 생략되었음.

***from the minute of the store's emptiness Morris had felt a gnawing anxiety**:「가게 문이 닫힌 때부터 모리스는 애가 타기 시작했다」

***asked him to please keep out another grocery**:「다른 식료품점이 들어오지 못하게 해 달라고 간청했다」

***gave it credit**=believed

another tailor or maybe a shoemaker, to rent to. He said so but the grocer didn't believe him. Yet weeks went by and the store stayed empty. Though Ida pooh-poohed* his worries, Morris could not overcome his underlying dread. Then one day, as he daily expected, there appeared a sign in the empty store window, announcing the coming of a new fancy delicatessen and grocery.

Morris ran to Karp. "What did you do to me?"*

The liquor dealer said with a one-shouldered shrug, "You saw how long stayed empty the store. Who will pay my taxes? But don't worry," he added, "he'll sell more delicatessen but you'll sell more groceries. Wait, you'll see he'll bring you in customers."

Morris groaned; he knew his fate.

Yet as the days went by, the store still sitting empty —emptier, he found himself thinking maybe the new business would never materialize.* Maybe the man had changed his mind. It was possible he had seen how poor the neighborhood was and would not attempt to open the new place. Morris wanted to ask Karp if he had guessed right but could not bear to humiliate himself further.*

Often after he had locked his grocery at night, he would go secretly around the corner and cross the quiet street. The empty store, dark and deserted, was one door to the left of the

---

***pooh-pooh**=treat (an idea) with contempt, laugh at 「비웃다」

***What did you do to me?**:「너는 나를 망쳐 놓을 작정인가?」라는 뜻.

***he found himself thinking maybe the new business would never materialize**:「그 새 가게가 결코 나타나지 않을 거라고 스스로 생각하고 있었다」 materialize=be realized, be carried out

***could not bear to humiliate himself further**:「그는 더 이상 망신당할 수 없었다」 humiliate oneself「면목을 잃다, 망신당하다」

corner drugstore;* and if no one was looking the grocer would peer through its dusty window, trying to see through shadows whether the emptiness had changed. For two months it stayed the same, and every night he went away reprieved.* Then one time—after he saw that Karp was, for once,* avoiding him—he spied a web of shelves sprouting from the rear wall,* and that shattered the hope he had climbed into.

In a few days the shelves stretched many arms along the other walls, and soon the whole tiered and layered place glowed with new paint.* Morris told himself to stay away but he could not help coming nightly to inspect, appraise, then guess the damage, in dollars, to himself. Each night as he looked, in his mind he destroyed what had been built, tried to make of it nothing,* but the growth was too quick. Every day the place flowered with new fixtures—streamlined counters, the latest refrigerator, fluorescent lights, a fruit stall, a chromium cash register; then from the wholesalers arrived a mountain of cartons and wooden boxes of all sizes, and one night there appeared in the white light a stranger, a gaunt German with a German pompadour,* who spent the silent night hours, a dead cigar stuck in his teeth, packing out

---

***one door to the left of the corner drugstore**:「길 모퉁이 약방의 왼쪽」

***he went away reprieved**:「일시 모면된 느낌으로 돌아갔다」

***for once**:「특별히」

***he spied a web of shelves sprouting from the rear wall**:「뒷벽에서 여러 겹의 선반이 튀어나와 있음을 발견했다」

***the whole tiered and layered place glowed with new paint**:「계단식으로 겹겹이 선반을 맨 온 장소는 페인트칠을 새로 하여 환히 빛나고 있었다」

***tried to make of it nothing**:「그것이 아무 소용 없을 거라고 생각하려 했다」 make of=think of, understand by

***a gaunt German with a German pompadour**:「독일식으로 머리를 빗어 올린 호리호리한 독일인」

symmetrical rows of brightly labeled cans,* jars, gleaming bottles. Though Morris hated the new store, in a curious way he loved it too, so that sometimes as he entered his own old-fashioned place of business, he could not stand the sight of it; and now he understood why Nick Fuso had that morning run around the corner and crossed the street—to taste the newness of the place and be waited on by Heinrich Schmitz, an energetic German dressed like a doctor, in a white duck jacket. And that was where many of his other customers had gone, and stayed, so that his own poor living was cut in impossible half.

Morris tried hard to sleep but couldn't and grew restless in bed. After another quarter of an hour he decided to dress and go downstairs, but there drifted into his mind,* with ease and no sorrow, the form and image of his boy Ephraim, gone so long from him, and he fell deeply and calmly asleep.

Helen Bober squeezed into a subway seat between two women* and was on the last page of a chapter when a man dissolved in front of her and another appeared;* she knew without looking that Nat Pearl was standing there. She thought she would go on reading, but couldn't, and shut her book.

"Hello, Helen." Nat touched a gloved hand to a new hat.

***packing out symmetrical rows of brightly labeled cans**:「화려하게 라벨이 붙은 통조림 통들을 대칭이 되게 줄줄이 쌓아 올리면서」

***there drifted into his mind**:「그의 마음속에 떠올랐다」

***squeezed into a subway seat between two women**:「지하철 차 속에서 두 여자 사이의 자리에 비집고 앉았다」

***a man dissolved in front of her and another appeared**:「그녀 앞의 남자가 어느새 사라지고 딴 남자가 나타났다」

He was cordial but as usual held back something—his future.* He carried a fat law book, so she was glad to be protected with a book of her own. But not enough protected, for her hat and coat felt suddenly shabby, a trick of the mind, because on her they would still do.*

"Don Quixote?"

She nodded.

He seemed respectful, then said in an undertone, "I haven't seen you a long time. Where've you been keeping yourself?"

She blushed under her clothes.

"Did I offend you in some way or other?"*

Both of the women beside her seemed stolidly deaf. One held a rosary in her heavy hand.

"No." The offense was hers against herself.*

"So what's the score?"* Nat's voice was low, his gray eyes annoyed.

"No score,"* she murmured.

"How so?"

"You're you, I'm me."

This he considered a minute, then remarked, "I haven't much of a head for oracles."*

But she felt she had said enough.

***as usual held back something—his future**:「그에게는 여전히 무언가—자신의 미래만은 혼자 간직해 두려는 기색이 보였다」 hold back=refrain from revealing

***her hat and coat felt . . . they would still do**:「그녀의 모자와 코트가 갑자기 초라하게 느껴졌다. 그러나 이것은 심리작용일 것이다. 왜냐하면 모자와 코트는 아직도 그녀에게 꼭 맞았기 때문이다」

***Did I offend you in some way or other?**:「내가 뭔가 당신의 감정을 상하게 했나요?」

***The offense was hers against herself**:「그녀는 자기 자신에 대해 화를 내고 있었다」

***So what's the score**:「그럼 왜 그러지?」 score「진상, 실정, 내막」

***No score**:「아무렇지도 않아요」

***I haven't much of a head for oracles**:「나는 신탁(神託)을 제대로 이해 못하는데」

He tried another way. "Betty asks for you."*

"Give her my best." She had not meant it but this sounded funny because they all lived on the same block, separated by one house.*

Tight-jawed, he opened his book. She returned to hers, hiding her thoughts behind the antics of a madman until memory overthrew him and she found herself ensnared in scenes of summer that she would gladly undo,* although she loved the season; but how could you undo what you had done again in the fall, unwillingly willing?* Virginity she thought she had parted with without sorrow, yet was surprised by torments of conscience, or was it disappointment at being valued under her expectations?* Nat Pearl, handsome, cleft-chinned, gifted, ambitious, had wanted without too much trouble a lay and she, half in love, had obliged and regretted.* Not the loving, but that it had taken her so long to realize how little he wanted.* Not her, Helen Bober.

Why should he?—magna cum laude,* Columbia, now in his

***Betty asks for you**:「베티가 당신을 만나고 싶어 하더군」

***because they all lived on the same block, separated by one house**:「그들은 모두 같은 블록에 살고 거기다 한 집 건너 이웃이었기 때문이다」

***she found herself ensnared in scenes of summer that she would gladly undo**:「없었더라면 좋았을 뻔한 지난 여름의 장면이 그녀의 마음을 사로잡았다」

***how could you undo what you had done again in the fall, unwillingly willing?**:「하기 싫어하면서도 또 한편으로는 스스로 원하여 되풀이한 그 짓을 어떻게 없었던 것으로 할 수 있겠는가?」

***was it disappointment at being valued under her expectations?**:「자기가 기대한 이하로 평가를 받아 실망한 것일까?」

***she, half in love, had obliged and regretted**:「상당히 그를 사랑하고 있었던 그녀는 그의 말을 들어주고 후회했다」 oblige「~의 소원을 들어주다」

***Not the loving, but that it had taken her so long to realize how little he wanted**:「그를 사랑했기 때문이 아니라, 그가 자기를 원하는 정도가 얼마나 미미한지 깨닫는데, 그토록 긴 시간이 걸렸음이 한탄스러웠다」

***magna cum laude**:「2등으로」

second year at law school, she only a high school graduate with a year's evening college credit mostly in lit; he with first-rate prospects, also rich friends he had never bothered to introduce her to; she as poor as her name sounded, with little promise of a better future. She had more than once asked herself if she had meant by her favors to work up a claim on him.* Always she denied it. She had wanted, admittedly, satisfaction, but more than that—respect for the giver of what she had to give,* had hoped desire would become more than just that. She wanted, simply, a future in love. Enjoyment she had somehow had, felt very moving the freedom of fundamental intimacy with a man. Though she wished for more of the same, she wanted it without aftermath of conscience, or pride, or sense of waste. So she promised herself next time it would go the other way; first mutual love, then loving, harder maybe on the nerves, but easier in memory. Thus she had reasoned, until one night in September, when coming up to see his sister Betty, she had found herself alone in the house with Nat and had done again what she had promised herself she wouldn't. Afterward she fought self-hatred. Since then, to this day, without telling him why, she had avoided Nat Pearl.

Two stations before their stop, Helen shut her book, got up in silence and left the train. On the platform, as the train moved away, she caught a glimpse of Nat standing before her empty seat, calmly reading. She walked on, lacking, wanting,

---

***She had . . . him**:「그의 말을 들어줌으로서 그에게 결혼을 요구할 생각이 아니었을까 하고 몇 번이나 자문했다」

***respect for the giver of what she had to give**:「그녀가 허락했던 것—그걸 준 사람에 대한 존경」

not wanting, not happy.*

Coming up the subway steps, she went into the park by a side entrance, and despite the sharp wind and her threadbare coat, took the long way home. The leafless trees left her with unearned sadness.* She mourned the long age before spring and feared loneliness in winter. Wishing she hadn't come, she left the park, searching the faces of strangers although she couldn't stand their stares. She went quickly along the Parkway, glancing with envy into the lighted depths of private houses that were, for no reason she could give, except experience, not for her. She promised herself she would save every cent possible and register next fall for a full program at NYU, night.*

When she reached her block, a row of faded yellow brick houses, two stories squatting on ancient stores, Sam Pearl, stifling a yawn,* was reaching into his corner candy store window to put on the lamp. He snapped the string* and the dull glow from the fly-specked globe fell upon her. Helen quickened her step. Sam, always sociable, a former cabbie, bulky, wearing bifocals and chewing gum, beamed at her but she pretended no see. Most of the day he sat hunched over dope sheets* spread out on the soda fountain counter, smok-

---

***She walked on, lacking, wanting, not wanting, not happy**:「그녀는 무언가 부족하고 무언가 필요함을 느끼며 동시에 또 그것을 부인하며 불행한 느낌을 맛보면서 걸어갔다」

***The leafless trees left her with unearned sadness**:「잎이 없는 나무들이 아무 이유 없이 그녀를 슬프게 했다」

***register next fall for a full program at NYU, night**:「내년 가을에 뉴욕 대학교 야간부의 모든 과정에 등록하다」

***stifling a yawn**:「하품을 죽이면서」

***He snapped the string**:「그는 줄을 잡아당겼다」

***he sat hunched over dope sheets**:「그는 등을 구부리고 앉아서 경마정보의 신문을 보고 있었다」

ing as he chewed gum, making smeary marks with a pencil stub under horses' names. He neglected the store; his wife Goldie was the broad-backed one, yet she did not much complain, because Sam's luck with the nags was exceptional* and he had nicely supported Nat in college until the scholarships started rolling in.

Around the corner, through the many-bottled window that blinked in neon "KARP wines and liquors," she glimpsed paunchy Julius Karp, with bushy eyebrows and an ambitious mouth, blowing imaginary dust off a bottle as he slipped a deft fifth of something into a paper bag,* while Louis, slightly popeyed son and heir, looking up from clipping to the quick his poor fingernails,* smiled amiably upon a sale. The Karps, Pearls and Bobers, representing attached houses and stores, but otherwise detachment, made up the small Jewish segment of this gentile community. They had somehow, her father first, then Karp, later Pearl, drifted together here where no other Jews dwelt, except on the far fringes of the neighborhood. None of them did well and were too poor to move elsewhere until Karp, who with a shoe store that barely made him a living, got the brilliant idea after Prohibition gurgled down the drain* and liquor licenses were offered to the public, to borrow cash from a whitebearded rich uncle and put in for

---

***Sam's luck with the nags was exceptional**:「샘의 경마에 대한 운은 보기 드물 정도로 좋았다」 exceptional=unusual

***as he slipped a deft fifth of something into a paper bag**:「무언가 1/5갈론쯤되는 것을 종이봉지에 넣으면서」

***clip to the quick his poor fingernails**:「그의 빈약한 손톱을 바싹 짜르다」」 quick:「손톱밑의 속살」 (the tender part of the flesh below the nail)

***after Prohibition gurgled down the drain**:「금주령이 폐지된 후」 go down the drain「없어지다, 사라지다」

one.* To everybody's surprise he got the license, though Karp, when asked how, winked a heavy-lidded eye and answered nothing. Within a short time after cheap shoes had become expensive bottles, in spite of the poor neighborhood—or maybe because of it, Helen supposed—he became astonishingly successful and retired his overweight wife from the meager railroad flat above the store to a big house on the Parkway—from which she hardly ever stepped forth—the house complete with two-car garage and Mercury;* and at the same time as Karp changed his luck—to hear her father tell it—he became wise without brains.*

The grocer, on the other hand, had never altered his fortune, unless degrees of poverty meant alteration,* for luck and he were, if not natural enemies, not good friends. He labored long hours, was the soul of honesty—he could not escape his honesty, it was bedrock; to cheat would cause an explosion in him, yet he trusted cheaters—coveted nobody's nothing and always got poorer. The harder he worked—his toil was a form of time devouring time*—the less he seemed to have. He was Morris Bober and could be nobody more fortunate. With that name you had no sure sense of property, as if it were in your blood and history not to possess, or if by some miracle to own

---

***put in for one**=put in for a liquor license:「주류판매면허를 신청하다」

***the house complete with two-car garage and Mercury**:「두 대의 차가 들어갈 차고와 머큐리 고급승용차가 완비된 집」 complete with ～「～이 완비된」

***he became wise without brains**:「그는 이해성 없이 약삭빠르게만 되었다」

***unless degrees of poverty meant alteration**:「빈곤의 정도가 운명의 변화를 의미하지 않는다면」

***his toil was a form of time devouring time**:「그의 노동은 시간을 더 허비하는 시간의 한 형태였다」 일하는 시간만 늘어나지 수입은 없다는 뜻.

something, to do so on the verge of loss.* At the end you were sixty and had less than at thirty. It was, she thought, surely a talent.

Helen removed her hat as she entered the grocery. "Me," she called, as she had from childhood. It meant that whoever was sitting in the back should sit and not suddenly think he was going to get rich.*

Morris awoke, soured by the long afternoon sleep. He dressed, combed his hair with a broken comb and trudged downstairs, a heavy-bodied man with sloping shoulders and bushy gray hair in need of a haircut.* He came down with his apron on. Although he felt chilly he poured out a cup of cold coffee, and backed against the radiator,* slowly sipped it. Ida sat at the table, reading.

"Why you let me sleep so long?" the grocer complained.

She didn't answer.

"Yesterday or today's paper?"

"Yesterday."

He rinsed the cup and set it on the top of the gas range. In the store he rang up "no sale" and took a nickel out of the drawer. Morris lifted the lid of the cash register, struck a match on the underside of the counter, and holding the flame cupped in his palm, peered at the figure of his earnings.* Ida

---

***if by some miracle to own something, to do so on the verge of loss**:「어떤 기적으로 무언가 소유한다 해도 상실될 위험에 직면하면서 겨우 소유하게 된다」

***It meant that . . . rich**:「뒷방에 앉아 있는 사람이 누구이든 그대로 앉아 있어도 되며, 부자가 되리라고 갑자기 생각해서는 안 된다는 뜻이었다」

***bushy gray hair in need of a haircut**:「이발해야 할 덥수룩한 센 머리」

***backed against the radiator**:「난로에 기댔다」

***holding the flame cupped in his palm, peered at the figure of his earnings**:「손바닥

had taken in three dollars. Who could afford a paper?

Nevertheless he went for one, doubting the small pleasure he would get from it. What was so worth reading about the world? Through Karp's window, as he passed, he saw Louis waiting on a customer while four others crowded the counter. Der oilem iz a goilem. Morris took the *Forward* from the newsstand and dropped a nickel into the cigar box. Sam Pearl, working over a green racing sheet, gave him a wave of his hammy hand.* They never bothered to talk. What did he know about race horses? What did the other know of the tragic quality of life? Wisdom flew over his hard head.*

The grocer returned to the rear of his store and sat on the couch, letting the diminishing light in the yard fall upon the paper. He read nearsightedly, with eyes stretched wide, but his thoughts would not let him read long. He put down the newspaper.

"So where is your buyer?" he asked Ida.

Looking absently into the store she did not reply.

"You should sell long ago the store," she remarked after a minute.

"When the store was good, who wanted to sell? After came bad times, who wanted to buy?"*

"Everything we did too late. The store we didn't sell in time. I said, 'Morris, sell now the store.' You said, 'Wait.' What for?

을 오목하게 하여 불을 가리면서 판매고의 숫자를 들여다 봤다」

***Pearl, working over a green racing sheet, gave him a wave of his hammy hand**:「초록색 경마예매표를 자세히 조사하고 있던 Pearl은 그를 보자 햄같이 살찐 손을 흔들었다」 work over「철저히 조사하다」

***Wisdom flew over his hard head**:「지혜는 그의 돌대가리에서 흘러가 버렸다」

***After came bad times, who wanted to buy?**:「불경기가 된 후에 누가 사려고 하겠소?」

The house we bought too late, so we have still a big mortgage that it's hard to pay every month.* 'Don't buy,' I said, 'times are bad.' 'Buy,' you said, 'will get better. We will save rent.' "

He answered nothing. If you had failed to do the right thing, talk was useless.

When Helen entered, she asked if the buyer had come. She had forgotten about him but remembered when she saw her mother's dress.

Opening her purse, she took out her pay check and handed it to her father. The grocer, without a word, slipped it under his apron into his pants pocket.

"Not yet," Ida answered, also embarrassed. "Maybe later."

"Nobody goes in the night to buy a store," Morris said. "The time to go is in the day to see how many customers. If this man comes here he will see with one eye the store is dead, then he will run home."

"Did you eat lunch?" Ida asked Helen.

"Yes."

"What did you eat?"

"I don't save menus, Mama."*

"Your supper is ready." Ida lit the flame under the pot on the gas range.

"What makes you think he'll come today?" Helen asked her.

"Karp told me yesterday. He knows a refugee that he looks to buy a grocery. He works in the Bronx, so he will be here late."

***we have still a big mortgage that it's hard to pay every month** :「매월 지불하기에 벅찬 저당을 짊어지고 있지」

***I don't save menus, Mama** :「메뉴를 잊어 버렸어요, 엄마」

Morris shook his head.

"He's a young man," Ida went on, "maybe thirty—thirty-two. Karp says he saved a little cash. He can make alterations,* buy new goods, fix up modern,* advertise a little and make here a nice business."

"Karp should live so long,"* the grocer said.

"Let's eat." Helen sat at the table.

Ida said she would eat later.

"What about you, Papa?"

"I am not hungry." He picked up his paper.

She ate alone. It would be wonderful to sell out and move but the possibility struck her as remote.* If you had lived so long in one place, all but two years of your life, you didn't move out overnight.

Afterward she got up to help with the dishes but Ida wouldn't let her. "Go rest," she said.

Helen took her things and went upstairs.

She hated the drab five-room flat; a gray kitchen she used for breakfast so she could quickly get out* to work in the morning. The living room was colorless and cramped; for all its overstuffed furniture of twenty years ago it seemed barren because it was lived in so little,* her parents being seven days out of seven in the store; even their rare visitors, when invited

---

***make alterations**:「개조하다」

***fix up modern**:「현대식으로 꾸미다」

***Karp should live so long**:「(그런 날이 오려면) Karp가 오래 살아야 되겠군」

***the possibility struck her as remote**:「그럴 가능성은 희박하다는 생각이 들었다」 strike=occur to, come to the mind of

***get out**=leave

***it seemed barren . . . little**:「그 방은 사람이 거의 살지 않고 있기 때문에 적적해 보였다」 *e.g.* This room does not seem to be lived in.「이 방에는 사람이 살고 있지 않는 것 같다」

upstairs, preferred to remain in the back. Sometimes Helen asked a friend up, but she went to other people's houses if she had a choice. Her bedroom was another impossibility, tiny, dark, despite the two by three foot opening in the wall,* through which she could see the living room windows; and at night Morris and Ida had to pass through her room to get to theirs, and from their bedroom back to the bathroom. They had several times talked of giving her the big room, the only comfortable one in the house, but there was no place else that would hold their double bed. The fifth room was a small icebox off the second floor stairs,* in which Ida stored a few odds and ends of clothes and furniture.* Such was home. Helen had once in anger remarked that the place was awful to live in, and it had made her feel bad that her father had felt so bad.

She heard Morris's slow footsteps on the stairs. He came aimlessly into the living room and tried to relax in a stiff armchair. He sat with sad eyes, saying nothing, which was how he began when he wanted to say something.*

When she and her brother were kids, at least on Jewish holidays Morris would close the store and venture forth* to Second Avenue to see a Yiddish play, or take the family

---

***despite the two by three foot opening in the wall**:「세로 2피트, 가로 3피트의 창구멍이 벽에 나 있었지만」

***The fifth room was a samll icebox off the second stairs**:「다섯번째 방은 2층 층계 곁에 있는 작은 냉장고 만한 방이었다」

***Ida stored a few odds and ends of clothes and furniture**:「Ida는 의류와 가구 등의 잡동사니를 넣어두었다」

***He sat with . . . something**:「그는 말없이 슬픈 눈을 하고 앉아 있었다. 그러나 그가 무언가 할 말이 있을 때엔 이와 같이 해서 입을 여는 것이었다」 which was how he began～=which was the way in which he began～

***venture forth**:「과감하게 나아가다」

visiting; but after Ephraim died he rarely went beyond the corner. Thinking about his life always left her with a sense of the waste of her own.*

She looks like a little bird, Morris thought. Why should she be lonely? Look how pretty she looks. Whoever saw such blue eyes?*

He reached into his pants pocket and took out a five-dollar bill.

"Take," he said, rising and embarrassedly handing her the money. "You will need for shoes."

"You just gave me five dollars downstairs."

"Here is five more."

"Wednesday was the first of the month, Pa."

"I can't take away from you all your pay."

"You're not taking, I'm giving."

She made him put the five away.* He did, with renewed shame.* "What did I ever give you? Even your college education I took away."

"It was my own decision not to go, yet maybe I will yet You can never tell."

"How can you go? You are twenty-three years old."

"Aren't you always saying a person's never too old to go to school?"

"My child," he sighed, "for myself I don't care, for you I want the best but what did I give you?"

***Thinking about his life always left her with a sense of the waste of her own**:「그의 인생을 생각하면, 그녀는 언제나 자신의 인생도 낭비되고 있다는 생각이 들었다」
***Whoever saw such a blue eyes?**:「누가 그런 푸른 눈을 보았겠는가?」
***She made him put the five away**:「그녀는 아버지가 5불을 도로 집어넣도록 했다」
***He did, with renewed shame**:「그는 새삼스레 부끄러워하며 돈을 도로 넣었다」

"I'll give myself," she smiled. "There's hope."

With this he had to be satisfied. He still conceded her a future.*

But before he went down, he said gently, "What's the matter you stay home so much lately? You had a fight with Nat?"

"No." Blushing, she answered, "I don't think we see things in the same way."*

He hadn't the heart to ask more.

Going down, he met Ida on the stairs and knew she would cover the same ground.*

In the evening there was a flurry of business.* Morris's mood quickened and he exchanged pleasantries with* the customers. Carl Johnsen, the Swedish painter, whom he hadn't seen in weeks, came in with a wet smile and bought two dollars' worth of beer, cold cuts and sliced Swiss cheese. The grocer was at first worried he would ask to charge*—he had never paid what he owed on the books before Morris had stopped giving trust—but the painter had the cash. Mrs. Anderson, an old loyal• customer, bought for a dollar. A stranger then came in and left eighty-eight cents. After him

---

***He still conceded her a future**:「그는 딸에게 아직 밝은 미래가 있다고 생각하고 있었다」 concede=allow a person to have

***I don't think we see things in the same way**:「우리 둘은 사물을 똑같은 관점에서 보는 게 아니어요」

***he . . . knew she would cover the same ground**:「그녀도 같은 문제를 딸에게 물어볼 것을 그는 알아차렸다」

***a flurry of business**:「일이 분주해짐」

***exchange pleasantries with ~**:「~와 농담을 주고 받다」 pleasantry「익살, 농담」

***The grocer was at first worried he would ask to charge**:「식료품점 주인은 그가 외상으로 해달라고 요구할까봐 처음에는 걱정했다」 *e.g.* Charge the cost to me.「비용은 내 앞으로 달아 놓으시오」

two more customers appeared. Morris felt a little surge of hope. Maybe things were picking up.* But after half-past eight his hands grew heavy with nothing to do.* For years he had been the only one for miles around who stayed open at night and had just about made a living from it, but now Schmitz matched him hour for hour. Morris sneaked a little smoke, then began to cough. Ida pounded on the floor upstairs, so he clipped the butt and put it away. He felt restless and stood at the front window, watching the street. He watched a trolley go by. Mr. Lawler, formerly a customer, good for at least a fiver* on Friday nights, passed the store. Morris hadn't seen him for months but knew where he was going. Mr. Lawler averted his gaze and hurried along. Morris watched him disappear around the corner. He lit a match and again checked the register—nine and a half dollars, not even expenses.*

Julius Karp opened the front door and poked his foolish head in.*

"Podolsky came?"

"Who Podolsky?"

"The refugee."

Morris said in annoyance,* "What refugee?

With a grunt Karp shut the door behind him. He was short, pompous, a natty dresser in his advanced age. In the past, like

---

***Maybe things were picking up.**=Business conditions were looking up. 「아마도 경기가 좋아지고 있었다」

***his hands grew heavy with nothing to do**:「할 일이 없어 그의 두 손은 활기를 잃기 시작했다」

***good for at least a fiver**:「적어도 5불 정도는 팔아 줄」

***nine and a half dollars, not even expenses**:「9불 50센트—비용도 안 되는 금액이었다」

***poked his foolish head in**:「그의 미련한 머리를 디밀었다」

***in annoyance**:「화가 나서, 기분이 상하여, 짜증이 나서」

Morris, he had toiled long hours in his shoe store, now he stayed all day in silk pajamas until it came time to relieve Louis before supper.* Though the little man was insensitive and a blunderer, Morris had got along fairly well with him, but since Karp had rented the tailor shop to another grocer, sometimes they did not speak. Years ago Karp had spent much time in the back of the grocery, complaining of his poverty as if it were a new invention and he its first victim. Since his success with wines and liquors he came in less often, but he still visited Morris more than his welcome entitled him to,* usually to run down* the grocery and spout unwanted advice. His ticket of admission was his luck,* which he gathered wherever he reached, at a loss, Morris thought, to somebody else.* Once a drunk had heaved a rock at Karp's window, but it had shattered his. Another time, Sam Pearl gave the liquor dealer a tip on a horse,* then forgot to place a bet* himself. Karp collected five hundred for his ten-dollar bill. For years the grocer had escaped resenting the man's good luck, but lately he had caught himself wishing on him some small misfortune.*

***until it came time to relieve Louis before supper**:「저녁식사 전에 Louis와 교대할 시간이 될 때까지」

***he still visited Morris more than his welcome entitled him to**:「Morris가 그에게 표하는 환대의 정도에 비해서 더 자주 그를 찾아왔다」 별로 환대하지 않는데도 자주 찾아왔다는 뜻.

***run down**=criticize severely「혹평하다」

***His ticket of admission was his luck**:「그가 뻔뻔스레 들어올 수 있는 것은 운이 좋았기 때문이었다」

***which he gathered . . . else**:「Morris의 생각에는, 그는 손해를 딴 사람에게 전가시키면서 어디서나 행운을 긁어 모았다」

***tip on a horse**:「경마에 관한 정보」

***place a bet**:「돈을 걸다」

***lately he had caught . . . misfortune**:「최근에는 그에게 약간의 불운이 나타나기를 원

"Podolsky is the one I called up to take a look at your gesheft," Karp answered.

"Who is this refugee, tell me, an enemy yours?"

Karp stared at him unpleasantly.

"Does a man," Morris insisted, "send a friend he should buy such a store that you yourself took away from it the best business?"*

"Podolsky ain't you," the liquor dealer replied. "I told him about this place. I said, 'The neighborhood is improving. You can buy cheap and build up this store. It's run down for years,* nobody changed anything there for twenty years.' "

"You should live so long how much I changed—"* Morris began but he didn't finish, for Karp was at the window, peering nervously into the dark street.

"You saw that gray car that just passed," the liquor dealer said. "This is the third time I saw it in the last twenty minutes." His eyes were restless.

Morris knew what worried him. "Put in a telephone* in your store," he advised, "so you will feel better."

Karp watched the street for another minute and worriedly replied, "Not for a liquor store in this neighborhood. If I had a telephone, every drunken bum would call me to make deliveries,* and when you go there they don't have a cent."

하게 되었다」

***a store that you yourself took away from it the best business**:「잘 되는 장사를 네 자신이 망쳐놓은 가게」

***It's run down for years**:「가게는 수년간 장사가 통 안 되었다」

***You should live so long how much I changed**:「내가 얼마나 개선해 놓았는지 알 만큼 자네는 오래 살아야 해」

***Put in a telephone**:「전화를 가설하게」

***call me to make deliveries**:「배달해 달라고 나에게 전화하다」

He opened the door but shut it in afterthought.* "Listen, Morris," he said, lowering his voice, "if they come back again, I will lock my front door and put out my lights. Then I will call you from the back window so you can telephone the police."

"This will cost you five cents," Morris said grimly.

"My credit is class A."*

Karp left the grocery, disturbed.

God bless Julius Karp, the grocer thought. Without him I would have my life too easy.* God made Karp so a poor grocery man will not forget his life is hard. For Karp, he thought, it was miraculously not so hard, but what was there to envy? He would allow the liquor dealer his bottles and gelt just not to be him. Life was bad enough.

At nine-thirty a stranger came in for a box of matches. Fifteen minutes later Morris put out the lights in his window. The street was deserted except for an automobile parked in front of the laundry across the car tracks. Morris peered at it sharply but could see nobody in it. He considered locking up and going to bed, then decided to stay open the last few minutes. Sometimes a person came in at a minute to ten. A dime was a dime.*

A noise at the side door which led into the hall frightened him.

"Ida?"

***in afterthought**:「생각을 고쳐서」

***My credit is class A**:「내 신용은 A급이야」

***Without him I would have my life too easy**:「저 놈만 없으면 내 인생은 아주 평안해질 것이다」

***A dime was a dime**:「10센트도 그 만한 가치는 있다」

The door opened slowly. Tessie Fuso came in in her housecoat, a homely Italian girl with a big face.

"Are you closed, Mr. Bober?" she asked embarrassedly.

"Come in," said Morris.

"I'm sorry I came through the back way but I was undressed and didn't want to go out in the street."

"Don't worry."

"Please give me twenty cents' ham for Nick's lunch tomorrow."

He understood. She was making amends for Nick's trip around the corner* that morning. He cut her an extra slice of ham.

Tessie bought also a quart of milk, package of paper napkins and loaf of bread. When she had gone he lifted the register lid. Ten dollars. He thought he had long ago touched bottom but now knew there was none.*

I slaved my whole life for nothing, he thought.

Then he heard Karp calling him from the rear. The grocer went inside, worn out.

Raising the window he called harshly, "What's the matter there?"

"Telephone the police," cried Karp. "The car is parked across the street."

"What car?"

"The holdupniks."*

***She was making amends for Nick's trip around the corner**:「Nick가 모퉁이를 돌아 딴 상점으로 간 것이 미안해서, 그녀는 보상해 주려 하고 있었다」 make amends (for)=make up (for some harm done to another)

***He thought . . . none**:「그는 오래 전에 불경기의 밑바닥까지 내려갔다고 생각했지만 이제는 얼마나 내려가야 바닥이 있는지 알 수 없었다」

***The holdupniks**:「강도의 차」

"There is nobody in this car, I saw myself."

"For God's sake, I tell you call the police. I will pay for the telephone."

Morris shut the window. He looked up the phone number and was about to dial the police when the store door opened and he hurried inside.

Two men were standing at the other side of the counter, with handkerchiefs over their faces. One wore a dirty yellow clotted one, the other's was white.* The one with the white one began pulling out the store lights.* It took the grocer a half-minute to comprehend that he, not Karp, was their victim.

Morris sat at the table, the dark light of the dusty bulb falling on his head, gazing dully at the few crumpled bills before him, including Helen's check, and the small pile of silver. The gunman with the dirty handkerchief, fleshy, wearing a fuzzy black hat, waved a pistol at the grocer's head. His pimply brow was thick with sweat; from time to time with furtive eyes he glanced into the darkened store. The other, a taller man in an old cap and torn sneakers, to control his trembling leaned against the sink, cleaning his fingernails with a matchstick.* A cracked mirror hung behind him on the wall above the sink and every so often he turned to stare into it.

***One wore a dirty yellow clotted one, the other's was white**:「한 놈은 더러운 황색의 얼룩진 손수건을 얼굴에 가리우고 또 한 놈은 흰 색의 것을 가리웠다」

***The one . . . lights**:「흰 손수건으로 가린 놈이 가게의 불을 끄기 시작했다」

***cleaning his fingernails with a matchstick**:「성냥개비로 손톱의 때를 긁어내고 있었다」

"I know damn well this ain't everything you took in," said the heavy one to Morris, in a hoarse, unnatural voice. "Where've you got the rest hid?"

Morris, sick to his stomach, couldn't speak.*

"Tell the goddam truth." He aimed the gun at the grocer's mouth.

"Times are bad," Morris muttered.

"You're a Jew liar."

The man at the sink fluttered his hand, catching the other's attention.* They met in the center of the room, the other with the cap hunched awkwardly over the one in the fuzzy hat, whispering into his ear.

"No," snapped the heavy one sullenly.

His partner bent lower, whispering earnestly through his handkerchief.

"I say he hid it," the heavy one snarled, "and I'm gonna get it if I have to crack his goddam head."

At the table he whacked the grocer across the face.

Morris moaned.

The one at the sink hastily rinsed a cup and filled it with water. He brought it to the grocer, spilling some on his apron as he raised the cup to his lips.

Morris tried to swallow but managed only a dry sip.* His frightened eyes sought the man's but he was looking elsewhere.

"Please," murmured the grocer.

***Morris, sick to his stomach, couldn't speak**:「Morris는 욕지기가 나서 말할 수 없었다」

***catching the other's attention**:「또 한 놈의 주의를 끌었다」

***managed only a dry sip**:「물을 마시려 했으나 소리만 났지 실제로 마시지는 못했다」

"Hurry up," warned the one with the gun.

The tall one straightened up and gulped down the water. He rinsed the cup and placed it on a cupboard shelf.

He then began to hunt among the cups and dishes there and pulled out the pots on the bottom. Next, he went hurriedly through the drawers of an old bureau in the room, and on hands and knees searched under the couch.* He ducked into the store,* removed the empty cash drawer from the register and thrust his hand into the slot, but came up with nothing.

Returning to the kitchen he took the other by the arm and whispered to him urgently.

The heavy one elbowed him aside.

"We better scram out of here."*

"Are you gonna go chicken on me?"*

"That's all the dough he has, let's beat it."

"Business is bad," Morris muttered.

"Your Jew ass is bad, you understand?"

"Don't hurt me."

"I will give you your last chance. Where have you got it hid?"

"I am a poor man." He spoke through cracked lips.

The one in the dirty handkerchief raised his gun. The other, staring into the mirror, waved frantically, his black eyes bulging,* but Morris saw the blow descend and felt sick of

---

***he went hurriedly through . . . couch**:「그는 방안의 낡은 책상의 서랍을 서둘러 뒤지고, 또 네 발 걸음 자세로 침대의자 밑을 뒤졌다」

***He ducked into the store**:「슬쩍 몸을 굽혀 그는 가게 안으로 들어갔다」

***We better scram out of here**:「여기서 도망치는 게 나을거야」

***Are you gonna go chicken on me?**:「병아리처럼 비겁해진 거야?」 chicken=coward

***his black eyes bulging**:「검은 눈이 튀어나올 듯하면서」 부대상황의 독립분사 구문임.

himself, of soured expectations, endless frustration,* the years gone up in smoke, he could not begin to count how many. He had hoped for much in America and got little. And because of him Helen and Ida had less. He had defrauded them, he and the bloodsucking store.*

He fell without a cry. The end fitted the day. It was his luck, others had better.*

***felt sick of himself, of soured expectations, endless frustration, . . .**:「자기 자신에 대하여, 어그러진 기대와 끝없는 좌절감 …등에 대하여 그는 욕지기를 느꼈다」

***He had defrauded them, he and the bloodsucking store**:「그는 그들을 속여 빼앗어 왔다. 그와 피를 빨아 먹는 가게가」

***It was his luck, others had better**:「그것이 Morris의 운이고, 더 나은 운은 다른 사람의 것이었다」

2

During the week that Morris lay in bed with a thickly bandaged head, Ida tended the store fitfully.* She went up and down twenty times a day until her bones ached and her head hurt with all her worries. Helen stayed home Saturday, a half-day in her place, and Monday, to help her mother, but she could not risk longer than that, so Ida, who ate in snatches and had worked up a massive nervousness,* had to shut the store for a full day, although Morris angrily protested. He needed no attention, he insisted, and urged her to keep open at least half the day or he would lose his remaining few customers; but Ida, short of breath,* said she hadn't the strength, her legs hurt. The grocer attempted to get up and pull on his pants but was struck by a violent headache and had to drag himself back to bed.*

On the Tuesday the store was closed a man appeared in the neighborhood, a stranger who spent much of his time standing on Sam Pearl's corner with a toothpick in his teeth, intently observing the people who passed by; or he would drift down

---

***Ida tended the store fitfully**:「Ida는 가게를 발작적으로 보고 있었다」

***ate in snatches and had worked up a massive nervousness**:「서둘러 식사했고 점차 심한 신경과민에 빠져 들어갔다」 *e.g.* He worked himself up into a passion.:「그는 서서히 화를 내기 시작했다」

***short of breath**=out of breath「숨을 헐떡이며」

***had to drag himself back to bed**:「도로 침대로 기어들어가지 않으면 안 되었다」

the long block of stores, some empty, from Pearl's to the bar at the far end of the street. Beyond that was a freight yard, and in the distance, a bulky warehouse. After an occasional slow beer in the tavern,* the stranger turned the corner and wandered past the high-fenced coal yard; he would go around the block until he got back to Sam's candy store. Once in a while the man would walk over to Morris's closed grocery, and with both hands shading his brow, stare through the window;* sighing, he went back to Sam's. When he had as much as he could take of the corner* he walked around the block again, or elsewhere in the neighborhood.

Helen had pasted a paper on the window of the front door, that said her father wasn't well but the store would open on Wednesday. The man spent a good deal of time studying this paper. He was young, dark-bearded, wore an old brown rain-stained hat, cracked patent leather shoes and a long black overcoat that looked as if it had been lived in.* He was tall and not bad looking, except for a nose that had been broken and badly set, unbalancing his face.* His eyes were melancholy. Sometimes he sat at the fountain with Sam Pearl, lost in his thoughts, smoking from a crumpled pack of cigarettes he had bought with pennies. Sam, who was used to all kinds

---

***After an occasional slow beer in the tavern**:「이따금 술집에서 느긋하게 맥주를 마신 다음」

***with both hands shading his brow, stare through the window**:「두 손을 이마에 대어 햇빛을 가리고 유리창 속을 들여다 보았다」

***when he had as much as he could take of the corner**:「그 골목에서 너무 오래 시간을 보낸 것 같이 생각되었을 때」

***a long black overcoat that looked as if it had been lived in**:「입고 잔 것같이 보이는 긴 검은 외투」

***except for a nose . . . , unbalancing his face**:「얻어 맞아 코가 비뚤어져서 얼굴의 균형이 깨어진 점을 제외하고」

of people, and had in his time seen many strangers appear in the neighborhood and as quickly disappear, showed no special concern for the man, though Goldie, after a full day of his presence complained that too much was too much; he didn't pay rent. Sam did notice that the stranger sometimes seemed to be under stress,* sighed much and muttered inaudibly to himself. However, he paid the man scant attention—everybody to their own troubles. Other times the stranger, as if he had somehow squared himself with himself,* seemed relaxed, even satisfied with his existence. He read through Sam's magazines, strolled around in the neighborhood and when he returned, lit a fresh cigarette as he opened a paper-bound book from the rack* in the store. Sam served him coffee when he asked for it, and the stranger, squinting from the smoke of the butt in his mouth,* carefully counted out five pennies to pay. Though nobody had asked him he said his name was Frank Alpine and he had lately come from the West, looking for a better opportunity. Sam advised if he could qualify for* a chauffeur's license, to try for work as a hack driver.* It wasn't a bad life. The man agreed but stayed around as if he was expecting something else to open up. Sam put him down as a moody gink.*

***seemed to be under stress**:「고민 거리가 있는 듯했다」

***as if he had somehow squared himself with himself**:「자기의 과거를 자기 나름대로 청산한 것처럼」 square oneself「과거를 청산하다, 범한 잘못을 스스로 청산하다」

***from the rack**:「서가에서」

***squinting from the smoke of the butt in his mouth**:「입에 문 담배연기 때문에 눈을 가늘게 뜨고」

***qualify for**:「면허를 받다, 자격을 얻다」

***hack driver**:「택시 운전수」

***Sam put him down as a moody gink**:「Sam은 그를 변덕스러운 놈이라고 간주했다」 put～down=regard～as

The day Ida reopened the grocery the stranger disappeared but he returned to the candy store the next morning, and seating himself at the fountain, asked for coffee. He looked bleary, unhappy, his beard hard, dark, contrasting with the pallor of his face; his nostrils were inflamed* and his voice was husky. He looks half in his grave,* Sam thought. God knows what hole he slept in last night.

As Frank Alpine was stirring his coffee, with his free hand he opened a magazine lying on the counter, and his eye was caught by a picture in color of a monk. He lifted the coffee cup to drink but had to put it down, and he stared at the picture for five minutes.

Sam, out of curiosity, went behind him with a broom, to see what he was looking at. The picture was of a thin-faced, dark-bearded monk in a coarse brown garment, standing barefooted on a sunny country road. His skinny, hairy arms were raised to a flock of birds that dipped over his head.* In the background was a grove of leafy trees; and in the far distance a church in sunlight.

"He looks like some kind of a priest," Sam said cautiously.

"No, it's St. Francis of Assisi. You can tell from that brown robe he's wearing and all those birds in the air. That's the time he was preaching to them. When I was a kid, an old priest used to come to the orphans' home where I was raised, and every time he came he read us a different story about St. Francis. They are clear in my mind to this day."

"Stories are stories," Sam said.

***his nostrils were inflamed**:「그의 콧구멍은 염증이 나 있었다」

***He looks half in his grave**:「그는 반쯤 죽은 거나 다름없다」 in one's grave=dead

***dipped over his head**:「그의 머리 위에 내려 앉았다」

"Don't ask me why I never forgot them."

Sam took a closer squint at the picture. "Talking to the birds? What was he—crazy? I don't say this out of any harm.*

The stranger smiled at the Jew. "He was a great man. The way I look at it, it takes a certain kind of a nerve* to preach to birds."

"That makes him great, because he talked to birds?"

"Also for other things. For instance, he gave everything away that he owned, every cent, all his clothes off his back. He enjoyed to be poor. He said poverty was a queen and he loved her like she was a beautiful woman."

Sam shook his head. "It ain't beautiful, kiddo.* To be poor is dirty work."

"He took a fresh view of things."

The candy store owner glanced again at St. Francis, then poked his broom into a dirty corner.* Frank, as he drank his coffee, continued to study the picture. He said to Sam, "Every time I read about somebody like him I get a feeling inside of me I have to fight to keep from crying. He was born good, which is a talent if you have it."

He spoke with embarrassment, embarrassing Sam.

Frank drained his cup and left.

That night as he was wandering past Morris's store he glanced through the door and saw Helen inside, relieving her mother.* She looked up and noticed him staring at her

---

***I don't say this out of any harm**:「악의로 하는 말은 아닐세」

***a certain kind of a nerve**:「어떤 종류의 용기」

***kiddo**:「여보게」 호칭으로 쓰임.

***poked his broom into a dirty corner**:「빗자루를 더러운 구석에 쑤셔넣었다」

***saw Helen inside, relieving her mother**:「안에서 Helen이 그녀의 어머니를 돕고 있는 모습을 보았다」

through the plate glass. His appearance startled her; his eyes were haunted, hungry, sad; she got the impression he would come in and ask for a handout* and had made up her mind to give him a dime, but instead he disappeared.

On Friday Morris weakly descended the stairs at six A.M., and Ida, nagging, came after him. She had been opening at eight o'clock and had begged him to stay in bed until then, but he had refused, saying he had to give the Poilisheh her roll.

"Why does three cents for a lousy roll mean more to you than another hour sleep?" Ida complained.

"Who can sleep?"

"You need rest, the doctor said."

"Rest I will take in my grave."

She shuddered. Morris said, "For fifteen years she gets here her roll, so let her get."

"All right, but let me open up. I will give her and you go back to bed."

"I stayed in bed too long. Makes me feel weak."

But the woman wasn't there and Morris feared he had lost her to the German. Ida insisted on dragging in the milk boxes, threatening to shout if he made a move for them.* She packed the bottles into the refrigerator. After Nick Fuso they waited hours for another customer. Morris sat at the table, reading the paper, occasionally raising his hand gently to feel the bandage

---

***ask for a handout**:「동냥을 요구하다」 handout=money or food given to a beggar

***Ida insisted on dragging . . . them**:「Ida는 스스로 우유상자를 끌어들이겠다고 고집을 부리고 만일 그가 우유상자 때문에 몸을 움직이면 고함을 치겠다고 위협했다」

around his head. When he shut his eyes he still experienced moments of weakness. By noon he was glad to go upstairs and crawl into bed and he didn't get up until Helen came home.

The next morning he insisted on opening alone. The Poilisheh* was there. He did not know her name. She worked somewhere in a laundry and had a little dog called Polaschaya. When she came home at night she took the little Polish dog for a walk around the block. He liked to run loose in the coal yard.* She lived in one of the stucco houses nearby. Ida called her die antisemitke,* but that part of her* didn't bother Morris. She had come with it from the old country, a different kind of anti-Semitism from in America.* Sometimes he suspected she needled him a little by asking for a "Jewish roll,"* and once or twice, with an odd smile, she wanted a "Jewish pickle." Generally she said nothing at all. This morning Morris handed her her roll and she said nothing. She didn't ask him about his bandaged head though her quick beady eyes* stared at it, nor why he had not been there for a week; but she put six pennies on the counter instead of three. He figured she had taken a roll from the bag one of the days the store hadn't opened on time. He rang up six-cent sale.

---

*__The Poilisheh__ :「폴란드 여자」

*__He liked to run loose in the coal yard__ :「개는 석탄을 쌓아두는 마당에서 제멋대로 뛰어다니기를 좋아했다」

*__die antisemitke__ :「유태인을 싫어하는 사람」

*__that part of her__ :「그녀가 지닌 그런 속성」 *e.g.* the better part of a man's nature「인간의 선성(善性)」

*__a different kind of anti-Semitism from in America__ :「미국의 반유태주의와는 종류가 다른 것」

*__she needled him a little by asking for a "Jewish roll"__ :「유태빵을 달라고 말하여 그를 약간 약올렸다」 needle=provoke by making cruel comments

*__her quick beady eyes__ :「날카롭고 반짝이는 작고 동그란 눈」

Morris went outside to pull in the two milk cases. He gripped the boxes but they were like rocks, so he let one go and tugged at the other.* A storm cloud formed in his head and blew up to the size of a house. Morris reeled* and almost fell into the gutter, but he was caught by Frank Alpine, in his long coat, steadied and led back into the store. Frank then hauled in the milk cases and refrigerated the bottles. He quickly swept up behind the countr and went into thc back. Morris, recovered, warmly thanked him.* Frank said huskily, his eyes on his scarred and heavy hands,* that he was new to the neighborhood but living here now with a married sister. He had lately come from the West and was looking for a better job.

The grocer offered him a cup of coffee, which he at once accepted. As he sat down Frank placed his hat on the floor at his feet, and he drank the coffee with three heaping spoonfuls of sugar, to get warm quick, he said. When Morris offered him a seeded hard roll, he bit into it hungrily. "Jesus, this is good bread." After he had finished he wiped his mouth with his handkerchief, then swept the crumbs off the table with one hand into the other,* and though Morris protested, he rinsed the cup and saucer at the sink, dried them and set them on top of the gas range, where the grocer had got them.*

***so he let one go and tugged at the other**:「그래서 그는 하나는 그대로 두고, 다른 하나를 잡아당겼다」

***Morris reeled**:「Morris는 비틀거렸다」

***warmly thanked him**:「그에게 진심으로 감사했다」

***his eyes on . . . hands**:「자기의 흉터가 있는 육중한 손을 보면서」 his 앞에 with를 넣어 해석할 것.

***swept the crumbs off . . . other**:「테이블의 부스러기를 한 손으로 쓸어서 다른 손의 손바닥에 담았다」

***where the grocer had got them**:「식료품점 주인이 그것들을 꺼냈던 장소」

"Much obliged for everything." He had picked up his hat but made no move to leave.

"Once in San Francisco I worked in a grocery for a couple of months," he remarked after a minute, "only it was one of those supermarket chain store deals."

"The chain store kills the small man."*

"Personally I like a small store myself. I might someday have one."

"A store is a prison. Look for something better."

"At least you're your own boss."

"To be a boss of nothing is nothing."*

"Still and all,* the idea of it appeals to me. The only thing is I would need experience on what goods to order. I mean about brand names,* and et cetera. I guess I ought to look for a job in a store and get more experience."

"Try the A&P,"* advised the grocer.

"I might."

Morris dropped the subject.* The man put on his hat.

"What's the matter," he said, staring at the grocer's bandage, "did you have some kind of an accident to your head?"

Morris nodded. He didn't care to talk about it, so the stranger, somehow disappointed, left.

He happened to be in the street very early on Monday when Morris was again struggling with the milk cases. The stranger

---

***The chain store kills the small man**:「연쇄점이 영세상인을 짓밟아 버린다」
***To be a boss of nothing is nothing**:「아무것도 없는 주인이 되어봤자 아무것도 아니지」
***Still and all**:「그래도, 결국」
***brand name**=trade name「상표이름」
***the A&P**=the Atlantic and Pacific Co(미국에서 유명한 식료품 소매 연쇄점)
***Morris dropped the subject**:「Morris는 더 이상 그 이야기를 하지 않았다」

tipped his hat* and said he was off to the city to find a job but he had time to help him pull in the milk. This he did and quickly left. However, the grocer thought he saw him pass by in the other direction about an hour later. That afternoon when he went for his *Forward* he noticed him sitting at the fountain with Sam Pearl. The next morning, just after six, Frank was there to help him haul in the milk bottles and he willingly accepted when Morris, who knew a poor man when he saw one, invited him for coffee.

"How is going now the job?" Morris asked as they were eating.

"So-so," said Frank, his glance shifting.* He seemed preoccupied, nervous.* Every few minutes he would set down his cup and uneasily look around. His lips parted as if to speak, his eyes took on a tormented expression, but then he shut his jaw as if he had decided it was better never to say what he intended.* He seemed to need to talk, broke into sweat—his brow gleamed with it—his pupils widening as he struggled. He looked to Morris like someone who had to retch—no matter where;* but after a brutal interval his eyes grew dull.* He sighed heavily and gulped down the last of his coffee. After, he brought up a belch. This for a moment satisfied him.

***tipped his hat**:「모자에 손을 대고 인사했다」

***his glance shifting**:「눈에는 침착성이 없었다」

***He seemed preoccupied, nervous**:「그는 무슨 생각에 마음이 빼앗기고 또 무슨 걱정이 있는 듯했다」

***he shut his jaw . . . intended**:「말하려 한 것을 입 밖에 내지 않는 편이 낫다고 결심한 듯이 그는 입을 다물었다」

***He looked to Morris . . . where**:「구역질이 나서 아무데나 토해 버리려는 사람처럼 Morris를 쳐다보았다」 retch=make efforts to vomit

***after a brutal interval his eyes grew dull**:「격렬한 고통의 순간이 지나자 그의 눈빛이 다시 몽롱해졌다」

Whatever he wants to say, Morris thought, let him say it to somebody else. I am only a grocer. He shifted in his chair, fearing to catch some illness.*

Again the tall man leaned forward, drew a breath and once more was at the point of speaking, but now a shudder passed through him, followed by a fit of shivering.*

The grocer hastened to the stove and poured out a cup of steaming coffee. Frank swallowed it in two terrible gulps. He soon stopped shaking, but looked defeated, humiliated, like somebody, the grocer felt, who had lost out on something he had wanted badly.*

"You caught a cold?" he asked sympathetically.

The stranger nodded, scratched up a match on the sole of his cracked shoe, lit a cigarette and sat there, listless.

"I had a rough life,"* he muttered, and lapsed into silence.

Neither of them spoke. Then the grocer, to ease the other's mood,* casually inquired, "Where in the neighborhood lives your sister? Maybe I know her."

Frank answered in a monotone.* "I forget the exact address. Near the park somewheres."

"What is her name?"

"Mrs. Garibaldi."

"What kind name is this?"

"What do you mean?" Frank stared at him.

***He shifted in his chair, fearing to catch some illness**:「무슨 병에 걸릴까봐 두려워서, 그는 의자에 앉은 채 몸을 움직였다」

***a fit of shivering**:「떠는 발작」

***looked defeated . . . badly**:「식료품점 주인이 느낀 바로는, 그는 몹시 바랬던 것을 놓쳐버린 사람처럼, 패배당하고 모욕을 받은 듯한 표정을 짓고 있었다」

***a rough life**:「고된 생활」

***to ease the other's mood**:「상대방의 기분을 진정시켜 주기 위해」

***in a monotone**:「단조로운 목소리로」

"I mean the nationality?"

"Italian. I am of Italian extraction.* My name is Frank Alpine—Alpinto in Italian."

The smell of Frank Alpine's cigarette compelled Morris to light his butt. He thought he could control his cough and tried but couldn't. He coughed till he feared his head would pop off.* Frank watched with interest. Ida banged on the floor upstairs, and the grocer ashamedly pinched his cigarette and dropped it into the garbage pail.

"She don't like me to smoke," he explained between coughs. "My lungs ain't so healthy."

"Who don't?"

"My wife. It's a catarrh some kind.* My mother had it all her life and lived till eighty-four. But they took a picture of my chest last year and found two dried spots. This frightened my wife."

Frank slowly put out his cigarette. "What I started out to say before about my life," he said heavily, "is that I have had a funny one, only I don't mean funny. I mean I've been through a lot.* I've been close to some wonderful things —jobs, for instance, education, women, but close is as far as I go."* His hands were tightly clasped between his knees. "Don't ask me why, but sooner or later everything I think is worth having gets away from me in some way or other. I work

---

***I am of Italian extraction**:「나는 이탈리아계입니다」 *e.g.* an American of Korean estraction「한국계 미국인」

***He coughed till he feared his head would pop off**:「그는 머리가 터질까 두려울 정도로 기침을 했다」

***It's a catarrh some kind**:「그건 일종의 기관지염이지」

***I mean I've been through a lot**:「나는 어떤 운명의 길을 줄곧 걸어온 셈입니다」

***close is as far as I go**:「바로 곁까지만 나는 갑니다」 목표에 이르기 직전에 실패한다는 뜻.

like a mule for what I want, and just when it looks like I am going to get it I make some kind of a stupid move, and everything that is just about nailed down tight blows up in my face."*

"Don't throw away your chance for education," Morris advised. "It's the best thing for a young man."

"I could've been a college graduate by now, but when the time came to start going, I missed out because something else turned up that I took instead. With me one wrong thing leads to another and it ends in a trap.* I want the moon so all I get is cheese."

"You are young yet."

"Twenty-five," he said bitterly.

"You look older."

"I feel old—damn old."

Morris shook his head.

"Sometimes I think your life keeps going the way it starts out on you," Frank went on. "The week after I was born my mother was dead and buried. I never saw her face, not even a picture. When I was five years old, one day my old man leaves this furnished room where we were staying, to get a pack of butts. He takes off and that was the last I ever saw of him. They traced him years later but by then he was dead. I was raised in an orphans' home and when I was eight they farmed me out* to a tough family.* I ran away ten times, also from the

---

***everything that is just about nailed down tight blows up in my face**:「거의 결정적으로 될 모든 것이 눈앞에서 수포로 돌아가고 맙니다」

***end in a trap**:「함정 속으로 빠져들다」

***farm out**:「(아이를) 맡기다」

***a tough family**:「인정 없는 집안」

next people I lived with. I think about my life a lot. I say to myself, 'What do you expect to happen after all of that?' Of course, every now and again, you understand, I hit some nice good spots in between,* but they are few and far, and usually I end up like I started out, with nothing."

The grocer was moved. Poor boy.

"I've often tried to change the way things work out for me* but I don't know how, even when I think I do. I have it in my heart to do more than I can remember." He paused, cleared his throat and said, "That makes me sound stupid but it's not as easy as that. What I mean to say is that when I need it most something is missing in me, in me or on account of me.* I always have this dream where I want to tell somebody something on the telephone so bad it hurts, but then when I am in the booth, instead of a phone being there, a bunch of bananas is hanging on a hook."

He gazed at the grocer then at the floor. "All my life I wanted to accomplish something worthwhile—a thing people will say took a little doing,* but I don't. I am too restless—six months in any one place is too much for me. Also I grab at everything too quick—too impatient. I don't do what I have to—that's what I mean. The result is I move into a place with nothing, and I move out with nothing. You understand me?"

***I hit some nice good spots in between**:「그 사이에 약간의 만족스러운 환경에서 지낼 때도 있었죠」

***I've often tried . . . me**:「내게 닥쳐오는 운명을 바꾸어보려고 자주 힘써보았읍니다」 work out「으로 되다」 *e.g.* Things didn't work out as we had expected.「사태는 우리가 기대하던 대로 되지 않았다」

***something is missing in me, in me or on account of me**:「어떤 것이 내게 없죠—내 안에라고 할까요 아니면 내 탓이라고 할까요」

***a thing people will say took a little doing**:「힘든 일을 했다고 말할 만한 일」

"Yes," said Morris.

Frank fell into silence. After a while he said, "I don't understand myself. I don't really know what I'm saying to you or why I am saying it."

"Rest yourself," said Morris.

"What kind of a life is that for a man my age?"

He waited for the grocer to reply—to tell him how to live his life, but Morris was thinking, I am sixty and he talks like me.*

"Take some more coffee," he said.

"No, thanks." Frank lit another cigarette and smoked it to the tip. He seemed eased yet not eased, as though he had accomplished something (What? wondered the grocer) yet had not. His face was relaxed, almost sleepy, but he cracked the knuckles* of both hands and silently sighed.

Why don't he go home? the grocer thought. I am a working man.

"I'm going." Frank got up but stayed.

"What happened to your head?" he asked again.

Morris felt the bandage. "This Friday before last I had here a holdup."*

"You mean they slugged you?"

The grocer nodded.

"Bastards like that ought to die." Frank spoke vehemently.

Morris stared at him.

Frank brushed his sleeve.* "You people are Jews, aren't

***I am sixty and he talks like me**:「나는 60세인데 그는 60세인 나처럼 말을 하고 있다」
***crack the knuckles**:「손가락 마디를 딱딱 소리나게 꺾다」
***I had here a holdup**:「강도가 여기에 들어왔었지」
***Frank brushed his sleeve**:「프랭크는 자기의 옷소매를 털었다」

you?"

"Yes," said the grocer, still watching him.

"I always liked Jews." His eyes were downcast.

Morris did not speak.

"I suppose you have some kids?" Frank asked.

"Me?"

"Excuse me for being curious."

"A girl." Morris sighed. "I had once a wonderful boy but he died from an ear sickness that they had in those days."

"Too bad." Frank blew his nose.

A gentleman, Morris thought with a watery eye.*

"Is the girl the one that was here behind the counter a couple of nights last week?"

"Yes," the grocer replied, a little uneasily.

"Well, thanks for all the coffee."

"Let me make you a sandwich. Maybe you'll be hungry later."

"No thanks."

The Jew insisted, but Frank felt he had all he wanted from him at the moment.

Left alone, Morris began to worry about his health. He felt dizzy* at times, often headachy. Murderers, he thought. Standing before the cracked and faded mirror at the sink he unwound the bandage from his head. He wanted to leave it off but the scar was still ugly, not nice for the customers, so he tied a fresh bandage around his skull. As he did this he thought of that night with bitterness, recalling the buyer who

---

***with a watery eye**:「눈물어린 눈을 하고」 watery=tearful「눈물어린」

***feel dizzy**:「현기증이 나다」 dizzy=giddy「어질어질하여」

hadn't come, nor had since then, nor ever would. Since his recovery, Morris had not spoken to Karp. Against words the liquor dealer had other words, but silence silenced him.*

Afterward the grocer looked up from his paper and was startled to see somebody out front washing his window with a brush on a stick. He ran out with a roar to drive the intruder away, for there were nervy window cleaners who did the job without asking permission,* then held out their palms to collect. But when Morris came out of the store he saw the window washer was Frank Alpine.

"Just to show my thanks and appreciation." Frank explained he had borrowed the pail from Sam Pearl and the brush and squeegee from the butcher next door.

Ida then entered the store by the inside door, and seeing the window being washed, hurried outside.

"You got rich all of a sudden?" she asked Morris, her face inflamed.*

"He does me a favor," the grocer replied.

"That's right," said Frank, bearing down on the squeegee.*

"Come inside, it's cold." In the store Ida asked, "Who is this goy?"

"A poor boy, an Italyener he looks for a job. He gives me a help in the morning with the cases milk."

"If you sold containers* like I told you a thousand times, you wouldn't need help."

***Against words the liquor dealer . . . silenced him**:「그 술장사는 Morris가 말을 걸면 말대꾸를 했지만, Morris가 침묵을 지키면 그도 말이 없었다」

***without asking permission**:「허락도 받지 않고」

***her face inflamed**:「그녀의 얼굴을 붉히면서」

***bearing down on the squeegee**:「고무 청소기를 누르면서」

***container**:「(우유를 담는 종이로 된) 용기(容器)」

"Containers leak. I like bottles."

"Talk to the wind," Ida said.

Frank came in blowing his breath on water-reddened fists.* "How's it look now, folks,* though you can't really tell till I do the inside."

Ida remarked under her breath,* "Pay now for your favor."

"Fine," Morris said to Frank. He went to the register and rang up "no sale."

"No, thanks," Frank said, holding up his hand. "For services already rendered."*

Ida reddened.

"Another cup coffee?" Morris asked.

"Thanks. Not as of now."*

"Let me make you a sandwich?"

"I just ate."

He walked out, threw the dirty water into the gutter, returned the pail and brush, then came back to the grocery. He went behind the counter and into the rear, pausing to rap on the doorjamb.*

"How do you like the clean window?" he asked Ida.

"Clean is clean." She was cool.

"I don't want to intrude here but your husband was nice to me, so I just thought maybe I could ask for one more small favor. I am looking for work and I want to try some kind of

---

***water-reddened fists**:「물이 묻어 빨개진 주먹」

***folks**:「여보세요」

***under her breath**=in a whisper

***For services already rendered**:「친절에 대한 보답이었읍니다」

***Not as of now**:「지금은 마시지 않겠읍니다」

***He went behind the counter and into the rear, pausing to rap on the doorjamb**:「그는 카운터 뒤로 뒷방으로 들어가더니 멈춰 서서 문설주를 툭툭 두드렸다」

a grocery job just for size.* Maybe I might like it, who knows? It happens I forgot some of the things about cutting and weighing and such, so I am wondering if you would mind me working around here for a couple-three weeks without wages just so I could learn again? It won't cost you a red cent. I know I am a stranger but I am an honest guy. Whoever keeps an eye on me* will find that out in no time.* That's fair enough, isn't it?"

Ida said, "Mister, isn't here a school."

"What do you say, pop?" Frank asked Morris.

"Because somebody is a stranger don't mean they ain't honest," answered the grocer. "This subject don't interest me. Interests me what you can learn here.* Only one thing"—he pressed his hand to his chest—"a heartache."

"You got nothing to lose on my proposition, has he now, Mrs?" Frank said. "I understand he don't feel so hot* yet, and if I helped him out a short week or two it would be good for his health, wouldn't it?"

Ida didn't answer.

But Morris said flatly, "No. It's a small, poor store. Three people would be too much."

Frank flipped an apron off a hook* behind the door and before either of them could say a word, removed his hat and

---

***I want to try some kind of a grocery job just for size**:「제게 꼭 알맞는 식료품점 일을 해보고 싶습니다」

***Whoever keeps an eye on me**:「저를 지켜 보는 사람이면 누구나」

***in no time**:「곧」

***Interests me what you can learn here**:「당신이 여기서 무엇을 배울 것이냐 하는 점이 내 관심거리오」

***hot**=very good 「아주 건강한」

***flip an apron off a hook**:「고리에서 앞치마를 홱 벗기다」

dropped the loop over his head. He tied the apron strings around him.

"How's that for fit?"*

Ida flushed, and Morris ordered him to take it off and put it back on the hook.

"No bad feelings, I hope,"* Frank said on his way out.

Helen Bober and Louis Karp walked, no hands touching, in the windy dark on the Coney Island boardwalk.

Louis had, on his way home for supper that evening, stopped her in front of the liquor store, on her way in from work.

"How's about a ride in the Mercury, Helen? I never see you much anymore. Things were better in the bygone days in high school."

Helen smiled. "Honestly, Louis, that's so far away." A sense of mourning at once oppressed her, which she fought to a practiced draw.*

"Near or far, it's all the same for me." He was built with broad back and narrow head, and despite prominent eyes was presentable.* In high school, before he quit,* he had worn his wet hair slicked straight back.* One day, after studying a picture of a movie actor in the *Daily News,* he had run a part

---

***How's that for fit?**:「제게 맞습니까?」

***No bad feelings, I hope**:「노하지 마시기 바랍니다」

***A sense of mourning . . . draw**:「순간적으로 슬픈 마음이 들었지만 그녀는 자주 했듯이 그 슬픔을 억제해 버렸다」

***despite prominent eyes was presentable**:「눈이 툭 튀어 나와 있었지만 못생긴 외모는 아니었다」

***before he quit**:「중퇴하기 전에」

***he had worn his wet hair slicked straight back**:「그는 젖은 머리를 뒤로 깨끗이 빗어 넘겼다」 slick back (down)「머리카락을 잘 매만지다」

across his head.* This was as much change as she had known in him. If Nat Pearl was ambitious, Louis made a relaxed living letting the fruit of his father's investment fall into his lap.*

"Anyway," he said, "why not a ride for old-times' sake?"*

She thought a minute, a gloved finger pressed into her cheek; but it was a fake gesture because she was lonely.

"For old-times' sake, where?"

"Name your scenery—continuous performance."*

"The Island?"

He raised his coat collar. "Brr, it's a cold, windy night. You wanna freeze?"*

Seeing her hesitation, he said, "But I'll die game.* When'll I pick you up?"

"Ring my bell after eight and I'll come down."

"Check," Louis said. "Eight bells."*

They walked to Seagate, where the boardwalk ended. She gazed with envy through a wire fence at the large lit houses fronting the ocean. The Island was deserted, except here and there an open hamburger joint or pinball machine concession.* Gone from the sky was the umbrella of rosy light

---

***he had run a part across his head**:「그는 머리에 가리마를 탔다」

***letting the fruit of his father's investment fall into his lap**:「아버지가 한 투자의 수익이 자기 앞으로 굴러 오게 하면서」

***for old-times' sake**:「옛정을 생각해서」

***Name your scenery—continuous performance**:「갈 곳을 말해 봐요—연속적으로 보여줄 테니」

***Brr, it's a cold, windy night. You wanna freeze?**:「우—, 춥고 바람부는 밤인데 너는 꽁꽁 얼고 싶으니?」 wanna=want to

***But I'll die game**:「그러나 끝까지 분발해야지」 추워도 끝까지 드라이브를 시켜준다는 뜻. die game=fight bravely to the last

***Eight bells**:「여덟 번 초인종을 누르지」

***an open hamburger joint or pinball machine concession**:「개점중인 햄버거 상점 또

that glowed over the place in summertime. A few cold stars gleamed down. In the distance a dark Ferris wheel looked like a stopped clock. They stood at the rail of the boardwalk, watching the black, restless sea.

All during their walk she had been thinking about her life, the difference between her aloneness now and the fun when she was young and spending every day of summer in a lively crowd of kids on the beach. But as her high school friends had got married, she had one by one given them up; and as others of them graduated from college, envious, ashamed of how little she was accomplishing, she stopped seeing them too. At first it hurt to drop people but after a time it became a not too difficult habit.* Now she saw almost no one, occasionally Betty Pearl, who understood, but not enough to make much difference.

Louis, his face reddened by the wind, sensed her mood.* "What's got in you, Helen?"* he said, putting his arm around her.

"I can't really explain it. All night I've been thinking of the swell times* we had on this beach when we were kids. And do you remember the parties? I suppose I'm blue* that I'm no longer seventeen."

"What's so wrong about twenty-three?"

"It's old, Louis. Our lives change so quickly. You know

는 회전당구기계가 있는 오락장」 joint「사람이 모이는 곳」 concession「영업장소」

***At first it hurt . . . habit**:「친구와 교제를 끊는 것은 처음에는 괴로왔지만 얼마 후에는 별로 어렵지 않은 버릇이 되었다」 *e.g.* drop an acquaintance「절교하다」

***sensed her mood**:「그녀의 기분을 알아차렸다」

***What's got in you, Helen?**:「어떻게 된 거야, Helen?」

***swell times**:「즐거웠던 시절」

***blue**=sad, discouraged

what youth means?"

"Sure I know. You don't catch me giving away nothing for nothing.* I got my youth yet."

"When a person is young he's privileged," Helen said, "with all kinds of possibilities. Wonderful things might happen, and when you get up in the morning you feel they will. That's what youth means, and that's what I've lost. Nowadays I feel that every day is like the day before, and what's worse, like the day after."

"So now you're a grandmother?"

"The world has shrunk for me."*

"What do you wanna be—Miss Rheingold?"

"I want a larger and better life. I want the return of my possibilities."

"Such as which ones?"*

She clutched the rail, cold through her gloves. "Education," she said, "prospects. Things I've wanted but never had."

"Also a man?"

"Also a man."

His arm tightened around her waist. "Talk is too cold, baby, how's about a kiss?"

She brushed his cold lips, then averted her head. He did not press* her.

"Louis," she said, watching a far-off light on the water, "what do you want out of your life?"

***You don't catch me giving away nothing for nothing**:「나는 무익하게 아무것도 낭비하지는 않아」 for nothing=uselessly, in vain

***The world has shrunk for me**:「나에게는 세상이 쪼그러 들었어요」

***Such as which ones?**:「예를 들면 어떤 것이지?」

***press**=force

He kept his arm around her. "The same thing I got—plus."

"Plus what?"

"Plus more, so my wife and family can have also."

"What if she wanted something different than you do?"

"Whatever she wanted I would gladly give her."

"But what if she wanted to make herself a better person, have bigger ideas, live a more worthwhile life? We die so quickly, so helplessly. Life *has* to have some meaning."

"I ain't gonna stop anybody from being better,"* Louis said, "That's up to them."*

"I suppose," she said.

"Say, baby, let's drop this deep philosophy and go trap a hamburger.* My stomach complains."

"Just a little longer. It's been ages since I came here this late in the year."*

He pumped his arms.* "Jesus, this wind, it flies up my pants. At least gimme* another kiss." He unbuttoned his overcoat.

She let him kiss her. He felt her breast. Helen stepped back out of his embrace. "Don't, Louis."

"Why not?" He stood there awkwardly, annoyed.

"It gives me no pleasure."

"I suppose I'm the first guy that ever gave it a nip?"*

***I ain't gonna stop anybody from being better**:「누구든 훌륭하게 되는 것을 막지는 않겠어요」 I ain't gonna～=I am not going to～

***That's up to them**:「그것은 각자가 할 일이죠」

***go trap a hamburger**:「햄버거를 먹다」

***this late in the year**:「(일년 중) 이렇게 늦은 계절에」

***He pumped his arms**:「그는 펌프의 핸들처럼 손을 상하로 움직였다」

***gimme**=give me

***give ～ a nip**:「꼬집다」

"Are you collecting statistics?"

"Okay," he said, "I'm sorry. You know I ain't a bad guy, Helen."

"I know you're not, but please don't do what I don't like."

"There was a time you treated me a whole lot better."

"That was the past, we were kids."

It's funny, she remembered, how necking made glorious dreams.*

"We were older than that, up till the time Nat Pearl started in college, then you got interested in him. I suppose you got him in mind for the future?"*

"If I do, I don't know it."

"But he's the one you want, ain't he? I like to know what that stuck-up has got beside a college education?* I work for my living."

"No, I don't want him, Louis." But she thought, Suppose Nat said I love you? For magic words a girl might do magic tricks.*

"So if that's so, what's wrong with me?"

"Nothing. We're friends."

"Friends I got all I need."

"What do you need, Louis?"

"Cut out the wisecracks, Helen.* Would it interest you that

***It's funny, . . . dreams**:「그녀의 기억에, 목을 껴안고 애무하는 것이 얼마나 멋있는 꿈을 주었는지, 지금 생각하면 우스웠다」

***I suppose you got him in mind for the future?**:「내가 보기에, 너는 그를 장래의 남편으로 삼을 생각이지?」

***I like to know what that stuck-up has got beside a college education?**:「대학교육을 받은 것 이외에 그 건방진 자가 무엇이 잘났는지 알고 싶구만」

***For magic words a girl might do magic tricks**:「마법과 같은 말에 대하여 소녀도 마법과 같은 재주를 부릴지도 모른다」

***Cut out the wisecracks, Helen**:「신 소리 그만 둬, Helen」 wisecrack=witticism,

I would honestly like to marry you?" He paled at his nerve.*

She was surprised, touched.

"Thank you," she murmured.

"Thank you ain't good enough. Give me yes or no."

"No, Louis."

"That's what I thought." He gazed blankly* at the ocean.

"I never guessed you were at all remotely interested.* You go with girls who are so different from me."

"Please, when I go with them you can't see my thoughts."

"No," she admitted.

"I can give you a whole lot better than you got."

"I know you can, but I want a different life from mine now, or yours. I don't want a storekeeper for a husband."

"Wines and liquors ain't exactly pisher groceries."*

"I know."

"It ain't because your old man don't like mine?"*

"No."

She listened to the wind-driven, sobbing surf. Louis said, "Let's go get the hamburgers."

"Gladly." She took his arm but could tell from the stiff way he walked that he was hurt.

As they drove home on the Parkway, Louis said, "If you

---

sarcasm

***He paled at his nerve**:「그는 자기의 용기에 자기도 놀라 얼굴이 창백해졌다」 nerve=boldness

***blankly**:「멍하니」

***I never guessed you were at all remotely interested**:「네가 나한테 조금이라도 관심이 있는지 난 전혀 생각해 보지 않았어」

***pisher groceries**:「시시한 식료품점」

***It ain't because your old man don't like mine**:「네 아버지가 나의 아버지를 좋아하지 않기 때문에 싫다는 건 아니겠지」

can't have everything you want, at least take something. Don't be so goddam proud."

Touché. "What shall I take, Louis?"

He paused. "Take less."

"Less I'll never take."

"People got to compromise."

"I won't with my ideals."*

"So what'll you be then, a dried-up prune of an old maid?* What's the percentage of that?"

"None."

"So what'll you do?"

"I'll wait. I'll dream. Something will happen."

"Nuts,"* he said.

He let her off in front of the grocery.

"Thanks for everything."

"You'll make me laugh." Louis drove off.

The store was closed, upstairs dark. She pictured her father asleep after his long day, dreaming of Ephraim. What am I saving myself for?* She asked herself. What unhappy Bober fate?

It snowed lightly the next day—too early in the year, complained Ida, and when the snow had melted it snowed again. The grocer remarked, as he was dressing in the dark,

---

***I won't with my ideals**:「난 내 이상과 타협할 수는 없어요」 won't 다음에 compromise가 생략됨.

***a dried-up prune of an old maid**:「시들어버린 얼간이 노처녀」 a prune=a dull or otherwise unpleasant person

***Nuts**:「바보 같은 소리, 제기랄(nonsense, nerts)」 증오·경멸·실망·거절 등을 나타냄.

***What am I saving myself for?**:「무엇 때문에 나는 내 몸을 소중히 하고 있을까?」

that he would shovel after he had opened the store. He enjoyed shoveling snow. It reminded him that he had practically lived in it in his boyhood; but Ida forbade him to exert himself* because he still complained of dizziness. Later, when he tried to lug the milk cases through the snow, he found it all but* impossible. And there was no Frank Alpine to help him, for he had disappeared after washing the window.

Ida came down shortly after her husband, in a heavy cloth coat, a woolen scarf pinned around her head and wearing galoshes. She shoveled a path through the snow and together they pulled in the milk. Only then did Morris notice that a quart bottle was missing from one of the cases.

"Who took it?" Ida cried.

"How do I know?"

"Did you count yet the rolls?"

"No."

"I told you always to count right away."

"The baker will steal from me? I know him twenty years."

"Count what everybody delivers,* I told you a thousand times."

He dumped the rolls out of the basket and counted them. Three were missing and he had sold only one to the Poilisheh. To appease* Ida he said they were all there.

The next morning another quart of milk and two rolls were gone. He was worried but didn't tell Ida the truth when she asked him if anything else was missing. He often hid un-

---

***exert oneself**:「힘써 일하다, 노력하다(endeavor, make efforts)」
***all but**=almost
***Count what everybody delivers**:「누가 배달하든지 모두 세어 보세요」
***appease**=soothe, calm「진정시키다」

pleasant news from her because she made it worse. He mentioned the missing bottle to the milkman, who answered, "Morris, I swear I left every bottle in that case. Am I responsible for this lousy neighborhood?"

He promised to cart the milk cases into the vestibule for a few days.* Maybe whoever was stealing the bottles would be afraid to go in there. Morris considered asking the milk company for a storage box.* Years ago he had had one at the curb, a large wooden box in which the milk was padlocked; but he had given it up after developing a hernia lifting the heavy cases out,* so he decided against a box.

On the third day, when a quart of milk and two rolls had again been taken, the grocer, much disturbed, considered calling the police. It wasn't the first time he had lost milk and rolls in this neighborhood. That had happened more than once—usually some poor person stealing a breakfast. For this reason Morris preferred not to call the police but to get rid of the thief by himself. To do it, he would usually wake up very early and wait at his bedroom window in the dark. Then when the man—sometimes it was a woman—showed up and was helping himself to the milk, Morris would quickly raise the window and shout down, "Get outa here,* you thief you." The thief, startled—sometimes it was a customer who could afford to buy the milk he was stealing—would drop the bottle and run. Usually he never appeared again—a lost customer

---

***He promised to cart the milk cases into the vestibule for a few days**:「그는 며칠간 우유궤짝을 문간방까지 운반하겠다고 약속했다」

***a storage box**:「보관상자」

***after developing a hernia lifting the heavy cases out**:「무거운 궤짝을 드느라고 탈장(脫腸)에 걸린 후」

***Get outa here**:「썩 꺼져 버려」

cut another way*—and the next goniff was somebody else.

So this morning Morris arose at four-thirty, a little before the milk was delivered, and sat in the cold in his long underwear, to wait. The street was heavy with darkness as he peered down. Soon the milk truck came, and the milkman, his breath foggy, lugged the two cases of milk into the vestibule. Then the street was silent again, the night dark, the snow white. One or two people trudged by. An hour later, Witzig, the baker, delivered the rolls, but no one else stopped at the door. Just before six Morris dressed hastily and went downstairs. A bottle of milk was gone, and when he counted the rolls, so were two of them.

He still kept the truth from Ida.* The next night she awoke and found him at the window in the dark.

"What's the matter?" she asked, sitting up in bed.

"I can't sleep."

"So don't sit in your underwear in the cold. Come back to bed."

He did as she said. Later, the milk and rolls were missing.

In the store he asked the Poilisheh whether she had seen anyone sneak into the vestibule* and steal a quart of milk. She stared at him with small eyes, grabbed the sliced roll and slammed* the door.

Morris had a theory that the thief lived on the block.* Nick

***a lost customer cut another way**:「사라진 고객은 다른 상점으로 가기 마련이었다」

***He still kept the truth from Ida**:「그래도 그는 Ida에게 그 사실을 알리지 않았다」

***sneak into the vestibule**:「문간방으로 몰래 들어오다」

***slam**=shut with force and noise

***Morris had a theory that the thief lived on the block**:「Morris는 도둑이 그 블록에 살고 있다고 확신했다」 that이하는 theory의 동격절임.

Fuso wouldn't do such a thing; if he did Morris would have heard him going down the stairs, the coming up again. The thief was somebody from outside. He sneaked along the street close to the houses, where Morris couldn't see him because of the cornice that hung over the store;* then he softly opened the hall door, took the milk, two rolls from the bag, and stole away, hugging the house fronts.*

The grocer suspected Mike Papadopolous, the Greek boy who lived on the floor above Karp's store. He had served a reformatory sentence at eighteen.* A year later he had in the dead of night climbed down the fire escape overhanging Karp's back yard, boosted himself up on the fence* and forced a window into the grocery. There he stole three cartons of cigarettes, and a roll of dimes that Morris had left in the cash register. In the morning, as the grocer was opening the store, Mike's mother, a thin, old-looking woman, returned the cigarettes and dimes to him. She had caught her son coming in with them and had walloped* his head with a shoe. She clawed his face, making him confess what he had done. Returning the cigarettes and dimes, she had begged Morris not to have the boy arrested and he had assured her he wouldn't do such a thing.

On this day that he had guessed it might be Mike taking the

***because of the cornice that hung over the store**:「가게 위로 나와 있는 처마 언저리의 벽에 붙은 장식에 가려져」

***stole away, hugging the house fronts**:「집쪽으로 몸을 바싹 붙여서 슬쩍 빠져 나갔다」 hug=keep close to~

***He had served a reformatory sentence at eighteen**:「그는 18세에 소년원에 복역했다」 serve one's sentence「형을 치르다, 복역하다」

***boost oneself up on the fence**:「담을 기어오르다」

***wallop**=beat soundly, thrash「후려패다」

milk and rolls, shortly after eight A.M., Morris went up the stairs and knocked reluctantly on Mrs. Papadopolous' door.

"Excuse me that I bother you," he said, and told her what had been happening to his milk and rolls.

"Mike work all nights in restaurants," she said. "No come home till nine o'clock in mornings. Sleep all days." Her eyes smoldered.* The grocer left.

Now he was greatly troubled. Should he tell Ida and let her call the police? They were bothering him at least once a week with questions about the holdup but had produced nobody. Still, maybe it would be best to call them, for this stealing had gone on for almost a week. Who could afford it? Yet he waited, and that night as he was leaving the store by the side door, which he always padlocked after shutting the front door from inside, he flicked on the cellar light* and as he peered down the stairs, his nightly habit, his heart tightened with foreboding* that somebody was down there. Morris unlocked the lock, went back into the store and got a hatchet. Forcing his courage,* he slowly descended the wooden steps. The cellar was empty. He searched in the dusty storage bins, poked around all over, but there was no sign of anybody.

In the morning he told Ida what was going on and she, calling him big fool, telephoned the police. A stocky,* red-faced detective came, Mr. Minogue, from a nearby precinct,*

***Her eyes smoldered**:「그녀의 눈에는 분한 기색이 나타났다」 smolder=show a suppressed emotion

***flick on the cellar light**:「지하실 전등을 찰칵 키다」

***his heart tightened with foreboding** ~:「~의 예감 때문에 마음이 죄었다」

***Forcing his courage**:「억지로 용기를 내어」

***stocky**=strongly built 「몸집이 건장한」

***a nearby precinct**:「인근 경찰서」

who was in charge of investigating Morris's holdup. He was a soft-spoken, unsmiling man, bald, a widower who had once lived in this neighborhood. He had a son Ward, who had gone to Helen's junior high school, a wild boy, always in trouble for manhandling girls.* When he saw one he knew playing in front of her house, or on the stoop, he would come swooping down* and chase her into the hall. There, no matter how desperately the girl struggled, or tenderly begged him to stop, Ward forced his hand down her dress and squeezed her breast till she screamed. Then by the time her mother came running down the stairs he had ducked* out of the hall, leaving the girl sobbing. The detective, when he heard of these happenings, regularly beat up his son, but it didn't do much good. Then one day, about eight years ago, Ward was canned* from his job for stealing from the company. His father beat him sick and bloody with his billy* and drove him out of the neighborhood. After that, Ward disappeared and nobody knew where he had gone. People felt sorry for the detective, for he was a strict man and they knew what it meant to him to have such a son.

Mr. Minogue seated himself at the table in the rear and listened to Ida's complaint. He slipped on his glasses and wrote in a little black notebook. The detective said he would have a cop watch the store mornings after the milk was delivered, and if there was any more trouble to let him know.

***a wild boy, always in trouble for manhandling girls**:「소녀들을 못 살게 들볶아 항상 두통거리인 난폭한 소년」 manhandle=handle roughly
***swoop down**:「마구 덤비다」
***duck**=move out quickly
***be canned**=be fired「해고당하다」
***billy**=truncheon「경찰봉」

As he was leaving, he said, "Morris, would you recognize Ward Minogue if you happened to see him again? I hear he's been seen around but whereabouts I don't know."

"I don't know," said Morris. "Maybe yes or maybe no. I didn't see him for years."

"If I ever meet up with him," said the detective, "I might bring him in to you for identification."*

"What for?"

"I don't know myself—just for possible identification."

Ida said afterward that if Morris had called the police in the first place, he might have saved himself a few bottles of milk that they could hardly afford to lose.

That night, on an impulse,* the grocer closed the store an hour later than usual. He snapped on the cellar light* and cautiously descended the stairs, gripping his hatchet. Near the bottom hc uttered a cry and the hatchet fell from his hands. A man's drawn and haggard face* stared up at him in dismay.* It was Frank Alpine, gray and unshaven. He had been asleep with his hat and coat on, sitting on a box against the wall. The light had awakened him.

"What do you want here?" Morris cried out.

"Nothing," Frank said dully. "I have just been sleeping in the cellar. No harm done."

"Did you steal from me my milk and rolls?"

"Yes," he confessed. "On account of I was hungry."

"Why didn't you ask me?"

***for identification**:「확인하기 위해서」
***on an impulse**:「충동에 이끌려서」
***snap on ~ light**:「전등불을 켜다」
***A man's drawn and haggard face**:「남자의 일그러지고 수척한 얼굴」
***in dismay**:「당황해서」

Frank got up. "Nobody has any responsibility to take care of me but myself. I couldn't find any job. I used up every last cent I had. My coat is too thin for this cold and lousy climate. The snow and the rain get in my shoes so I am always shivering. Also, I had no place to sleep. That's why I came down here."

"Don't you stay any more with your sister?"

"I have no sister. That was lie I told you. I am alone by myself."

"Why you told me you had a sister?"

"I didn't want you to think I was a bum."*

Morris regarded the man silently. "Were you ever in prison sometimes?"

"Never, I swear to Christ."

"How you came to me in my cellar?"

"By accident.* One night I was walking around in the snow so I tried the cellar door and found out you left it unlocked, then I started coming down at night about an hour after you closed the store. In the morning, when they delivered the milk and rolls, I sneaked up through the hall, opened the door and took what I needed for breakfast. That's practically all I ate all day. After you came down and got busy with some customer or a salesman, I left by the hallway with the empty milk bottle under my coat. Later I threw it away in a lot.* That's all there is to it.* Tonight I took a chance* and came in while you were

---

***I didn't want you to think I was a bum**:「당신이 나를 부랑자로 여기지 않기를 바랐읍니다」 you는 to think의 의미상 주어임. a bum=a tramp「부랑자」

***By accident**=by chance「우연히」

***in a lot**:「빈 터에」

***That's all there is to it**:「할 이야기는 이것이 전부입니다」

***take a chance**=make a venture「모험을 하다」

still in the back of the store, because I have a cold and don't feel too good."

"How can you sleep in such a cold and drafty cellar?"*

"I slept in worse."*

"Are you hungry now?"

"I'm always hungry."

"Come upstairs."

Morris pickd up his hatchet, and Frank, blowing his nose in his damp handkerchief, followed him up the stairs.

Morris lit a light in the store and made two fat liverwurst sandwiches with mustard,* and in the back heated up a can of bean soup. Frank sat at the table in his coat, his hat lying at his feet. He ate with great hunger, his hand trembling as he brought the spoon to his mouth. The grocer had to look away.*

As the man was finishing his meal, with coffee and cup cakes, Ida came down in felt slippers and bathrobe.

"What happened?" she asked in fright, when she saw Frank Alpine.

"He's hungry," Morris said.

She guessed at once. "He stole the milk!"

"He was hungry," explained Morris. "He slept in the cellar."

"I was practically starving," said Frank.

"Why didn't you look for a job?" Ida asked.

"I looked all over."

***drafty cellar**:「외풍이 들어오는 지하실」
***I slept in worse**:「저는 더 지독한 곳에서도 잤읍니다」
***liverwurst sandwiches with mustard**:「겨자를 바른 간 소시지 샌드위치」
***look away**=turn the eyes away「눈을 딴 데로 돌리다」

After, Ida said to Frank, "When you finish, please go someplace else." She turned to her husband. "Morris, tell him to go someplace else. We are poor people."

"This he knows."

"I'll go away," Frank said, "as the lady wishes."

"Tonight is already too late," Morris said. "Who wants he should walk all night in the streets?"

"I don't want him here." She was tense.*

"Where you want him to go?"

Frank set his coffee cup on the saucer and listened with interest.

"This ain't my businss," Ida answered.

"Don't anybody worry," said Frank. "I'll leave in ten minutes' time. You got a cigarette, Morris?"

The grocer went to the bureau and took out of the drawer a crumpled pack of cigarettes.*

"It's stale,"* he apologized.

"Don't make any difference."* Frank lit a stale cigarette, inhaling with pleasure.

"I'll go after a short while," he said to Ida.

"I don't like trouble," she explained.

"I won't make any. I might look like a bum in these clothes, but I am not. All my life I lived with good people."

"Let him stay here tonight on the couch," Morris said to Ida.

"No. Give him better a dollar he should go someplace else."

***She was tense**:「그녀는 긴장되어 있었다」
***a crumpled pack of cigarettes**:「구겨진 담뱃갑」
***stale**=musty「곰팡내 나는」
***Don't make any difference**:「상관없읍니다」

"The cellar would be fine," Frank remarked.

"It's too damp.* Also rats."

"If you let me stay there one more night I promise I will get out the first thing in the morning.* You don't have to be afraid to trust me.* I am an honest man."

"You can sleep here," Morris said.

"Morris, you crazy," shouted Ida.

"I'll work it off for you,"* Frank said. "Whatever I cost you I'll pay you back. Anything you want me to do, I'll do it."

"We will see," Morris said.

"No," insisted Ida.

But Morris won out, and they went up, leaving Frank in the back, the gas radiator left lit.

"He will clean out the store,"* Ida said wrathfully.

"Where is his truck?" Morris asked, smiling. Seriously he said, "He's a poor boy. I feel sorry for him."

They went to bed. Ida slept badly. Sometimes she was racked by* awful dreams. Then she awoke and sat up in bed, straining to hear noises in the store—of Frank packing huge bags of groceries to steal. But there was no sound. She dreamed she came down in the morning and all the stock was gone, the shelves as barren as the picked bones of dead birds. She dreamed, too, that the Italyener had sneaked up into the

---

***damp**—slightly wet「습기찬, 축축한」

***I will get out the first thing in the morning**:「내일 아침이 되면 곧 나가겠읍니다」

***You don't have to be afraid to trust me.**=You need not be afraid to trust me.「걱정 말고 믿어 주시오」

***I'll work it off for you**:「저는 일해서 신세를 갚겠읍니다」*e.g.* I'll work off a debt.「저는 일 해서 빚을 갚겠읍니다」

***He will clean out the store**:「그는 가게를 다 쓸어 가 버릴 거요」

***be racked by** ～:「～으로 고통을 받다」

house and was peeking through the keyhole of Helen's door. Only when Morris got up to open the store did Ida fall fitfully asleep.

The grocer trudged down the stairs with a dull pain in his head. His legs felt weak. His sleep had not been refreshing.

The snow was gone from the streets and the milk boxes were again lying on the sidewalk near the curb. None of the bottles were missing. The grocer was about to drag in the milk cases when the Poilisheh came by. She went inside and placed three pennies on the counter. He entered with the brown bag of rolls, cut up one and wrapped it. She took it wordlessly and left.

Morris looked through the window in the wall. Frank was asleep on the couch in his clothes, his coat covering him. His beard was black, his mouth loosely open.

The grocer went out into the street, grabbed both milk boxes and yanked.* The shape of a black hat blew up in his head, flared into hissing light, and exploded.* He thought he was rising but felt himself fall.

Frank dragged him in and laid him on the couch. He ran upstairs and banged on the door. Helen, holding a housecoat over her nightdress, opened it. She suppressed a cry.

"Tell your mother your father just passed out.* I called the ambulance."

She screamed. As he ran down the stairs he could hear Ida

***yank**=give a sharp pull to「확 잡아당기다」

***The shape of a black hat . . . and exploded**:「검은 모자의 형상이 머리 안에서 부풀더니 쉿쉿 소리나는 번쩍이는 빛이 되고 마침내 폭발했다」 *e.g.* blow up a tire「타이어에 바람을 넣다」

***nass out**=become unconscious, faint「의식을 잃다」

moaning. Frank hurried into the back of the store. The Jew lay white and motionless on the couch. Frank gently removed his apron. Draping the loop over his own head,* he tied the tapes around him.*

"I need the experience," he muttered.

***Draping the loop over his own head**:「apron의 고리로 된 끈을 머리로부터 쓰고」
***he tied the tapes around him**:「그는 납작한 끈을 몸에 매었다」

3

Morris had reopened the wound on his head. The ambulance doctor, the same who had treated him after the holdup, said he had got up too soon last time and worn himself out.* He again bandaged the grocer's head, saying to Ida, "This time let him lay in bed a good couple of weeks till his strength comes back." "You tell him, doctor," she begged, "he don't listen to me." So the doctor told Morris, and Morris weakly nodded. Ida, in a gray state of collapse,* remained with the patient all day. So did Helen, after calling the ladies' underthings concern where she worked.* Frank Alpine stayed competently downstairs in the store. At noon Ida remembered him and came down to tell him to leave. Recalling her dreams, she connected him with their new misfortune. She felt that if he had not stayed the night, this might not have happened.

Frank was clean-shaven in the back, having borrowed Morris's safety razor, his thick hair neatly combed, and when she appeared he hopped up to ring open the cash register,*

***he had got up too soon last time and worn himself out**:「요전번에 너무 일찍 일어나서 과로했다」

***in a gray state of collapse**:「침울한 허탈상태에서」

***after calling the ladies' underthings concern where she worked**:「그녀가 근무하는 여자 내의 회사에 전화를 건 다음」

***he hopped up to ring open the cash register**:「그는 벌떡 일어나서 금전등록기를 열었다」

showing her a pile of puffy bills.*

"Fifteen," he said, "count every one."

She was astonished. "How is so much?"

He explained, "We had a busy morning. A lot of people stopped in to ask about Morris's accident."

Ida had planned to replace him with Helen* for the time being, until she herself could take over, but she was now of two minds.*

"Maybe you can stay," she faltered, "if you want to, till tomorrow."

"I'll sleep in the cellar, Mrs. You don't have to worry about me. I am as honest as the day."

"Don't sleep in the cellar," she said with a tremble to her voice, "my husband said on the couch. What can anybody steal here? We have nothing."

"How is he now?" Frank asked in a low voice.

She blew her nose.

The next morning Helen went reluctantly to work. Ida came down at ten to see how things were. This time there were only eight dollars in the drawer, but still better than lately. He apologized, "Not so good today, but I wrote down every article I sold so you'll know nothing stuck to my fingers."* He produced a list of goods sold, written on wrapping paper. She happened to notice that it began with three cents for a roll. Glancing around, Ida saw he had packed out the few cartons

---

***a pile of puffy bills**:「두툼한 지폐뭉치」 puffy=swollen, fat

***Ida had planned to replace him with Helen**:「Ida는 Helen으로 하여금 그를 대신하게 하려고 했다」

***she was now of two minds**:「그녀는 이제 마음이 두 갈래로 갈라졌다」

***so you'll know nothing stuck to my fingers**:「제가 하나도 훔친 것이 없음을 알 수 있도록」

delivered yesterday, swept up, washed the window from the inside and had straightened the cans on the shelves. The place looked a little less dreary.*

During the day he also kept himself busy with odd jobs. He cleaned the trap of the kitchen sink,* which swallowed water slowly, and in the store fixed a light whose chain wouldn't pull,* making useless one lamp. Neither of them mentioned his leaving. Ida, still uneasy, wanted to tell him to go but she couldn't ask Helen to stay home any more, and the prospect of two weeks alone in the store, with her feet and a sick man in the bargain* to attend upstairs, was too much for her. Maybe she would let the Italian stay ten days or so. With Morris fairly well recovered there would be no reason to keep him after that. In the meantime he would have three good meals a day and a bed, for being little more than a watchman.* What business, after all, did they do here? And while Morris was not around she would change a thing or two she should have done before. So when the milkman stopped by for yesterday's empties, she ordered containers brought from now on. Frank Alpine heartily approved. "Why should we bother with bottles?" he said.

Despite all she had to do upstairs, and her recent good impressions of him, Ida haunted the store,* watching his every move. She was worried because, now, not Morris but she was responsible for the man's presence in the store. If something

---

***The place looked a little less dreary**:「가게가 전보다 좀 덜 쓸쓸해 보였다」
***the trap of the kitchen sink**:「부엌 싱크대의 트랩장치」
***fixed a light whose chain wouldn't pull**:「줄이 당겨지지 않는 전구 하나를 수리했다」
***in the bargain**=besides「게다가, 그 위에 또」
***for being little more than a watchman**:「야경꾼 정도의 일을 한 댓가로」
***Ida haunted the store**:「Ida는 가게에 자주 나타났다」

bad happened, it would be her fault. Therefore, though she climbed the stairs often to tend to her husband's needs, she hurried back down, arriving pale and breathless to see what Frank was up to. But anything he happened to be doing was helpful. Her suspicions died slowly, though they never wholly died.

She tried not to be too friendly to him, to make him feel that a distant relationship meant a short one.* When they were in the back or for a few minutes together behind the counter she discouraged conversation,* took up something to do, or clean, or her paper to read. And in the matter of teaching him the business there was also little to say. Morris had price tags displayed under all items on the shelves, and Ida supplied Frank with a list of prices for meats and salads and for the miscellaneous unmarked things like loose coffee, rice or beans. She taught him how to wrap neatly and efficiently, as Morris had long ago taught her, how to read the scale and to set and handle the electric meat slicer. He caught on quickly;* she suspected he knew more than he said he did. He added rapidly and accurately, did not overcut meats or overload the scale on bulk items, as she had urged him not to do, and judged well the length of paper needed to wrap with, and what number bag to pack goods into, conserving* the larger bags which cost more money. Since he learned so fast, and since she had seen in him not the least evidence of dishonesty (a hungry

---

***to make him feel that a distant relationship meant a short one**:「서먹서먹한 관계는 오래 가지 못한다는 것을 그로 하여금 깨닫게 하기 위해」
***she discouraged conversation**:「그녀는 대화를 나누려 하지 않았다」
***He caught on quickly**:「그는 신속히 배웠다」
***conserve**:「절약하다, 보존하다」

man who took milk and rolls, though not above suspicion,* was not the same as a thief), Ida forced herself to remain upstairs with more calm, in order to give Morris his medicine, bathe her aching feet and keep up the house, which was always dusty from the coal yard. Yet she felt, whenever she thought of it, always a little troubled at the thought of a stranger's presence below, a goy,* after all, and she looked forward to the time when he was gone.

Although his hours were long—six to six, at which time she served him his supper—Frank was content. In the store he was quits with the outside world, safe from cold, hunger and a damp bed.* He had cigarettes when he wanted them and was comfortable in clean clothes Morris had sent down, even a pair of pants that fitted him after Ida lengthened and pressed the cuffs.* The store was fixed, a cave, motionless.* He had all his life been on the move, no matter where he was; here he somehow couldn't be. Here he could stand at the window and watch the world go by, content to be here.

It wasn't a bad life. He woke before dawn. The Polish dame was planted at the door like a statue, distrusting him with beady eyes to open the place in time for her to get to work.* Her he didn't like; he would gladly have slept longer. To get

---

***though not above suspicion**:「의심하지 않을 수는 없지만」

***goy**=gentile「이교도」 non-Jew「이방인」

***In the store he was quits with . . . and a damp bed**:「가게에 있는 한, 그는 밖의 세상을 두려워할 필요가 없었고 추위, 배고픔, 습기찬 침대 등을 걱정하지 않아도 되었다」 be quits with=be on even terms「비기다, 피장파장이다」

***after Ida lengthened and pressed the cuffs**:「Ida가 바지의 접단을 펴서 다린 후에」

***The store was fixed, a cave, motionless**:「가게는 안정되어 있었고, 하나의 움직이지 않는 동굴과 같았다」

***distrusting him . . . work**:「그녀가 일을 시작하는데 늦지 않게끔 그가 제시간에 맞추어 가게 문을 열지를 구슬 같은 눈동자로 못 미더워하면서」

up in the middle of the night for three lousy cents was a joke but he did it for the Jew. After packing away the milk containers, turning bottomside up the occasional one that leaked,* he swept the store and then the sidewalk. In the back he washed, shaved, had coffee and a sandwich, at first made with meat from a ham or roast pork butt, then after a few days, from the best cut. As he smoked after coffee he thought of everything he could do to improve this dump* if it were his. When somebody came into the store he was up with a bound,* offering service with a smile. Nick Fuso, on Frank's first day, was surprised to see him there, knowing Morris could not afford a clerk. But Frank said that though the pay was scarce there were other advantages. They spoke about this and that, and when the upstairs tenant learned Frank Alpine was a paisan,* he told him to come up and meet Tessie. She cordially invited him for macaroni* that same night, and he said he would come if they let him bring the macs.*

Ida, after the first few days, began to go down at her regular hour, around ten, after she had finished the housework; and she busied herself with writing in a notebook which bills they had got and which paid.* She also wrote out, in a halting

---

***After packing away . . . one that leaked**:「통이 새는 것을 거꾸로 세워서, 우유 저장함에 집어 넣은 후에」

***dump**:「보잘것없는 집 또는 건물」

***he was up with a bound**:「그는 벌떡 일어났다」

***paisan**:「이탈리아계 미국인」

***macaroni**:「이탈리아 국수」

***if they let him bring the macs**:「자기가 macaroni 재료를 가져오는 것을 그들이 허락해 준다면」

***writing in a notebook which bills they had got and which paid**:「가게에 어떤 청구서가 들어왔고 어떤 청구서를 지불했는지 공책에·기록하느라고」

hand, a few meager special-account checks for bills* that could not be paid in cash directly to the drivers, mopped the kitchen floor, emptied the garbage pail into the metal can on the curb outside and prepared salad if it was needed. Frank watched her shred* cabbage on the meat slicer for coleslaw,* which she made in careful quantity, because if it turned sour it had to be dumped into the garbage. Potato salad was a bigger job, and she cooked up a large pot of new potatoes, which Frank helped her peel hot in their steaming jackets.* Every Friday she prepared fish cakes and a panful of home-made baked beans, first soaking the little beans overnight, pouring out the water, then spreading brown sugar on top before baking. Her expression as she dipped in among the soggy beans* pieces of ham from a butt she had cut up caught his eye,* and he felt for her repugnance* for hating to touch the ham, and some for himself because he had never lived this close to Jews before. At lunchtime there was a little "rush,"* which meant that a few dirty-faced laborers from the coal yard and a couple of store clerks from on the block wanted sand-wiches and containers of hot coffee. But the "rush", for which they both went behind the counter, petered out* in a matter of

---

***a few meager special-account checks for bills**:「청구서에 대한 몇 장의 소액 특별 당좌수표」

***shred**:「조각조각으로 끊다」

***coleslaw**:「cabbage로 만든 salad」

***Frank helped her peel hot in their steaming jackets**:「Frank는 그녀가 김 나는 감자 껍질을 벗기는 것을 도왔다」 *e.g.* potatoes boiled in their jackets「껍질 째 삶은 감자」

***soggy beans**:「물에 불은 콩」

***Her expression as . . . caught his eye**:「그녀가 …할 때의 표정이 그의 시선을 끌었다」

***he felt for her repugnance**:「그녀의 혐오감에 대하여 그는 동정했다」 feel for= sympathize

***a little "rush"**:「약간의 혼잡시간」

***peter out**=slowly end or disappear *e.g.* My enthusiasm petered out.「내 열성도 사

minutes and then came the dead hours of the afternoon. Ida said he ought to take some time off, but he answered that he had nowhere special to go and stayed in the back, reading the *Daily News* on the couch, or flipping through* some magazines that he had got out of the public library, which he had discovered during one of his solitary walks in the neighborhood.

At three, when Ida departed for an hour or so to see if Morris needed something, and to rest, Frank felt relieved. Alone, he did a lot of casual eating, sometimes with unexpected pleasure. He sampled* nuts, raisins, and small boxes of stale dates or dried figs, which he liked anyway; he also opened packages of crackers, macaroons, cupcakes and doughnuts, tearing up their wrappers into small pieces and flushing them down the toilet.* Sometimes in the middle of eating sweets he would get very hungry for something more substantial, so he made a thick meat and Swiss cheese sandwich on a seeded hard roll spread with mustard, and swallowed it down with a bottle of ice-cold beer. Satisfied, he stopped roaming in the store.

Now and then there were sudden unlooked-for flurries of customers,* mostly women, whom he waited on attentively, talking to them about all kinds of things. The drivers, too, liked his sociability and cheery manner and stayed to chew the fat.* Otto Vogel, once when he was weighing a ham, warned

---

그러지고 말았다」
***flip through**:「책장을 빨리 넘기다」
***sample**:「시식하다, 시음하다」
***flushing them down the toilet**:「포장지가 수세식 변소에서 씻겨 내려가게 했다」
***sudden unlooked-for flurries of customers**:「갑자기 뜻하지 않게 손님들이 몰려옴」
***to chew the fat**=to chatter「재갈거리기 위하여」

him in a low voice, "Don't work for a Yid,* kiddo. They will steal your ass while you are sitting on it." Frank, though he said he didn't expect to stay long, felt embarrassed for being there; then, to his surprise, he got another warning, from an apologetic* Jew salesman of paper products, Al Marcus, a prosperous, yet very sick and solemn character who wouldn't stop working. "This kind of a store is a death tomb, positive," Al Marcus said. "Run out while you can. Take my word,* if you stay six months, you'll stay forever."

"Don't worry about that," answered Frank.

Alone afterward, he stood at the window, thinking thoughts about his past, and wanting a new life. Would he ever get what he wanted? Sometimes he stared out of the back yard window at nothing at all, or at the clothesline above, moving idly in the wind, flying Morris's scarecrow union suits, Ida's hefty bloomers, modestly folded lengthwise, and her housedresses guarding her daughter's flower-like panties and restless brassières.*

In the evening, whether he wanted to or not, he was "off."* Ida insisted, fair was fair.* She fed him a quick supper and allowed him, with apologies because she couldn't afford more, fifty cents spending money. He occasionally passed the time upstairs with the Fusos or went with them to a picture at the local movie house. Sometimes he walked, in spite of the cold,

---

***a Yid**=a Jew
***apologetic**=diffident「소심한, 내성적인, 자신이 없는」
***Take my word**:「내 말을 믿으시오」
***her housedresses . . . and restless brassières**:「딸의 꽃같이 아름다운 팬티와 흔들리는 브래지어를 가려주고 있는 그녀의 실내복」
***he was "off"**:「그는 퇴근을 했다」
***Ida insisted, fair was fair**:「Ida는 규정은 규정대로 지켜야 한다고 고집을 부렸다」

and stopped off at a poolroom* he knew, about a mile and a half from the grocery store. When he got back, always before closing, for Ida wouldn't let him keep a key to the store in his pocket, she counted up the day's receipts,* put most of the cash into a small paper bag and took it with her, leaving Frank five dollars to open up with in the morning. After she had gone, he turned the key in the front door lock, hooked the side door through which she had left,* put out the store lights and sat in his undershirt in the rear, reading tomorrow's pink-sheeted paper that he had picked off Sam Pearl's stand on his way home. Then he undressed and went restlessly to bed in a pair of Morris's bulky, rarely used, flannel pajamas.

The old dame, he thought with disgust, always hurried him out of the joint* before her daughter came down for supper.

The girl was in his mind a lot. He couldn't help it, imagined seeing her in the things that were hanging on the line—he had always had a good imagination. He pictured her as she came down the stairs in the morning; also saw himself standing in the hall after she came home, watching her skirts go flying as she ran up the stairs. He rarely saw her around, had never spoken to her but twice, on the day her father had passed out. She had kept her distance—who could blame her, dressed as he was and what he looked like then?* He had the feeling as he spoke to her, a few hurried words, that he knew more about

---

***a poolroom**:「당구장」
***the day's receipts**:「그 날의 수입액」
***hooked the side door through which she had left**:「그녀가 나간 옆 문을 잠그었다」
***always hurried him out of the joint**:「항상 그를 가게 밖으로 서둘러 내보냈다」
***She had kept her . . . then?**:「그녀는 그와의 사이에 거리를 두었다—그의 옷차림이나 그 당시의 그의 모습으로 판단해 볼 때 누가 그녀를 탓할 수 있겠는가?」

her than anybody would give him credit for.* He had got this thought the first time he had ever laid eyes on her, that night he saw her through the grocery window. When she had looked at him he was at once aware of something starved about her,* a hunger in her eyes he couldn't forget because it made him emember his own, so he knew how wide open she must be.* But he wouldn't try to push anything, for he had heard that these Jewish babes could be troublemakers and he was not looking for any of that now—at least no more than usual; besides, he didn't want to spoil anything before it got started. There were some dames you had to wait for—for them to come to you.

His desire grew to get to know her, he supposed because she had never once come into the store in all the time he was there except after he left at night. There was no way to see and talk to her to her face, and this increased his curiosity. He felt they were both lonely but her old lady kept her away from him as if he had a dirty disease; the result was he grew more impatient to find out what she was like, get to be friends with her* for whatever it was worth. So, since she was never around, he listened and watched for her. When he heard her walking down the stairs he went to the front window and stood there waiting for her to come out; he tried to look casual, as if he

---

***he knew more about her than anybody would give him credit for**:「다른 사람이 그가 알고 있으리라고 생각하는 이상으로 그는 Helen에 대하여 더 많이 알고 있었다」 *e.g.* I gave you credit for being more sensible.「나는 너를 사리를 좀더 아는 사람으로 생각했었다」

***When she had looked at him . . . starved about her**:「그녀가 그를 쳐다보았을 때 그는 즉시 그녀에게 무언가 굶주린 기색이 있음을 알아차렸다」

***so he knew how wide open she must be**:「그 결과 그녀가 유혹에 빠지기 쉽다는 사실을 그는 알아냈다」

***get to be friends with her**:「그녀와 친구가 되다」

weren't watching, just in case she happened to glance back* and see him; but she never did, as if she liked nothing about the place enough to look back on. She had a pretty face and a good figure, small-breasted, neat, as if she had meant herself to look that way. He liked to watch her brisk, awkward walk till she turned the corner. It was a sexy walk, with a wobble* in it, a strange movement, as though she might dart sideways although she was walking forward. Her legs were just a bit bowed, and maybe that was the sexy part of it. She stayed in his mind after she had turned the corner; her legs and small breasts and the pink brassières that covered them. He would be reading something or lying on his back on the couch, smoking, and she would appear in his mind, walking to the corner. He did not have to shut his eyes to see her. Turn around, he said out loud, but in his thoughts she wouldn't.*

To see her coming toward him he stood at the lit grocery window at night, but often before he could catch sight of her she was on her way upstairs, or already changing her dress in her room, and his chance was over for the day. She came home about a quarter to six, sometimes a little earlier, so he tried to be at the window around then, which wasn't so easy because that was the time for Morris's few supper customers to come in. So he rarely saw her come home from work, though he always heard her on the stairs. One day things were slower than usual in the store,* it was dead at five-thirty, and Frank

---

***happen to glance back**:「우연히 돌아다보다」

***wobble**:「비틀거림」

***Turn around, he said out loud, but in his thoughts she wouldn't**:「그는 큰 소리로 돌아서라고 명령했지만 그의 머리 속에 나타나는 그녀는 말을 들어주지 않았다」

***things were slower than usual in the store**:「평상시보다 가게가 한가했다」

said to himself, Today I will see her. He combed his hair in the toilet so that Ida wouldn't notice, changed into a clean apron, lit a cigarette, and stood at the window, visible in its light.* At twenty to six, just after he had practically shoved a woman out of the joint, a dame who had happened to walk in off the trolley,* he saw Helen turn Sam Pearl's corner. Her face was prettier than he had remembered and his throat tightened as she walked to within a couple of feet of him, her eyes blue, her hair, which she wore fairly long, brown, and she had an absent-minded way of smoothing it back off the side of her face. He thought she didn't look Jewish, which was all to the good.* But her expression was discontented, and her mouth a little drawn.* She seemed to be thinking of something she had no hope of ever getting. This moved him, so that when she glanced up and saw his eyes on her,* his face plainly showed his emotion. It must have bothered her because she quickly walked, without noticing him further, to the hall and disappeared inside.

The next morning he didn't see her—as if she had sneaked out on him—and at night he was waiting on somebody when she returned from work; regretfully he heard the door slam behind her. Afterward he felt downhearted; every sight lost to a guy who lived with his eyes was lost for all time.* He

---

***visible in its light**:「전등불로 볼 수 있는」

***a dame who had happened to walk in off the trolley**:「전차에서 내려 우연히 가게에 들어온 여자」 앞의 woman과 dame은 동격.

***He thought she didn't look Jewish, which was all to the good**:「그녀는 유태인답지 않다고 그는 생각했으며 그건 더욱 잘 된 일이었다」

***a little drawn**:「약간 일그러진」

***saw his eyes on her**:「그녀를 보고 있는 그의 눈을 (그녀가) 보았다」

***every sight lost to a guy who lived with his eyes was lost for all time**:「보고 싶은 욕망 때문에 사는 놈이 볼 것을 볼 수 없게 되면, 언제나 인생에 실패한다」 이 문장의

thought up different ways to meet her and exchange a few words. What he had on his mind to say to her about himself was beginning to weigh on him,* though he hadn't clearly figured out* the words. Once he thought of coming in on her unexpectedly while she was eating her supper, but then he would have Ida to deal with. He also had the idea of opening the door the next time he saw her and calling her into the store; he could say that some guy had telephoned her, and after that talk about something else, but nobody did call her. She was in her way a lone bird, which suited him fine, though why she should be with her looks he couldn't figure out. He got the feeling that she wanted something big out of life, and this scared him. Still, he tried to think of schemes of getting her inside the store, even planning to ask her something like did she know where her old man kept his saw; only she mightn't like that, her mother being around all day to tell him. He had to watch out not to scare her any farther away than the old dame had done.

For a couple of nights after work he stood in a hallway next door to the laundry across the street in the hope that she would come out to do some errand, then he would cross over, tip his hat and ask if he could keep her company to where she was going.* But this did not pay off either, because she didn't leave the house. The second night he waited fruitlessly until Ida put out the lights in the grocery window.

동사는 was lost임.

***was beginning to weigh on him**:「그를 괴롭히기 시작했다」 weigh on「괴롭히다, 무거운 짐이 되다」

***figure out**:「생각해 내다, 해결하다, 이해하다」

***ask if he could keep her company to where she was going**:「그녀가 가는 곳까지 동반해도 좋으냐고 묻다」 keep ~ company=accompany「동반하다」

One evening toward the end of the second week after Morris's accident, Frank's loneliness burdened him to the point of irritation.* He was eating his supper a few minutes after Helen had returned from work, while Ida happened to be upstairs with Morris. He had seen Helen come round the corner and had nodded to her as she approached the house. Caught by surprise, she half-smiled,* then entered the hall. It was then the lonely feeling gripped him. While he was eating, he felt he had to get her into the store before her old lady came down and it was time for him to leave. The only excuse he could think of was to call Helen to answer the phone and after he would say that the guy must've hung up. It was a trick but he had to do it. He warned himself not to, because it would be starting out the wrong way with her and he might someday regret it. He tried to think of a better way but time was pressing him and he couldn't.*

Frank got up, went over to the bureau, and took the phone off its cradle.* He then walked out into the hall, opened the vestibule door, and holding his breath,* pressed the Bober bell.

Ida looked over the banister. "What's the matter?"

"Telephone for Helen."

He could see her hesitate, so he returned quickly to the

***Frank's loneliness burdened him to the point of irritation**:「Frank의 고독감은 신경질이 날 정도로 그를 괴롭혔다」

***Caught by surprise, she half-smiled**:「그녀는 어쩔줄 모르고 반쯤 미소를 지었다」

***time was pressing him and he couldn't**:「시간이 얼마 없어 그는 묘안을 생각해 낼 수 없었다」

***took the phone off its cradle**:「수화기를 대에서 내려놓았다」 cradle=rest「대」

***hold one's breath**=stop breathing「숨을 죽이다」

store. He sat down, pretending to be eating, his heart whamming* so hard it hurt. All he wanted, he told himself, was to talk to her a minute so the next time would be easier.

Helen eagerly entered the kitchen. On the stairs she had noticed the excitement that flowed through her.* My God, it's gotten to be that a phone call is an event.*

If it's Nat, she thought, I might give him another chance.

Frank half-rose as she entered, then sat down.

"Thanks," she said to him as she picked up the phone.

"Hello." While she waited he could hear the buzz in the receiver.

"There's nobody there," she said, mystified.

He laid down his fork. "This girl called you," he said gently.

But when he saw the disappointment in her eyes, how bad she felt, he felt bad.

"You must've been cut off."*

She gave him a long look. She was wearing a white blouse that showed the firmness of her small breasts. He wet his dry lips, trying to figure out some quick way to square himself,* but his mind, usually crowded with all sorts of schemes, had gone blank.* He felt very bad, as he had known he would, that

---

***wham**:「쾅쾅 치다, 쾅하고 부딪

***she had noticed the excitement that flowed through her**:「그녀는 자기가 홍분하고 있음을 알아차렸다」

***My God, it's gotten . . . event**:「참 같이지, 전화 하나 걸려오는 것이 무슨 사건이 일어난 것같이 되었네」

***You must've been cut off**:「저쪽에서 끊었음에 틀림없군요」

***trying to figure out some quick way to square himself**:「자기가 저지른 잘못을 넘길 묘안을 생각해 내려 힘썼다」 square oneself「잘못을 보상하다, 과거를 청산하다, 변명하다」

***his mind, usually crowded with all sorts of schemes, had gone blank**:「평소에 그

he had done what he had.* If he had it to do over he wouldn't do it this way.

"Did she leave you her name?" Helen asked.

"No."

"It wasn't Betty Pearl?"

"No."

She absently brushed back her hair. "Did she say anything to you?"

"Only to call you." He paused. "Her voice was nice—like yours. Maybe she didn't get me straight* when I said you were upstairs but I would ring your doorbell, and that's why she hung up."

"I don't know why anybody would do that."

Neither did he. He wanted to step clear of his mess* but saw no way other than to keep on lying. But lying made their talk useless. When he lied he was somebody else lying to somebody else.* It wasn't the two of them as they were. He should have kept that in his mind.

She stood at the bureau, holding the telephone in her hand as if still expecting the buzz to become a voice; so he waited for the same thing, a voice to speak and say he had been telling the truth, that he was a man of fine character. Only that didn't happen either.

의 머리에는 여러 묘안이 가득 차 있었지만 지금은 백지 같은 상태였다」 *e.g.* My memory was completely blank. 「나는 아무것도 생각해낼 수 없었다」

***He felt very bad, as he had known he would, that he had done what he had**:「미리 예상한 것이지만, 그가 저지른 짓으로 인하여 아주 미안하게 되었다고 그는 느꼈다」 that 이하는 He felt very bad의 원인을 나타내는 부사절임.

***she didn't get me straight**:「그녀는 내 말을 잘못 알아들었다」

***step clear of one's mess**:「난처한 입장에서 벗어나다」

***When he lied he was somebody else lying to somebody else**:「그가 거짓말을 했을 때 그는 다른 사람에게 거짓말을 하는 딴 사람이 되는 것이다」

He gazed at her with dignity as he considered saying the simple truth, starting from there, come what would, but the thought of confessing what he had done almost panicked* him.

"I'm sorry," he said brokenly, but by then she was gone, and he was attempting to fix in his memory what she had looked like so close.*

Helen too was troubled. Not only could she not explain why she believed yet did not fully believe him, nor why she had lately become so conscious of his presence among them,* though he never strayed from the store, but she was also disturbed by her mother's efforts to keep her away from him. "Eat when he leaves," Ida had said. "I am not used to goyim* in my house." This annoyed Helen because of the assumption that she would keel over* for somebody just because he happened to be a gentile. It meant, obviously, her mother didn't trust her. If she had been casual about him, Helen doubted she would have paid him any attention to speak of. He was interesting looking, true, but what except a poor grocery clerk? Out of nothing Ida was trying to make something.*

Though Ida was still concerned at having the young Italian

***panicked**:「당황케 했다」

***what she had looked like so close**:「그토록 가까이에서 본 그녀의 모습」

***why she had lately become so conscious of his presence among them**:「왜 가족들 중에서, 그녀가 최근에 그의 존재를 그토록 의식하게 되었는지」

***goyim**=goys (goy의 복수)

***keel over**:「타락하다, 실패하다, 졸도하다」

***Out of nothing Ida was trying to make something**:「아무것도 아닌 것을 가지고 Ida는 말썽을 일으키려고 하는 것이다」

around the place, she observed with pleased surprise how, practically from the day of his appearance, the store had improved. During the first week there were days when they had taken in from five to seven dollars more than they were averaging daily in the months since summer. And the same held for the second week. The store was of course still a poor store, but with this forty to fifty a week more they might at least limp along* until a buyer appeared. She could at first not understand why more people were coming in, why more goods were being sold. True, the same thing had happened before. Without warning, after a long season of dearth,* three or four customers, lost faces, straggled in one days, as if they had been let out of their poor rooms* with a few pennies in their pockets. And others, who had skimped on food,* began to buy more. A storekeeper could tell almost at once when times were getting better. People seemed less worried and irritable, less in competition for the little sunlight in the world. Yet the curious thing was that business, according to most of the drivers, had not very much improved anywhere. One of them said that Schmitz around the corner was having his troubles too; furthermore he wasn't feeling so good. So the sudden pickup of business in the store,* Ida thought, would not have happened without Frank Alpine. It took her a while to admit this to herself.

***limp along**:「간신히 꾸려나가다」

***a long season of dearth**:「긴 궁핍의 계절」 dearth=scarceness「결핍, 부족」

***as if they had been let out of their poor rooms**:「초라한 방에서 밖으로 나가도록 그들이 허락을 받기나 한 것처럼」 let out「해방시키다, 면제시키다, 자유롭게 하다」

***skimp on food**:「음식을 찔끔찔끔 사다」 skimp「감질나게 주다, 인색하게 굴다」

***the sudden pickup of business in the store**:「갑작스런 가게 경기의 호전」 pickup= improvement, a getting better

The customers seemed to like him. He talked a lot as he waited on them, sometimes saying things that embarrassed Ida but made the customers, the gentile housewives, laugh. He somehow drew in people she had never before seen in the neighborhood, not only women, men too. Frank tried things that Morris and she could never do, such as attempting to sell people more than they asked for, and usually he succeeded. "What can you do with a quarter of a pound?" he would say. "A quarter is for the birds—not even a mouthful. Better make it a half." So they would make it a half. Or he would say, "Here's a new brand of mustard that we just got in today. It weighs two ounces more than the stuff they sell you in the supermarkets for the same price. Why don't you give it a try? If you don't like it, bring it back and I will gargle* it." And they laughed and bought it. This made Ida wonder if Morris and she were really suited to the grocery business. They had never been salesmen.

One of the women customers called Frank a supersalesman, a word that brought a pleased smile to his lips. He was clever and worked hard. Ida's respect for him reluctantly grew; gradually she became more relaxed in his presence. Morris was right in recognizing that he was not a bum but a boy who had gone through bad times.* She pitied him for having lived in an orphan asylum. He did his work quickly, never complained, kept himself neat and clean now that he had soap and water around, and answered her politely. The one or two times, just lately, that he had briefly talked to Helen in her

---

***gargle**:「목을 가시다, 양치질하다」
***a boy who had gone through bad times**:「불행한 세월을 살아 온 소년」

presence, he had spoken like a gentleman and didn't try to stretch a word into a mouthful.* Ida discussed the situation with Morris and they raised his "spending money" from fifty cents a day to five dollars for the week. Despite her good will to him, this worried Ida, but, after all, he was bringing more money into the store, the place looked spic and span*—let him keep five dollars of their poor profit. Bad as things still were,* he willingly did so much extra around the store—how could they not pay him a little something? Besides, she thought, he would soon be leaving.

Frank accepted the little raise with an embarrassed smile. "You don't have to pay me anything more, Mrs, I said I would work for nothing to make up for* past favors from your husband and also to learn the business. Besides that, you give me my bed and board, so you don't owe me a thing."

"Take," she said, handing him a crumpled five-dollar bill. He let the money lie on the counter till she urged him to put it into his pocket. Frank felt troubled about the raise because he was earning something for his labor that Ida knew nothing of, for business was a little better than she thought. During the day, while she was not around, he sold at least a buck's worth, or a buck and a half, that he made no attempt to ring up on the register.* Ida guessed nothing; the list of sold items he had supplied her with in the beginning they had discontinued as impractical. It wasn't hard for him to scrape up* here a bit of

---

***stretch a word into a mouthful**:「한 마디로 끝나는 것을 길게 중언 부언하다」
***spic and span**:「잘 정돈된」
***Bad as things still were**:「경기는 아직도 나쁘지만」
***make up for**=compensate for「~을 보상하다」
***ring up on the register** :「금전등록기에 돈을 넣다」
***scrape up**:「긁어 모으다」

change, there a bit. At the end of the second week he had ten dollars in his pocket. With this and the five she gave him he bought a shaving kit,* a pair of cheap brown suede shoes, a couple of shirts and a tie or two; he figured that if he stayed around two more weeks he would own an inexpensive suit. He had nothing to be ashamed of, he thought—it was practically his own dough he was taking. The grocer and his wife wouldn't miss it because they didn't know they had it, and they wouldn't have it if it wasn't for his hard work. If he weren't working there, they would have less than they had with him taking what he took.

Thus he settled it in his mind only to find himself remorseful.* He groaned, scratching the backs of his hands with his thick nails. Sometimes he felt short of breath and sweated profusely. He talked aloud to himself when he was alone, usually when he was shaving or in the toilet, exhorted himself to be honest.* Yet he felt a curious pleasure in his misery, as he had at times in the past when he was doing something he knew he oughtn't to, so he kept on dropping quarters into his pants pocket.*

One night he felt very bad about all the wrong he was doing and vowed to set himself straight.* If I could do one right thing, he thought, maybe that would start me off; then he

---

***a shaving kit**:「면도기구」

***Thus he settled it . . . remorseful**:「이렇게 그 일을 마음속에서 해결했지만 양심의 가책은 여전했다」

***exhorted himself to be honest**:「정직해야 한다고 자신에게 타일렀다」

***he kept on dropping quarters into his pants pocket**:「그는 바지 주머니에 계속 25센트의 은화를 집어넣었다」

***vowed to set himself straight**:「올바른 사람이 되려고 마음속으로 맹세했다」

thought if he could get the gun and get rid of it he would at least feel better. He left the grocery after supper and wandered restlessly in the foggy streets, feeling cramped in the chest* from his long days in the store and because his life hadn't changed much since he had come here. As he passed by the cemetery, he tried to keep out of his mind the memory of the holdup but it kept coming back in. He saw himself sitting with Ward Minogue in the parked car, waiting for Karp to come out of the grocery, but when he did his store lights went out and he hid in the back among the bottles. Ward said to drive quick around the block so they would flush the Jew out,* and he would slug* him on the sidewalk and take his fat wallet away; but when they got back, Karp's car was gone with him in it, and Ward cursed him into an early grave. Frank said Karp had beat it,* so they ought to scram,* but Ward sat there with heartburn,* watching, with his small eyes, the grocery store, the one lit place on the block besides the candy store on the corner.

"No," Frank urged, "it's just a little joint, I got my doubts if they took in thirty bucks today."

"Thirty is thirty," Ward said. "I don't care if it's Karp or Bober, a Jew is a Jew."

"Why not the candy store?"

Ward made a face.* "I can't stand penny candy."

***feeling cramped in the chest**:「마음이 울적하고 괴로왔다」
***flush ~ out**:「~을 몰아내다」
***slug**:「세게 후려치다」
***Karp had beat it**:「Karp는 도망쳤다」 beat it=run away, hurry away
***scram**:「(주로 명령형으로) 도망쳐라」
***with heartburn**:「분한 듯이」 heartburn=heartburning「분함, 불만, 불평, 원한」
***Ward made a face**:「Ward는 얼굴을 찌푸렸다」

"How do you know his name?" asked Frank.

"Who?"

"The Jew grocer."

"I used to go to school with his daughter. She has a nice ass."

"Then if that's so, he will recognize you."

"Not with a rag around my snoot,* and I will rough up my voice. He ain't seen me for eight or nine years. I was a skinny* kid then."

"Have it your way.* I will keep the car running."

"Come in with me," Ward said. "The block is dead. Nobody will expect a stickup* in this dump."

But Frank hesitated. "I thought you said Karp was the one you were out after?"*

"I will take Karp some other time. Come on."

Frank put on his cap and crossed the car tracks with Ward Minogue. "It's your funeral," he said, but it was really his own.*

He remembered thinking as they went into the store, a Jew is a Jew, what difference does it make? Now he thought, I held him up because he was a Jew. What the hell are they to me so that I gave them credit for it?*

***Not with a rag around my snoot**:「얼굴에 누더기를 감으면 몰라 볼 거야」 snoot「얼굴」

***skinny**=very thin, very lean「깡마른」

***Have it your way**:「네 마음대로 해」

***a stickup**=hold up「권총강도」

***you said Karp was the one you were out after**:「네가 노리는 사람이 Karp라고 말했지」

***"It's your funeral," he said, but it was really his own**:「"잘못하면 너는 끝장이야" 하고 Frank는 말했다. 그러나 그건 사실상 그의 끝장이 되고 말았다」

***What the hell are they to me so that I gave them credit for it?**:「도대체 그들이 무엇이기에 내가 그들을 감싸주어야 하나?」

But he didn't know the answer and walked faster, from time to time glancing through the spiked iron fence at the shrouded gravestones. Once he felt he was being followed and his heart picked up a hard beat. He hurried past the cemetery and turned right on the first street after it, hugging the stoops of the stone houses* as he went quickly down the dark street. When he reached the poolroom he felt relieved.

Pop's poolroom was a dreary four-table joint, owned by a glum* old Italian with a blue-veined bald head and droopy* hands, who sat close to his cash register.

"Seen Ward yet?" Frank said.

Pop pointed to the rear where Ward Minogue, in his fuzzy black hat and a bulky overcoat, was practicing shots alone at a table. Frank watched him place a black ball at a corner pocket and aim a white at it. Ward leaned tensely forward, his face strained,* a dead butt hanging from his sick mouth. He shot but missed. He banged his cue on the floor.*

Frank had drifted past the players at the other tables. When Ward looked up and saw him, his eyes lit with fear. The fear drained* after he recognized who it was. But his pimply face was covered with sweat.

He spat his butt to the floor. "What have you got on your feet, you bastard, gumshoes?"

***hugging the stoops of the stone houses**:「석조건물의 현관 입구의 계단쪽에 몸을 바싹 붙이고」 stoop「현관 입구의 계단, 현관, 포치」

***glum**=sullen「침울한」

***droopy**:「축 쳐진」

***his face strained**:「얼굴을 긴장시키고」 his 앞에 with를 보충해서 해석할 것.

***He banged his cue on the floor** :「그는 큐로 마룻바닥을 쾅 쳤다」 *e.g.* bang one's fist on the table「주먹으로 테이블을 쾅 치다」

***The fear drained**:「공포의 빛이 사라졌다」

"I didn't want to spoil your shot."

"Anyway you did."

"I've been looking for you about a week."

"I was on my vacation." Ward smiled in the corner of his mouth.

"On a drunk?"

Ward put his hand to his chest and brought up a belch.* "I wish to hell it was.* Somebody tipped* my old man I was around here, so I hid out for a while. I had a rough time. My heartburn is acting up."* He hung up his cue, then wiped his face with a dirty handkerchief.

"Why don't you go to a doctor?" Frank said.

"The hell with them."*

"Some medicine might help you."

"What will help me is if my goddam father drops dead."

"I want to talk to you, Ward," Frank said in a low voice.

"So talk."

Frank nodded toward the players at the next table.

"Come out in the yard," Ward said. "I got something I want to say to you."

Frank followed him out the rear door into a small enclosed back yard with a wooden bench against the building. A weak bulb shone down on them from the top of the doorjamb.*

Ward sat down on the bench and lit a cigarette. Frank did the same, from his own pack. He puffed but got no pleasure

---

***bring up a belch**:「트림을 하다」
***I wish to hell it was**:「그랬었으면 오죽 좋겠나!」
***tip**=give secret information「밀고하다」
***My heartburn is acting up**:「가슴앓이가 더 심해지고 있지」
***The hell with them**:「의사들은 있으나 마나야」
***doorjamb**=doorpost「문설주」

from the butt, so he threw it away.

"Sit down," said Ward.

Frank sat on the bench. Even in the fog he stinks, he thought.

"What do you want me for?" Ward asked, his small eyes restless.

"I want my gun, Ward. Where is it?"

"What for?"

"I want to throw it in the ocean."

Ward snickered.* "Cat got your nuts?"*

"I don't want some dick* coming around and asking me do I own it."

"I thought you said you bought the rod off a fence."*

"That's right."

"Then nobody's got a record of it, so what are you scared of?"

"If you lost it," Frank said, "they trace them even without a record."

"I won't lose it," Ward said. After a minute he ground his cigarette into the dirt. "I will give it back to you after we do this job I have on my mind."

Frank looked at him. "What kind of a job?"

"Karp. I want to stick him up."

"Why Karp?—there are bigger liquor stores"

"I hate that Jew son of a bitch and his popeyed Louis.

***snicker**=giggle「숨 죽여 웃다」

***Cat got your nuts?**:「너 겁쟁이가 되었니?」

***dick**:「형사, 탐정」detective의 단축형.

***I thought you said you bought the rod off a fence**:「그 권총을 장물매매소에서 샀다고 네가 말한 것으로 난 생각하는데」 the rod「권총」 a fence「장물매매소」

When I was a kid all I had to do was go near banjo eyes and they would complain to my old man and get me beat up."*

"They would recognize you if you go in there."

"Bober didn't. I will use a handkerchief and wear some different clothes. Tomorrow I will go out and pick up a car. All you got to do is drive and I will make the heist."*

"You better stay away from that block," Frank warned. "Somebody might recognize you."

Ward moodily rubbed his chest. "All right, you sold me.* We will go somewheres else."

"Not with me," Frank said.

"Think it over."

"I've had all I want."*

Ward showed his disgust. "The minute I saw you I knew you would puke all over."*

Frank didn't answer.

"Don't act so innocent," Ward said angrily. "You're hot, the same as me."*

"I know," Frank said.

"I slugged him because he was lying where he hid the rest of the dough," Ward argued.

"He didn't hide it. It's a poor, lousy store."

***When I was a kid . . . beat up**:「내가 어렸을 때 그 밴죠 같은 눈깔 곁에 가기만 해도 놈들은 내 늙은이에게 불평하여 날 얻어맞게 했어」

***heist**=robbery, holdup

***All right, you sold me**:「좋아, 네 말도 일리가 있어」 sell=convince, persuade. *e.g.* sell one's children on reading「아이들에게 독서의 재미를 설득하다」

***I've had all I want**:「하고 싶은 건 다 해 봤어」

***The minute I saw you I knew you would puke all over**:「너를 처음 만났을 때부터 난 네가 싫어할 줄 알았지」 puke「혐오하다, 토하다」

***You're hot, the same as me**:「너도 경찰에 쫓기고 있는 거야, 나처럼」 hot=wanted by the police「지명수배된」

"I guess you know all about that."

"What do you mean?"

"Can the crud.* I know you been working there."

Frank drew a breath. "You following me again, Ward?"

Ward smiled. " I followed you one night after you left the poolroom. I found out you were working for a Jew and living on bird crap."*

Frank slowly got up. "I felt sorry for him after you slugged him, so I went back to give him a hand while he was in a weak condition. But I won't be staying there long."

"That was real sweet of you.* I suppose you gave him back the lousy seven and a half bucks that was your part of the take?"

"I put it back in the cash register. I told the Mrs the business was getting better."

"I never thought I would meet up with a goddam Salvation Army soldier."*

"I did it to quiet my conscience," Frank said.

Ward rose. "That ain't your conscience you are worried about."*

"No?"

"It's something else. I hear those Jew girls make nice ripe lays."*

***Can the crud**:「시치미 떼지 마」

***living on bird crap**:「푼돈을 받고 살고 있더군」 bird crap「새똥」여기서는 푼돈이라는 의미.

***That was real sweet of you**:「참말 착한 사람이군」

***Salvation Army**:「구세군」

***That ain't your conscience you are worried about**:「네가 고민하는 것은 양심의 가책 때문이 아니야」

***lay**:「성교, 그 상대」

Frank went back without his gun.

Helen was with her mother as Ida counted the cash.

Frank stood behind the counter, cleaning his fingernails with his jackknife blade, waiting for them to leave so he could close up.*

"I think I'll take a hot shower before I go to bed," Helen said to her mother. "I've felt chilled all night."

"Good night," Ida said to Frank. "I left five dollars change for the morning."

"Good night," said Frank.

They left by the rear door and he heard them go up the stairs. Frank closed the store and went into the back. He thumbed through tomorrow's *News,* then got restless.*

After a while he went into the store and listened at the side door; he unlatched the lock, snapped on the cellar light, closed the cellar door behind him so no light would leak out into the hall, then quietly descended the stairs.

He found the air shaft* where an old unused dumb-waiter* stood, pushed the dusty box back and gazed up the vertical shaft. It was pitch-dark. Neither the Bobers' bathroom window nor the Fusos' showed any light.

Frank struggled against himself but not for long. Shoving the dumb-waiter back as far as it would go, he squeezed into*

***close up**=shut up for the night「닫아 버리다」

***He thumbed through tomorrow's *News,* then got restless**:「그는 내일 날짜의 뉴스지를 넘기며 훑어보고 있다가 점점 마음이 들뜨기 시작했다」*e.g.* thumb through the book「재빨리 페이지를 넘기며 책을 훑어보다」

***air shaft**:「환기구멍」

***dumb-waiter**:「도르래를 통한 밧줄로 물건을 달아 올리는 운반기구」

***squeeze into**=force into too small a space「(비좁은 곳에) 억지로 비집고 들어가다」

the shaft and then boosted himself up on top of the box. His heart shook him with its beating.

When his eyes got used to the dark he saw that her bathroom window was only a couple of feet above his head. He felt along* the wall as high as he could reach and touched a narrow ledge* around the air shaft. He thought he could anchor himself on it* and see into the bathroom.

But if you do it, he told himself, you will suffer.

Though his throat hurt and his clothes were drenched in sweat, the excitement of what he might see forced him to go up.

Crossing himself,* Frank grabbed both of the dumb-waiter ropes and slowly pulled himself up, praying the pulley at the skylight* wouldn't squeak too much.

A light went on over his head.

Holding his breath, he crouched motionless,* clinging to the swaying ropes. Then the bathroom window was shut with a bang. For a while he couldn't move, the strength gone out of him. He thought he might lose his grip and fall, and he thought of her opening the bathroom window and seeing him lying at the bottom of the shaft in a broken, filthy heap.*

It was a mistake to do it, he thought.

But she might be in the shower before he could get a look

***feel along**:「손으로 더듬다」

***ledge**=shelf「선반」

***he could anchor himself on it**:「그는 그 위에 올라 앉을 수 있었다」

***Crossing himself**:「십자를 긋고 나서」

***the pulley at the skylight**:「천창에 달린 활차」

***he crouched motionless**:「꼼짝 않고 그는 쪼그려 앉았다」 crouch=stoop with the limbs close to the body

***in a broken, filthy heap**:「박살난 더러운 시체가 되어」

at her, so, trembling, he began again to pull himself up. In a few minutes he was straddling the ledge,* holding onto the ropes to steady himself yet keep his full weight off the wood.*

Leaning forward, though not too far, he could see through the uncurtained crossed sash window* into the old-fashioned bathroom. Helen was there looking with sad eyes at herself in the mirror. He thought she would stand there forever, but at last she unzippered her housecoat, stepping out of it.

He felt a throb of pain at her nakedness, an overwhelming desire to love her, at the same time an awareness of loss, of never having had what he had wanted most,* and other such memories he didn't care to recall.

Her body was young, soft, lovely, the breasts like small birds in flight, her ass like a flower. Yet it was a lonely body in spite of its lovely form, lonelier. Bodies are lonely, he thought, but in bed she wouldn't be. She seemed realer to him now than she had been, revealed without clothes, personal, possible. He felt greedy as he gazed, all eyes at a banquet, hungry so long as he must look. But in looking he was forcing her out of reach,* making her into a thing only of his seeing, her eyes reflecting his sins, rotten past, spoiled ideals, his passion poisoned by his shame.*

Frank's eyes grew moist and he wiped them with one hand.

***straddle the ledge**=sit astride of the ledge「선반에 걸터 앉다」

***keep his full weight off the wood**:「그의 전 체중이 나무 궤짝에 실리지 않게 하다」

***the uncurtained crossed sash window**:「커튼을 안 친 십자형 내리닫이 창」

***an awareness of loss, of never having had what he had wanted most**:「무언가 놓쳐 버린 느낌, 가장 바라던 것을 가져 보지 못한 애석한 느낌」

***in looking he was forcing her out of reach**:「쳐다봄으로써 그는 손이 닿지 않는 곳으로 그녀를 밀어제치고 있었다」

***his passion poisoned by his shame**:「치욕으로 더러워진 정욕」

When he gazed up again she seemed, to his horror, to be staring at him through the window, a mocking smile on her lips, her eyes filled with scorn, pitiless. He thought wildly of jumping, bolting, broken-boned, out of the house;* but she turned on the shower and stepped into the tub, drawing the flowered plastic curtain around her.

The window was quickly covered with steam. For this he was relieved, grateful. He let himself down silently. In the cellar, instead of the grinding remorse* he had expected to suffer, he felt a moving joy.

***He thought wildly of jumping, bolting, broken-boned, out of the house**:「그는 자리에서 뛰어 내려 뼈가 부서진 채 집 밖으로 달아나버릴까하고 미친듯이 생각했다」

***grinding remorse**:「괴로운 양심의 가책」grinding=tormenting *e.g.* grinding toothache「고통스러운 치통」

4

On a Saturday morning in December, Morris, after a little more than two impatient weeks upstairs, came down with his head healed.* The night before, Ida told Frank he would have to leave in the morning, but when Morris later learned this they had an argument. Although he hadn't said so to Ida, the grocer, after his long layoff,* was depressed at the prospect of having to take up his dreary existence* in the store. He dreaded the deadweight of hours, mostly sad memories of his lost years of youth. That business was better gave him some comfort but not enough, for he was convinced from all Ida had told him that business was better only because of their assistant, whom he remembered as a stranger with hungry eyes, a man to be pitied. Yet the why of it* was simple enough—the store had improved not because this cellar dweller was a magician, but because he was not Jewish. The goyim in the neighborhood were happier with one of their own.* A Jew stuck in their throats.* Yes, they had, on and off, patronized

---

***came down with his head healed**:「머리의 상처가 나아서 (가게로) 내려왔다」
***after his long layoff**:「오래 쉬고 난 후에」
***take up one's dreary existence**:「따분한 생활을 시작하다」
***the why of it**:「그 이유」
***The goyim···own**:「이 근처의 이방인들은 그들과 같은 이방인이 하나 있어야 더 즐거워하는 것이다」
***A Jew stuck in their throats**:「유태인은 못마땅한 존재였다」 stick in one's throat「마음에 들지 않다」

his store, called him by his first name and asked for credit as if he were obliged to give it,* which he had, in the past, often foolishly done; but in their hearts they hated him. If it weren't so, Frank's presence could not have made such a quick difference in income. He was afraid that the extra forty-five dollars weekly would melt away overnight if the Italian left and he vehemently said so to Ida. She, though she feared he was right, still argued that Frank must be let go.* How could they, she asked, keep him working seven days a week, twelve hours a day, for a miserable five dollars? It was unjust. The grocer agreed, but why push the boy into the street if he wanted to stay longer? The five dollars, he admitted, was nothing, but what of the bed and board, the free packs of cigarettes, the bottles of beer she said he guzzled* in the store? If things went on well, he would offer him more, maybe even a small commission, very small—maybe on all they took in over a hundred and fifty a week,* a sum they had not realized since Schmitz had opened up around the corner; meantime he would give him his Sundays off and otherwise reduce his hours. Since Morris was now able to open the store, Frank could stay in bed till nine. This proposition was no great bargain but the grocer insisted that the man have the chance

---

***asked for credit as if he were obliged to give it**:「마치 Morris가 마땅히 주어야 할 의무라도 있는 듯이, 외상을 달라고 그들은 요구했다」

***still argued that Frank must be let go**:「Frank를 내보내야 한다고 여전히 주장했다」

***guzzle**=drink and eat greedily

***he would offer him . . . week**:「그는 더 많이 줄 수도 있고, 아마 아주 적은 수수료이긴 하나, 매주 150불 이상의 매상고에 대하여 그에 상응하는 수수료를 줄 수도 있다」
e.g. They allowed him a commission of 5 per cent on the sales made.「그들은 그에게 매상에 대하여 5%의 수수료를 냈다」

to take or refuse it.*

Ida, a red flush spreading on her neck,* said, "Are you crazy, Morris? Even with the forty more that comes in, which we give him away five dollars, our little profit, who can afford to keep him here? Look what he eats. It's impossible."

"We can't afford to keep him but we can't afford to lose him, on account he might improve more the business if he stays," Morris answered.

"How can three people work in such a small store?" she cried.

"Rest your sick feet," he answered. "Sleep longer in the morning and stay more upstairs in the house. Who needs you should be so tired every night?"

"Also," Ida argued, "who wants him in the back all night so we can't go inside after the store is closed when we forget something?"

"This I thought about also. I think I will take off from Nick's rent upstairs a couple dollars and tell him he should give Frank the little room to sleep in. They don't use it for nothing, only storage.* There, with plenty blankets he will be comfortable, with a door which it goes right in the hall so he can come in and go out with his own key without bothering anybody. He can wash himself here in the store."

"A couple dollars less from the rent comes also from our poor pocket," Ida replied, pressing her clasped hands to her

---

***the man have the chance to take or refuse it**:「그 제안을 받아들이느냐 거절하느냐 하는 것은 그 사람의 의사에 달려 있다」 insisted의 목적절 내의 동사이므로 has가 아니라 have임.

***a red flush spreading on her neck**:「목을 붉혀가며」

***They don't use it for nothing, only storage**:「그들은 그 방을 창고로밖에 쓰지 않는다」

bosom.* "But the most important is I don't want him here on account of Helen. I don't like the way he looks on her."*

Morris gazed at her. "So you like maybe how Nat looks on her, or Louis Karp? That's the way they look, the boys. Tell me better, how does she look on him?"

She shrugged stiffly.

"This is what I thought. You know yourself Helen wouldn't be interested in such a boy. A grocery clerk don't interest her. Does she go out with the salesmen where she works, that they ask her? No. She wants better—so let her have better."

"Will be trouble,"* she murmured.

He belittled her fears, and when he came down on Saturday morning, spoke to Frank about staying on for a while. Frank had arisen before six and was sitting dejectedly on the couch when the grocer came in. He agreed at once to continue on in the store under the conditions Morris offered.

More animated now,* the clerk said he liked the idea of living upstairs near Nick and Tessie; and Morris that day arranged it, in spite of Ida's misgivings, by promising three dollars off their rent.* Tessie lugged out of the room a trunk, garment bags and a few odds and ends of furniture; after, she dusted and vacuumed.* Between what she offered, and what Morris got out of his bin* in the cellar, they supplied a bed

---

***pressing her clasped hands to her bosom**:「깍지 낀 두 손을 가슴에 꼭 대면서」
***I don't like the way he looks on her**:「그가 Helen을 보는 눈초리가 좋지 않아요」
***Will be trouble**:「문제가 생길 거예요」
***More animated now** = As he was more animated now「점원은 힘을 되찾고」
***by promising three dollars off their rent**:「그들의 집세에서 3불을 덜 받을 것을 약속함으로써」
***vacuum**:「진공 청소기로 청소하다」
***bin**:「큰 상자, 궤」

with a fairly good mattress, a usable chest of drawers,* chair, small table, electric heater and even an old radio Nick had around. Although the room was cold, because it had no radiator and was locked off from the Fusos' gas-heated bedroom, Frank was satisfied. Tessie worried about what would happen if he had to go to the bathroom at night, and Nick talked the matter over with Frank, saying apologetically that she was ashamed to have him go through their bedroom, but Frank said he never woke up at night. Anyway, Nick had a key made to the front door patent lock.* He said if Frank ever had to get up he could walk across the hall and let himself in through the front without waking them. And he could also use their bathtub, just so long as he told them when he would want it.

This arrangement suited Tessie.* Everyone was satisfied but Ida, who was unhappy with herself for having kept Frank on. She made the grocer promise he would send the clerk away before the summer. Business was always more active in the summertime, so Morris agreed. She asked him to tell Frank at once that he would be let go then,* and when the grocer did, the clerk smiled amiably and said the summer was a long ways off but anyway it was all right with him.

The grocer felt his mood change. It was a better mood than he had expected. A few of his old customers had returned. One

---

***a usable chest of drawers**:「쓸 수 있는 장롱」

***Nick had a key made to the front door patent lock**:「Nick는 앞 문의 특허자물쇠에 맞는 열쇠를 만들게 했다」

***This arrangement suited Tessie**:「이 결정은 Tessie의 마음에 들었다」

***She asked him to tell Frank at once that he would be let go then**:「Frank가 그때 나가야 한다는 것을 그에게 즉시 말하라고 그녀는 남편에게 요구했다」

woman told him that Schmitz was not giving as good service as he once did; he was having trouble with his health and was thinking of selling the store. Let him sell, thought Morris. He thought, let him die, then severely struck his chest.*

Ida stayed upstairs most of the day, reluctantly at first, less so as time went by.* She came down to prepare lunch and supper—Frank still ate before Helen—or to make a salad when it was needed. She attended to little else in the store;* Frank did the cleaning and mopping. Upstairs, Ida took care of the house, read a bit, listened to the Jewish programs on the radio and knitted. Helen bought some wool and Ida knitted her a sweater. In the night, after Frank had gone, Ida spent her time in the store, added up the accounts in her notebook* and left with Morris when he closed up.

The grocer got along well with his assistant. They divided tasks and waited on alternate customers,* though the waiting in between was still much too long. Morris went up for naps to forget the store. He too urged Frank to take some time off* in the afternoon, to break the monotony of the day. Frank, somewhat restless, finally began to. Sometimes he went up to his room and lay on the bed, listening to the radio. Usually he put his coat on over his apron and visited one of the other stores on the block. He liked Giannola, the Italian barber

---

***He thought, let him die, then severely struck his chest**:「죽으라면 죽으라지 하고 그는 생각했다. 그리고 나서(양심의 가책을 받아) 자기의 가슴을 세게 때렸다」

***reluctantly at first, less so as time went by**:「처음에는 마지못해 그랬으나 시간이 흘러가자 그렇게 하는 것이 싫지 않았다」

***She attended to little else in the store**:「그녀는 가게에서 그밖의 일은 거의 안했다」
attend to=apply oneself to「몰두하다, 온 힘을 기울이다」

***added up the accounts in her notebook**:「장부에 수입을 집계했다」

***waited on alternate customers**:「교대로 손님을 접대했다」

***take ~ off**=leave

across the street, an old man who had recently lost his wife and sat in the shop all day, even when it was long past time to go home; the old barber gave a fine haircut. Occasionally Frank dropped in on Louis Karp and gassed* with him, but generally Louis bored him. Sometimes he went into the butcher store, next door to Morris, and talked in the back room with Artie, the butcher's son, a blond fellow with a bad complexion who was interested in riding horses. Frank said he might go riding with him sometime but he never did though Artie invited him. Once in a while he drank a beer in the bar on the corner, where he liked Earl, the bartender. Yet when the clerk got back* to the grocery he was glad to go in.

When he and Morris were together in the back they spent a lot of time talking. Morris liked Frank's company;* he liked to hear about strange places, and Frank told him about some of the cities he had been to, in his long wandering, and some of the different jobs he had worked at. He had passed part of his early life in Oakland, California, but most of it across the bay in a home in San Francisco.* He told Morris stories about his hard times as a kid. In this second family the home had sent him to, the man used to work him hard in his machine shop. "I wasn't twelve," Frank said, "and he kept me out of school as long as he could get away with."*

***gas**=talk nonsense at great length「잡담을 길게 하다」

***get back**=come back, return

***Morris liked Frank's company**:「Morris는 Frank와 함께 있는 것을 좋아했다」 *e.g.* I enjoyed your company.「함께 지내서 매우 즐거웠읍니다」

***most of it across the bay in a home in San Francisco**:「대부분의 시간은 만(灣) 건너의 San Francisco의 고아원에서 (보냈다)」

***he kept me out of school as long as he could get away with**:「법에 걸리지 않는 한 그는 나를 학교에 보내지 않았죠」 get away with=succeed in doing (something) without being punished

After staying with that family for three years, he took off. "Then began my long period of travels." The clerk fell silent, and the ticking clock, on the shelf above the sink, sounded flat and heavy. "I am mostly self-educated," he ended.

Morris told Frank about life in the old country. They were poor and there were pogroms.* So when he was about to be conscripted* into the czar's army his father said, "Run to America." A landsman,* a friend of his father, had sent money for his passage. But he waited for the Russians to call him up, because if you left the district before they had conscripted you, then your father was arrested, fined and imprisoned. If the son got away after induction,* then the father could not be blamed; it was the army's responsibility. Morris and his father, a peddler in butter and eggs, planned that he would try to get away on his first day in the barracks.*

So on that day, Morris said, he told the sergeant, a peasant with red eyes and a bushy mustache which smelled of tobacco, that he wanted to buy some cigarettes in the town. He felt scared but was doing what his father had advised him to do. The half-drunk sergeant agreed he could go, but since Morris was not yet in uniform he would have to go along with him. It was a September day and had just rained. They walked along a muddy road till they reached the town. There, in an inn, Morris bought cigarettes for himself and the sergeant; then, as he had planned it with his father, he invited the

---

***pogrom** :「유태인 대학살」
***be conscripted** :「군대에 징집되다」
***landsman** :「동향인」
***If the son got away after induction** :「아들이 징집된 후에 도망치면」
***on his first day in the barracks** :「그가 병영에 들어간 첫 날에」

soldier to drink some vodka with him. His stomach became rigid at the chance he was taking.* He had never drunk in an inn before, and he had never before tried to deceive anybody to this extent. The sergeant, filling his glass often, told Morris the story of his life, crying when he came to the part where, through forgetfulness,* he had not attended his mother's funeral. Then he blew his nose, and wagging a thick finger in Morris's face,* warned him if he had any plans to skip,* he had better forget them if he expected to live. A dead Jew was of less consequence than a live one. Morris felt a heavy gloom descend on him. In his heart he surrendered* his freedom for years to come. Yet once they had left the inn and were trudging in the mud back to the barracks, his hopes rose as the sergeant, in his stupor, kept falling behind.* Morris walked slowly on, then the sergeant would cup his hands to his mouth, and cursing, haloo for him to wait. Morris waited. They would go on together, the sergeant muttering to himself, Morris uncertain what would happen next. Then the soldier stopped to urinate into a ditch in the road. Morris pretended to wait but he walked on, every minute expecting a bullet to crash through his shoulders and leave him lying in the dirt, his future with the worms. But then, as if seized by his fate, he began to run. The halooing and cursing grew louder as the

---

***His stomach became rigid at the chance he was taking**:「그가 할 모험을 생각하니 위가 뻣뻣하게 굳어지는 듯했다」 chance=risk「모험」

***through forgetfulness**:「건망증으로 인하여」

***wagging a thick finger in Morris's face**:「굵은 손가락으로 Morris의 얼굴에 삿대질을 하면서」

***skip**=escape, leave hurriedly

***surrender**=abandon, give up

***as the sergent, in his stupor, kept falling behind**:「취해서 정신이 몽롱해진 하사관이 계속 뒤로 처지자」 stupor「마비, 혼수, 인사불성」.

red-faced sergeant, waving a revolver, stumbled after him; but when he reached the bend of the tree-lined road where he had last seen Morris, nobody was there but a yellow-bearded peasant driving a nag pulling a load of hay.

Telling this story excited the grocer. He lit a cigarette and smoked without coughing. But when he had finished, when there was no more to say, a sadness settled on him.* Sitting in his chair, he seemed a small, lonely man. All the time he had been upstairs his hair had grown bushier and he wore a thick pelt of it at the back of his neck.* His face was thinner than before.

Frank thought about the story Morris had just told him. That was the big jig in his life* but where had it got him? He had escaped out of the Russian Army to the U.S.A. but once in a store he was like a fish fried in deep fat.*

"After I came here I wanted to be a druggist," Morris said. "I went for a year in night school. I took algebra, also German and English. '"Come," said the wind to the leaves one day, "come over the meadow with me and play."' This is a poem I learned. But I didn't have the patience to stay in night school, so when I met my wife I gave up my chances." Sighing, he said, "Without education you are lost."

Frank nodded.

"You're still young," Morris said. "A young man without a family is free. Don't do what I did."

"I won't," Frank said.

***a sadness settled on him**:「그는 슬픈 마음이 들었다」

***he wore a thick pelt of it at the back of his neck**:「그의 목덜미까지 머리털이 많이 나 있었다」 pelt「(털이 많이 난) 피부」

***That was the big jig in his life**:「그 사건은 그의 일생에서 큰 전기(轉機)였다」

***a fish fried in deep fat**:「진한 기름으로 튀겨진 물고기」

But the grocer didn't seem to believe him. It made the clerk uncomfortable to see the wet-eyed old bird brooding over* him. His pity leaks out of his pants, he thought, but he would get used to it.

When they were behind the counter together, Morris kept an eye on Frank and tried to improve some of the things Ida had taught him. The clerk did very well what he was supposed to.* As if ashamed somebody could learn the business so easily, Morris explained to him how different it had been to be a grocer only a few years ago. In those days one was more of a macher,* a craftsman. Who was ever called on nowadays to slice up a loaf of bread for a customer,* or ladle out a quart of milk?

"Now is everything in containers, jars, or packages. Even hard cheeses that they cut them for hundreds of years by hand come now sliced up in cellophane packages. Nobody has to know anything any more."*

"I remember the family milk cans,"* Frank said, "only my family sent me out to get beer in them."

But Morris said it was a good idea that milk wasn't sold loose any more.* "I used to know grocers that they took out

---

***brood over**=fret over「걱정하다, 속태우다」

***what he was supposed to**:「그가 해야 할 일」 be supposed to do=be expected to do「~하기로 되어 있다」

***a macher**:「제조자」 der Macher「제조자, 제작인」

***Who was ever called on nowadays to slice up a loaf of bread for a customer . . . ?**:「오늘날 누가 손님에게 빵을 썰어줄 것을 주문받고 있는가?」

***Nobody has to know anything any more**:「더 이상의 일은 몰라도 되지」

***the family milk cans**:「가정용 우유통」 *e.g.* a garbage can「쓰레기통」

***Morris said it was a good idea that milk wasn't sold loose any more**:「더 이상 우유를 되로 팔지 않게 되어 잘 되었다고 Morris는 말했다」 *e.g.* loose milk「되로 되어 파는 우유」

a quart or two cream from the top of the can, then they put in water. This water-milk they sold at the regular price."*

He told Frank about some other tricks he had seen. "In some stores they bought two kinds loose coffee and two kinds tub butter.* One was low grade, the other was medium, but the medium they put half in the medium bin and half in the best. So if you bought the best coffee or the best butter you got medium—nothing else."

Frank laughed. "I'll bet some of the customers came back saying that the best butter tasted better than the medium."

"It's easy to fool people," said Morris.

"Why don't you try a couple of those tricks yourself, Morris? Your amount of profit is small."

Morris looked at him in surprise. "Why should I steal from my customers? Do they steal from me?"

"They would if they could."*

"When a man is honest he don't worry when he sleeps. This is more important than to steal a nickel."

Frank nodded.

But he continued to steal. He would stop for a few days then almost with relief* go back to it. There were times stealing made him feel good. It felt good to have some change in his pocket, and it felt good to pluck a buck from under the Jew's nose.* He would slip it into his pants pocket so deftly that

---

***at the regular price**:「정가로」

***two kinds loose coffee and two kinds tub butter**:「두 종류의 되로 파는 커피와 두 종류의 통에 든 버터」

***They would if they could**:「그들도 속일 수 있다면 속이겠죠」

***with relief**:「안도감을 느끼고」

***it felt good to pluck a buck from under the Jew's nose**:「유태인 코 앞에서 1불을 훔쳐서 기분 좋았다」 pluck=plunder「훔치다, 빼앗다」

he had to keep himself from laughing. With this money, and what he earned, he bought a suit and hat, and got new tubes for Nick's radio. Now and then, through Sam Pearl, who telephoned it in for him, he laid a two-buck bet on a horse,* but as a rule he was careful with the dough. He opened a small savings account in a bank near the library and hid the bankbook under his mattress. The money was for future use.

When he felt pepped up about stealing,* it was also because he felt he had brought them luck. If he stopped stealing he bet business would fall off again. He was doing them a favor, at the same time making it a little worth his while to stay on and give them a hand.* Taking this small cut* was his way of showing himself he had something to give. Besides, he planned to return everything sometime or why would he be marking down the figure of what he took? He kept it on a small card in his shoe. He might someday plunk down a tenner or so on some longshot* and then have enough to pay back every lousy cent of what he had taken.

For this reason he could not explain why, from one day to another, he should begin to feel bad about snitching the bucks from Morris, but he did. Sometimes he went around with a

---

***he laid a two-buck bet on a horse**:「경마의 말에 2불을 걸었다」 lay a bet on ~「~에 걸다」

***When he felt pepped up stealing**:「도둑질하고 싶은 마음이 일어날 때에는」 pep up「격려하다, 원기를 북돋우다」

***at the same time making it a little worth his while to stay on and give them a hand**:「동시에 그는 가게에 머물며 그들을 도와 주고 있는 것에 대한 약간의 보수를 받고 있는 것이다」 *e.g.* He will make it worth your while.=He will reward you in some way.「그는 네 수고에 보답할 것이다」

***Taking this small cut**:「이처럼 약간 떼어 먹는 것」

***plunk down a tenner or so on some longshot**:「승산이 없는 말에다 10불 정도를 걸다」 tenner「10불짜리 지폐」 longshot「경마에서 이길 것 같지 않은 말」

quiet grief in him, as if he had just buried a friend and was carrying the fresh grave within himself. This was an old feeling of his. He remembered having had something like it for years back. On days he felt this way he sometimes got headaches and went around muttering to himself. He was afraid to look into the mirror for fear it would split apart and drop into the sink. He was wound up so tight he would spin for a week if the spring snapped.* He was full of sudden rages at himself. These were his worst days and he suffered trying to hide his feelings. Yet they had a curious way of ending. The rage he felt disappeared like a windstorm that quietly pooped out,* and he felt a sort of gentleness creeping in. He felt gentle to the people who came into the store, especially the kids, whom he gave penny crackers to for nothing. He was gentle to Morris, and the Jew was gentle to him. And he was filled with a quiet gentleness for Helen and no longer climbed the air shaft to spy on her, naked in the bathroom.

And there were days when he was sick to death of everything.* He had had it, up to here. Going downstairs in the morning he thought he would gladly help the store burn if it caught on fire.* Thinking of Morris waiting on the same lousy customers day after day throughout the years, as they picked out with dirty fingers the same cheap items they ate every day

---

***He was wound up . . . snapped**:「그의 몸안의 태엽이 너무 세게 감겨졌기 때문에, 만일 용수철이 뚝 끊어지면 1주일쯤 몸이 빙빙 돌 것 같은 기분이었다」

***poop out**:「가라앉다, 지쳐 버리다, 고갈하다」

***there were days when he was sick to death of everything**:「모든 일이 다 귀찮은 날이 있었다」 *e.g.* I was sick to death of it.「그것엔 정말 넌더리가 났다」

***if it caught on fire**:「가게에 불이 나면」

of their flea-bitten lives,* then when they were gone, waiting for them to come back again, he felt like leaning over the banister and throwing up.* What kind of a man did you have to be born to shut yourself up in an overgrown coffin* and never once during the day, so help you, outside of going for your Yiddish newspaper, poke your beak out of the door for a snootful of air?* The answer wasn't hard to say—you had to be a Jew. They were born prisoners. That was what Morris was, with his deadly patience, or endurance, or whatever the hell it was; and it explained Al Marcus, the paper products salesman, and that skinny rooster Breitbart,* who dragged from store to store his two heavy cartons full of bulbs.

Al Marcus, who had once, with an apologetic smile, warned the clerk not to trap himself in a grocery, was a well-dressed man of forty-six, but he looked, whenever you saw him, as if he had just lapped up cyanide.* His face was the whitest Frank had ever seen, and what anybody saw in his eyes if he took a good look, would not help his appetite. The truth of it was, the grocer had confided to Frank, that Al had cancer and was supposed to be dead in his grave a year ago, but he fooled the doctors; he stayed alive if you could call it that.* Although he had a comfortable pile, he wouldn't quit working and

---

***the same cheap items they ate every day of their flea-bitten lives**:「벼룩에 물리는 시시한 생활을 하면서 매일 같이 그들이 먹는 똑같은 싸구려 식품」

***throw up**=vomit「토하다」

***an overgrown coffin**:「너무 크게 짠 관」

***poke your beak out of the door for a snootful of air**:「공기 한 모금 마시려고 문에서 주둥이를 내밀다」 poke「쑥 내밀다, 쑥 넣다」

***that skinny rooster Breitbart**:「저 말라 빠진 수탉 같은 Breitbart」

***lap up cyanide**:「청산가리를 핥아먹다」

***he stayed alive if you could call it that**:「그의 삶을 사는 것이라고 할 수 있다면, 그는 아직도 살아 있었다」

showed up regularly once a month to take orders for paper bags, wrapping paper and containers. No matter how bad business was, Morris tried to have some kind of little order waiting for him. Al would suck on* an unlit cigar, scribble an item or two on a pink page in his metal covered salesbook, then stand around a few minutes, making small talk, his eyes far away from what he was saying;* and after that, tip his hat and take off for the next place. Everybody knew how sick he was, and a couple of the storekeepers earnestly advised him to quit working, but Al, smiling apologetically, took his cigar out of his mouth and said, "If I stay home, somebody in a high hat* is gonna walk up the stairs and put a knock on my door. This way let him at least move his bony ass around and try and find me."

As for Breitbart, according to Morris, nine years ago he had owned a good business, but his brother ran it into the ground, gambling,* then he took off with what was left of the bank account,* persuading Breitbart's wife to come along and keep it company. That left him with a drawerful of bills and no credit;* also a not too bright five-year-old boy. Breitbart went bankrupt; his creditors plucked every feather.* For months he and the boy lived in a small, dirty furnished room, Breitbart

---

***suck on**:「빨다」

***his eyes far away from what he was saying**:「그의 이야기와는 상관 없는 딴 곳을 바라보면서」 his앞에 with를 보충해서 해석할 것.

***somebody in a high hat**:「실크해트를 쓰신 분(죽음의 사자(使者))」

***his brother ran it into the ground, gambling**:「그의 동생이 도박을 해서 가게를 파멸의 구렁텅이로 몰아넣었다」

***what was left of the bank account**:「은행예금 잔액」

***That left him with a drawerful of bills and no credit**:「그 결과 그에게는 예금은 없고, 서랍에 가득 찬 청구서 뭉치만이 남았다」

***his creditors plucked every feather**:「채권자는 마지막 한 푼까지 뜯어 갔다」

not having the heart to go out to look for work. Times were bad. He went on relief and later took to peddling.* He was now in his fifties but his hair had turned white and he acted like an old man. He bought electric bulbs at wholesale and carried two cartons of them slung, with clothesline rope, over his shoulder.* Every day, in his crooked shoes, he walked miles, looking into stores and calling out in a mournful voice, "Lights for sale." At night he went home and cooked supper for his Hymie, who played hooky* whenever he could from the vocational school where they were making him into a shoemaker.

When Breitbart first came to Morris's neighborhood and dropped into the store, the grocer, seeing his fatigue, offered him a glass of tea with lemon. The peddler eased the rope off his shoulder and set his boxes on the floor. In the back he gulped the hot tea in silence, warming both hands on the glass. And though he had, besides his other troubles, the seven-year itch,* which kept him awake half the night, he never complained. After ten minutes he got up, thanked the grocer, fitted the rope onto his lean and itchy shoulder and left. One day he told Morris the story of his life and they both wept.

That's what they live for, Frank thought, to suffer. And the one that has got the biggest pain in the gut* and can hold onto

---

***He went on relief and later took to peddling**:「그는 정부의 구제를 받아 살았고 후에 행상을 하게 되었다」

***carried two cartons of them slung, with clothesline rope, over his shoulder**:「전구 두 상자를 빨래줄로 묶어 어깨에 메고 다녔다」 *e.g.* sling a gun over one's shoulder「총을 어깨에 메다」

***play hookey**=play truant「학교를 빼먹다」

***the seven-year itch**:「7년이나 된 옴」

***the one that has got the biggest pain in the gut**:「창자에서 가장 큰 고통을 받고 있는 자」 즉, 가장 배고픔을 당한 사람.

it the longest without running to the toilet is the best Jew. No wonder they got on his nerves.*

Winter tormented Helen. She ran from it, hid in the house. In the house she revenged herself on December by crossing off the calendar all its days.* If Nat would only call, she thought endlessly, but the telephone was deaf and dumb. She dreamed of him nightly, felt deeply in love, famished for him;* would gladly have danced into his warm white bed if only he nodded, or she dared ask him to ask her; but Nat never called. She hadn't for a minute glimpsed him since running into him on the subway early in November. He lived around the corner but it might as well be Paradise.* So with a sharp-pointed pencil she scratched out each dead day while it still lived.

Though Frank hungered for her company he rarely spoke to her. Now and then he passed her on the street. She murmured hello and walked on with her books, conscious of his eyes following her. Sometimes in the store, as if in defiance of her mother,* she stopped to talk for a minute with the clerk. Once he startled her by abruptly mentioning this book he was reading. He longed to ask her to go out with him, but never dared; the old lady's eyes showed distrust of the goings on.* So he waited. Mostly he watched for her at the window. He

---

***No wonder they got on his nerves**:「유태인들이 그의 신경을 건드리는 것도 놀랄 것이 못 된다」

***by crossing off the calendar all its days**:「달력의 모든 날짜에 ×표를 함으로써」 *e.g.* Please cross my name off the program.「프로그램에서 내 이름을 지워 주시오」

***famished for him**:「(그를 못 만나) 그에 대하여 굶주려 있었다」

***He lived around the corner but it might as well be Paradise**:「그는 바로 길모퉁이에서 살고 있었는데, 그곳은 바로 천국처럼이나 먼 곳이었다」

***as if in defiance of her mother**:「마치 그녀의 어머니에게 도전하듯이」

***goings on**=behavior(태도), action(행동)

studied her hidden face, sensed her lacks, which deepened his own, but didn't know what to do about it.

December yielded nothing to spring. She awoke to each frozen, lonely day with dulled feeling. Then one Sunday afternoon winter leaned backward for an hour* and she went walking. Suddenly she forgave everyone everything. A warmish breath of air was enough to inspire; she was again grateful for living. But the sun soon sank and it snowed pellets.* She returned home, leaden.* Frank was standing at Sam Pearl's deserted corner but she seemed not to see him though she brushed by.* He felt very bad. He wanted her but the facts made a terrible construction.* They were Jews and he was not. If he started going out with Helen her mother would throw a double fit* and Morris another. And Helen made him feel, from the way she carried herself,* even when she seemed most lonely, that she had plans for something big in her life —nobody like F. Alpine. He had nothing, a backbreaking past, had committed a crime against her old man, and in spite of his touchy conscience, was stealing from him too. How complicated could impossible get?*

***winter leaned backward for an hour**:「한 시간쯤 겨울 추위가 누그러졌다」 lean over backward「반대의 태도를 취하다」

***it snowed pellets**:「작은 탄알 같은 눈이 내렸다」

***She returned home, leaden**:「그녀는 무거운 마음으로 집으로 돌아왔다」

***though she brushed by**:「그녀는 스치듯이 지나갔지만」

***the facts made a terrible construction**:「여러 가지 사실들이 무서운 방해물이 되어 있었다」

***throw a double fit**:「노발대발하다」 throw a fit=behave as one who is infuriated

***from the way she carried herself**:「그녀의 거동으로 봐서」 carry oneself=behave, conduct oneself

***How complicated could impossible get?**:「어찌할 수 없는 것들이 어디까지 얽혀야만 하나?」

He saw only one way of squeezing through the stone knot;* start by shoveling out* the load he was carrying around in his mind by admitting to Morris that he was one of the guys that had held him up. It was a funny thing about that; he wasn't really sorry they had stuck up a Jew but he hadn't expected to be sorry that they had picked on this particular one, Bober; yet now he was. He had not minded, if by mind you meant in expectation, but what he hadn't minded no longer seemed to matter. The matter was how he now felt, and he now felt bad he had done it. And when Helen was around he felt worse.

So the confession had to come first—this stuck like a bone through the neck. From the minute he had tailed* Ward Minogue into the grocery that night, he had got this sick feeling that he might someday have to vomit up in words,* no matter how hard or disgusting it was to do, the thing he was then engaged in doing. He felt he had known this, in some frightful way, a long time before he went into the store, before he had met Minogue, or even come east; that he had really known all his life he would sometime, through throat blistered with shame,* his eyes in the dirt, have to tell some poor son of a bitch that he was the one who had hurt or betrayed him. This thought had lived in him with claws;* or like a thirst he could never spit out, a repulsive need to get out of his system

---

***He saw only one way of squeezing through the stone knot**:「그 난국을 빠져나갈 길은 하나밖에 없을 것 같았다」 *e.g.* Gordian knot「난제」

***shovel out**:「퍼서 치워 버리다」

***tail**=follow closely behind

***vomit up in words**:「(말로) 자백하다」

***through throat blistered with shame**:「부끄러움으로 고통을 느끼는 목구멍을 통해서」

***This thought had lived in him with claws**:「이 생각이 갈고리처럼 그의 마음속에 얽혀 있었다.」

all that had happened*—for whatever had happened had happened wrong; to clean it out of his self and bring in a little peace, a little order; to change the beginning, beginning with the past that always stupendously stank up the now*—to change his life before the smell of it suffocated him.

Yet when the chance came to say it, when he was alone with Morris that November morning in the back of the store, as they were drinking the coffee that the Jew had served him, and the impulse came on him to spill everything now, *now,* he had strained to heave it up,* but it was like tearing up your whole life, with the broken roots and blood; and a fear burned in his gut that once he had got started saying the wrongs he had done he would never leave off until he had turned black;* so instead he had told him a few hurried things about how ass-backward his life had gone,* which didn't even begin to say what he wanted. He had worked on Morris's pity* and left halfway satisfied, but not for long, because soon the need to say it returned and he heard himself groaning, but groans weren't words.

He argued with himself that he was smart in not revealing

***a repulsive need to get out of his system all that had happened**:「과거에 일어난 모든 일들을 그의 몸 밖으로 쏟아 버려야 할 불쾌한 욕구」

***beginning with the past that always stupendously stank up the now**:「현재를 항상 심한 악취로 채우고 있는 과거로부터 시작해서」

***he had strained to heave it up**:「모든 것을 불어 버리려고 힘썼다」 heave up「토해내다」

***he would never leave off until he had turned black**:「그 자신이 까맣게 타 버릴 때까지 고백을 계속할 것이다」 leave off=cease to ~「~을 끝내다」

***about how ass-backward his life had gone**:「자기의 인생이 얼마나 그릇된 방향으로 흘러 갔는지에 대하여」

***He had worked on Morris's pity**:「그는 Morris의 동정심을 일으켰다」

to the grocer more than he had. Enough was enough;* besides, how much of a confession was the Jew entitled to for the seven and a half bucks he had taken, then put back into his cash register drawer, and for the knock on the head he had got from Ward, whom he himself had come with unwillingly? Maybe willing, but not to do what had finally been done. That deserved some consideration, didn't it?* Furthermore, he had begged the creep* not to hurt anybody, and had later turned him down* when he cooked up another scheme of stickup* against Karp, who they were out to get in the first place. That showed his good intentions for the future, didn't it? And who was it, after all was said and done, that had waited around shivering in his pants in the dark cold, to pull in Morris's milk boxes, and had worked his ass to a frazzle twelve hours a day* while the Jew lay upstairs resting in his bed? And was even now keeping him from starvation in his little rat hole? All that added up to something too.

That was how he argued with himself, but it didn't help for long, and he was soon again fighting out how to jump free of what he had done. He would someday confess it all—he promised himself. If Morris accepted his explanation and solemn apology, it would clear the rocks out of the road for

---

*__Enough was enough__ :「그것으로 충분했다」

*__That deserved some consideration, didn't it?__ :「그 사실은 정상이 참작되어야 하지 않겠는가 ?」

*__creep__ :「나쁜 놈」

*__turn down__=reject, refuse to accept

*__cook up another scheme of stickup__ :「또 다른 강도질 계획을 꾸미다」 cook up=make up, invent

*__had worked his ass to a frazzle twelve hours a day__ :「하루에 12시간씩 뼈 빠지게 일했다」 frazzle「닳아 헤어짐, 곤핍(困乏)」

the next move.* As for his present stealing from the cash register, he had decided that once he had told the grocer all there was to say about the holdup, he would at the same time start paying back into the drawer, out of his little salary and the few bucks he had put away in the bank, what he had taken, and that would fix that.* It wouldn't necessarily mean that Helen Bober would then and there* fall for* him—the opposite could happen—but if she *did,* he wouldn't feel bad about it.

He knew by heart* what he would say to the grocer once he got to say it. One day while they were talking in the back, he would begin, as he had once done, about how his life was mostly made up of lost chances, some so promising he could still not stand to remember them.* Well, after certain bad breaks through various causes, mostly his own mistakes—he was piled high with regrets*—after many such failures, though he tried every which way to free himself from them, usually he failed; so after a time he gave up and let himself be a bum.* He lived in gutters, cellars if he was lucky, slept in lots, ate what the dogs wouldn't, or couldn't, and what he scrounged out of garbage cans.* He wore what he found, slept where he flopped and guzzled anything.

***for the next move**:「다음의 행동을 위하여」
***that would fix that**:「그것으로 그 문제는 해결될 것이다」
***then and there**=at the very moment「즉시」
***fall for**=fall in love with「~에 반하다」
***He knew by heart**:「그는 암기했다」
***some so promising he could still not stand to remember them**:「기억하는 것조차 견딜 수 없을 정도로 유망했던 기회들」promising 다음에 that가 생략됨.
***he was piled high with regrets**:「후회하는 마음으로 가득 차 있었다」
***let himself be a bum**:「드디어 부랑자가 되고 말았다」
***what he scrounged out of garbage cans**:「쓰레기통에서 주운 것」

By rights* this should have killed him, but he lived on, bearded, smelly, dragging himself through the seasons without a hope to go by. How many months he had existed this way he would never know. Nobody kept the score of it.* But one day while he lay in some hole he had crawled into, he had this terrific idea that he was really an important guy, and was torn out of his reverie with the thought that he was living this kind of life only because he hadn't known he was meant for something a whole lot better—to do something big, different. He had not till that minute understood this. In the past he had usually thought of himself as an average guy, but there in this cellar it came to him he was wrong. That was why his luck had so often curdled,* because he had the wrong idea of what he really was and had spent all his energy trying to do the wrong things. Then when he had asked himself what should he be doing, he had another powerful idea, that he was meant for crime.* He had at times teased himself with this thought,* but now it wouldn't let go of him. At crime he would change his luck, make adventure, live like a prince. He shivered with pleasure as he conceived robberies, assaults—murders if it had to be—each violent act helping to satisfy a craving that somebody suffer as his own fortune improved. He felt in-

---

***By rights**=by good rights「당연히」

***Nobody kept the score of it**:「아무도 그 숫자를 기록하지 않았다」 keep the score「득점을 기록하다」

***That was why his luck had so often curdled**:「그것이 바로 그의 운이 피지 못한 이유였다」 curdle「응결하다, 악화하다」

***he had another powerful idea, that he was meant for crime**:「자기는 범죄로 성공할 운명이라는 또 다른 강한 생각이 그를 사로잡았다」

***He had at times teased himself with this thought**:「그는 때때로 이 생각으로 괴로와했다」

finitely relieved, believing that if a person figured for himself something big, something different in his life, he had a better chance to get it than some poor jerk* who couldn't think that high up.

So he gave up his outhouse existence.* He began to work again, got himself a room, saved and bought a gun. Then he headed east, where he figured he could live the way he wanted —where there was money, nightclubs, babes.* After a week of prowling around in Boston, not sure where he ought to start off, he hopped a freight to Brooklyn and a couple of days after he got there met Ward Minogue. As they were shooting pool* one night, Ward cannily detected the gun on him and made him the proposition that they do a holdup together. Frank welcomed the idea of some kind of start but said he wanted to think about it more. He went to Coney Island, and while sitting on the boardwalk, worrying about what he ought to do, got this oppressive feeling he was being watched.* When he turned around it was Ward Minogue. Ward sat down and told him that it was a Jew he planned to rob, so Frank agreed to go with him.

But on the night of the holdup he found himself nervous. In the car Ward sensed it and cursed him. Frank felt he had to stick it out,* but the minute they were both in the grocery and tying handkerchiefs around their mouths, the whole idea

---

***jerk**:「얼간이, 멍청이」

***outhouse existence**:「거지생활」

***babe**=young woman

***shoot pool**:「당구를 치다」

***got this oppressive feeling he was being watched**:「자기가 감시를 받고 있다는 우울한 느낌이 들었다」

***stick out**=be insistent and not give in「끝까지 해내다」

seemed senseless. He could feel it poop out in his mind. His plans of crime lay down and died. He could hardly breathe in his unhappiness, wanted to rush out into the street and be swallowed up out of existence,* but he couldn't let Ward stay there alone. In the back, nauseated by the sight of the Jew's bloodied head, he realized he had made the worst mistake yet, the hardest to wipe out. And that ended his short life of violent crime, another pipe dream,* and he was trapped tighter in the tangle of his failures.* All this he thought he would someday tell Morris. He knew the Jew well enough to feel sure of his mercy.

Yet there were times when he imagined himself, instead, telling it all to Helen. He wanted to do something that would open her eyes to his true self, but who could be a hero in a grocery store? Telling her would take guts and guts was something.* He continued to feel he deserved a better fate, and he would find it if he only once—*once*—did the right thing —the thing to do at the right time. Maybe if they were ever together for any decent amount of time, he would ask her to listen. At first she might be embarrassed, but when he started telling her about his life, he knew she would hear him to the end. After that—who knew? With a dame all you needed was a beginning.*

***be swallowed up out of existence**:「무엇인가에 삼켜져서 세상에서 없어지다」 go out of existence「소멸되다」

***pipe dream**=day-dream「백일몽」 castle in the air「공상」

***in the tangle of his failures**:「실패의 곤경 속에서」

***Telling her would take guts and guts was something**:「그녀에게 고백하려면 용기가 필요할 것이며 용기란 누구에게나 있는 것이 아니었다」

***With a dame all you needed was a beginning**:「여자와 교제하려면 가장 중요한 것은 시작하는 일이었다」

But when the clerk caught himself coldly and saw the sentimentality of his thinking—he was a sentimental wop at heart*—he knew he was having another of his hopped-up dreams. What kind of a chance did he think he would have with her after he had admitted the stickup of her old man? So he figured the best thing was to keep quiet. At the same time a foreboding crept into him* that if he said nothing now, he would someday soon have a dirtier past to reveal.

A few days after Christmas, on the night of a full moon, Frank, dressed in his new clothes, hurried to the library, about a dozen blocks from the grocery. The library was an enlarged store, well lit, with bulging shelves of books that smelled warm on winter nights. In the rear there were a few large reading tables. It was a pleasant place to come to out of the cold. His guess was good, soon Helen arrived. She wore a red woolen scarf on her head, one end thrown over her shoulder. He was at a table reading. She noticed him as she closed the door behind her; he knew it. They had met here, briefly, before. She had wondered what he read at the table, and once in passing, glanced quickly over his shoulder. She had guessed *Popular Mechanics,* but it was the life of somebody or other. Tonight, as usual, she was aware of his eyes on her as she moved about from shelf to shelf. When, after an hour, she left, he caught a tight hidden glance in his direction.* Frank got

---

***he was a sentimental wop at heart**:「그는 실제로는 감상적인 이탈리아 이주민이었다」

***a foreboding crept into him**:「그에게 예감이 들었다」

***he caught a tight hidden glance in his direction**:「그는 자기 쪽을 쳐다보는, 그녀의 아주 은밀한 시선을 느꼈다」

up and checked out a book.* She was halfway down the street before he caught up with her.*

"Big moon." He reached up to tip his hat and awkwardly discovered he wasn't wearing any.

"It feels like snow," Helen answered.

He glanced at her to see if she was kidding,* then at the sky. It was cloudless, flooded with moonlight.

"Maybe." As they approached the street corner, he remarked, "We could take a walk in the park if it's okay with you."

She shivered at the suggestion, yet turned with a nervous laugh* at the corner, and walked by his side. She had said almost nothing to him since the night he had called her to answer the empty phone. Who it had been she would never know; the incident still puzzled her.

Helen felt for him, as they walked, an irritation bordering on something worse.* She knew what caused it—her mother, in making every gentile, by definition,* dangerous; therefore he and she, together, represented some potential evil. She was also annoyed that his eating eyes* were always on her, for he saw, she felt, more than his occasionally trapped gaze revealed. She fought her dislike of him,* reasoning it wasn't

---

***checked out a book**:「책을 빌렸다(도서관에서)」
***he caught up with her**:「그녀를 따라잡았다」 catch up with=overtake
***kid**=jolly「놀리다, 농담하다」
***a nervous laugh**:「소심한 웃음」
***an irritation bordering on something worse**:「아주 심한 짜증」 border on「~와 유사하다, ~와 같다, 인접하다」
***by definition**:「당연히」
***his eating eyes**:「그의 탐욕스러운 시선」 *e.g.* friendly eyes「다정스러운 시선」
***She fought her dislike of him**:「그녀는 그를 싫어하는 자기의 감정을 없애려고 애썼다」

his fault if her mother had made him into an enemy; and if he was always looking at her, it meant at least he saw something attractive or why would he look? Considering her lonely life, for that she owed him gratitude.

The unpleasant feeling passed and she glanced guardedly up at him. He was walking unmarked in moonlight, innocent of her reaction to him.* She felt then—this thought had come to her before—that there might be more to him than she had imagined. She felt ashamed she had never thanked him for the help he had given her father.

In the park the moon was smaller, a wanderer* in the white sky. He was talking about winter. "It's funny you mentioned snow before," Frank said. "I was reading about the life of St. Francis in the library, and when you mentioned the snow it made me think about this story where he wakes up one winter night, asking himself did he do the right thing to be a monk. My God, he thought, supposing I met some nice young girl and got married to her and by now I had a wife and a family? That made him feel bad so he couldn't sleep. He got out of his straw bed and went outside of the church or monastery or wherever he was staying. The ground was all covered with snow. Out of it he made this snow woman, and he said, 'There, that's my wife.' Then he made two or three kids out of the snow. After, he kissed them all and went inside and laid down in the straw. He felt a whole lot better and fell asleep."

The story surprised and touched her.

"Did you just read that?"

***innocent of her reaction to him**:「자기에 대한 그녀의 반응도 깨닫지 못하고」

***a wanderer**:「방랑자」

"No. I remember it from the time I was a kid. My head is full of those stories, don't ask me why. A priest used to read them to the orphans in his home I was in, and I guess I never forgot them. They come into my thoughts for no reason at all."

He had had a haircut and in his new clothes was hardly recognizable as her father's baggy-pants assistant* who had slept a week in their cellar. Tonight he looked like somebody she had never seen before. His clothes showed taste,* and he was, in his way, interesting looking. Without an apron on he seemed younger.

They passed an empty bench. "What do you say if we sit down?" Frank said.

"I'd rather walk."

"Smoke?"

"No."

He lit a cigarette, then caught up with her.

"Sure is some night."*

"I want to say thanks for helping my father," Helen said, "You've been very kind. I should have mentioned it before."

"Nobody has to thank me. Your father did me some good favors." He felt uncomfortable.

"Anyway, don't make a career of a grocery,*" she said. "There's no future in it."

***her father's baggy-pants assistant**:「그녀의 아버지의 헐렁헐렁한 바지를 입고 있는 점원」

***His clothes showed taste**:「그의 복장은 고상한 취미를 나타내고 있었다」

***Sure is some night**:「아주 상쾌한 밤이군요」

***don't make a career of a grocery**:「식료품상으로 출세할 생각은 마세요」 make a career of「출세하다」

He puffed with a smile on his lips.* "Everybody warns me. Don't worry, my imagination is too big for me to get stuck in a grocery. It's only temporary work."

"It isn't what you usually do?"

"No." He set himself to be honest. "I'm just taking a breather,* you could call it. I started out wrong and have to change my direction where I am going. The way it happened I landed up in your father's store, but I'm only staying there till I figure out* what's my next move."

He remembered the confession he had considered making to her, but the time wasn't ready yet. You could confess as a stranger, and you could confess as a friend.

"I've tried about everything," he said, "now I got to choose one thing and stick with it. I'm tired of being on the move all the time."

"Isn't it a little late for you to be getting started?"

"I'm twenty-five. There are plenty of guys who start that late and some I have read about started later. Age don't mean a thing.* It doesn't make you less than anybody else."*

"I never said so." At the next empty bench she paused. "We could sit here for a few minutes if you like."

"Sure." Frank wiped the seat with his handkerchief before she sat down. He offered her his cigarettes.

***He puffed with a smile on his lips**:「그는 입가에 미소를 띠고 담배를 뻐끔뻐끔 피웠다」

***I'm just taking a breather**:「나는 잠깐 쉬고 있는 겁니다」 have(take) a breather「잠깐 쉬다」

***figure out**=think out「생각해 내다, 고안하다」

***Age don't mean a thing**:「나이가 문제되는 것이 아닙니다」

***It doesn't make you less than anybody else**:「나이 때문에 남보다 뒤떨어지는 것은 아닙니다」

"I said I don't smoke."

"Sorry, I thought you didn't want to smoke while you were walking. Some girls don't like to." He put his pack* away.

She noticed the book he was carrying. "What are you reading?"

He showed it to her.

"*The Life of Napoleon?*"

"That's right."

"Why him?"

"Why not—he was great, wasn't he?"

"Others were in better ways."*

"I'll read about them too," Frank said.

"Do you read a lot?"

"Sure. I am a curious guy. I like to know why people tick.* I like to know the reason they do the things they do, if you know what I mean."

She said she did.

He asked her what book she was reading.

"*The Idiot.* Do you know it?"

"No. What's it about?"

"It's a novel."

"I'd rather read the truth," he said.

"It's a novel."

"I'd rather read the truth," he said.

"It is the truth."

Helen asked, "Are you a high school graduate?"

***pack**:「담뱃갑」

***Others were in better ways**:「다른 사람들은 더 나은 방법으로 위대했죠」

***tick**:「알 수 없는 행동을 하다」 *e.g.* What makes him tick?「왜 그는 저와 같이 행동하는가?」

He laughed. "Sure I am. Education is free in this country."

She blushed. "It was a silly question."

"I didn't mean any wisecrack,"* he said quickly.

"I didn't take it as such."

"I went to high school in three different states and finally got finished up at night—in a night school. I planned on going to college but this job came along that I couldn't turn down, so I changed my mind, but it was a mistake."

"I had to help my mother and father out," Helen said, "so I couldn't go either. I've taken courses in NYU at night —mostly lit courses—and I've added up about a year's credit, but it's very hard at night. My work doesn't satisfy me. I would still like to go full time in the day."*

He flipped his butt away.* "I've been thinking about starting in college lately, even if I am this age. I know a guy who did it."

"Would you go at night?" she asked.

"Maybe, maybe in the day if I could get the right kind of a job—in an all-night cafeteria or something like that, for instance. This guy I just mentioned did that—assistant manager or something. After five or six years he graduated and engineer. Now he's making his pile, working all over the country."*

"It's hard doing it that way—very hard."

***I didn't mean any wisecrack**:「나는 무슨 재치있는 말을 하려고 한 것은 아닙니다」 wisecrack=a smart remark, a witticism

***I would still like to go full time in the day**:「지금도 주간에 착실하게 학교에 다니고 싶어요」

***flip ~ away**:「툭 던져 버리다」

***Now he's making his pile, working all over the country**:「온 나라를 돌아다니며 일을 하여 많은 돈을 벌고 있읍니다」 make one's pile「돈을 많이 모으다」

"The hours are rough but you get used to it. When you got something good to do, sleep is waste of time."

"It takes years at night."

"Time don't mean anything to me."

"It does to me."

"The way I figure, anything is possible. I always think about the different kinds of chances I have. This has stuck in my mind—don't get yourself trapped in one thing,* because maybe you can do something else a whole lot better. That's why I guess I never settled down so far. I've been exploring conditions.* I still have some very good ambitions which I would like to see come true. The first step to that, I know for sure now, is to get a good education. I didn't use to think like that, but the more I live the more I do. Now it's always on my mind."

"I've always felt that way," Helen said.

He lit another cigarette, throwing the burnt match away. "What kind of work do you do?"

"I'm a secretary."

"You like it?" He smoked with half-closed eyes. She sensed he knew she didn't care for her job and suspected he had heard her father or mother say so.

After a while, she answered, "No, I don't. The job never changes. And I could live happily without seeing some of those characters I have to deal with all day long, the salesmen, I mean."

"They get fresh?"*

***don't get yourself trapped in one thing**:「한 가지 일에만 매이지 마시오」
***I've been exploring conditions**:「나는 여러 경우를 살펴 보았읍니다」
***They get fresh?**:「그들은 건방진가요?」 fresh=impudent「건방진」

"They talk a lot. I'd like to be doing something that feels useful—some kind of social work or maybe teaching. I have no sense of accomplishment* in what I'm doing now. Five o'clock comes and at last I go home. That's about all I live for, I guess."

She spoke of her daily routine, but after a minute saw he was only half-listening. He was staring at the moon-drenched trees in the distance,* his face drawn, his lit eyes elsewhere.

Helen sneezed, unwound her scarf and wrapped it tightly around her head.

"Shall we go now?"

"Just till I finish my cigarette."

Some fat nerve,* she thought.

Yet his face, even with the broken nose, was sensitive in the dark light. What makes me so irritable? She had had the wrong idea of him but it was her own fault, the result of staying so long apart from people.

He drew a long jagged breath.

"Is something the matter?" she asked.

Frank cleared his throat but his voice was hoarse. "No, just something popped into my mind* when I was looking at the moon. You know how your thoughts are."

"Nature sets you thinking?"

"I like scenery."

"I walk a lot for that reason."

***sense of accomplishment**:「성취감」

***the moon-drenched trees in the distance**:「달빛을 흠뻑 받고 먼 곳에 서 있는 나무」

***Some fat nerve**:「두툼한 배짱」

***just something popped into my mind**:「바로 어떤 생각이 떠올랐죠」 pop「후딱 들어오다」

"I like the sky at night, but you see more of it in the West. Out here the sky is too high, there are too many big buildings."

He squashed his cigarette with his heel and wearily rose, looking now like someone who had parted with his youth.

She got up and walked with him, curious about him. The moon moved above them in the homeless sky.

After a long silence, he said as they were walking, "I like to tell you what I was thinking about."

"Please, you don't have to."*

"I feel like talking," he said. "I got to thinking about this carnie outfit* I worked for one time when I was about twenty-one. Right after I got the job I fell for a girl in an acrobatic act.* She was built something like you—on the slim side,* I would say. At first I don't think I rated with her. I think she thought I wasn't a serious type of guy. She was kind of a complicated girl,* you know, moody, with lots of problems in her mind that she kept to herself. Well, one day we got to talking and she told me she wanted to be a nun. I said, 'I don't think it will suit you.' 'What do you know about me?' she said. I didn't tell her, although I know people pretty well, don't ask me why, I guess you are born with certain things.* Anyway, the whole summer long I was nuts about* her but she wouldn't give me another look though there was nobody else

---

***you don't have to**=you need not「꼭 할 필요는 없다」
***carnie outfit**:「순회 서커스단」
***an acrobatic act**:「곡예」
***on the slim side**:「가냘픈 편인」
***She was kind of a complicated girl**:「그녀는 복잡한 성격의 소녀였다」
***be born with certain things**:「어떤 재능을 가지고 태어나다」
***be nuts about**=be dead nuts on「아주 좋아하다, 열중하다」

around that I saw she went with. 'Is it my age?' I asked her. 'No, but you haven't lived,' she answered me. 'If you only could see in my heart all I have lived through,' I said, but I have my doubts if she believed me. All we ever did was talk like that. Once in a while I would ask her for a date, not thinking I would ever get one, and I never did. 'Give up,' I said to myself, 'all she is interested in is herself.'

"Then one morning, when it was getting to be around fall and you could smell the season changing, I said to her I was taking off when the show closed. 'Where are you going?' she asked me. I said I was going to look for a better life. She didn't answer anything to that. I said, 'Do you still want to be a nun?' She got red and looked away, then she answered she wasn't sure about that any more. I could see she had changed but I wasn't fool enough to think it was account of me. But I guess it really was, because by accident our hands sort of* touched, and when I saw the way she looked at me, it was hard to breathe. My God, I thought, we are both in love. I said to her, 'Honey, meet me here after the show tonight and let's go where we will be alone.' She said yes. Before she left she gave me a quick kiss.

"Anyway, that same afternoon she took off in her old man's jalopy* to buy a blouse she had seen in some store window in the last town, but on the way back it started to rain. Exactly what happened I don't know. I guess she misjudged a curve or something and went flying off the road. The jalopy bounced down* the hill, and her neck was broken . . . That's how it

---

***sort of**=somewhat, to some extent, more or less

***jalopy**:「낡은 자동차」

***bounced down**:「굴러 떨어졌다」

ended."

They walked in silence. Helen was moved. But why, she thought, all the sad music?*

"I'm awfully sorry."

"It was years ago."

"It was a tragic thing to happen."

"I couldn't expect better," he said.

"Life renews itself."

"My luck stays the same."

"Go on with your plans for an education."

"That's about it," Frank said. "That's what I got to do."

Their eyes met, she felt her scalp prickle.*

Then they left the park and went home.

Outside the dark grocery store she quickly said good night.

"I'll stay out a little longer," Frank said. "I like to see the moon."

She went upstairs.

In bed she thought of their walk, wondering how much to believe of what he had told her about his ambitions and plans for college. He could not have said anything to make a better impression on her. And what was the purpose of the sad tale of the carnival girl* "built something like you"? Who was he mixing up with* his carnival girls? Yet he had told the story simply, without any visible attempt to work on her

---

***But why, she thought, all the sad music?**:「그러나 왜 슬픈 이야기만 하는 것일까 하고 그녀는 생각했다」

***she felt her scalp prickle**:「그녀는 머리 가죽이 따끔따끔 쑤시는 것을 느꼈다」

***the carnival girl**:「써커스단의 소녀」

***mix up with**:「혼동하다」

sympathy.* Probably it was a true memory, recalled because he happened to be feeling lonely. She had had her own moonlit memories to contend with.* Thinking about Frank, she tried to see him straight but came up with a confusing image: the grocery clerk with the greedy eyes, on top of* the ex-carnival hand and future serious college student, a man of possibilities.

On the verge of sleep she sensed a desire on his part to involve her in his life. The aversion* she felt for him before returned, but she succeeded without too much effort in dispelling* it. Thoroughly awake now, she regretted she could not see the sky from her window in the wall, or look down into the street. Who was he making into a wife out of snowy moonlight?*

***without any visible attempt to work on her sympathy**:「그녀의 동정심을 유발시키려는 어떠한 명백한 눈치도 보이지 않고」

***She had had her own moonlit memories to contend with**:「그녀도 그의 회상에 못지않을, 달빛 어린 추억을 지니고 있었다」

***on top of**=in addition to「~에 덧붙여」

***aversion**:「혐오감」

***dispel**=drive away

***Who was he making into a wife out of snowy moonlight?**:「그는 눈 같은 달빛으로 누구를 자기의 아내로 만들려는 것일까?」

5

Earnings in the grocery, especially around Christmas and New Year's, continued to rise. For the last two weeks in December Morris averaged an unusual one hundred and ninety. Ida had a new theory to explain the spurt of business:* an apartment house had opened for rentals a few blocks away;* furthermore, she had heard that Schmitz was not so attentive to his store as he was before. An unmarried storekeeper was sometimes erratic.* Morris didn't deny these things but he still attributed their good fortune mostly to his clerk. For reasons that were clear to him the customers liked Frank, so they brought in their friends. As a result, the grocer could once more meet his running expenses,* and with pinching and scrimping,* even pay off some outstanding bills.* Grateful to Frank—who seemed to take for granted the upswing of business—he planned to pay him more than the measly five dollars they shamefacedly gave him, but cautiously

---

***a new theory to explain the spurt of business**:「장사가 갑자기 잘 되는 것을 설명하는 새로운 이론」 spurt=a jet or burst

***an apartment house had opened for rentals a few blocks away**:「몇 블럭 떨어진 곳에 임대 아파트가 생겼다」 *e.g.* a rental car「세 놓는 자동차」

***erratic**=capricious「변덕스러운」, not fixed

***running expenses**=current expenses「경상비」 *e.g.* school expenses「학비」

***with pinching and scrimping**:「줄이고 절약하여」 pinch「바싹 줄이다」 scrimp「절약하여 쓰다」

***some outstanding bills**:「약간의 지불하지 못한 청구서」 *e.g.* outstanding debts「부채」

decided to see if the added income would continue in January, when business usually slackened off.* Even if he regularly took in two hundred a week, with the slight profit he made he could hardly afford a clerk. Before things were easier they had to take in a minimum of two-fifty or three hundred, an impossibility.

Since, though, the situation was better, Morris told Helen that he wanted her to keep more of her hard-earned twenty-five dollars; he said she must now keep fifteen, and if business stayed as it was maybe he would not need her assistance any more. He hoped so. Helen was overwhelmed at having fifteen a week to spend on herself. She needed shoes badly and could use a new coat—hers was little better than a rag—and a dress or two. And she wanted to put away* a few dollars for future tuition at NYU. She felt like her father about Frank—he had changed their luck. Remembering what he had said in the park that night about his ambitions and desire for education, she felt he someday would get what he wanted because he was obviously more than just an ordinary person.

He was often at the library. Almost every time Helen went there she saw him sitting over an open book at one of the tables; she wondered if all he did in his spare time was come here and read.* She respected him for it. She herself averaged two weekly visits,* each time checking out only a book or

---

***when business usually slackened off**:「보통 장사가 침체해 질 때」

***put away**=keep or save for future use

***all he did in his spare time was come here and read**:「한가할 때에 그가 하는 것은 여기에 와서 독서하는 것 뿐이었다」 주부에 do가 있을 때 보어가 될 부정사는 원형부정사를 쓸 때가 많음(미국식 용법).

***She herself averaged two weekly visits**:「그녀는 평균 매주 두 번 방문했다」

two, because it was one of her few pleasures to return for another. Even at her loneliest* she liked being among books, although she was sometimes depressed to see how much there was to read that she hadn't. Meeting Frank so often, she was at first uneasy: he haunted* the place, for what? But a library was a library; he came here, as she did, to satisfy certain needs. Like her he read a lot because he was lonely, Helen thought. She thought this after he had told her about the carnival girl. Gradually her uneasiness left her.

Although he left, as a rule, when she did, if she wanted to walk home alone, he did not intrude. Sometimes he rode back on the trolley while she walked. Sometimes she was on the trolley and saw him walking. But generally, so long as the weather was not too bad, they went home together, a couple of times turning off into the park. He told her more about himself. He had lived a different life from most people she had known, and she envied him all the places he had been to. Her own life, she thought, was much like her father's, restricted by his store, his habits, hers. Morris hardly ever journeyed past the corner, except on rare occasions, usually to return something a customer had left on the counter. When Ephraim was alive, when they were kids, her father liked to go bathing Sunday afternoons at Coney Island; and on Jewish holidays they would sometimes see a Yiddish play, or ride on the subway to the Bronx to call on landsleit. But after Ephraim died Morris had for years gone nowhere. Neither had she, for other reasons. Where could she go without a cent? She read

---

***Even at her loneliest**:「그녀가 가장 외로울 때에도」
***haunt**=frequent「자주 가다」

with eagerness of far-off places but spent her life close to home. She would have given much to visit* Charleston, New Orleans, San Francisco, cities she had heard so much about, but she hardly ever got beyond the borough of Manhattan. Hearing Frank talk of Mexico, Texas, California, other such places, she realized anew the meagerness of her movements: every day but Sunday on the BMT* to Thirty-fourth Street and back. Add to that a twice-weekly visit to the library at night. In summer, the same as before, except a few times —usually during her vacation—to Manhattan Beach; also, if she were lucky, to a concert or two at Lewisohn Stadium. Once when she was twenty and worn out, her mother had insisted she go for a week to an inexpensive adult camp in New Jersey. Before that, while in high school, she had traveled to Washington, D.C., with her American history class for a week end of visiting government buildings. So far and no further in the open world.* To stick so close to where she had lived her whole life was a crime. His stories made her impatient—she wanted to travel, experience, live.

One night as they were sitting on an bench in an enclosed part of the park beyond the tree-lined plaza, Frank said he had definitely made up his mind to start college in the fall. This excited her, and for hours afterward Helen couldn't stop thinking about it. She imagined all the interesting courses he could take, envied him the worthwhile people he'd meet in his

---

***She would have given much to visit** ~ :「~을 방문할 수 있었다면 비싼 댓가를 치루어도 개의치 않았을 것이다」
***on the BMT**:「BMT 선 (New York 지하철의 1노선)을 타고」
***So far and no further in the open world**:「이 넓은 세상에서 그 이상은 가 보지 못했다」

classes, the fun he'd have studying. She pictured him in nice clothes, his hair cut shorter, maybe his nose straightened, speaking a more careful English, interested in music and literature, learning about politics, psychology, philosophy; wanting to know more the more he knew, in this way growing in value to himself and others.* She imagined herself invited by him to a campus concert or play, where she would meet his college friends, people of promise. Afterward as they crossed the campus in the dark, Frank would point out the buildings his classes met in, classes taught by distinguished professors. And maybe if she closed her eyes she could see a time —miracle of miracles—when Helen Bober was enrolled here, not just a stranger on the run, pecking at a course or two at night,* and tomorrow morning back at Levenspiel's Louisville Panties and Bras. At least he made her dream.*

To help him prepare for college Helen said he ought to read some good novels, some of the great ones. She wanted Frank to like novels, to enjoy in them what she did. So she checked out *Madame Bovary, Anna Karenina* and *Crime and Punishment,* all by writers he had barely heard of, but they were very satisfying books, she said. He noticed she handled each yellow-paged volume* as though she were holding in her respectful hands the works of God Almighty. As if—according to her—you could read in them everything you couldn't

---

***in this way growing in value to himself and others**:「이런 식으로 자기 자신뿐만 아니라 다른 사람에게도 가치 있는 사람으로 성장해 가는」

***not just a stranger on the run, pecking at a course or two at night**:「밤에 겨우 한두 강좌 들으며 분주히 뛰어다니는 낯선 사람이 아니라」 on the run=busy

***At least he made her dream**:「적어도 그는 Helen이 꿈을 갖도록 해주었다」

***yellow-paged volume**:「누렇게 색이 바랜 책」

afford not to know*—the Truth about Life. Frank carried the three books up to his room, and huddled in a blanket to escape the cold that seeped in through the loose window frames, had rough going.* The stories were hard to get into because the people and places were strange to him, their crazy names difficult to hold in his mind* and some of the sentences were so godawful* complicated he forgot the beginning before he got to the end. The opening pages irritated him as he pushed through forests of odd facts and actions.* Though he stared for hours at the words, starting one book, then another, then the third—in the end, in exasperation,* he flung them aside.

But because Helen had read and respected these books, it shamed him that he hadn't, so he picked one up from the floor and went back to it. As he dragged himself through the first chapters, gradually the reading became easier and he got interested in the people—their lives in one way or another wounded—some to death. Frank read, at the start, in snatches,* then in bursts of strange hunger,* and before too long he had managed to finish the books. He had started *Madame Bovary* with some curiosity, but in the end he felt disgusted, wearied, left cold. He did not know why people

---

***everything you couldn't afford not to know**:「당신이 몰라서는 안 될 모든 것」
***had rough going**:「고생했다, 고전했다」 *e.g.* She had a bit of rough going.「그녀는 좀 고생했다」
***difficult to hold in his mind**:「기억하기 힘든」
***godawful**:「지독한」
***as he pushed through forests of odd facts and actions**:「기묘한 사실들과 행동들로 원시림처럼 뒤얽힌 부분을 읽어 나아갈 때」
***in exasperation**=in anger「화가 나서」
***in snatches**:「(생각난 듯이) 이따금」 *e.g.* work in snatches「찔끔찔끔 일하다」
***in bursts of strange hunger**:「기묘한 공복감이 갑자기 일어나서」

would want to write about that kind of a dame. Yet he felt a little sorry for her and the way things had happened, till there was no way out of it but her death. *Anna Karenina* was better; she was more interesting and better in bed.* He didn't want her to kill herself under the train in the end. Still, although Frank felt he could also take the book or leave it, he was moved at the deep change that came over Levin in the woods just after he had thought of hanging himself. At least he wanted to live. *Crime and Punishment* repelled yet fascinated him, with everybody in the joint confessing to something every time he opened his yap*—to some weakness, or sickness, or crime. Raskolnikov, the student, gave him a pain, with all his miseries. Frank first had the idea he must be a Jew and was surprised when he found he wasn't. He felt, in places in the book, even when it excited him, as if his face had been shoved into dirty water in the gutter;* in other places, as if he had been on a drunk for a month.* He was glad when he was finished with the book, although he liked Sonia, the prostitute, and thought of her for days after he had read it.

Afterward Helen suggested other novels by the same writers, so he would know them better, but Frank balked,* saying he wasn't sure that he had understood those he had read. "I'm sure you have," she answered, "if you got to know the people." "I know them," he muttered. But to please her he worked

---

***better in bed**:「침대에 있을 때 더 매력이 있었다」

***yap**=mouth

***as if his face had been shoved into dirty water in the gutter**:「마치 도랑의 더러운 물 속에 그의 얼굴이 쳐박혀진 것처럼」

***as if he had been on a drunk for a month**:「마치 한 달간이나 그가 술에 취해 있었던 것처럼」

***balk**=hesitate

through two more thick books, sometimes tasting nausea on his tongue,* his face strained as he read, eyes bright black, frowning, although he usually felt some relief at the end of the book. He wondered what Helen found so satisfying in all this goddamned human misery, and suspected her of knowing he had spied on her in the bathroom and was using the books to punish him for it. But then he thought it was an unlikely idea. Anyway, he could not get out of his thoughts how quick some people's lives went to pot* when they couldn't make up their minds what to do when they had to do it; and he was troubled by the thought of how easy it was for a man to wreck his whole life in a single wrong act. After that the guy suffered forever, no matter what he did to make up for the wrong.* At times, as the clerk had sat in his room late at night, a book held stiffly in his reddened hands, his head numb although he wore a hat, he felt a strange falling away from the printed page* and had this crazy sensation that he was reading about himself. At first this picked him up* but then it deeply depressed him.

One rainy night, as Helen was about to go up to Frank's room to ask him to take back something he had given her that she didn't want, before she could go the phone rang, and Ida hastened out into the hall to call her. Frank, lying on his bed

---

***sometimes tasting nausea on his tongue**:「때때로 입에서 구역질이 나고」
***go to pot**=be destroyed「파멸되다」
***to make up for the wrong**:「그 잘못을 보상하기 위해」 make up for=compensate, make amends for「보상하다」
***he felt a strange falling away from the printed page**:「그 책에서 자기가 멀리 떨어져 나가는 듯한 이상한 느낌이 들었다」
***At first this picked him up**:「처음에는 이 생각 때문에 힘이 솟아났다」

in this room, watching the rainy window, heard her go downstairs. Morris was in the store waiting on someone as Helen came in, but her mother sat in the back over a cup of tea.*

"It's Nat," Ida whispered, not moving.

She'll tell herself she isn't listening, thought Helen.*

Her first feeling was that she didn't want to talk to the law student, but his voice was warm, which for him meant extended effort,* and a warm voice on a wet night was a warm voice. She could easily picture what he looked like as he spoke into the phone. Yet she wished he had called her in December, when she had so desperately wanted him, for now she was again aware of a detachment in herself that she couldn't account for.*

"Nobody sees you any more, Helen," Nat began. "Where've you disappeared to?"

"Oh, I've been around," she said, trying to hide a slight tremble in her voice. "And you?"

"Is somebody there where you're talking that you sound so restrained?"

"That's right."

"I thought so. So let me make it quick and clean. Helen, it's

---

***her mother sat in the back over a cup of tea**:「그녀의 어머니는 뒷방에 앉아 차를 마시고 있었다」

***She'll tell herself she isn't listening, thought Helen**:「어머니는 남의 전화를 엿듣지 않는다고 스스로 말하겠지 하고 Helen은 생각했다」

***his voice was warm, which for him meant extended effort**:「그의 목소리는 다정했는데 이 사실은 그가 몹시 애써서 말하고 있음을 나타내고 있었다」 extended effort「집중적인 노력」 which의 선행사는 앞의 문장임.

***she was again aware of . . . account for**:「그녀는 이제 설명할 수 없는 어떤 냉정한 감정을 그에 대하여 다시 느끼고 있었다」

been a long time. I want to see you. What do you say if we take in a play* this Saturday night? I can stop off for tickets on my way uptown* tomorrow."

"Thanks, Nat. I don't think so." She heard her mother sigh.

Nat cleared his throat. "Helen, I honestly want to know how somebody's supposed to defend himself when he hasn't any idea what's in the indictment against him?* What kind of a crime have I committed? Yield the detalis."

"I'm not a lawyer—I don't make indictments."

"So call it a cause*—what's the cause? One day we're close to each other, the next I'm alone on an island, holding my hat. What did I do, please tell me?"

"Let's drop this subject."

Here Ida rose and went into the store, softly closing the door behind her. Thanks, thought Helen. She kept her voice low so they wouldn't hear her through the window in the wall.

"You're a funny kid," Nat was saying. "You've got some old-fashioned values about some things. I always told you punish yourself too much. Why should anybody have such a hot and heavy conscience* in these times? People are freer in the twentieth century. Pardon me for saying it but it's true."

She blushed. His insight was to his credit.* "My values are my values," she replied.

***take in a play**:「연극을 구경하다」 take in=see or watch

***I can stop off for tickets on my way uptown**:「주택구역으로 가는 도중, 차에서 내려 표를 살 수 있지」

***I honestly want to know . . . him?**:「어떤 사람이 자기에 대한 고발내용도 모를 때 어떻게 자신을 변호할 수 있는지 나는 진실로 알고 싶소」

***So call it a cause**:「그렇다면 그걸 이유라고 해둡시다」

***have such a hot and heavy conscience**:「심한 양심의 가책을 받다」

***His insight was to his credit**:「그의 통찰력은 날카로운 편이었다」

"What," Nat argued, "would people's lives be like if everybody regretted every beautiful minute of all that happened? Where's the poetry of living?"

"I hope you're alone," she said angrily, "where you're so blithely* discussing this subject."

He sounded weary, hurt. "Of course I'm alone. My God, Helen, how low have I fallen in your opinion?"*

"I told you what was going on at this end.* Up to a minute ago my mother was still in the room."

"I'm sorry, I forgot."

"It's all right now."

"Look, girl," he said affectionately, "the telephone is no place to hash out* our personal relations. What do you say if I run upstairs and see you right away? We got to come to some kind of a sensible understanding. I'm not exactly a pig, Helen. What you don't want is your privilege, if I may be so frank. So you don't want, but at least let's be friends and go out once in a while. Let me come up and talk to you."

"Some other time, Nat, I have to do something now."

"For instance?"

"Some other time," she said.

"Why not?" Nat answered amiably.

When he had hung up, Helen stood at the phone, wondering if she had done right. She felt she hadn't.*

Ida entered the kitchen. "What did he want—Nat?"

***blithely**=gaily, cheerfully「즐겁게」

***Helen, how low have I fallen in your opinion?**:「Helen, 내가 이처럼 당신에게 경멸을 받아야 해?」

***I told you what was going on at this end**:「이쪽의 사정은 제가 말씀해 드렸지」

***hash out**:「엉망진창으로 만들다」

***She felt she hadn't**: hadn't 다음에 done right가 생략됨.

"Just to talk."

"He asked you to go out?"

She admitted it.

"What did you answer him?"

"I said I would some other time."

"What do you mean 'some other time?'" Ida said sharply. "What are you already, Helen, an old lady? What good is it to sit so many nights alone upstairs? Who gets rich from reading? What's the matter with you?"

"Nothing's the matter, Mama." She left the store and went into the hall.

"Don't forget you're twenty-three years old," Ida called after her.

"I won't."

Upstairs her nervousness grew. When she thought what she had to do she didn't want to, yet felt she must.

They had met, she and Frank, last night at the library, the third time in eight days.* Helen noticed as they were leaving that he clumsily carried a package she took to contain some shirts or underwear, but on the way home Frank flung away his cigarette, and under a street lamp handed it to her.

"Here, this is for you."

"For me? What is it?"

"You'll find out."

She took it half-willingly, and thanked him. Helen carried it awkwardly the rest of the way home, neither of them saying much. She had been caught by surprise.* If she had given

---

***the third time in eight days**:「8일 동안에 세번째」

***She had been caught by surprise**:「그녀는 기습을 받은 격이었다」

herself a minute to think, she would have refused it on grounds that it was wise just to stay friends; because, she thought, neither of them really knew the other. But once she had the thing in her hands she hadn't the nerve to ask him to take it back. It was a medium-sized box of some sort with something heavy in it—she guessed a book; yet it seemed too big for a book. As she held it against her breast, she felt a throb of desire for Frank* and this disturbed her. About a block from the grocery, nervously saying good night, she went on ahead. This was how they parted when the store window was still lit.

Ida was downstairs with Morris when Helen came into the house, so no questions were asked. She shivered a little as she unwrapped the box on her bed, ready to hide it the minute she heard a footstep on the stairs. Lifting the carton lid, she found two packages in it, each wrapped in white tissue paper and tied with red ribbons with uneven bows,* obviously by Frank. When she had untied the first present, Helen gasped at the sight of* a long, hand-woven scarf—rich black wool interlaced with gold thread.* She was startled to discover that the second present was a red leather copy of Shakespeare's plays. There was no card.

She sat weakly down on the bed. I can't, she told herself. They were expensive things, probably had cost him every

---

***felt a throb of desire for Frank**:「Frank를 받아들이고 싶은 충동을 느꼈다」

***tied with red ribbons with uneven bows**:「고르지 못한 나비꼴 매듭의 붉은 리본으로 매어져 있었다」

***Helen gasped at the sight of ~**:「Helen은 ~을 보고 숨을 헐떡였다」 gasp=pant, struggle for breathe

***rich black wool interlaced with gold thread**:「금실로 섞어 짠 짙은 검은 색 털실」 rich=vivid 「짙은, 선명한」

penny of the hard-earned money he was saving for college. Even supposing he had enough for that, she still couldn't take his gifts. It wasn't right, and coming from him, it was, somehow, less than not right.*

She wanted then and there to go up to his room and leave them at the door with a note, but hadn't the heart to the very night he had given them to her.

The next evening, after a day of worry, she felt she must return them; and now she wished she had done it before Nat had called, then she might have been more relaxed on the phone.

Helen got down on her hands and knees* and reached under the bed for the carton* with Frank's scarf and book in it. It touched her that he had given her such lovely things—so much nicer than anyone else ever had. Nat, at his best, had produced a half-dozen small pink roses.

For gifts you pay, Helen thought. She drew a deep breath, and taking the box went quietly up the stairs. She tapped hesitantly on Frank's door. He had recognized her step and was waiting behind the door. His fists were clenched, the nails cutting his palms.*

When he opened the door and his glance fell on what she was carrying, he frowned as though struck in the face.

Helen stepped awkwardly into the little room, quickly

***coming from him, it was, somehow, less than not right**:「그로부터 받은 것이기 때문에, 어쨌든, 더욱 정당치 못한 것이었다」
***Helen got down on her hands and knees**:「Helen은 손을 짚고 엎드렸다」
***reached under the bed for the carton**:「침대 밑의 종이상자를 잡으려고 손을 뻗었다」
e.g. He reached for the branch「그는 나뭇가지를 잡으려고 손을 뻗쳤다」
***the nails cutting his palms**:「손톱이 손바닥을 파고 들어갔다」

shutting the door behind her. She suppressed a shudder at the smallness and barrenness of the place. On his unmade* bed lay a sock he had been trying to mend.

"Are the Fusos home?" she asked in a low voice.

"They went out." He spoke dully, his eyes hopelessly stuck to the things he had given her.

Helen handed him the box with the presents. "Thanks so much, Frank," she said, trying to smile, "but I really don't think I ought to take them. You'll need every cent for your college tuition in the fall."

"That's not the reason you mean," he said.

Her face reddened. She was about to explain that her mother would surely make a scene if she saw his gifts, but instead said, "I can't keep them."

"Why not?"

It wasn't easy to answer and he didn't make it easier, just held the rejected presents in his big hands as if they were living things that had suddenly died.

"I can't," she got out. "Your taste is so nice, I'm sorry."

"Okay," he said wearily. He tossed the box on the bed and the Shakespeare fell to the floor. She stooped quickly to pick it up and was unnerved to see it had opened to "Romeo and Juliet."*

"Good night." She left his room and went hastily downstairs. In her room she thought she heard the distant sound of a man crying. She listened tensely, her hand on her throbbing throat, but no longer heard it.

***unmade**:「정돈되지 않은」

***was unnerved to see it had opened to "Romeo and Juliet"**:「펼쳐진 곳이 "로미오와 쥬리엘"인 것을 보고 힘이 빠져 버렸다」 unnerve=unman「낙담시키다」

Helen took a shower to relax, then got into a nightgown and housecoat. She picked up a book but couldn't read. She had noticed before signs he might be in love with her, but now she was almost sure of it. Carrying his package as he had walked with her last night, he had been somebody different, though the hat and overcoat were the same. There seemed to be about him a size and potentiality she had not seen before.* He did not say love but love was in him. When the insight came to her, at almost the minute he was handing her the package, she had reacted with gooseflesh.* That it had gone this far was her own fault. She had warned herself not to get mixed up with him but hadn't obeyed her warning. Out of loneliness she had encouraged him. What else, going so often to the library, knowing he would be there? And she had stopped off with him, on their walks, for pizzas and coffee;* had listened to his stories, discussed with him plans for college, talked at length about books he was reading; at the same time she had been concealing these meetings from her father and mother. He knew it, no wonder he had built up hopes.

The strange thing was there were times she felt she liked him very much. He was, in many ways, a worthwhile person, and where a man gave off honest feeling, was she a machine to shut off her own?* Yet she knew she mustn't become seriously

---

***There seemed to be . . . before**:「그녀가 전에 보지 못한 크기와 잠재력을 Frank가 지니고 있는 듯했다」

***she had reacted with gooseflesh**:「온 몸에 소름이 쫙 끼쳤다」

***for pizzas and coffee**:「이탈리아 파이와 커피를 들기 위하여」

***where a man gave off honest feeling, was she a machine to shut off her own?**:「남자가 자기의 솔직한 감정을 보이는 데 그 대상인 여자로서 자신의 감정을 억제하는 기계가 될 수 있겠는가?」

attracted to him because there would be trouble in buckets.* Trouble, thank you, she had had enough of. She wanted now a peaceful life without worry—any more worries. Friends they could be, in a minor key;* she might on a moonlit night even hold hands with him, but beyond that nothing. She should have said something of the sort;* he would have saved his presents for a better prospect and she would not now be feeling guilt at having hurt him. Yet in a way he had surprised her by his apparent depth of affection. She had not expected anything to happen so quickly, because, for her, things had happened in reverse order.* Usually she fell in love first, then the man, if he wasn't Nat Pearl, responded. So the other way around was nice for a change,* and she wished it would happen more often, but with the right one.* She must go, she decided, less to the library; he would then understand, if he didn't already, and give up any idea of having her love.* When he realized what was what he would get over his pain, if he really felt any.* But her thoughts gave her no peace, and though she tried often, she could still not concentrate on her books. When Morris and Ida trudged through her room, her

---

***trouble in buckets**:「많은 어려운 문제」

***in a minor key**:「낮은 정도로, 평범한 관계로」

***She should have said something of the sort**:「그녀는 이런 뜻의 말을 했어야 했다」

***in reverse order**:「거꾸로」

***So the other way around was nice for a change**:「그러므로 그 반대의 순서도 기분전환이 되어 좋았다」

***but with the right one**:「그러나 알맞는 상대라야 한다」

***and give up any idea of having her love**:「그녀의 사랑을 얻으려는 어떠한 생각도 버릴 것이다」

***When he realized . . . if he really felt any**:「그가 사정을 깨닫게 되면 그가 비록 어떠한 고통을 받고 있다 해도 그것을 극복하게 될 것이다」 *e.g.* My friend told me what was what.「내 친구는 나에게 일의 진상을 알려주었다」

light was out and she seemed to be sleeping.

As she left the house for work the next morning, to her dismay she spied the carton containing his presents on top of some greasy garbage bags in the stuffed rubbish can* at the curb. The cover of the can apparently had been squeezed down on the box but had fallen off and now lay on the sidewalk. Lifting the carton cover, Helen saw the two gifts, loosely covered with the tissue paper. Angered by the waste, she plucked the scarf and book out of the crushed cardboard box and went quickly into the hall with them. If she took them upstairs Ida would want to know what she had, so she decided to hide them in the cellar. She turned on the light and went quietly down, trying to keep her high heels from clicking on the stairs.* Then she removed the tissue paper and hid the presents, neither of which had been harmed, in the bottom drawer of a broken chiffonier in their bin.* The dirty tissue paper and red ribbons she rolled up* in a sheet of old newspaper, then went upstairs and pressed it into the garbage can. Helen noticed her father at the window, idly watching her. She passed into the store, said good morning, washed her hands and left for work. On the subway she felt despondent.*

After supper that night, while Ida was washing dishes, Helen sneaked down into the cellar, got the scarf and book and carried them up to Frank's room. She knocked and

---

***in the stuffed rubbish can**:「꽉 찬 쓰레기통 안에」

***trying to keep her high heels from clicking on the stairs**:「계단에서 그녀의 하이힐이 삐걱거리지 않게 조심하면서」

***in the bottom drawer of a broken chiffonier in their bin**:「지하실 포도주 저장소에 있는 부서진 장롱의 제일 아래 서랍 속에」

***roll up**:「똘똘 싸다」

***she felt despondent**:「그녀는 기운이 빠져 버렸다」

nobody answered. She considered leaving them at the door but felt he would throw them away again unless she spoke to him first.

Tessie opened her door. "I heard him go out a while before, Helen." Her eyes were on the things in her hands.

Helen blushed. "Thanks, Tessie."

"Any message?"

"No." She returned to her floor and once more pushed the gifts under her bed. Changing her mind, she put the book and scarf in different bureau drawers, hiding them under her underwear. When her mother came up she was listening to the radio.

"You going someplace tonight, Helen?"

"Maybe, I don't know. Maybe to the library."

"Why so much to the library? You went a couple days ago."

"I go to meet Clark Gable, Mama."

"Helen, don't get fresh."*

Sighing, she said she was sorry.

Ida sighed too. "Some people want their children to read more. I want you to read less."

"That won't get me married any faster."*

Ida knitted but soon grew restless and went down to the store again. Helen got out Frank's things, packed them in heavy paper she had bought on her way home, tied the bundle with cord, and took the trolley to the library. He wasn't there.

***Helen, don't get fresh**:「Helen 건방지게 굴지 마」 fresh=presumptuous, brazen「뻔뻔스러운」

***That won't get me married any faster**:「책을 덜 읽는다고 제가 빨리 결혼하는 것도 아니죠」

The next night she tried first his room, then when she was able to slip out of the house, again the library, but found him in neither place.

"Does Frank still work here?" she asked Morris in the morning.

"Of course he works."

"I haven't seen him for a while," she said. "I thought he might be gone."

"In the summer he leaves."

"Did he say that?"

"Mama says."

"Does he know?"

"He knows. Why you ask me?"

She said she was just curious.

As Helen came into the hall that evening she heard the clerk descending the stairs and waited for him at the landing.* Lifting his hat, he was about to pass when she spoke.

"Frank, why did you throw your two presents into the garbage?"

"What good were they to me?"

"It was a terrible waste. You should have got your money back."

He smiled in the corners of his mouth. "Easy come, easy go."*

"Don't joke. I took them out of the rubbish and have them in my room for you. They weren't damaged."

"Thanks."

***at the landing**:「층계참에서」
***Easy come, easy go**:「쉽게 번 돈은 쉽게 나가기 마련이죠」

"Please give them back and get your money. You'll need every penny for the fall."

"Since I was a kid I hate to go back with stuff I bought."*

"Then let me have the sales checks* and I'll return them during my lunch hour."

"I lost them," he answered.

She said gently, "Frank, sometimes things turn out other than we plan. Don't feel hurt."

"When I don't feel hurt, I hope they bury me."*

He left the house, she walked up the stairs.

Over the week end Helen went back to crossing off the days on the calendar. She found she had crossed nothing since New Year's. She fixed that. On Sunday the weather turned fair and she grew restless. She wished again for Nat to call her; instead his sister did and they walked, in the early afternoon, on the Parkway.

Betty was twenty-seven and resembled Sam Pearl. She was large-boned and on the plain side* but made good use of reddish hair and a nice nature. She was in her ideas, Helen thought, somewhat dull. They had not too much in common and saw each other infrequently, but liked to talk once in a while, or go to a movie together. Recently Betty had become engaged to a CPA* in her office and was with him most of the

---

***Since I was a kid I hate to go back with stuff I bought**:「나는 어렸을 때부터, 산 물건을 무르러 가는 것을 싫어합니다」 stuff=상품

***sales check**=sales slip「매상전표」

***When I don't feel hurt, I hope they bury me**:「상처를 입지 않게 될 때는, 내가 죽어 장사 지내게 될 때이겠죠」

***on the plain side**:「못생긴 편인」

***a CPA**=a Certified Public Accountant「공인회계사」

time. Now she sported* a prosperous diamond ring on her stylish finger. Helen, for once, envied her, and Betty, as if she had guessed, wished her the same good luck.

"And it should happen soon," she said.

"Many thanks, Betty."

After they had gone a few blocks, Betty said, "Helen, I don't like to butt in* somebody else's private business but for a long time I wanted to ask you what happened between you and my brother Nat. I once asked him and he gave me double talk."*

"You know how such things go."

"I thought you liked him?"

"I did."

"Then why don't you see him any more? Did you have some kind of a fight?"

"No fights. We didn't have the same things in mind."

Betty asked no more. Later, she remarked, "Sometime give him another chance, Helen. Nat really has the makings of a good person.* Shep, my boy friend, thinks so too. His worst fault is he thinks his brains entitle him to certain privileges.* You'll see, in time he'll get over it."

"I may," Helen said. "We'll see sometime."

They returned to the candy store, where Shep Hirsch, Betty's stout, eyeglassed, future husband was waiting to take her for

---

***sport**=show off「자랑해 보이다」

***butt in**=meddle in「참견하다, 간섭하다」

***he gave me double talk**:「앞뒤가 안 맞는 말을 했다」 double=equivocal, deceitful, insincere

***Nat really has the makings of a good person**:「Nat는 사실 착한 사람이 될 소질을 가지고 있지」 makings「소질, 요소」 *e.g.* He has the makings of a statesman.「그에겐 정치가의 소질이 있다」

***he thinks his brains entitle him to certain privileges**:「그는 자기의 명석한 머리 때문에 어떤 특전을 누릴 수 있다고 생각한다」

a drive in his Pontiac.

"Come along, Helen," said Betty.

"With pleasure." Shep tipped his hat.

"Go, Helen," advised Goldie Pearl.

"Thanks, all, from the bottom of my heart," said Helen, "but I have some of my underthings to iron."

Upstairs, she stood at the window, looking out at the back yards. The remnants of last week's dirty snow. No single blade of green, or flower to light the eye or lift the heart. She felt as if she were made of knots* and in desperation got on her coat, tied a yellow kerchief around her head and left the house again, not knowing which way to go. She wandered toward the leafless park.

At the approach to the park's main entrance there was a small island in the street, a concrete triangle formed by intersecting avenues.* Here people sat on benches during the day and tossed peanuts or pieces of bread to the noisy pigeons that haunted the place. Coming up the block, Helen saw a man squatting by one of the benches, feeding the birds. Otherwise, the island was deserted. When the man rose, the pigeons fluttered up* with him, a few landing on his arms and shoulders, one perched on his fingers, pecking peanuts from his cupped palm. Another fat bird sat on his hat. The man clapped his hands when the peanuts were gone and the birds, beating their wings, scattered.

***She felt as if she were made of knots**:「온 몸이 옹이로 이루어진 것같이 그녀는 느꼈다」

***a concrete triangle formed by intersecting avenues**:「가로수길이 교차되어 이루어진 삼각형의 콘크리트」

***flutter up**:「날개를 파닥거리며 날아오르다」

When she recognized Frank Alpine, Helen hesitated. She felt in no mood to see him, but remembering the package hidden in her bureau drawer, determined once and for all* to get rid of it. Reaching the corner, she crossed over to the island.

Frank saw her coming and wasn't sure he cared one way or the other.* The return of his presents had collapsed his hopes. He had thought that if she ever fell for him it would change his life in the way he wanted it to happen, although at times the very thought of another change, even in this sense of it, made him miserable. Yet what was the payoff,* for instance, of marrying a dame like her and having to do with Jews the rest of his life? So he told himself he didn't care one way or the other.

"Hi," Helen said.

He touched his hat. His face looked tired but his eyes were clear and his gaze steady, as if he had been through something and had beat it.* She felt sorry if she had caused him any trouble.

"I had a cold," Frank remarked.

"You should get more sun."

Helen sat down on the edge of the bench, as if she were afraid, he thought, she would be asked to take a lease on it;*

***once and for all**=decisively「단호히, 확실하게」 *e.g.* Tell him so once for all.「그에게 확실하게 말해라」

***wasn't sure he cared one way or the other**:「그녀를 만나고 싶은지 그렇지 않은지 사신도 몰랐다」

***payoff**=return, recompense「보답, 보수」

***as if he had been through something and had beat it**:「마치 무언가 해내고 극복한 것처럼」

***as if she were afraid, he thought, she would be asked to take a lease on it**:「그의 생각에는 마치 그것을 세 놓도록 요구받을까봐 그녀가 두려워하는 것처럼」 *e.g.* He took

and he sat a little apart from her. One of the pigeons began to chase another running in circles and landed on its back. Helen looked away but Frank idly watched the birds until they flew off.

"Frank," she said, "I hate to sound like a pest on this subject,* but if there's anything I can't stand it's waste. I know you're not Rockefeller, so would you mind giving me the names of the stores where you bought your kind presents so that I can return them? I think I can without the sales checks."

Her eyes, he noticed, were a hard blue, and though he thought it ridiculous, he was a little scared of her, as if she were far too determined, too dead serious for him. At the same time he felt he still liked her. He had not thought so, but with them sitting together like this he thought again that he did. It was in a way a hopeless feeling, yet it was more than that because he did not exactly feel hopeless. He felt, as he sat next to her and saw her worn, unhappy face, that he still had a chance.

Frank cracked his knuckles one by one. He turned to her. "Look, Helen, maybe I try to work too fast. If so, I am sorry. I am the type of a person, who if he likes somebody, has to show it. I like to give her things, if you understand that, though I do know that not everybody likes to take. That's their business. My nature is to give and I couldn't change it even if I wanted. So okay. I am also sorry I got sore* and

---

a lease of the building.「그는 그 빌딩을 임차했다」

***I hate to sound like a pest on this subject**:「이 문제에 대해서 귀찮게 들먹거려 죄송합니다」 pest=a nuisance「성가신 것」

***get sore**:「화를 내다」 *e.g.* He is very sore about his defeat.「그는 패배하여 아주 분하게 생각하고 있다」

dumped your presents in the can and you had to take them out. But what I want to say is this. Why don't you just go ahead and keep one of those thing that I got for you? Let it be a little memory of a guy you once knew that wants to thank you for the good books you told him to read. You don't have to worry that I expect anything for what I give you."

"Frank . . ." she said, reddening.

"Just let me finish. How's this for a deal?* If you keep one of those things, I will take the other back to the store and get what I paid for it. What do you say?"

She was not sure what to say, but since she wanted to be finished with it, nodded at his proposal.

"Fine," Frank said. "Now what do you want the most?"

"Well, the scarf is awfully nice, but I'd rather keep the book."

"So keep the book then," he said. "You can give me the scarf anytime you want and I promise I will bring it back."

He lit a cigarette and inhaled deeply.

She considered whether to say good-by, now that the matter had been settled, and go on with her walk.

"You busy now?" he asked.

She guessed a short stroll.* "No."

"How about a movie?"

It took her a minute to reply. Was he starting up once more? She felt she must quickly set limits* to keep him from again creeping too close. Yet out of respect for his already hurt feelings, she thought it best that she think out exactly what to

---

***How's this for a deal?**:「타협을 하면 어떻겠읍니까?」
***She guessed a short stroll**:「짧은 산보를 하자고 그가 제안할 것으로 그녀는 생각했다」
***set limits**:「한계를 정하다」

say and tactfully say it, later on.

"I'll have to be back early."

"So let's go," he said, getting up.

Helen slowly untied her kerchief, then knotted it, and they went off together.

As they walked she kept wondering if she hadn't made a mistake in accepting the book. In spite of what he had said about expecting nothing she felt a gift was a claim, and she wanted none on her.* Yet, when, almost without noticing, she once more asked herself if she liked him at all, she had to admit she did a little. But not enough to get worried about; she liked him but not with an eye to* the possibility of any deeper feeling. He was not the kind of man she wanted to be in love with. She made that very clear to herself, for among his other disadvantages there was something about him, evasive, hidden.* He sometimes appeared to be more than he was, sometimes less. His aspirations, she sensed, were somehow apart from the self he presented normally when he wasn't trying,* though he was always more or less trying; therefore when he was trying less. She could not quite explain this to herself, for if he could make himself seem better, broader, wiser when he tried, then he had these things in him because

***she felt a gift was a claim, and she wanted none on her**:「선물은 권리가 따르는 것인데, 그녀는 상대방이 권리를 주장해 오지 않기를 바랬다」

***with an eye to ～ = with a view to ～**:「～을 목적으로 하여, ～을 꾀하여」 *e.g.* He did it with an eye to deceiving me.「그는 나를 속일 목적으로 그 짓을 했다」

***among his other disadvantages . . . evasive, hidden**:「그의 다른 결점 중에서도, 그에게는 어딘가 남의 눈을 피하는, 비밀스러운 데가 있었다」

***His aspirations···when he wasn't trying**:「그의 야망은, 그가 훌륭하게 보이려고 하지 않을 때, 그가 보통 보여주는 자신의 모습과는 심한 차이가 있다고 그녀는 느꼈다」

you couldn't make them out of nothing.* There was more to him than his appearance. Still, he hid what he had and he hid what he hadn't. With one hand the magician showed his cards, with the other he turned them into smoke. At the very minute he was revealing himself, saying who he was, he made you wonder if it was true. You looked into mirrors and saw mirrors and didn't know what was right or real or important. She had gradually got the feeling that he only pretended to be frank about himself, that in telling so much about his experiences, his trick was to hide his true self.* Maybe not purposely —maybe he had no idea he was doing it.* She asked herself whether he might have been married already. He had once said he never was. And was there more to the story of the once-kissed, tragic carnival girl? He had said no. If not, what made her feel he had done something—committed himself in a way she couldn't guess?

As they were approaching the movie theater, a thought of her mother crossed her mind and she heard herself say, "Don't forget I'm Jewish."*

"So what?" Frank said.

Inside in the dark, recalling what he had answered her, he felt this elated feeling,* as if he had crashed head on through a brick wall but hadn't bruised himself.

***because you couldn't make them out of nothing**:「왜냐하면 무에서 장점을 만들어 낼 수 없었기 때문에」

***his trick was to hide his true self**:「그의 계략은 자기의 진짜 모습을 감추려는 데 있었다(는 느낌)」 in telling 앞의 that는 the feeling에 연결됨.

***maybe he had no idea he was doing it**:「아마도 그는 자기가 그런 짓을 하고 있다고 생각하지 않을 것이다」

***she heard herself say, "Don't forget I'm Jewish"**:「"내가 유태인임을 잊지 마세요" 라고 그녀는 혼잣말을 했다」

***elated feeling**:「의기양양한 기분」 elated=exultant「크게 우쭐대는」

She had bitten her tongue but made no reply.

Anyway, by summer he'd be gone.

Ida was very unhappy that she had kept Frank on when she could have got rid of him so easily. She was to blame and she actively worried. Though she had no evidence, she suspected Helen was interested in the clerk. *Something* was going on between them. She did not ask her daughter what, because a denial would shame her.* And though she had tried she felt she could not really trust Frank. Yes, he had helped the business, but how much would they have to pay for it? Sometimes when she came upon him alone in the store, his expression, she told herself, was sneaky.* He sighed often, muttered to himself, and if he saw he was observed, pretended he hadn't. Whatever he did there was more in it than he was doing. He was like a man with two minds. With one he was here, with the other someplace else. Even while he read he was doing more than reading. And his silence spoke a language she couldn't understand. Something bothered him and Ida suspected it was her daughter. Only when Helen happened to come into the store or the back while he was there, did he seem to relax, become one person.* Ida was troubled, although she could not discover in Helen any response to him. Helen was quiet in his presence, detached, almost cold to the clerk. She gave him for his restless eyes, nothing—her back.* Yet for this reason, too, Ida worried.

***because a denial would shame her**:「딸이 부인하면 창피할 것 같았기 때문에」

***sneaky**=sneaking, mean「비열한」

***did he seem to relax, become one person**:「그는 마음이 놓이고, 또 두 마음 아닌 한 마음을 가진 사람이 되는 것 같았다」

***She gave him for his restless eyes, nothing—her back**:「그의 침착치 못한 시선에 대하여 그녀는 아무런 반응도 보이지 않았다—그녀의 등을 돌리는 것 이외에는」

One night, after Helen had left the house, when her mother heard the clerk's footsteps going down the stairs, she quickly got into a coat, wrapped a shawl around her head and trudged through a sprinkle of snow after him. He walked to the movie house several blocks away, paid his money, and passed in. Ida was almost certain that Helen was inside, waiting for him. She returned home with nails in her heart* and found her daughter upstairs, ironing. Another night she followed Helen to the library. Ida waited across the street, shivering for almost an hour in the cold, until Helen emerged, then followed her home. She chided herself for her suspicions but they would not fly from her mind. Once, listening from the back, she heard her daughter and the clerk talking about a book. This annoyed her. And when Helen later happened to mention that Frank had plans to begin college in the autumn, Ida felt he was saying that only to get her interested in him.*

She spoke to Morris and cautiously asked if he had noticed anything developing between Helen and the clerk.

"Don't be foolish," the grocer replied. He had thought about the possibility, at times felt concerned, but after pondering how different they were, had put the idea out of his head.

"Morris, I am afraid."

"You are afraid of everything, even which it don't exist."

"Tell him to leave now—business is better."

"So is better," he muttered, "but who knows how will be next week. We decided he will stay till summer."

"Morris, he will make trouble."

***with nails in her heart**:「몹시 괴로와하면서」
***to get her interested in him**:「그녀가 자기에게 관심을 갖도록 하기 위하여」

"What kind trouble will he make?"

"Wait," she said, clasping her hands, "a tragedy will happen."

Her remark at first annoyed, then worried him.

The next morning the grocer and his clerk were sitting at the table, peeling hot potatoes. The pot had been drained of water and dumped on its side; they sat close to the steaming pile of potatoes, hunched over, ripping off the salt-stained skins* with small knives. Frank seemed ill at ease.* He hadn't shaved and had dark blobs* under his eyes. Morris wondered if he had been drinking but there was never any smell of liquor about him. They worked without speaking, each lost in his thoughts.*

After a half-hour, Frank squirming* restlessly in his chair, remarked, "Say, Morris, suppose somebody asked you what do the Jews believe in, what would you tell them?"

The grocer stopped peeling, unable at once to reply.

"What I like to know is what is a Jew anyway?"

Because he was ashamed of his meager education* Morris was never comfortable with such questions, yet he felt he must answer.

"My father used to say to be a Jew all you need is a good heart."

***ripping off the salt-stained skins**:「소금물이 밴 껍질을 벗기면서」
***Frank seemed ill at ease**:「Frank는 불안한 것 같았다」
***dark blobs**:「검은 그늘」
***each lost in his thoughts**:「각각 자기의 생각에 잠긴 채」 독립분사구문이며 lost 앞에 being을 넣어서 생각할 것.
***squirm**=twist the body as in pain:「고통스러운 듯이 몸을 뒤틀다」
***meager education**:「빈약한 교육」

"What do you say?"

"The important thing is the Torah. This is the Law—a Jew must believe in the Law."

"Let me ask you this," Frank went on. "Do you consider yourself a real Jew?"

Morris was startled, "What do you mean if I am a real Jew?"*

"Don't get sore about this," Frank said, "But I can give you an argument that you aren't.* First thing, you don't go to the synagogue*—not that I have ever seen. You don't keep your kitchen kosher and you don't eat kosher.* You don't even wear one of those little black hats like this tailor I knew in South Chicago. He prayed three times a day. I even hear the Mrs say you kept the store open on Jewish holidays, it makes no difference if she yells her head off."*

"Sometimes," Morris answered, flushing, "to have to eat, you must keep open on holidays. On Yom Kippur* I don't keep open. But I don't worry about kosher, which is to me old-fashioned. What I worry is to follow the Jewish Law."

"But all those things are the Law, aren't they? And don't the Law say you can't eat any pig, but I have seen you taste ham."

***What do you mean if I am a real Jew?**:「내가 진짜 유태인이냐고? 그게 무슨 뜻인가?」

***I can give you an argument that you aren't**:「저는 당신이 유태인이 아니라고 증명할 수 있읍니다」

***the synagogue**:「유태인 교회」

***You don't keep your kitchen kosher and you don't eat kosher**:「당신은 부엌을 유태인 율법에 따라 관리하지 않고 율법에 따라 만든 음식을 먹지 않습니다」 kosher「(형) 유태교의 율법에 맞는, (명)유태교의 율법에 따라 만든 음식」

***if she yells her head off**:「그녀가 아무리 큰 소리로 반대해도」 one's head off= excessively「심하게」

***Yom Kippur**:「유태교의 속죄일」

"This is not important to me if I taste pig or if I don't. To some Jews is this important but not to me. Nobody will tell me that I am not Jewish because I put in my mouth once in a while, when my tongue is dry, a piece ham. But they will tell me, and I will believe them, if I forget the Law. This means to do what is right, to be honest, to be good. This means to other people. Our life is hard enough. Why should we hurt somebody else? For everybody should be the best, not only for you or me. We ain't animals. This is why we need the Law. This is what a Jew believes."

"I think other religions have those ideas too," Frank said. "But tell me why it is that the Jews suffer so damn much, Morris? It seems to me that they like to suffer, don't they?"

"Do you like to suffer? They suffer because they are Jews."

"That's what I mean, they suffer more than they have to."

"If you live, you suffer. Some people suffer more, but not because they want. But I think if a Jew don't suffer for the Law, he will suffer for nothing."

"What do you suffer for, Morris?" Frank said.

"I suffer for you," Morris said calmly.

Frank laid his knife down on the table. His mouth ached. "What do you mean?"

"I mean you suffer for me."

The clerk let it go at that.*

"If a Jew forgets the Law," Morris ended, "he is not a good Jew, and not a good man."

Frank picked up his knife and began to tear the skins off the potatoes. The grocer peeled his pile in silence. The clerk

---

***The clerk let it go at that**:「점원은 더 이상 캐묻지 않았다」

When the potatoes were cooling, Morris, troubled by their talk, asked himself why Frank had brought up this subject.* A thought of Helen, for some reason, crossed his mind.*

"Tell me the truth," he said, "why did you ask me such questions?"

Frank shifted in his chair. He answered slowly, "To be truthful to you,* Morris, once I didn't have much use for the Jews."*

Morris looked at him without moving.

"But that was long ago," said Frank, "before I got to know what they were like. I don't think I understood much about them."

His brow was covered with sweat.

"Happens like this many times,"* Morris said.

But his confession had not made the clerk any happier.

One afternoon, shortly after lunch, happening to glance at himself in the mirror, Morris saw how bushy his hair was and how thick the pelt on his neck; he felt ashamed. So he said to Frank he was going across the street to the barber. The clerk, studying the racing page of the *Mirror,** nodded, Morris hung

---

***asked himself why Frank had brought up this subject**:「왜 Frank가 이 문제를 꺼냈을까 하고 자문해 보았다」

***A thought of Helen, for some reason, crossed his mind**:「무슨 이유에서인지 Helen의 생각이 그의 머리를 스쳐갔다」

***To be truthful to you**:「솔직히 말씀드리자면」

***Morris, once I didn't have much use for the Jews**:「Morris씨, 이전에 저는 유태인을 별로 좋아하지 않았읍니다」 have little use「싫어하다, 가치를 인정하지 않다」 *e. g.* He had very little use for music.「그는 음악에 거의 관심이 없었다」

***Happens like this many times**:「그런 일은 흔히 있을 수 있지」

studying the racing page of the *Mirror:「*Mirror*지의 경마란을 자세히 살펴보면서」

up his apron and went into the store to get some change from the cash register. After he took a few quarters out of the drawer, he checked the receipts for the day and was pleased. He left the grocery and crossed the car tracks* to the barber shop.

The chair was empty and he didn't have to wait. As Mr. Giannola, who smelled of olive oil, worked on him and they talked, Morris, though embarrassed at all the hair that had to be cut by the barber,* found himself thinking mostly of his store. If it would only stay like this—no Karp's paradise,* but at least livable, not the terrible misery of only a few months ago—he would be satisfied. Ida had again been nagging him to sell, but what was the use of selling until things all over got better and he could find a place he would have confidence in?* Al Marcus, Breitbart, all the drivers he talked to, still complained about business. The best thing was not to look for trouble* but stay where he was. Maybe in the summer, after Frank left, he would sell out and search for a new place.

As he rested in the barber's chair, the grocer, watching through the window his own store, saw with satisfaction that at least three customers had been in since he had sat down. One man left with a large lumpy bag,* in which Morris imagined at least six bottles of beer. Also, two women had come out with heavy packages, one carrying a loaded market

---

***the car tracks**:「차도」
***though embarrassed at all the hair that had to be cut by the barber**:「이발사로부터 수북한 머리를 깎기는 것이 좀 창피했지만」
***no Karp's paradise**:「Karp의 상점처럼 번창하고 있지는 않았지만」
***have confidence in**=place trust in「신뢰하다」
***look for trouble**:「긁어 부스럼을 만들다」
***a large lumpy bag**:「큰 우툴두툴한 봉지」

bag.* Figuring, let's say, at least two dollars apiece for the women, he estimated he had taken in a nice fiver* and earned his haircut. When the barber unpinned the sheet around him and Morris returned to the grocery, he struck a match over the cash register and peered with anticipation at the figures. To his great surprise he saw that only a little more than three dollars had been added to the sum he had noted on leaving the store. He was stunned. How could it be only three if the bags had been packed tight with groceries? Could it be they contained maybe a couple of boxes of some large item like cornflakes, that came to nothing? He could hardly believe this and felt upset to the point of illness.*

In the back he hung up his overcoat, and with fumbling fingers tied his apron strings.

Frank glanced up from the racing page with a smile. "You look different without all the kelp* on you, Morris. You look like a sheep that had the wool clipped off it."

The grocer, ashen, nodded.*

"What's the matter your face is so pale?"

"I don't feel so good."

"Whyn't you go up then and take your snooze?"

"After."

He shakily poured himself a cup of coffee.

"How's business?" he asked, his back to the clerk.

***a loaded market bag**:「두둑한 시장 바구니」

***he estimated he had taken in a nice fiver**:「그는 5불 한 장은 벌었을 거라고 어림잡았다」

***felt upset to the point of illness**:「정신이 혼란해 질 정도로 쇼크를 받았다」

***kelp**:「켈프(해초의 일종)」 여기서는 머리털을 의미함.

***The grocer, ashen, nodded**:「안색이 창백해 진 식료품점 주인은 고개를 끄덕였다」 ashen「창백한, 잿빛의」

"So-so," said Frank.

"How many customers you had since I went to the barber?"

"Two or three."

Unable to meet Frank's eye, Morris went into the store and stood at the window, staring at the barber shop, his thoughts in a turmoil,* tormented by anxiety. Was the Italyener stealing from the cash register? The customers had come out with stuffed bags, what was there to show for it? Could he have given things on credit? They had told him never to. So what then?

A man entered and Morris waited on him. The man spent forty-one cents. When Morris rang up the sale, he saw it added correctly to the previous total. So the register was not broken. He was now almost certain that Frank had been stealing, and when he asked himself how long, he was numbed.*

Frank went into the store and saw the dazed grocer* at the window.

"Don't you feel any better, Morris?"

"It will go away."

"Take care of yourself. You don't want to get sick any more."

Morris wet his lips but made no reply. All day he went around, dragging his heart.* He had said nothing to Ida, he

---

***his thoughts in a turmoil**:「그의 생각은 혼동을 일으켰고」 turmoil「소란, 혼란」in 앞에 being이 생략되었음. *e.g.* The town was in a turmoil during the election.「그 도시는 선거기간중 대소란이었다」

***he was numbed**:「그는 제 정신이 아니었다」 *e.g.* Her heart was numbed with grief.「그녀의 마음은 슬픔으로 얼이 빠졌다」

***the dazed grocer**:「어리벙벙한 식료품점 주인」

***All day he went around, dragging his heart**:「종일 그는 의기소침해져서 돌아다녔다」

didn't dare.*

For the next few days he carefully watched the clerk. He had decided to give him the benefit of doubt* yet not rest till he knew the truth. Sometimes he sat at the table inside, pretending to be reading, but he was carefully listening to each item the customer ordered. He jotted down the prices and when Frank packed the groceries, quickly calculated the approximate sum. After the customer had gone he went idly to the register and secretly examined the amount the clerk had rung up. Always it was near the figure he had figured, a few pennies more or less. So Morris said he would go upstairs for a few minutes, but instead stationed himself in the hall, behind the back door. Peering through a crack in the wood, he could see into the store. Standing here, he added in his head the prices of the items ordered, and later, about fifteen minutes, casually checked the receipts and found totaled there the sum he had estimated. He began to doubt his suspicions. He may have wrongly guessed the contents of the customers' bags when he was at the barber's. Yet he could still not believe they had spent only three dollars; maybe Frank had caught on and was being wary.*

Morris then thought, yes, the clerk could have been stealing, but if so it was more his fault than Frank's. He was a grown man with a man's needs and all he was paying him, including his meager commission, was about six or seven dollars a week.

***he didn't dare**:「그는 말할 용기가 나지 않았다」

***give him the benefit of doubt**:「의심스러운 점을 그 사람에게 유리하게 해석해 주다, 그 사람을 선의로 해석해 주다」

***maybe Frank had caught on and was being wary**:「아마 Frank가 낌새를 알아채고 조심하고 있는지도 몰랐다」 catch on=sense, become aware of「눈치채다, 알아채다」

True, he got his room and meals free, plus cigarettes, but what was six or seven dollars to anybody in times like these, when a decent pair of shoes cost eight to ten? The fault was therefore his for paying slave wages for a workman's services, including the extra things Frank did, like last week cleaning out the stopped sewer pipe in the cellar with a long wire* and so saving five or ten dollars that would surely have gone to the plumber, not to mention how his presence alone had improved the store.

So although he worked on a slim markup,* one late afternoon when he and Frank were packing out some cartons of goods that had just been delivered,* Morris said to his assistant standing on the stepladder, "Frank, I think from now on till it comes summer I will raise you your wages to straight fifteen dollars without any commission. I would like to pay you more, but you know how much we do here business."*

Frank looked down at the grocer. "What for, Morris? The store can't afford to pay me any more than I am getting. If I take fifteen your profit will be shot.* Let it go the way it is now.* I am satisfied."

"A young man needs more and he spends more."

"I got all I want."

***cleaning out the stopped sewer pipe in the cellar with a long wire**:「지하실의 막힌 하수관을 긴 철사로 뚫는 것」

***So although he worked on a slim markup**:「그래서 비록 근소한 판매이윤으로 장사를 하고 있지만」 markup「판매 이윤폭」

***that had just been delivered**:「방금 배달된」

***I would like to pay . . . business**:「나는 더 주고 싶지만, 우리의 요즘 장사 형편은 자네도 알고 있을 거야」

***If I take fifteen your profit will be shot**:「제가 만일 15불을 받는다면 당신의 이익은 전혀 없어질 겁니다」 shoot=exhaust「다 써 버리다」, dissipate「낭비하다」

***Let it go the way it is now**:「지금대로 두십시오」

"Let it be like I said."

"I don't want it," said the clerk, annoyed.

"Take," insisted the grocer.

Frank finished his packing then got down, saying he was going to Sam Pearl's. His eyes were averted as he went past the grocer.

Morris continued to pack the cans of the shelves. Rather than admit Frank's raise to Ida and start a fuss, he decided to withhold from the register the money he would need to pay him,* a little every day so it would not be noticed. He would privately give it to the clerk sometime on Saturday, before Ida handed him his regular wages.

***withhold from the register the money he would need to pay him**:「그가 Frank에게 지불하는 데 필요한 돈을 금전등록기에서 미리 떼어두다」

6

Helen felt herself, despite the strongest doubts, falling in love with Frank. It was a dizzying dance,* she didn't want to. The month was cold—it often snowed—she had a rough time, fighting* hesitancies, fears of a disastrous mistake. One night she dreamed their house had burned down and her poor parents had nowhere to go. They stood on the sidewalk, wailing* in their underwear. Waking, she fought an old distrust of the broken-faced stranger, without success. The stranger had changed, grown unstrange. That was the clue to what was happening to her. One day he seemed unknown, lurking at the far end of an unlit cellar: the next he was standing in sunlight, a smile on his face, as if all she knew of him and all she didn't, had fused into a healed and easily remembered whole.* If he was hiding anything, she thought, it was his past pain, his orphanhood and consequent suffering. His eyes were quieter, wiser. His crooked nose fitted his face* and his face fitted him. It stayed on straight. He was gentle, waiting for whatever he awaited with a grace she respected.

***a dizzying dance**:「현기증나게 하는 춤」

***she had a rough time, fighting** ~ :「~와 싸우면서 고통스러운 시간을 보냈다」

***wail**=express sorrow「슬퍼하다, 비탄하다」

***as if all she knew . . . whole**:「그녀가 그에 관해서 알고 있는 것과 모르고 있는 모든 것이, 치유되고 쉽사리 기억되는 하나의 전체 안에 융합된 것처럼」

***His crooked nose fitted his face**:「그의 비뚤어진 코도 그의 얼굴에 어울렸다」

She felt she had changed him and this affected her. That she had willed to stay free of him made little difference now.* She felt tender to him, wanted him close by. She had, she thought, changed in changing him.

After she had accepted his gift of a book their relationship had subtly altered. What else, if whenever she read in her Shakespeare, she thought of Frank Alpine,* even heard his voice in the plays? Whatever she read, he crept into her thoughts; in every book he haunted the words, a character in a plot somebody else had invented, as if all associations had only one end.* He was, to begin with, everywhere.* So, without speaking of it, they met again in the library. That they were meeting among books relieved her doubt,* as if she believed, what possible wrong can I do among books, what possible harm can come to me here?

In he library he too seemed surer of himself—though once they were on their way home he became almost remote, strangely watchful, looking back from time to time as though they were being followed, but who or what would follow them? He never took her as far as the store; as before, by

---

***That she had willed to stay free of him made little difference now**:「그녀가 그로부터 떨어져 있으려고 결심했던 사실이 이제는 아무 문제도 되지 않았다」 will「(타동사) 바라다, 의도하다, 결심하다」 *e.g.* If he wills success, he can find it.「그가 성공을 결심한다면, 그것을 찾아낼 수 있을 것이다」

***What else, . . . she thought of Frank Alpine?**:「Shakespeare를 읽을 때마다 그녀는 Frank Alpine 이외의 누구를 생각할 수 있겠는가?」 *e.g.* What else can it be?「그것이 아니면 무엇이겠는가?」

***as if all associations had only one end**:「마치 모든 연상이 오직 하나의 결말을 가진 것처럼」

***He was, to begin with, everywhere**:「무엇보다도 Frank가 모든 곳에 있었던 것처럼 생각되었다」

***relieved her doubt**:「그녀의 의심을 덜어주었다」

mutual consent, she went on ahead, then he walked around the block and entered the hall from the other way so he wouldn't have to go past the grocery window and possibly be seen coming from the direction she had come from. Helen interpreted his caution to mean he sensed victory and didn't want to endanger it.* It meant he valued her more than she was altogether sure she wanted to be.

Then one night they walked across a field in the park and turned to one another.* She tried to awaken in herself a feeling of danger, but danger was dulled, beyond her, in his arms.* Pressed against him, responsive to his touch, she felt the cold ebb out of the night, and a warmth come over her. Her lips parted—she drew from his impassioned* kiss all she had long desired. Yet at the moment of sweetest joy she felt again the presence of doubt, almost a touch of illness. This made her sad. The fault was her. It meant she still could not fully accept him. There were still signals signaling no. She had only to think of them and they would work in her, pinching the nerves.* On their way home she could not forget the first happiness of their kiss. But why should a kiss become anxiety? Then she saw that his eyes were sad, and she wept when he wasn't looking. Would it never come spring?

She stalled love with arguments, only to be surprised at

***didn't want to endanger it**:「그것을 위태롭게 하려고 하지 않았다」 it는 victory를 가리킴.

***turned to one another**:「서로 마주섰다」

***in his arms**:「그의 팔에 안겨」

***impassioned**=ardent「열렬한」

***She had only to think of them and they would work in her, pinching the nerves**:「그녀가 그 신호를 생각하기만 하면, 그 신호가 그녀에게 작용하여 신경을 괴롭히는 것이었다」 pinch=cause discomfort

their swift dissolution;* found it difficult to keep her reasons securely nailed down, as they were before. They flew up in the mind, shifted, changed, as if something had altered familiar weights, values, even experience. He wasn't, for instance, Jewish. Not too long ago this was the greatest barrier, her protection against ever taking him seriously; now it no longer seemed such an urgently important thing—how could it in times like these? How could anything be important but love and fulfillment? It had lately come to her that her worry he was a gentile was less for her own sake than for her mother and father. Although she had only loosely been brought up as Jewish she felt loyal to the Jews, more for what they had gone through than what she knew of their history or theology*—loved them as a people, thought with pride of herself as one of them; she had never imagined she would marry anybody but a Jew. But she had recently come to think that in such unhappy times—when the odds were so high against personal happiness*—to find love was miraculous, and to fulfill it as best two people could was what really mattered.* Was it more important to insist a man's religious beliefs be exactly hers (if it was a question of religion), or that the two of them have in common ideals, a desire to keep love in their lives, and to

---

***She stalled love with arguments, only to be surprised at their swift dissolution**:「그녀는 여러 이유를 들어 사랑을 피게하려 했으나 그 이유가 순식간에 사라지는 것을 보고 놀랄 뿐이었다」 stall「피하다, 얼버무리다」

***more for what they . . . their history or theology**:「유태민족의 역사나 신학에 관해서 그녀가 알고 있는 것보다도 그들이 지내온 과거의 역사 때문에」

***when the odds were so high against personal happiness**:「개인의 행복을 얻을 가능성이 아주 희박했던 때」 *e.g.* The odds are in his favor.「그가 이길 것 같다」 The odds are against his returning safe.「그가 무사히 돌아올 가능성은 없다」

***to fulfill it as best two people could was what really mattered**:「두 사람이 가능한한 훌륭하게 그 사랑을 완성시키는 것이 정말로 중요한 것이다」

preserve in every possible way what was best in themselves? The less difference among people, the better; thus she settled it for herself yet was dissatisfied for those for whom she hadn't settled it.

But her logic, if it was logic, wouldn't decide a thing for her unhappy parents once they found out what was going on. With Frank enrolled in college maybe some of Ida's doubts of his worth as a person might wither away, but college was not the synagogue, a B.A. not a bar mitzvah;* and her mother and even her father with his liberal ideas would insist that Frank had to be what he wasn't.* Helen wasn't at all sure she could handle them if it ever came to a showdown.* She dreaded the arguments, their tear-stained pleas and her own misery for taking from the small sum of peace they had in the world, adding to the portion of their unhappiness. God knows they had had enough of that. Still, there was just so much time to live, so little of youth among the years; one had to make certain heartbreaking choices.* She foresaw the necessity of upholding her own,* enduring pain yet keeping to her decisions. Morris and Ida would be grievously hurt, but before too long their pain would grow less and perhaps leave them; yet she could not help but hope* her own children would someday marry Jews.

***a bar mitzvah**:「13세가 된 유태인 소년의 성년축하식」

***would insist that Frank had to be what he wasn't**:「Frank가 될 수 없는 어떤 인물로 그가 되어야 한다고 주장할 것이다」

***if it ever came to a showdown**:「그 일이 최종 단계에 이르렀을 때」 a showdown= a final test

***certain heartbreaking choices**:「어떤 가슴 아픈 선택」

***the necessity of upholding her own**:「그녀 자신의 선택을 밀고 나가야 할 필요성」

***she could not help but hope ～**:「～을 원하지 않을 수 없었다」

And if she married Frank, her first job would be to help him realize his wish to be somebody.* Nat Pearl wanted to be "somebody," but to him this meant making money to lead the life of some of his well-to-do friends at law school. Frank, on the other hand, was struggling to realize himself as a person, a more worthwhile ambition. Though Nat had an excellent formal education, Frank knew more about life and gave the impression of greater potential depth. She wanted him to become what he might, and conceived a plan to support him through college. Maybe she could even see him through a master's degree,* once he knew what he wanted to do. She realized this would mean the end of her own vague plans for going to day college, but that was really lost long ago, and she thought she would at last accept the fact once Frank had got what she hadn't. Maybe after he was working, perhaps as an engineer or chemist, she could take a year of college just to slake her thirst.* By then she would be almost thirty, but it would be worth postponing having a family to give him a good start and herself a taste of what she had always wanted. She also hoped they would be able to leave New York. She wanted to see more of the country. And if things eventually worked out, maybe Ida and Morris would someday sell the store and come to live near them. They might all live in California, her parents in a little house of their own where they could take life easy and be near their grandchildren. The

---

***his wish to be somebody**:「훌륭한 사람이 되려는 그의 소원」

***Maybe she could even see him through a master's degree**:「아마 그녀는 그가 석사 학위를 따도록 끝까지 도와줄 수 있을 것이다」 see ~ through「~을 끝까지 도와주다, ~을 도와 곤란을 극복케 하다」 *e.g.* I'll see you through the difficulty.「그 곤란을 극복할 수 있도록 계속 너의 힘이 되어 주겠다」

***to slake her thirst**:「그녀의 향학열을 만족시키기 위해」

future offered more in the way of realizable possibilities, Helen thought, if a person dared take a chance* with it. The question was, did she?*

She postponed making any important decision. She feared most of all the great compromise—she had seen so many of the people she knew settle for so much less than they had always wanted. She feared to be forced to choose beyond a certain point, to accept less of the good life than she had hungered for, appreciably less—to tie up with a fate far short of her ideals.* That she mustn't do, whether it meant taking Frank or letting him go. Her constant fear, underlying all others,* was that her life would not turn out as she had hoped, or would turn out vastly different. She was willing to change, make substitutions,* but she would not part with the substance of her dreams. Well, she would know by summertime what to do. In the meantime Frank went every third night to the library and there she was. But when the old-maid librarian smiled knowingly upon them, Helen felt embarrassed, so they met elsewhere. They met in cafeterias, movie houses, the pizza place—where it was impossible to say much, or hold him or be held. To talk they walked, to kiss they hid.

Frank said he was getting the college bulletins he had

***take a chance**:「모험을 하다」

***The question was, did she?**:「문제는 그녀에게 그런 용기가 있느냐 라는 점이었다」 she 다음에 dare가 생략되었음. *e.g.* He wanted to go, but he didn't dare.「그는 가고 싶었지만 갈 만한 용기가 없었다」 Wouldn't you dare?「너는 해 볼 만한 용기가 없느냐?」

***tie up with a fate far short of her ideals**:「그녀의 이상보다 훨씬 못한 선에서 운명과 타협하다」

***Her constant fear, underlying all others**:「그녀의 모든 다른 두려움의 밑에 깔린 끊임없는 공포」 *e.g.* political ideas underlying the revolution「그 혁명의 기초가 되어 있는 정치사상」

***make substitutions**:「대체하다」

written for, and around May he would have a transcript of his high school record* sent to whichever place they picked for him to go. He showed he knew she had plans for him. He didn't say much more, for he was always afraid the old jinx would grab hold of him* if he opened his mouth a little too wide.

At first he waited patiently. What else was there to do?* He had waited and was still waiting. He had been born waiting. But before long, though he tried not to show it, he was beginning to be fed up with his physical loneliness.* He grew tired of the frustrations of kissing in doorways, a cold feel on a bench in the park. He thought of her as he had seen her in the bathroom, and the memory became a burden. He was the victim of the sharp edge of his hunger. So he wanted her to the point where he thought up schemes* for getting her into his room and in bed. He wanted satisfaction, relief, a stake in the future.* She's not yours till she gives it to you, he thought. That's the way they all are. It wasn't always true, but it was true enough. He wanted an end to the torment of coming to a boil,* then thank you, no more. He wanted to take her completely.

***a transcript of his high school record**:「그의 고등학교 성적증명서」

***he was always afraid the old jinx would grab hold of him**:「자기를 괴롭혀 온 액운이 자기를 또 사로잡을지도 모른다고 그는 항상 두려워 했다」

***What else was there to do?**:「달리 할 일이 있었겠는가?」

***he was beginning to be fed up with his physical loneliness**:「그는 육체적 욕망을 채울 수 없어 진절머리가 나기 시작했다」 be fed up with=be utterly bored「진절머리 나다」

***think up schemes**:「계획을 세우다」

***a stake in the future**:「미래에 대한 포석」

***come to the boil**:「절정에 이르다」

They met more often now. At a bench on the Parkway, on street corners—in the wide windy world. When it rained or snowed, they stepped into doorways, or went home.

He complained one night, "What a joke. We leave the same warm house to meet out in the cold here."

She said nothing.

"Forget it," Frank said, looking into her troubled eyes, "we will take it the way it is."*

"This is our youth," she said bitterly.

He wanted then to ask her to come to his room but felt she wouldn't, so he didn't ask.

One cold, starry night she led him through the trees in the park near where they usually sat, onto a broad meadow where on summer nights lovers lay in the grass.

"Come on and sit down on the ground for a minute," Frank urged, "there's nobody here now."

But Helen wouldn't.

"Why not?" he asked.

"Not now," she said.

She realized, though he later denied it, that the situation had made him impatient. Sometimes he was moody for hours. She worried, wondering what rusty wound their homelessness had opened in him.*

One evening they sat alone on a bench on the Parkway, Frank with his arm around her; but because they were so close to home Helen was jumpy* and moved away whenever some-

---

***we will take it the way it is**:「이대로 참아 갑시다」

***she worried, . . . had opened in him**:「그들의 집 없는 서러움이 그의 낡은 상처에 다시 아픔을 준 것이 아닐까하고 생각하면서, 그녀는 괴로와했다」

***jumpy**=easily frightened, nervous

body passed by.

After the third time Frank said, "Listen, Helen, this is no good. Some night we will have to go where we can be inside."

"Where?" she asked.

"Where do you say?"

"I can't say anything, Frank. I don't know."

"How long is this going to keep up* like this?"

"As long as we like," she said, smiling faintly, "or as long as we like each other."

"I don't mean it that way. What I am talking about is not having any place private to go to."*

She answered nothing.

"Maybe some night we ought to sneak up to my room," he suggested. "We could do it easy enough—I don't mean tonight but maybe Friday, after Nick and Tessie go to the show and your mother is down in the store. I bought a new heater and the room keeps warm. Nobody will know you are there. We would be alone for once. We have never been alone that way."*

"I couldn't," Helen said.

"Why?"

"Frank, I can't."

"When will I get a chance to put my arms around you without being an acrobat?"*

***keep up**=continue

***What I am talking about . . . to**:「내가 말하는 것은 우리 둘만 갈 수 있는 곳이 아무데도 없다는 것이야」

***We have never been alone that way**:「우리들끼리만 있어 본 일은 이제껏 한번도 없었지」

***without being an acrobat**:「곡예사가 되지 않고」

"Frank," said Helen, "there's one thing I wish to make clear to you. I won't sleep with you now, if that's what you mean. It'll have to wait till I am really sure I love you, maybe till we're married, if we ever are."*

"I never asked you to," Frank said. "All I said was for you to come up to my room so we could spend the time more comfortable, not you bucking away* from me every time a shadow passes."

He lit a cigarette and smoked in silence.

"I'm sorry." After a minute she said, "I thought I ought to tell you how I feel on this subject. I was going to sometime anyway."*

They got up and walked, Frank gnawing* his wound.

A cold rain washed the yellow slush* out of the gutters. It rained drearily for two days. Helen had promised to see Frank on Friday night but she didn't like the thought of going out in the wet. When she came home from work, and got the chance, she slipped a note under his door, then went down. The note said that if Nick and Tessie did go to the movies, she would try to come up to his room for a while.

At half past seven Nick knocked on Frank's door and asked him if he wanted to go to the pictures. Frank said no, he thought he had seen the picture that was playing. Nick said good-by and he and Tessie, bundled in raincoats and carrying umbrellas, left the house. Helen waited for her mother to go

---

***if we ever are**:「우리가 결혼하게 된다면」 are 다음에 married가 생략됨.
***buck away**:「껑충 뛰어 물러나다」
***I was going to sometime anyway**:「어쨌든 언젠가는 말하려고 생각하고 있었죠」
***gnaw**=bite persistently at
***slush**:「녹기 시작하는 눈」

down to Morris, but Ida complained that her feet hurt, and said she would rest. Helen then went down herself, knowing Frank would hear her on the stairs and figure something had gone wrong. He would understand she could not go up to see him so long as anyone might hear her.*

But a few minutes later, Ida came down, saying she felt restless upstairs.* Helen then said she intended to drop in on Betty Pearl and might go along with her to the dressmaker who was making her wedding things.

"It's raining," said Ida.

"I know, Mama," Helen answered, hating her deceit.

She went up to her room, got her hat and coat, rubbers and an umbrella; then walked down, letting the door bang,* as if she had just left the house. She quietly opened it and went on tiptoe up the stairs.

Frank had guessed what was going on and opened his door to her quick tap. She was pale, obviously troubled, but very lovely. He held her hard and could feel her heartbeat against his chest.

She will let me tonight, he told himself.*

Helen was still uneasy. It took her a while to quiet her conscience for having lied to her mother. Frank had put out the light and tuned in the radio to soft dance music; now he lay on the bed, smoking. For a time she sat awkwardly in his chair, watching the glow of his cigarette, and when not that,

---

***so long as anyone might hear her**:「누군가가 그녀의 발 소리를 들을 수 있는 한」
***saying she felt restless upstairs**:「윗층에서는 안절부절 못한다고 말하면서」
***letting the door bang**:「문 소리를 광하고 냈다」
***She will let me tonight, he told himself**:「그녀는 오늘밤 내 말을 들어줄 것이라고 그는 생각했다」

the drops of lit rain on the window, reflecting the street light. But after he had rubbed his butt into an ash tray on the floor, Helen stepped out of her shoes and lay down beside him on the narrow bed, Frank moving over to the wall.*

"This is more like it," he sighed.

She lay with closed eyes in his arms, feeling the warmth of the heater like a hand on her back. For a minute she half-dozed, then woke to his kisses. She lay motionless, a little tense, but when he stopped kissing her, relaxed. She listened to the quiet sound of the rain in the street, making it in her mind into spring rain, though spring was weeks away; and within the rain grew all sorts of flowers; and amid the spring flowers, in this flowering dark—a sweet spring night—she lay with him in the open under new stars and a cry rose to her throat.* When he kissed her again, she responded with passion.*

"Darling."

"I love you, Helen, you are my girl."

They kissed breathlessly, then he undid the buttons of her blouse. She sat up to unhook her brassière but as she was doing it, felt his fingers under her skirt.

Helen grabbed his hand. "Please, Frank. Let's not get that hot and bothered."

"What are we waiting for, honey?" He tried to move his hand but her legs tightened and she swung her feet off the bed.*

He pulled her back, pressing her shoulders down. She felt

***Frank moving over to the wall**:「Frank는 벽쪽으로 몸을 움직였다」
***a cry rose to her throat**:「외치는 소리가 그녀의 목구멍까지 올라왔다」
***she responded with passion**:「그녀는 정열적으로 반응을 보였다」
***she swung her feet off the bed**:「그녀는 다리를 돌려 침대 밖으로 나갔다」

his body trembling on hers and for a fleeting minute thought he might hurt her; but he didn't.

She lay stiff, unresponsive on the bed. When he kissed her again she didn't move. It took a while before he lay back. She saw by the reflected glow of the heater how unhappy he looked.

Helen sat on the edge of the bed, buttoning her blouse.

His hands covered his face. He said nothing but she could feel his body shivering on the bed.

"Christ," he muttered.

"I'm sorry," she said softly. "I told you I wouldn't."

Five minutes passed. Frank slowly sat up. "Are you a virgin, is that what's eating you?"*

"I'm not," she said.

"I thought you were," he said, surprised. "You act like one."

"I said I wasn't."

"Then why do you act like one? Don't you know what it does to people?"

"I'm people."

"Then why do you do it for?"

"Because I believe in what I'm doing."*

"I thought you said you weren't a virgin?"

"You don't have to be a virgin to have ideals in sex."*

***Are you a virgin, is that what's eating you?**:「당신은 처녀야? 처녀성 때문에 마음을 놓지 못하는 거야?」 eat=trouble, worry. *e.g.* What's eating you?「무엇을 염려하고 있니?」

***Because I believe in what I'm doing**:「제가 하는 것이 옳다고 믿기 때문이죠」

***You don't have to be a virgin to have ideals in sex**:「이상적인 성관계를 갖는데 꼭 처녀이어야 할 필요는 없죠」

"What I don't understand is if you did it before, what's the difference if we do it now?"

"We can't, just because I did," she said, brushing her hair back. "That's the point. I did it and that's why I can't with you now. I said I wouldn't, that night on the Parkway."

"I don't get it," Frank said.

"Loving should come with love."

"I said I love you, Helen, you heard me say it."

"I mean I have to love you too. I think I do but sometimes I'm not sure."

He fell again into silence. She listened absent-mindedly to the radio but nobody was dancing now.

"Don't be hurt, Frank."*

"I'm tired of that," he said harshly.

"Frank," said Helen, "I said I slept with somebody before and the truth of it is, if you want to know, I'm sorry I did. I admit I had some pleasure, but after, I thought it wasn't worth it, only I didn't know at the time I would feel that way, because at the time I didn't know what I wanted. I suppose I felt I wanted to be free, so I settled for sex.* But if you're not in love sex isn't being free, so I made a promise to myself that I never would any more unless I really fell in love with somebody. I don't want to dislike myself. I want to be disciplined,* and you have to be too if I ask it. I ask it so I might someday love you without reservations."*

"Crap,*" Frank said, but then, to his surprise, the idea

***Don't be hurt, Frank**:「불쾌하게 생각지 마세요, Frank」
***so I settled for sex**:「그래서 저는 성에 대한 만족을 찾았죠」
***I want to be disciplined**:「나는 절제할 줄 아는 사람이 되고 싶어요」
***without reservations**:「거리낌없이, 무조건으로」
***Crap**=nonsense, lie

seized him. He thought of himself as disciplined, then wished he were. This seemed to him like an old and faraway thought, and he remembered with regret and strange sadness how often he had wished for better control over himself, and how little of it he had achieved.

He said, "I didn't mean to say what I just now did, Helen."*

"I know," she answered.

"Helen," he said huskily, "I want you to know I am a very good guy in my heart."

"I don't think otherwise."

"Even when I am bad I am good."*

She said she thought she knew what he meant.

They kissed, again and again. He thought there were a whole lot worse things than waiting for something that was going to be good once he got it.*

Helen lay back on the bed and dozed, awaking when Nick and Tessie came into their bedroom, talking about the movie they had seen. It was a love story and Tessie had liked it very much. After they undressed and got into bed their double bed creaked. Helen felt bad for Frank but Frank did not seem to feel bad. Nick and Tessie soon fell asleep. Helen, breathing lightly, listened to their heavy breathing, worrying how she was going to get down to her floor, because if Ida was awake she would hear her on the stairs. But Frank said in a low voice

---

***I didn't mean to say what I just now did, Helen**:「Helen, 방금 내가 한 말은 진심에서 한 말은 아니야」 *e.g.* I didn't mean you to do it.「너한테 그것을 시킬 생각은 아니었어」

***Even when I am bad I am good**:「내가 나쁜 짓을 할 때라도 마음은 착한 거야」

***waiting for something that was going to be good once he got it**:「자기 손에 넣으면 이익이 될 무엇인가를 기다리는 것」

that he would carry her to the vestibule, then she could go up after a few minutes, as if she had just come home from some place.

She put on her coat, hat and rubbers, and was careful to remember her umbrella. Frank carried her down the stairs. There were only his slow, heavy steps going down. And not long after they had kissed good night and he had gone for a walk in the rain, Helen opened the hall door and went up.

Then Ida fell asleep.

Thereafter Helen and Frank met outside the house.

It was snowing in the afternoon, when the front door opened and in came Detective Minogue, pushing before him this stocky handcuffed guy,* unshaven, and wearing a faded green wind-breaker* and denim slacks.* He was about twenty-seven, with tired eyes and no hat. In the store he lifted his manacled hands* to wipe the snow off his wet hair.

"Where's Morris?" the detective asked the clerk.

"In the back."

"Go on in," said Detective Minogue to the handcuffed man.

They went into the back. Morris was sitting on the couch, stealing a smoke.* He hurriedly put out the butt and dropped it into the garbage pail.

"Morris," said the detective, "I think I have got the one who hit you on the head."

***this stocky handcuffed guy**:「땅딸막한 수갑을 채운 놈」
***wind-breaker**:「스포츠용 자켓」
***denim slack**:「작업용 즈봉」
***his manacled hands**:「그의 수갑채워진 손」
***stealing a smoke**:「몰래 담배를 피우면서」

The grocer's face turned white as flour. He stared at the man but didn't approach him.

After a minute he muttered, "I don't know if it's him. He had his face covered with a handkerchief."

"He's a big son of a bitch," the detective said. "The one that hit you was big, wasn't he?"

"Heavy," said Morris. "The other was big."

Frank was standing in the doorway, watching.

Detective Minogue turned to him. "Who're you?"

"He's my clerk," explained Morris.

The detective unbuttoned his overcoat and took a clean handkerchief out of his suit pocket. "Do me a favor," he said to Frank. "Tie this around his puss."*

"I would rather not," Frank answered.

"As a favor. To save me the trouble of getting hit on the head with his cuffs."*

Frank took the handkerchief, and though not liking to, tied it around the man's face, the suspect holding himself stiffly erect.*

"How about it now, Morris?"

"I can't tell you," Morris said, embarrassed. He had to sit down.

"You want some water, Morris?" Frank asked.

"No."

"Take your time,"* said Detective Minogue, "look him over

***puss**=face

***To save me the trouble of getting hit on the head with his cuffs**:「그의 수갑으로 머리를 얻어 맞지 않으려고 그러는 거요」

***the suspect holding himself stiffly erect**:「혐의자는 몸을 딱딱하게 하고 서 있었다」

***Take your time.**=Don't hurry.

good."*

"I don't recognize him. The other acted more rough. He had a rough voice—not nice."

"Say something, son," the detective said.

"I didn't hold this guy up," said the suspect in a dead voice.

"Is that the voice, Morris?"

"No."

"Does he look like the other one—the heavy guy's partner?"

"No, this is a different man."

"How are you so sure?"

"The helper was a nervous man. He was bigger than this one. Also this one has got small hands. The helper had big heavy hands."

"Are you positive? We grabbed him on a job last night.* He held up a grocery with another guy who got away."*

The detective pulled the handkerchief off the man's face.

"I don't know him," Morris said with finality.*

Detective Minogue folded the handkerchief and tucked it into his pocket.* He slipped his eyeglasses into a leather case. "Morris, I think I asked you already if you saw my son Ward Minogue around here. Have you yet?"

"No," said the grocer.

Frank went over to the sink and rinsed his mouth with a cup of water.

***look him over good**:「그 놈을 잘 보십시요」

***We grabbed him on a job last night**:「어젯밤 그 놈이 강도질을 하는 중에 그 놈을 잡았죠」 job=robbery

***get away**:「도망치다, 달아나다」 get away=manage to escape

***Morris said with finality**:「Morris는 단언했다」 *e.g.* with an air of finality「결정적인 태도로」

***tucked it into his pocket**:「그것을 호주머니 속에 밀어넣었다」

"Maybe you know him?" the detective asked him.

"No," said the clerk.

"O.K., then." The detective unbuttoned his overcoat. "By the way,* Morris, did you ever find out who was stealing your milk that time?"

"Nobody steals any more," said Morris.

"Come on, son," said the detective to the suspect.

The handcuffed man went out of the store into the snow, the detective following him.

Frank watched them get into the police car, sorry for the guy. What if they arrested me now, he thought, although I am not the same guy I once was?*

Morris, thinking of the stolen milk bottles, gazed guiltily* at his assistant.

Frank happened to notice the size of his hands, then had to go to the toilet.

As he was lying in his bed after supper, thinking about his life, Frank heard footsteps coming up the stairs and someone banged on his door. For a minute his heart hammered with fear, but he got up and forced himself to open the door. Grinning* at him from under his fuzzy hat stood Ward Minogue, his eyes small and smeary. He had lost weight and looked worse.

Frank let him in and turned on the radio. Ward sat on the bed, his shoes dripping from the snow.

"Who told you I live here?" Frank asked.

***by the way**=incidentally「그런데」

***although I am not the same guy I once was**:「비록 나는 전과 같은 사람은 아니지만」

***guiltily**:「죄진 것처럼, 꺼림칙한 태도로」

***grin**=smile broadly showing the teeth「히죽히죽 웃다」

"I watched you go in the hall, opened the door and heard you go up the stairs," Ward said.

How am I ever going to get rid of this bastard, Frank thought.

"You better stay away from here," he said with a heavy heart. "If Morris recognizes you in that goddamned hat, we will both go to jail."

"I came to visit my popeyed* friend, Louis Karp," said Ward. "I wanted a bottle but he wouldn't give it to me because I am short on cash, so I thought my good-looking friend Frank Alpine will lend me some. He's an honest, hardworking bastard."

"You picked the wrong guy.* I am poor."

Ward eyed him craftily.* "I was sure you'd have saved up a pile by now, stealing from the Jew."

Frank stared at him but didn't answer.

Ward's glance shifted.* "Even if you are stealing his chicken feed,* it ain't any skin off me.* Why I came is this. I got a new job that we can do without any trouble."

"I told you I am not interested in your jobs, Ward."

"I thought you would like to get your gun back, otherwise it might accidentally get lost with your name on it."

Frank rubbed his hands.

"All you got to do is drive," Ward said amiably. "The job

***popeyed**:「퉁방울 눈의」
***You picked the wrong guy**:「너는 사람을 잘못 골랐어」
***craftily**:「교활하게」
***Ward's glance shifted**:「Ward의 시선이 움직였다」
***chicken feed**=small change「푼돈, 닭 모이」
***it ain't any skin off me**:「그것은 내가 알 바 아니지」 *e.g.* That's no skin off my nose. 「그건 내 관심사가 아니야」

is a cinch,* a big liquor joint in Bay Ridge. After nine o'clock they only keep one man on. The take will be over three hundred."

"Ward, you don't look to me in any kind of condition to do a stickup.* You look more like you need to be in a hospital."

"All I got is a bad heartburn."

"You better take care of yourself."

"You are making me cry."

"Why don't you start going straight?"*

"Why don't you?"

"I am trying to."

"Your Jew girl must be some inspiration."*

"Don't talk about her, Ward."

"I tailed you last week when you took her in the park. She's a nice piece. How often do you get it?"

"Get the hell out of here."

Ward got up unsteadily. "Hand over fifty bucks or I will fix you good with your Jew boss and your Jew girl.* I will write them a letter who did the stickup last November."

Frank rose, his face hard. Taking his wallet out of his pocket, he emptied it on the bed. There were eight single dollar bills. "That's all I have got."

Ward snatched up the money. "I'll be back for more."

***cinch**=easy thing

***you don't look to me in any kind of condition to do a stickup**:「어떤 조건이든 강도질을 하려고 나를 끌어들이려 하지는 마」

***Why don't you start going straight?**:「정직하게 살아보지 그래?」

***Your Jew girl must be some inspiration**:「네 유태인 처녀한테서 교화를 받았음에 틀림없군」 *e.g.* His wife was a constant inspiration to him.「그는 아내로부터 끊임없이 지적인 자극을 받았다」

***I will fix you good with your Jew boss and your Jew girl**:「유태인 주인과 그의 딸과 너와의 관계를 완전히 끝장나게 만들어 놓겠다」

"Ward," Frank said through tight teeth, "if you drag your ass up here any more to make trouble, or if you ever follow me and my girl again, or tell Morris anything, the first thing I will do is telephone your old man at the police station and tell him under which rock he can find you.* He was in the grocery asking about you today, and if he ever meets up with you, he looks like he will bust* your head off."

Ward with a moan* spat at the clerk and missed, the gob of spit* trickling down the wall.

"You stinking kike,"* he snarled. Rushing out into the hall, he all but fell down two flights of stairs.

The grocer and Ida ran out to see who was making the racket,* but by then Ward was gone.

Frank lay in bed, his eyes closed.

One dark and windy night when Helen left the house late, Ida followed her through the cold streets and across the plaza into the interior of the deserted park, and saw her meet Frank Alpine. There, in an opening between a semicircle of tall lilac shrubs and a grove of dark maples, were a few benches, dimly lit and private, where they liked to come to be alone. Ida watched them sitting together on one of the benches, kissing. She dragged herself home* and went upstairs, half-dead.

***under which rock he can find you**:「그가 너를 어디서 찾을 수 있는지」
***bust**=hit「치다」
***with a moan**:「신음소리를 내면서」
***the gob of spit**:「가래침 덩어리」
***kike**=Jew
***make a racket**=kick up a racket「큰 소동을 일으키다」
***She dragged herself home**:「그녀는 발을 질질 끌며 집으로 돌아왔다」 drag oneself along「무거운 발걸음으로 걷다」

Morris was asleep and she didn't want to wake him, so she sat in the kitchen, sobbing.

When Helen returned and saw her mother weeping at the kitchen table, she knew Ida knew, and Helen was both moved and frightened.

Out of pity she asked. "Mama, why are you crying?"

Ida at last raised her tear-stained face and said in despair, "Why do I cry? I cry for the world. I cry for my life that it went away wasted. I cry for you."

"What have I done?"

"You have killed me in my heart."

"I've done nothing that's wrong, nothing I'm ashamed of."

"You are not ashamed that you kissed a goy?"

Helen gasped. "Did you follow me, Mama?"

"Yes," Ida wept.

"How could you?"*

"How could you kiss a goy?"

"I'm not ashamed that we kissed."

She still hoped to avoid an argument. Everything was unsettled, premature.

Ida said, "If you marry such a man your whole life will be poisoned."

"Mama, you'll have to be satisfied with what I now say. I have no plans to marry anybody."

"What kind plans you got then with a man that he kisses you alone in a place where nobody can find you in the park?"

"I've been kissed before."

"But a goy, Helen, an Italyener."

***How could you?**:「어떻게 그런 행동을 할 수 있어요?」

"A man, a human being like us."

"A man is not good enough. For a Jewish girl must be a Jew."

"Mama, it's very late. I don't wish to argue. Let's not wake Papa."

"Frank is not for you. I don't like him. His eyes don't look at a person when he talks to them."

"His eyes are sad. He's had a hard life."

"Let him go and find someplace a shikse* that he likes, not a Jewish girl."

"I have to work in the morning. I'm going to bed."

Ida quieted down. When Helen was undressing she came into her room. "Helen," she said, holding back her tears, "the only thing I want for you is the best.* Don't make my mistake. Don't make worse and spoil your whole life, with a poor man that he is only a grocery clerk which we don't know about him nothing. Marry somebody who can give you a better life, a nice professional boy with a college education.* Don't mix up now with a stranger.* Helen, I know what I'm talking. Believe me, I know." She was crying again.

"I'll try my best," Helen said.

Ida dabbed at her eyes with a handkerchief. "Helen, darling, do me one favor."

"What is it? I am very tired."

"Please call up Nat tomorrow. Just to speak to him. Say

***shikse**:「유태인이 아닌 여성」

***the only thing I want for you is the best**:「내가 너를 위해서 바라는 것은 네가 잘 되는 것뿐이다」

***a nice professional boy with a college education**:「대학교육을 받은 훌륭한 전문직에 있는 남자」

***Don't mix up now with a stranger**:「잘 모르는 남자와 가까이 하지 마라」

hello, and if he asks you to go out with him, tell him yes. Give him a chance."

"I gave him one."

"Last summer you enjoyed so much with him. You went to the beach, to concerts. What happened?"

"Our tastes are different," Helen said wearily.

"In the summer you said your tastes were the same."

"I learned otherwise."*

"He is a Jewish boy, Helen, a college graduate. Give him another chance."

"All right," said Helen, "now will you go to sleep?"

"Also don't go no more with Frank. Don't let him kiss you, it's not nice."

"I can't promise."

"Please, Helen."

"I said I'd call Nat. Let that be an end of it now. Good night, Mama."

"Good night," Ida said sadly.

Though her mother's suggestion depressed her, Helen called Nat from her office the next day. He was cordial, said he had bought a secondhand car from his future brother-in-law* and invited her to go for a drive.

She said she would sometime.

"How about Friday night?" Nat asked.

She was seeing Frank on Friday. "Could you make it Saturday?"*

"I happen to have an engagement Saturday, also Thursday

***I learned otherwise**:「그렇지 않다는 것을 알게 됐어요」
***his future brother-in-law**:「그의 매부가 될 사람」
***Could you make it Saturday?**:「토요일로 하면 어떻겠어요?」

—something doing at the law school."

"Then Friday is all right." She agreed reluctantly, thinking it would be best to change the date with Frank, to satisfy her mother.

When Morris came up for his nap that afternoon Ida desperately begged him to send Frank away at once.

"Leave me alone on this subject ten minutes."*

"Morris," she said, "last night I went out when Helen went, and I saw she met Frank in the park, and they kissed each the other."

Morris frowned. "He kissed her?"

"Yes."

"She kissed him?"

"I saw with my eyes."

But the grocer, after thinking about it, said wearily, "So what is a kiss? A kiss is nothing."

Ida said furiously, "Are you crazy?"

"He will go away soon," he reminded her. "In the summer."

Tears sprang into her eyes. "By summer could happen here ten times a tragedy."

"What kind tragedy you expecting—murder?"

"Worse," she cried.

"His heart turned cold, he lost his temper. "Leave me alone on this subject, for God's sakes."

"Wait," Ida bitterly warned.

On Thursday of that week Julius Karp left Louis in the liquor store and stepped outside to peek through the grocery

---

***Leave me alone on this subject ten minutes**:「이 문제에 대해서 10분간이라도 좋으니, 날 좀 그냥 내버려 두세요」

window to see if Morris was alone. Karp had not set foot in Morris's store since the night of the holdup, and he uneasily considered the reception he might meet* if he were to go in now. Usually, after a time of not speaking to one another, it was Morris Bober, by nature unable to hold a grudge,* who gave in and spoke to Karp; but this time he had put out of his mind the possibility of seeking out the liquor dealer and re-establishing their fruitless relationship. While in bed during his last convalescence* he had thought much of Karp—an unwilling and distasteful thinking—and had discovered he disliked him more than he had imagined. He resented him as a crass* and stupid person who had fallen through luck into flowing prosperity. His every good fortune spattered others with misfortune, as if there was just so much luck in the world and what Karp left over wasn't fit to eat.* Morris was incensed by thoughts of the long years he had toiled without just reward.* Though this was not Karp's fault, it *was* that a delicatessen had moved in across the street to make a poor man poorer. Nor could the grocer forgive him the blow he had taken on the head in his place,* who could in health and

---

***the reception he might meet**:「그가 받게 될 대접」
***by nature unable to hold a grudge**:「성격상 남에게 원한을 품을 수 없었기 때문에」
***While in bed during his last convalescence**:「지난번 몸이 회복되어 갈 무렵 병상에 누워 있을 때」
***crass**=coarse「저속한」stupid「우둔한」
***His every good fortune spattered . . . eat**:「마치 세상에는 일정량의 행운이 있는데 Karp가 차지하고 남겨 놓은 행운은 다른 사람에겐 쓸모 없이 되는 것처럼, 그의 모든 행운은 다른 사람에게 불행을 안겨 주었다」
***Morris was incensed . . . without just reward**:「정당한 보수 없이 고생해 온 긴 세월을 생각하고 Morris는 화를 냈다」 be incensed by「~으로 인하여 화를 내다」
***Nor could the grocer···place**:「식료품점 주인은 Karp 대신 자기가 머리를 얻어 맞은 사실 때문에 그를 용서할 수가 없었다」

wealth better afford it.* Therefore it gave him a certain satisfaction not to have anything to do with the liquor dealer, though he was every day next door.

Karp, on the other hand, had been content to wait for Morris to loosen up* first. He pictured the grocer yielding his aloof silence while he enjoyed the signs of its dissolution, meanwhile pitying the poor Jew his hard luck life—in capital letters.* Some were born that way. Whereas Karp in whatever he touched now coined pure gold,* if Morris Bober found a rotten egg in the street, it was already cracked and leaking. Such a one needed someone with experience to advise him when to stay out of the rain. But Morris, whether he knew how Karp felt, or not, remained rigidly uncommunicative—offering not so much as a flicker of recognition* when on his way to the corner for his daily *Forward,* he passed the liquor dealer standing in front of his store or caught his* eye peeking into his* front window. As a month passed, now, quickly, almost four, Karp came to the uncomfortable conclusion that although Ida was still friendly to him, he would this time get nothing for free from Morris; he wasn't going to give in.* He

---

***afford**:「(~해도) 별 지장이 없다」 *e.g.* Now I can afford to die.「나는 지금 죽어도 별 지장이 없다」

***loosen up**:「(화를) 풀다」

***his hard luck life—in capital letters**:「그의 불운한 인생—그것도 아주 심한 정도로 불운한」

***Whereas Karp in whatever he touched now coined pure gold**:「요즘 Karp가 손을 대는 어떤 것에서도 순금을 만들어내는 반면에」

***offering not so much as a flicker of recognition**:「아는 척도 하지 않았다」 *e.g.* She saw a flicker of ridicule in his smile.「그녀는 그의 미소에서 희미한 조소하는 기색을 봤다」

***his**는 Karp를 나타냄.

***his**는 Morris를 나타냄.

***he wasn't going to give in**:「그는 양보하려 하지 않았다」

reacted coldly to this insight, would give back what he got —so let it be indifference. But indifference was not a commodity he was pleased to exchange. For some reason that was not clear to him Karp liked Morris to like him, and it soon rankled* that his down-at-the-heels neighbor* continued to remain distant. So he had been hit on the head in a holdup, but was the fault Karp's? *He* had taken care—why hadn't Morris, the shlimozel?* Why, when he had warned him there were two holdupniks across the street, hadn't he like a sensible person gone first to lock his door, then telephoned the police? Why?— because he was inept, unfortunate.

And because he was, his troubles grew like bananas in bunches. First, in another accident to his hard head, then through employing Frank Alpine. Karp, no fool, knew the makings of a bad situation* when he saw it. Frank, whom he had got acquainted with and considered a fly-by-night rolling stone,* would soon make trouble—of that he was certain. Morris's fly-specked, worm-eaten shop* did not earn half cnough to pay for a full-time helper, and it was idiotic extravagance for the grocer, after he was better, to keep the clerk working for him. Karp soon learned from Louis that his estimate of a bad situation was correct. He found out that

---

***rankle**:「괴롭히다」

***down-at-the-heels neighbor**:「장사가 전혀 안 되는 이웃」

***shlimozel**:「불운하고 실패만 저지르는 사람」

***the makings of a bad situation**:「불행한 사태로 빠져 가는 과정」 makings「발전과정」

***a fly-by-night rolling stone**:「믿을 수 없는 뜨내기」 fly-by-night=not to be trusted「믿을 수 없는, 일시적인(transitory)」

***Morris's fly-specked, worm-eaten shop**:「파리똥 투성이의 낡아빠진 Morris의 가게」 worm-eaten=worn-out「다 낡은」

Frank every so often invested in a bottle of the best stuff,* paying, naturally, cash—but whose? Furthermore Sam Pearl, another waster, had mentioned that the clerk would now and then paste a two-dollar bill on some nag's useless nose,* from which it blew off in the breeze. This done by a man who was no doubt paid in peanuts added up to only one thing—he stole.* Who did he steal from? Naturally from M. Bober, who had anyway nothing—who else? Rockefeller knew how to take care of his millions, but if Morris earned a dime he lost it before he could put it into his torn pocket. It was the nature of clerks to steal from those they were working for. Karp had, as a young man, privately peculated* from his empolyer, a half-blind shoe wholesaler; and Louis, he knew, snitched from him, but by Louis he was not bothered. He was, after all, a son; he worked in the business and would someday — it shouldn't be too soon—own it. Also, by strict warnings and occasional surprise inventories* he held Louis down to a bare minimum—beans.* A stranger stealing money was another matter—slimy. It gave Karp gooseflesh* to think of the Italian working for him.

***Frank every so often invested in a bottle of the best stuff**:「Frank는 가끔 최고급 술을 샀다」 invest in=buy

***would now and then paste a two-dollar bill on some nag's useless nose**:「이따금 경마에서 어떤 몹쓸 말에 2불을 걸었다」 nag「쓸모없는 말」

***This done by a man who was no doubt paid in peanuts added up to only one thing—he stole**:「분명히 보잘것없는 보수를 받고 있는 사람에 의하여 이루어진 이 낭비는 결국 다음의 사실을 의미하는 것이었다—즉 도둑질을 했다는 것이다」 peanuts「근소한 보수, 근소한 금액」 add up to ~「~을 의미한다」

***peculate**=embezzle「횡령하다, 잘라쓰다」

***occasional surprise inventories**:「때때로 하는 불시의 재고조사」

***he held Louis down to a bare minimum—beans**:「그는 Louis의 횡령을 최소한으로 억제시켰다—소액의 금액으로」 beans「소액의 금액」

***give ~ gooseflesh**:「소름끼치게 하다」

And since misfortune was the grocer's lot, the stranger would shovel on more, not less, for it was always dangerous to have a young goy around where there was a Jewish girl. This worked out by an unchangeable law that Karp would gladly have explained to Morris had they been speaking, and saved him serious trouble. That *this* trouble, too, existed he had confirmed twice in the last week. Once he saw Helen and Frank walking on the Parkway under the trees, and another time while driving home past the local movie house, he had glimpsed them coming out after a show, holding hands. Since then he had often thought about them, indeed with anxiety, and felt he would in some way like to assist the luckless Bober.

Without doubt Morris kept Frank on to make his life easier, and probably, being Bober, he had no idea what was happening behind his back. Well, Julius Karp would warn him of his daughter's danger. Tactfully he would explain him what was what. After, he would put in a plug* for Louis, who, Karp was aware, had long liked Helen but was not sure enough of himself to be successful with her. Swat Louis down and he retreated to tenderize his fingernails with his teeth.* In some things he needed a push.* Karp felt he could ease his son's way to Helen by making Morris a proposition he had had in the back of his head for almost a year. He would describe Louis' prospects after marriage in terms of cold cash and other advantages, and suggest that Morris speak to Helen on the

---

***put in a plug**:「마개를 꽂다」 여기서는「대책을 세우다」는 뜻임.

***Swat Louis down and he retreated to tenderize his fingernails with his teeth**:「누가 Louis를 때린다면, 그는 뒤로 물러서서 이빨로 자기의 손톱이나 물고 있을 것이다」 swat「때리다」 tenderize「연하게 하다」

***In some things he needed a push**:「어떤 일에 있어서 그는 박력이 필요했다」

subject of going with him seriously. If they went together a couple of months—Louis would give her an extravagant good time—and the combination worked out, it would benefit not only the daughter, but the grocer as well, for then Karp would take over Morris's sad gesheft* and renovate and enlarge it into a self-service market with the latest fixtures and goods. His tenant around the corner he would eliminate when his lease expired*—a sacrifice, but worthwhile. After that, with himself as the silent partner giving practical advice, it would take a marvelous catastrophe to keep the grocer from earning a decent living in his old age.

Karp foresaw that the main problem of this matter would be Helen, whom he knew as a strictly independent yet not unworthy girl, even if she had pretensions to* marriage with a professional—although she had got no place with Nat Pearl. To be successful, Nat needed what Louis Karp would have plenty of, not a poor girl. So he had acted in his best interests in gently shooing Helen away* when her thoughts got too warm—a fact Karp had picked up from Sam Pearl. Louis, on the other hand, could afford a girl like Helen, and Helen, independent and intelligent, would be good for Louis. The liquor store owner decided that when the opportunity came he would talk turkey*to her like a Dutch uncle.* He would

---

***gesheft**:「상점」
***when his lease expired**:「그의 임대기간이 만료되었을 때」
***have pretensions to ~** :「포부를 갖다, 자부하다」
***So he had acted in his best interests in gently shooing Helen away**:「그래서 그는 Helen을 쉬잇하여 쫓아 버림으로써 자기에게 최대한의 유리한 상황을 꾀하려 했다」 *e. g.* shoo a bird away (off)「쉬잇하고 새를 쫓다」
***talk turkey**=talk frankly or directly「솔직히 말하다」
***a Dutch uncle**:「엄하게 노골적으로 비난하는 사람」

patiently explain that her only future with Frank would be as an outcast, poorer even than her father and sharing his foolish fate; whereas with Louis she could have what she wanted and more—leave it to her father-in-law.* Karp felt that once Frank had gone she would listen to reason and appreciate the good life he was offering her. Twenty-three or -four was a dangerous age for a single girl. At that age she would not get younger; at that age even a goy looked good.

Having observed that Frank had gone into Sam Pearl's place, and that Morris was for the moment alone in the back of his store, Karp coughed clear his throat and stepped inside the grocery. When Morris, emerging from the rear, saw who it after all was, he experienced a moment of vindictive triumph,* but this was followed by annoyance that the pest was once more present, and at the same time by an uncomfortable remembrance that Karp never entered unaccompanied by bad news.* Therefore he stayed silent, waiting for the liquor dealer, in prosperous sport jacket and gabardine slacks which could not camouflage* his protrusive belly nor subtract from the foolishness of his face, to speak; but for once Karp's active tongue lay flat on its back* as, embarrassed in recalling the results of his very last visit here, he stared at the visible scar on Morris's head.

***leave it to her father-in-law**:「그 일은 시아버지에게 맡겨 두어라」
***a moment of vindictive triumph**:「복수했다는 순간적인 승리감」
***an uncomfortable remembrance . . . bad news**:「Karp는 항상 나쁜 소식을 가지고 온다는 불안스러운 기억」
***camouflage**=disguise「위장하다」
***for once Karp's active tongue lay flat on its back**:「이번만은 Karp의 잘 돌아가는 혓바닥도 꼼짝하지 않고 있었다」 on one's back「완전히 손들어」

In pity for him,* the grocer spoke, his tone friendlier than he would have guessed. "So how are you, Karp?"

"Thanks. What have I got to complain?" Beaming, he thrust a pudgy* hand across the counter and Morris found himself unwillingly weighing the heavy diamond ring that pressed his fingers.*

Since it did not seem sensible to Karp, one minute after their reconciliation, to blurt out news of a calamity concerning Morris's daughter, he fiddled around for words to say and came up with, "How's business?"*

Morris had hoped he would ask.* "Fine, and every day gets better."

Karp contracted his brows;* yet it occurred to him that Morris's business might have improved more than he had guessed, when peering at odd moments through the grocery window, he had discovered a customer or two instead of the usual dense emptiness. Now on the inside after several months, he noticed the store seemed better taken care of, the shelves solidly packed with stock. But if business was better he at once knew why.

Yet he casually asked, "How is this possible? You are maybe advertising in the paper?"

***In pity for him** :「그를 불쌍히 여기고」

***pudgy** :「땅딸막한」

***ring that pressed his fingers** :「그의 손가락에 끼어 있는 반지」

***he fiddled around for words to say and came up with, "How's business?"** :「그는 할 말을 이것 저것 찾다가 겨우 "장사는 어때 ? "하고 물었다」 fiddle around「만지작거리다, 빈들거리다」

***Morris had hoped he would ask** :「Morris는 그가 이 질문을 하기를 속으로 고대하고 있었다」

***Karp contracted his brows** :「Karp는 눈살을 찌푸렸다」

Morris smiled at the sad joke. Where there was no wit money couldn't buy it.* "By word of mouth," he remarked, "is the best advertising."

"This is according to what the mouth says."*

"It says," Morris answered without shame, "that I got a fine clerk who has pepped me up the business. Instead going down in the winter, every day goes up."

"Your clerk did this?" Karp said, thoughtfully scratching under one buttock.

"The customers like him. A goy brings in goyim."

"New customers?"

"New, old."

"Something else helps you also?"

"Also helps a little the new apartment house that it opened in December."

"Hmm," said Karp, "nothing more?"

Morris shrugged. "I don't think so. I hear your Schmitz don't feel so good and he don't give service like he used to give. Came back a few customers from him, but the most important help to me is Frank."

Karp was astonished. Could it be that the man didn't know what had happened practically under his nose? He then and there saw a God-given opportunity to boot the clerk out of the place forever.* "That wasn't Frank Alpine who improved you

---

***Where there was no wit money couldn't buy it**:「기지를 타고 나지 못하면 돈 주고도 못 사는 법이다」

***This is according to what the mouth says**:「그것은 입에서 어떤 말이 나오느냐에 달려있지」

***a God-given opportunity to boot the clerk out of the place forever**:「점원을 이 가게에서 영원히 추방할 절호의 기회」 boot out=kick out「차 내다」, dismiss「해고하다」

your business," he said decisively. "That was something else."

Morris smiled slightly. As usual the sage* knew every reason for every happening.

But Karp persisted. "How long does he work here?"

"You know when he came—in November."

"And right away the business started to pick up?"

"Little by little."

"This happened," Karp announced with excitement, "not because this goy came here. What did he know about the grocery business? Nothing. Your store improved because my tenant Schmitz got sick and had to close his store part of the day. Didn't you know that?"

"I heard he was sick," Morris answered, his throat tightening, "but the drivers said his old father came to give him a help."

"That's right," Karp said, "but in the middle December he went every morning to the hospital for treatments. First the father stayed in the store, then he got too tired so Schmitz didn't open till maybe nine, ten o'clock, instead of seven. And instead of closing ten o'clock at night, he closed eight. This went on like this till last month, then he couldn't open till eleven o'clock in the morning, and so he lost half a day's business.* He tried to sell the store but nobody would buy then. Yesterday he closed up altogether. Didn't somebody mention that to you?"

"One of the customers said," Morris answered, distressed, "but I thought it was temporary."

***the sage**:「현자인 체하는 사람」

***so he lost half a day's business**:「그래서 그는 반나절의 장사를 못했던 거야」

"He's very sick," said Karp solemnly. "He won't open again."

My God, thought Morris. For months he had watched the store when it was empty and while it was being altered, but never since its opening had he gone past Sam Pearl's corner to look at it. He hadn't the heart to.* But why had no one told him that the place had been closing part of the day for more than two months—Ida, Helen? Probably they had gone past it without noticing the door was sometimes closed. In their minds, as in his, it was always open for *his* business.

"I don't say," Karp was saying, "that your clerk didn't help your income, but the real reason things got better is when Schmitz couldn't stay open, some of his customers came here. Naturally, Frank wouldn't tell you that."

Filled with foreboding, Morris reflected on what the liquor dealer had said. "What happened to Schmitz?"

"He has a bad blood disease and lays now in the hospital."

"Poor man," the grocer sighed. Hope wrestled shame as he asked,* Will he give the store in auction?"*

Karp was devastating.* "What do you mean give in auction? It's a good store. He sold it Wednesday to two up-to-date Norwegian partners and they will open next week a modern fancy grocery and delicatessen. You will see where your business will go."

Morris, with clouded eyes, died slowly.

***He hadn't the heart to**:「그는 그렇게 할 용기가 없었다」

***Hope wrestled shame as he asked**:「그가 물었을 때 그는 희망과 부끄러움을 동시에 느꼈다」

***give the store in auction**:「가게를 경매에 부치다」

***Karp was devastating**:「Karp는 상대방을 압도해 버렸다」

Karp, to his horror, realized he had shot at* the clerk and wounded the grocer. He remarked hastily, "What could I do? I couldn't tell him to go in auction if he had a chance to sell."

The grocer wasn't listening. He was thinking of Frank with a violent sense of outrage, of having been deceived.

"Listen, Morris," Karp said quickly, "I got a proposition for you about your gesheft. Throw out first on his ass this Italyener that he fooled you, then tell Helen that my Louis—"

But when the ghost behind the counter cursed him* in a strange tongue for the tidings he had brought, Karp backed out of the store and was swallowed in his own*

After a perilous night at the hands of ancient enemies,* Morris escaped from his bed and appeared in the store at five A.M. There he faced the burdensome day alone. The grocer had struggled all night with Karp's terrible news—had tossed around like a red coal* why nobody had told him before how sick the German was—maybe one of the salesmen, or Breitbart, or a customer. Probably no one had thought it too important, seeing that Schmitz's store was until yesterday open daily. Sure he was sick, but somebody had already mentioned that, and why should they tell him again if they figured that people got sick but then they got better? Hadn't he himself been sick, but who had talked of it in the neighborhood?

***shoot at ～**:「～을 향해 총을 쏘다」

***when the ghost behind the counter cursed him**:「카운터 뒤의 유령 같은 남자가 그에게 욕설을 퍼붓게 되자」

***was swallowed in his own**:「자기 가게 안으로 사라져 버렸다」

***After a perilous night at the hands of ancient enemies**:「옛날부터 그를 괴롭혀 온 불면증 때문에 위험한 하룻밤을 지낸 후에」

***had tossed around like a red coal**:「불타는 석탄처럼 몸을 뒤치락거렸다」

Probably nobody. People had their own worries to worry about. As for the news that Schmitz had sold his store, the grocer felt that here he had nothing to complain of—he had been informed at once, like a rock dropped on his skull.*

As for what he would do with Frank, after long pondering the situation, thinking how the clerk had acted concerning their increase in business—as if he alone had created their better times—Morris at length decided that Frank had not—as he had assumed when Karp told him the news—tried to trick him into believing* that he was responsible for the store's change for the better. The grocer supposed that the clerk, like himself, was probably ignorant of the true reason for their change of luck. Maybe he shouldn't have been,* since he at least got out during the day, visited other places on the block, heard news, gossip—maybe he should have known, but Morris felt he didn't, possibly because he wanted to believe he was their benefactor. Maybe that was why he had been too blind to see what he should have seen,* too deaf to have heard what he had heard. It was possible.

After his first confusion and fright, Morris had decided he must sell the store—he had by eight o'clock already told a couple of drivers to pass the word around*—but he must

---

***he had been informed at once, like a rock dropped on his skull**:「머리 위에 바윗돌이 굴러떨어지듯 그는 그 소식을 곧 바로 들었던 것이다」

***tried to trick him into believing ~**:「~라고 그가 믿게끔 그를 속이려 했다」*e.g.* trick a person into consent「속여서 승락하게 하다」

***Maybe he shouldn't have been**:「아마 그가 몰랐을 리는 없을 것이다」 been 다음에 ignorant of가 생략되어 있음.

***Maybe that was why he had been too blind to see what he should have seen**:「아마도 그것이 그가 마땅히 보아야할 것을 보지 못한 이유였을 것이다」

***tell ~ to pass the word around**:「~에게 그 말을 퍼뜨려 달라고 부탁하다」

under no circumstances part with Frank* and must keep him here to do all he could to prevent the Norwegian partners, after they had reopened the store, from quickly calling back the customers of Schmitz who were with him now. He couldn't believe that Frank hadn't helped. It had not been proved in the Supreme Court that the German's sickness was the only source of their recent good fortune. Karp said so but since when did Karp speak the word of God? Of course Frank had helped the business—only not so much as they had thought.* Ida was not so wrong about that. But maybe Frank could hold onto a few people; the grocer doubted he himself could. He hadn't the energy, the nerve to be alone in the store during another time of change for the worse. The years had eaten away his strength.

When Frank came down he at once noticed that the grocer was not himself,* but the clerk was too concerned with his own problems to ask Morris what ailed him. Often since the time Helen had been in his room he had recalled her remark that he must discipline himself and wondered why he had been so moved by the word, why it should now bang around in his head like a stick against a drum.* With the idea of self-control came the feeling of the beauty of it—the beauty of a person being able to do things the way he wanted to, to do good if he wanted; and this feeling was followed by regret—of

---

***he must under no circumstances part with Frank**:「무슨 일이 있어도 그는 Frank를 내보내서는 안 된다」 part with「~와 헤어지다」

***only not so much as they had thought**:「그들이 전에 생각했던 만큼은 아니지만」

***the grocer was not himself**:「식료품점 주인은 제 정신이 아니었다」

***why it should now bang around in his head like a stick against a drum**:「북을 치는 막대기처럼, 왜 그 말이 그의 머리 속에서 지금 쾅쾅 울리는지」

the slow dribbling away, starting long ago, of his character,* without him lifting a finger to stop it. But today, as he scraped at his hard beard with a safety razor, he made up his mind to return, bit by bit until all paid up, the hundred and forty-odd bucks he had filched* from Morris in the months he had worked for him, the figure of which he had kept for this very purpose written on a card hidden in his shoe.

To clean up the slate in a single swipe,* he thought again of telling Morris about his part in the holdup. A week ago he was on the point of getting it past his teeth,* had even spoken aloud the grocer's name, but when Morris looked up Frank felt it was useless and said never mind. He was born he thought, with a worrisome conscience that had never done him too much good, although at times he had liked having the acid weight of it in him* because it had made him feel he was at least that different from other people. It made him want to set himself straight so he could build his love for Helen right, so it would stay right.

But when he pictured himself confessing, the Jew listening with a fat ear, he still could not stand the thought of it. Why should he make more trouble for himself than he could now handle, and end by defeating his purpose to fix things up and

---

***of the slow dribbling away, starting long ago, of his character**:「오래 전에 시작된 자기 성격의 점진적인 타락에 대한(후회심)」 앞의 of는 regret에 연결됨.

***filch**=pilfer「슬쩍하다」

***To clean up the slate in a single swipe**:「단번에 과거의 잘못을 청산하기 위해」 slate「(개인에 관한)기록」 a clean slate「흠 없는 경력, 전과가 없는 것」 swipe「한 번 치는 강타」

***he was on the point of getting it past his teeth**:「그는 그 말을 막 입 밖에 내려 했다」

***he had liked having the acid weight of it in him**:「그는 양심의 쓰라린 가책을 받는 것을 좋아했다」 it는 conscience를 가리킴.

have a better life?* The past was the past and the hell with it. He had unwillingly taken part in a holdup, but he was, like Morris, more of a victim of Ward Minogue. If alone, he wouldn't have done it. That didn't excuse him that he did, but it at least showed his true feelings. So what was there to confess if the whole thing had been sort of an accident? Let bygones be gone.* He had no control over the past—could only shine it up here and there and shut up as to the rest.* From now on he would keep his mind on tomorrow, and tomorrow take up the kind of life that he saw he valued more than how he had been living. He would change and live in a worthwhile way.

Impatient to begin, he waited to empty the contents of his wallet into the cash drawer. He thought he could try it when Morris was napping; but then for some cockeyed reason,* although there was nothing for her to do in the store today, Ida came down and sat in the back with him. She was heavy-faced, dispirited; she sighed often but said nothing, although she acted as if she couldn't stand the sight of him.* He knew why, Helen had told him, and he felt uncomfortable, as if he were wearing wet clothes she wouldn't let him take off; but the best thing was to keep his trap shut and let Helen handle her end of it.

Ida wouldn't leave, so he couldn't put the dough back

***by defeating his purpose to fix things up and have a better life**:「사태를 잘 수습하여 올바른 생활을 해보려는 그의 목표를 뒤엎음으로써」

***Let bygones be gone**:「지난 일은 물에 흘려 보내자」

***could only shine it up here and there and shut up as to the rest**:「여기저기 과거의 좋은 점은 돋보이게 하고 나머지는 입을 다물 수 있을 뿐이다」

***for some cockeyed reason**:「쓸데없는 이유로」

***as if she couldn't stand the sight of him**:「그녀는 그를 쳐다보는 것도 지겨운듯이」

although his itch to do so had grown into impatience.* Whenever somebody went into the store Ida insisted on waiting on them, but this last time after she came back* she said to Frank, stretched out on the couch with a butt in his mouth, that she wasn't feeling so well and was going up.

"Feel better," he said sitting up, but she didn't reply and at last left. He went quickly into the store, once he was sure she was upstairs. His wallet contained a five-dollar bill and a single, and he planned to put it all back in the register, which would leave him only with a few coins in his pocket but tomorrow was payday anyway. After ringing up the six bucks, to erase the evidence of an unlikely sale he rang up "no sale."* Frank then felt a surge of joy at what he had done and his eyes misted.* In the back he drew off his shoe, got out the card, and subtracted six dollars from the total amount he owed. He figured he could pay it all up in a couple-three months, by taking out of the bank the money—about eighty bucks—that was left there, returning it bit by bit, and when that was all used up, giving back part of his weekly salary till he had the debt squared.* The trick was to get the money back without arousing anybody's suspicion he was putting in the drawer more than the business was earning.

While he was still in a good mood over what he had done,

***although his itch to do so had grown into impatience**:「그렇게 하려는 그의 갈망은 이제 조바심으로 바뀌어 버렸지만」 itch=an impatient desire「갈망」

***but this last time after she came back**:「그러나 손님을 접대하고 마지막으로 그녀가 돌아오자」

***to erase the evidence of an unlikely sale he rang up "no sale"**:「있을 법하지 않은 매상의 증거를 없애려고 그는 "비매"란 단추를 눌렀다」

***his eyes misted**:「그는 눈물이 났다」 *e.g.* eyes misting with tears「눈물로 흐려진 눈」

***till he had the debt squared**:「그가 부채를 다 청산할 때까지」 square=settle one's debts「부채를 청산하다」

Helen called up.

"Frank," she said, "are you alone? If not say wrong number and hang up."*

"I am alone."

"Have you seen how nice it is today? I went for a walk at lunchtime and it feels like spring has arrived."

"It's still in February. Don't take your coat off too soon."

"After Washington's Birthday winter loses its heart.* Do you smell the wonderful air?"

"Not right now."

"Get outside in the sun," she said, "it's warm and wonderful."

"Why did you call me for?" he asked.

"Must I have an excuse to call?" she said softly.

"You never do."

"I called because I wished I were seeing you tonight instead of Nat."

"You don't have to go out with him if you don't want to."

"I'd better, because of my mother."

"Change it to some other time."

She thought a minute then said she had better to get it over with.*

"Do it any way like."

"Frank, do you think we could meet after I see Nat—maybe at half past eleven, or twelve at the latest? Would you like to

---

***If not say wrong number and hang up**:「만일 사람이 있으면 전화번호가 틀렸다고 말하고 끊어 버리세요」

***winter loses its heart**:「겨울은 그 기세가 꺾입니다」

***said she had better to get it over with**:「그녀는 그 일을 끝내 버리는 것이 낫겠다고 말했다」 get over with=finish「끝내 버리다」

meet me then?"

"Sure, but what's it all about?"

"I'll tell you when I see you," she said with a little laugh. "Should we meet on the Parkway or our regular place in front of the lilac trees?"

"Wherever you say. The park is okay."

"I really hate to go there since my mother followed us."

"Don't worry about that, honey." He said, "Have you got something nice to tell me?"

"Very nice," Helen said.

He thought he knew what it was. He thought he would carry her like a bride up to his room, then when it was over carry her down so she could go up alone without fear her mother suspected where she had been.

Just then Morris came into the store so he hung up.

The grocer inspected the figure in the cash register and the satisfying sum there set him sighing.* By Saturday they would surely have two-forty or fifty, but it wouldn't be that high any more once the Norwegians opened up.*

Noticing Morris peering at the register under the yellow flame of his match, Frank remembered that all he had left on him was about seventy cents. He wished Helen had called him before he had put back the six bucks in the drawer. If it rained tonight they might need a cab to get home from the park, or maybe if they went up in his room she would be hungry after and want a pizza or something. Anyway, he could borrow a buck from her if he needed it. He also thought of asking Louis

---

***the satisfying sum there set him sighing**:「거기에 기록된 만족스러운 금액을 보고 그는 한숨을 쉬었다」

***once the Norwegians opened up**:「노르웨이인들이 가게를 열게 되면」

Karp for a little loan but didn't like to.

Morris went out for his *Forward* and spread it before him on the table, but he wasn't reading. He was thinking how distracted he was about the future.* While he was upstairs, he had lain in bed trying to think of ways to cut down his expenses. He had thought of the fifteen dollars weekly he paid Frank and had worried over how large the sum was. He had also thought of Helen being kissed by the clerk, and of Ida's warnings, and all this had worked on his nerves.* He seriously considered telling Frank to go but couldn't make the decision to. He wished he had let him go long ago.*

Frank had decided he didn't like to ask Helen for any money—it wasn't a nice thing to do with a girl you liked. He thought it was better to take a buck out of the register drawer, out of the amount he had just put back. He wished he had paid back the five and kept himself the one-buck bill.

Morris sneaked a glance at his clerk sitting on the couch. Recalling the time he had sat in the barber's chair, watching the customers coming out of the grocery with big bags, he felt uneasy. I wonder if he steals from me, he thought. The question filled him with dread because he had asked it of himself many times yet had never answered it with certainty.

He saw through the window in the wall that a woman had come into the store. Frank got up from the couch. "I'll take this one, Morris."

***He was thinking how distracted he was about the future**:「장래의 일 때문에 자기가 얼마나 고심하고 있는지 그는 스스로 생각하고 있었다」 distracted=confused「어찌할 바를 모르는」, insane「미친」

***all this had worked on his nerves**:「이런 모든 것이 그의 신경을 건드렸다」

***He wished he had let him go long ago**:「오래 전에 Frank를 내보냈어야 했다고 그는 생각했다」

Morris spoke to his newspaper. "I got anyway something to clean up in the cellar."*

"What have you got there?"

"Something."

When Frank walked behind the counter, Morris went down into the cellar but didn't stay there. He stole up the stairs and stationed himself behind the hall door.* Peering through a crack in the wood, he clearly saw the woman and heard her ordering. He added up the prices of the items as she ordered them.

The bill came to $1.81. When Frank rang up the money, the grocer held his breath for a painful second, then stepped inside the store.

The customer, hugging* her bag of groceries, was on her way out of the front door. Frank had his hand under his apron, in his pants pocket. He gazed at the grocer with a startled expression.* The amount rung up on the cash register was eighty-one cents.

Morris groaned within himself.

Frank, though tense with shame,* pretended nothing was wrong. This enraged Morris. "The bill was a dollar more, why did you ring a dollar less?"

The clerk, after a time of long agony, heard himself say, "It's just a mistake, Morris."

***I got anyway something to clean up in the cellar**:「나는 아무래도 지하실에서 정리할 것이 있네」

***stationed himself behind the hall door**:「복도 문 뒤에 숨어 있었다」 *e.g.* The detective stationed himself among the bushes. 「탐정은 숲 속에 숨었다」

***hug**:「가슴에 안다」

***with a startled expression**:「놀란 표정을 하고」

***though tense with shame**:「수치심으로 긴장하고 었지만」

"No," thundered the grocer. "I heard behind the hall door how much you sold her. Don't think I don't know you did many times the same thing before."

Frank could say nothing.

"Give it here the dollar," Morris ordered, extending his trembling hand.

Anguished, the clerk tried lying. "You're making a mistake. The register owes me a buck. I ran short on nickels so I got twenty from Sam Pearl with my own dough.* After, I accidentally rang up one buck instead of 'no sale.' That's why I took it back this way. No harm done, I tell you."

"This is a lie," cried Morris. "I left inside a roll nickels in case anybody needed." He strode behind the counter, rang "no sale" and held up the roll of nickels. "Tell the truth."

Frank thought, This shouldn't be happening to me, for I am a different person now.

"I was short,* Morris," he admitted, "that's the truth of it. I figured I would pay you back tomorrow after I got my pay." He took the crumpled dollar out of his pants pocket and Morris snatched it from his hand.

"Why didn't you ask me to lend you a dollar instead to steal it?"

The clerk realized it hadn't occurred to him to borrow from the grocer. The reason was simple—he had never borrowed, he had always stolen.

"I didn't think about it. I made a mistake."

***I ran short on nickels so I got twenty from Sam Pearl with my own dough**:「5센트짜리가 부족해서 내 돈 1불을 가지고 Sam Pearl에게 가서 20개의 5센트 백통화로 바꿔 왔죠」

***short**:「돈이 부족한」 *e.g.* I am rather short today.「나는 오늘 돈이 좀 부족하다」

"Always mistakes," the grocer said wrathfully.

"All my life," sighed Frank.

"You stole from me since the day I saw you."

"I confess to it," Frank said, "but for God's sake, Morris, I swear I was paying it back to you. Even today I put back six bucks. That's why you got so much in the drawer from the time you went up to snooze until now. Ask the Mrs if we took in more than two bucks while you were upstairs. The rest I put in."

He thought of taking off his shoe and showing Morris how carefully he had kept track of the money he had taken,* but he didn't want to do that because the amount was so large it might anger the grocer more.

"You put it in," Morris cried, "but it belongs to me. I don't want a thief here." He counted fifteen dollars out of the register. "Here's your week's pay—the last. Please leave now the store."

His anger was gone. He spoke in sadness and fear of tomorrow.

"Give me one last chance," Frank begged, "Morris, please." His face was gaunt,* his eyes haunted,* his beard like night.

Morris, though moved by the man, thought of Helen.

"No."

Frank stared at the gray and broken* Jew and seeing,

***how carefully he had kept track of the money he had taken**:「자기가 훔친 돈을 얼마나 주의깊게 기록하고 있는지」 keep track of「기록하다, 뒤를 쫓다」 *e.g.* I kept track of what was going on.「진전되어 가는 사실을 나는 기록했다」

***gaunt**=thin and bony「수척한」

***haunted**:「고민에 찬」

***broken**:「쇠약한」

despite tears in his eyes, that he would not yield, hung up his apron on a hook and left.

The night's new beauty struck Helen with the anguish of loss* as she hurried into the lamplit park a half-hour after midnight. That morning as she had stepped into the street, wearing a new dress under her old coat, the fragrant day had moved her to tears and she felt then she was truly in love with Frank. Whatever the future held* it couldn't deny her the sense of release and fulfillment she had felt then. Hours later, when she was with Nat Pearl, as they stopped off for a drink at a roadside tavern, then at his insistence drove into Long Island, her thoughts were still on Frank and she was impatient to be with him.

Nat was Nat. He exerted himself tonight, giving out with charm.* He talked with charm and was hurt with charm. Unchanged after all the months she hadn't been with him, as they were parked on the dark shore overlooking the starlit Sound, after a few charming preliminaries* he had put his arms around her. "Helen, how can we forget what pleasure we had in the past?"

She pushed him away, angered. "It's gone, I've forgotten. If you're so much of a gentleman, Nat, you ought to forget it too.

***The night's new beauty struck Helen with the anguish of loss**:「밤의 신선한 아름다움이 Helen의 마음속에 괴로운 상실감을 불러일으켰다」 *e.g.* The sight struck him with horror.「그 광경을 보고 그는 두려움을 느꼈다」

***Whatever the future held**:「미래가 어떻게 되든간에」 *e.g.* The future may hold many sorrows for us.「우리의 미래에 여러 슬픔이 기다리고 있을지도 모른다」

***give out with charm**:「매력적으로 기분을 표현하다」

***after a few charming preliminaries**:「몇 번 매력적인 간사를 떨더니」 preliminary「예비적인 행위」

Was a couple of times in bed a mortgage on my future?"*

"Helen, don't talk like a stranger. For Pete's sake,* be human."

"I *am* human, please remember."

"We were once good friends. My plea is for friendship again."

"Why don't you admit by friendship you mean something different?"

"Helen . . ."

"No."

He sat back at the wheel. "Christ, you have become a suspicious character."

She said, "Things have changed—you must realize."

"Who have they changed for," he asked sullenly, "that dago* I hear you go with?"

Her answer was ice.

On the way home he tried to unsay* what he had said, but Helen yielded him only a quick good-by. She left him with relief and a poignant sense of all she had wasted of the night.*

Worried that Frank had had to wait so long, she hurried across the lit plaza and along a gravel path bordered by tall lilac shrubs, toward their meeting place. As she approached their bench, although she was troubled by a foreboding he would not be there, she couldn't believe it, then was painfully

---

***Was a couple of times in bed a mortgage on my future?**:「두 번 동침했다 해서 내 미래가 저당잡혀진 건가요?」

***For Pete's sake**=For God's sake「제발」

***dago**:「이탈리아계의 사람」

***unsay**:「한 말을 취소하다」

***a poignant sense of all she had wasted of the night**:「밤을 온통 허송했다는 뼈에 사무치는 괴로운 느낌」 poignant=very painful, bitter

disappointed to find that though others were present—it was true, he wasn't.

Could he have been and gone already? It didn't seem possible; he had always waited before, no matter how late she was. And since she had told him she had something important to say, nothing less than that she now knew she loved him,* surely he would want to hear what. She sat down, fearing he had had an accident.

Usually they were alone at this spot, but the almost warmish late-February night had brought out company. On a bench diagonally opposite Helen,* in the dark under budding branches, sat two young lovers locked in a long kiss.* The bench at her left was empty, but on the one beyond that a man was sleeping under a dim lamp. A cat nosed at his shadow and departed. The man woke with a grunt, squinted at* Helen, yawned and went back to sleep. The lovers at last broke apart and left in silence, the boy awkwardly trailing* the happy girl. Helen deeply envied her, an awful feeling to end the day with.

Glancing at her watch she saw it was already past one. Shivering, she rose, then sat down to wait five last minutes. She felt the stars clustered like a distant weight above her head.* Utterly lonely, she regretted the spring-like loveliness

---

***nothing less than that she now knew she loved him**:「그녀가 Frank를 사랑하고 있음을 이제야 알게 되었다는 바로 그 사실」 nothing less than=the same thing as

***On a bench diagonally opposite Helen**:「Helen이 있는 곳에서 비스듬히 맞은 편에 있는 벤치에」

***sat two young lovers locked in a long kiss**:「두 젊은 연인들이 앉아서 긴 키스를 하고 있었다」

***squint at**=look with the eyes half closed「눈을 가늘게 뜨고 보다」

***trail**:「어슬렁어슬렁 뒤를 따라가다」

***She felt the stars clustered like a distant weight above her head**:「그녀의 머리 위에서, 별들이 먼 곳에 있는 무거운 짐처럼 밀집해 있다고 그녀는 느꼈다」

of the night; it had gone, in her hands, to waste. She was tired of anticipation, of waiting for nothing.

A man was standing unsteadily before her, heavy, dirty, stinking of whiskey. Helen half-rose, struck with fright.

He flipped off his hat and said huskily, "Don't be afraid of me, Helen. I'm personally a fine guy—son of a cop. You remember me, don't you—Ward Minogue that went to your school? My old man beat me up once in the girls' yard."

Though it was years since she had seen him she recognized Ward, at once recalling the incident of his following a girl into a lavatory.* Instinctively Helen raised her arm to protect herself. She kept herself from screaming, or he might grab her. How stupid, she thought, to wait for this.

"I remember you, Ward."

"Could I sit down?"

She hesitated. "All right."

Helen edged as far away* from him as she could. He looked half-stupefied.* If he made a move she would run, screaming.

"How did you recognize me in the dark?" she asked, pretending to be casual as she glanced stealthily around to see how best to escape. If she could get past the trees, it was then another twenty feet along the shrub-lined path before she could be out in the open. Once on the plaza* there would be people around she could appeal to.

God only help me, she thought.

***the incident of his following a girl into a lavatory**:「그가 여학생을 뒤따라 변소에 들어갔던 사건」

***edge away**:「비스듬히 움직이다」

***He looked half-stupefied**:「그는 반쯤 정신이 나간 사람처럼 보였다」

***Once on the plaza**:「일단 광장에 도착하면」

"I saw you a couple of times lately," Ward answered, rubbing his hand slowly across his chest.

"Where?"

"Around. Once I saw you come out of your old man's grocery and I figured it was you. You have still kept your looks,"* he grinned.

"Thanks. Don't you feel so well?"

"I got gas pains in my chest and a goddam headache."

"In case you want one I have a box of aspirins in my purse."

"No, they make me puke."* She noticed that he was glancing toward the trees. She grew more anxious, thought of offering him her purse if he only wouldn't touch her.

"How's your boy friend, Frank Alpine?" Ward asked, with a wet wink.

She said in surprise, "Do you know Frank?"

"He's an old friend of mine," he answered. "He was here lookin' for you."

"Is—he all right?"

"Not so hot,"* said Ward. "He had to go home."

She got up. "I have to leave now."

But he was standing.

"Good night." Helen walked away from him.

"He told me to give you this paper." Ward thrust his hand into his coat pocket.

She didn't believe him but paused long enough for him to move forward. He grabbed her with astonishing swiftness,

---

***You have still kept your looks**:「너 아름다운 용모를 그대로 지니고 있구나」
***puke**=vomit「토하다」
***Not so hot**:「별로 좋지 않았어」

smothering her scream with his smelly hand, as he dragged her toward the trees.

"All I want is what you give that wop,"* Ward grunted.

She kicked, clawed, bit his hand, broke loose.* He caught her by her coat collar, ripped it off. She screamed again and ran forward but he pounced upon her and got his arm over her mouth. Ward shoved her hard against a tree, knocking the breath out of her.* He held her tightly by the throat as with his other hand he ripped open her coat and tore her dress off the shoulder, exposing her brassière.

Struggling, kicking wildly, she caught him between the legs with her knee. He cried out and cracked her across the face. She felt the strength go out of her and fought not to faint.* She screamed but heard no sound.

Helen felt his body shuddering against her. I am disgraced, she thought, yet felt curiously freed of his stinking presence, as if he had dissolved into a can of filth and she had kicked it away.* Her legs buckled* and she slid to the ground. I've fainted, went through her mind, although she felt she was still fighting him.

Dimly she realized that a struggle was going on near her. She heard the noise of a blow, and Ward Minogue cried out in great pain and staggered away.

***wop** :「이탈리아에서 온 이주민(경멸적인 뜻을 포함)」
***broke loose** :「풀려 났다」
***knocking the breath out of her** :「그녀를 깜짝 놀라게 했다」
***fought not to faint** :「실신하지 않으려고 있는 힘을 다했다」
***as if he had dissolved into a can of filth and she had kicked it away** :「마치 그가 쓰레기 깡통으로 사그라지고 그것을 그녀가 차 버린 것처럼」
***buckle** :「굽다, 휘어지다」

Frank, she thought with tremulous joy.* Helen felt herself gently lifted and knew she was in his arms. She sobbed in relief. He kissed her eyes and lips and he kissed her half-naked breast. She held him tightly with both arms, weeping, laughing, murmuring she had come to tell him she loved him.

He put her down and they kissed under the dark trees. She tasted whiskey on his tongue and was momentarily afraid.

"I love you, Helen," he murmured, attempting clumsily to cover her breast with the torn dress as he drew her deeper into the dark, and from under the trees onto the star-dark field.

They sank to their knees on the winter earth,* Helen urgently whispering, "Please not now, darling," but he spoke of his starved and passionate love, and all the endless heartbreaking waiting. Even as he spoke he thought of her as beyond his reach,* forever in the bathroom as he spied, so he stopped her pleas with kisses. . . .

Afterward, she cried, "Dog—uncircumcised* dog!"

***Frank, she thought with tremulous joy**:「Frank, 그녀는 떨리는 기쁨으로 바로 그를 생각했다」 tremulous=trembling「떨리는」

***They sank to their knees on the winter earth**:「그들은 언 겨울 땅 위에 무릎을 꿇고 말았다」

***he thought of her as beyond his reach**:「그녀는 자기의 손이 미치지 못하는 여자라고 그는 생각했다」

***uncircumcised**:「할례받지 않은, 이방인의」

7

While Morris was sitting alone in the back the next morning, a boy brought in a pink handbill* and left it on the counter. When the grocer picked it up he saw it announced the change of management and reopening on Monday, by Taast and Pederson,* of the grocery and fancy delicatessen around the corner. There followed, in large print, a list of specials* they were offering during their first week, bargains Morris could never hope to match, because he couldn't afford the loss the Norwegians were planning to take. The grocer felt he was standing in an icy draft* blowing from some hidden hole in the store. In the kitchen, though he stood with his legs and buttocks pressed against the gas radiator, it took an age to diminish the chill that had penetrated his bones.*

All morning he scanned* the crumpled handbill, muttering to himself; he sipped cold coffee, thinking of the future, and off and on, of Frank Alpine. The clerk had left last night without taking his fifteen dollars' wages. Morris thought he would come in for it this morning but, as the hours passed, knew he wouldn't, maybe having left it to make up some of

---

***a pink handbill**:「분홍색 전단」
***by Taast and Pederson**:「Taast와 Pederson의 공동경영으로」
***a list of specials**:「특매품의 리스트」
***an icy draft**:「얼음같이 찬 바람 구멍」
***the chill that had penetrated his bones**:「그의 뼈 속까지 스며든 냉기」
***scan**=examine with care

the money he had stolen;* yet maybe not. For the thousandth time the grocer wondered if he had done right in ordering Frank to go. True, he had stolen from him, but also true, he was paying it back. His story that he had put six dollars into the register and then found he had left himself without a penny in his pocket was probably the truth, because the sum in the register, when Morris counted it, was more than they usually took in during the dead part of the afternoon when he napped.* The clerk was an unfortunate man; yet the grocer was alternately glad and sorry the incident had occurred. He was glad he had finally let him go. For Helen's sake it had had to be done, and for Ida's peace of mind, as well as his own. Still, he felt unhappy to lose his assistant and be by himself when the Norwegians opened up.

Ida came down, puffy-eyed from poor sleep.* She felt a hopeless rage against the world. What will become of Helen? she asked herself, and cracked her knuckles against her chest. But when Morris looked up to listen to her complaints, she was afraid to say anything. A half-hour later, aware that something had changed in the store, she thought of the clerk.

"Where is he?" she asked.

"He left," Morris answered.

"Where did he leave?" she said in astonishment.

"He left for good."

She gazed at him. "Morris, what happened, tell me?"

***to make up some of the money he had stolen**:「그가 훔친 돈의 얼마라도 보상하기 위하여」

***during the dead part of the afternoon when he napped**:「그가 낮잠을 잤던 오후의 손님이 전혀 없는 시간」

***Ida came down, puffy-eyed from poor sleep**:「Ida는 잠이 부족하여 부은 눈을 하고 내려왔다」

"Nothing," he said, embarrassed. "I told him to leave."

"Why, all of a sudden?"

"Didn't you say you didn't want him here no more?"

"From the first day I saw him, but you always said no."

"Now I said yes."

"A stone falls off my heart."* But she was not satisfied. "Did he move out* of the house yet?"

"I don't know."

"I will go and ask the upstairske."

"Leave her alone. We will know when he moves."

"When did you tell him to leave?"

"Last night."

"So why didn't you tell me last night?" she said angrily. "Why you told me he went early to the movies?"

"I was nervous."

"Morris," she asked in fright. "Did something else happen? Did Helen—"

"Nothing happened."

"Does she know he left?"

"I didn't tell her. Why she went so early to work this morning?"

"She went early?"

"Yes."

"I don't know," Ida said uneasily.

He produced the handbill.* "This is why I feel bad."

She glanced at it, not comprehending.

***A stone falls off my heart**:「앓던 이가 빠졌군」

***move out**:「이사하다」

***He produced the handbill**:「그는 전단을 보여 주었다」 produce=present「제시하다, 내놓다」

"The German," he explained. "They bought him out, two Norwegians."*

She gasped. "When?"

"This week. Schmitz is sick. He lays now in the hospital."

"I told you," Ida said.

"You told me?"

"Vey is mir.* I told you after Christmas—when improved more the business. I told you the drivers said the German was losing customers. You said no, Frank improved the business. A goy brings in goyim, you said. How much strength I had to argue with you?"*

"Did you tell me he kept closed in the morning his store?"

"Who said? I didn't know this."

"Karp told me."

"Karp was here?"

"He came on Thursday to tell me the good news."

"What good news?"

"That Schmitz sold out."

"Is this good news?" she asked.

"Maybe to him but not to me."

"You didn't tell me he came."

"I tell you now," he said irritably. "Schmitz sold out Monday will open two Norwegians. Our business will go to hell again. We will starve here."

"Some helper you had," she said with bitterness. "Why

***They bought him out, two Norwegians**:「그들이 독일인 상점을 사 버렸어, 두 노르웨이 사람들이 말이야」

***Vey is mir**:「하느님 맙소사」

***How much strength I had to argue with you**:「당신과 말다툼할 힘이 내게 있었겠수?」

didn't you listen to me when I said let him go?"

"I listened," he said wearily.

She was silent, then asked, "So when Karp told you Schmitz sold his store you told Frank to leave?"

"The next day."

"Thank God."

"See if you say next week 'Thank God.' "*

"What is this got to do with Frank? Did he help us?"

"I don't know."

"You don't know," she said shrilly. "You just told me you said he should leave when you found out where came our business."*

"I don't know," he said miserably, "I don't know where it came."*

"It didn't come from him."

"Where it came I don't worry any more. Where will it come next week I worry." He read aloud the specials the Norweigians were offering.

She squeezed her hands white. "Morris, we must sell the store."

"So sell." Sighing, Morris removed his apron. "I will take my rest."

"It's only half past eleven."

"I feel cold." He looked depressed.

"Eat something first—your soup."

"Who can eat?"

***See if you say next week 'Thank God'**:「다음 주에도 '하느님 감사해요'라고 말할지 두고 봅시다」

***when you found out where came our business**:「당신이 우리 장사가 잘 되는 원인을 알게 되었을 때」

***I don't know where it came**:「가게가 잘 된 원인을 난 몰라」 it는 our business임.

"Drink a hot glass tea."

"No."

"Morris," she said quietly, "don't worry so much. Something will happen. We will always have to eat."

He made no reply, folded the handbill into a small square* and took it upstairs with him.

The rooms were cold. Ida always shut off the radiators when she went down and lit them again in the late afternoon about an hour before Helen returned. Now the house was too cold. Morris turned on the stopcock* of the bedroom radiator, then found he had no match in his pocket. He got one in the kitchen.

Under the covers he felt shivery.* He lay under two blankets and a quilt yet shivered. He wondered if he was sick but soon fell asleep. He was glad when he felt sleep come over him, although it brought night too quickly. But if you slept it was night, that's how things were. Looking, that same night, from the street into his store, he beheld Taast and Pederson—one with a small blond mustache, the other half-bald, a light shining on his head—standing behind *his* counter, poking into *his* cash register.* The grocer rushed in but they were gabbing* in German and paid no attention to his gibbering Yiddish.* At that moment Frank came out of the back with Helen. Though the clerk spoke a musical Italian, Morris

---

***into a small square**:「작은 네모꼴로」
***turned on the stopcock**:「꼭지를 열었다」
***Under the covers he felt shivery**:「이불을 덮었지만 그는 오싹오싹 추웠다」 shivery=chilly 「추운, 오한이 나는」
***poking into *his* cash register**:「그의 금전등록기를 뒤지면서」
***gab**:「허튼 소리를 지껄여대다」
***his gibbering Yiddish**:「뜻을 알 수 없는 Morris가 지껄이는 이디시 어」

recognized a dirty word.* He struck his assistant across the face and they wrestled furiously on the floor, Helen screaming mutely. Frank dumped him heavily on his back* and sat on his poor chest. He thought his lungs would burst. He tried hard to cry out but his voice cracked his throat and no one would help. He considered the possibility of dying and would have liked to.

Tessie Fuso dreamed of a tree hit by thunder and knocked over; she dreamed she heard someone groan terribly and awoke in fright, listened, then went back to sleep. Frank Alpine, at the dirty end of a long night, awoke groaning. He awoke with a shout*—awake, he thought, forever.* His impulse was to leap out of bed and rush down to the store; then he remembered that Morris had thrown him out. It was a gray, dreary winter morning. Nick had gone to work and Tessie, in her bathrobe, was sitting in the kitchen, drinking coffee. She heard Frank cry out again but had just discovered that she was pregnant, so did nothing more than wonder at his nightmare.*

He lay in bed with the blankets pulled over his head, trying to smother his thoughts but they escaped and stank. The more he smothered them the more they stank. He smelled garbage in the bed and couldn't move out of it. He couldn't because he

---

***a dirty word**:「외설스러운 말」
***Frank dumped him heavily on his back**:「Frank는 그를 뒤로 힘껏 넘어뜨렸다」
***He awoke with a shout**:「그는 소리를 지르다 잠이 깨었다」
***—awake, he thought, forever**:「자기는 영원히 잠이 깨어 있을 거라고 그는 생각했다」
***so did nothing more than wonder at his nightmare**:「그래서 그녀는 Frank가 악몽을 꾸고 있는가 하고 여겼을 뿐이었다」

was it—the stink in his own broken nose.* What you did was how bad you smelled. Unable to stand it he flung the covers aside and struggled to dress but couldn't make it. The sight of his bare feet utterly disgusted him. He thirsted for a cigarette but couldn't light one for fear of seeing his hand. He shut his eyes and lit a match. The match burned his nose. He stepped on the lit match with his bare feet* and danced in pain.

Oh my God, why did I do it? Why did I ever do it? Why did I do it?

His thoughts were killing him. He couldn't stand them. He sat on the edge of the twisted bed, his thoughtful head ready to burst in his hands.* He wanted to run. Part of him was already in flight, he didn't know where. He just wanted to run. But while he was running, he wanted to be back. He wanted to be back with Helen, to be forgiven. It wasn't asking too much. People forgave people—who else?* He could explain if she would listen. Explaining was a way of getting close to somebody you had hurt; as if in hurting them you were giving them a reason to love you. He had come, he would say, to the park to wait for her, to hear what she had to tell him. He felt he knew she would say she loved him; it meant they would soon sleep together. This stayed in his mind and he sat there waiting to hear her say it, at the same time in an agony that

---

***because he was it—the stink in his own broken nose**:「왜냐하면 그 자신이 그의 찌그러진 코 속에 있는 악취였기 때문이었다」 it는 the stink를 나타냄.

***He stepped on the lit match with his bare feet**:「그는 불 붙은 성냥깨비를 맨발로 밟았다」

***his thoughtful head ready to burst in his hands**:「생각에 잠긴 머리가 그의 두 손 안에서 방금 터질 것만 같은 상태에서」 his thoughtful head 앞에 with를 넣을 것.

***People forgave people—who else?**:「사람이 사람을 용서하는 것이다—그 외에 누가 용서하겠는가?」 *e.g.* Who else is coming?「그 외에 누가 오겠는가?」

she never would, that he would lose her the minute she found out why her father had kicked him out of the grocery. What could he tell her about that? He sat for hours trying to think what to say, at last growing famished.* At midnight he left to get a pizza but stopped instead in a bar. Then when he saw his face in the mirror he felt a nose-thumbing revulsion. Where have you ever been, he asked the one in the glass,* except on the inside of a circle? What have you ever done but always the wrong thing? When he returned to the park, there was Ward Minogue hurting her. He just about killed Ward. Then when he had Helen in his arms, crying, saying at last that she loved him, he had this hopeless feeling it was the end and now he would never see her again.* He thought he must love her before she was lost to him. She said no, not to, but he couldn't believe it the same minute she was saying she loved him. He thought, once I start she will come along with me. So then he did it. He loved her with his love. She should have known that. She should not have gone wild, beat his face with her fists, called him dirty names, run from him, his apologies, pleadings, sorrow.*

Oh Jesus, what did I do?

He moaned; had got instead of a happy ending, a bad smell. If he could root out what he had done, smash and destroy it;

***at last growing famished**=and at last he grew famished「드디어 그는 배가 고파졌다」

***he asked the one in the glass**:「그는 거울에 비친 자에게 물었다」

***he had this hopeless feeling···again**:「그는 이제 이것이 마지막이며 앞으로 그녀를 만나지 못할 거라는 절망감에 빠져 버렸다」 feeling 뒤에 that가 생략되었으며 이것은 feeling의 동격절인 명사절을 인도함.

***She should not have . . . run from him, his apologies, pleadings, sorrow**:「그녀는 …그로부터, 그리고 그의 사과, 탄원, 비탄 등에서 도망치지 말았어야 했다」

but it was done, beyond him to undo.* It was where he could never lay hands on* it any more—in his stinking mind. His thoughts would forever suffocate him. He had failed once too often. He should somewhere have stopped and changed the way he was going, his luck, himself, stopped hating the world, got a decent education, a job, a nice girl. He had lived without will, betrayed every good intention. Had he ever confessed the holdup to Morris? Hadn't he stolen from the cash register till the minute he was canned?* In a single terrible act in the park hadn't he murdered the last of his good hopes, the love he had so long waited for—his chance at a future? His goddamned life had pushed him wherever it went; he had led it nowhere. He was blown around in any breath that blew, owned nothing, not even experience to show for the years he had lived. If you had experience you knew at least when to start and where to quit; all he knew was how to mangle himself more.* The self he had secretly considered valuable was, for all he could make of it, a dead rat. He stank.

This time his shout frightened Tessie. Frank got up on the run but he had run everywhere. There was no place left to escape to. The room shrank. The bed was flying up at him.* He felt trapped—sick, wanted to cry but couldn't. He planned to kill himself, at the same minute had a terrifying insight: that

---

***but it was done, beyond him to undo**:「그러나 그 행동은 이미 저질러진 것이고 그가 그것을 취소함은 불가능했다」

***lay hands on ～**:「～에 손대다, 잡다」

***till the minute he was canned**:「해고되는 마지막 순간까지」 be canned＝be fired「해고되다」

***all he knew was how to mangle himself more**:「그가 아는 것은 자기 자신을 더 엉망으로 만드는 것뿐이었다」

***The bed was flying up at him**:「침대가 그에게로 날아왔다」

all the while he was acting like he wasn't, he was really a man of stern morality.*

Ida had awakened in the night and heard her daughter crying. Nat did something to her, she thought wildly, but was ashamed to go to Helen and beg her to say what. She guessed he had acted like a lout*—it was no wonder Helen had stopped seeing him. All night she blamed herself for having urged her to go out with the law student. She fell into an unhappy sleep.

It was growing light when Morris left the flat. Helen dragged herself out of bed and sat with reddened eyes in the bathroom, sewing on her coat collar. Once near the office* she would give it to a tailor to fix so the tear couldn't be seen. With her new dress she could do nothing. Rolling it into a hopeless ball, she hid it under some things in her bottom bureau drawer.* Monday she would buy one exactly like it and hang it in her closet. Undressing for a shower—her third in hours—she burst into tears at the sight of her body. Every man she drew to her dirtied her. How could she have encouraged him? She felt a violent self-hatred for trusting him, when from the very beginning she had sensed he was untrustable. How could she have allowed herself to fall in love with anybody like him? She was filled with loathing at the fantasy she had created, of making him into what he couldn't be

---

***that all the while . . . a man of stern morality**:「즉 그는 언제나 도덕적 인간이 아닌 것처럼 행동해 왔으나 사실은 그가 엄격한 도덕적 인간이라는 사실」

***a lout**=an awkward, stupid fellow

***Once near the office**:「회사 근처에 가게 되면」

***Rolling it into a hopeless ball, she hid···drawer**:「체념하고 그것을 돌돌 말아, 장롱의 가장 아래 서랍 속의 어떤 물건 밑에 숨겼다」

—educable, promising, kind and good, when he was no more than a bum. Where were her wits, her sense of elemental self-preservation?*

Under the shower she soaped herself heavily, crying as she washed. At seven, before her mother awakened, she dressed and left the house, too sickened to eat. She would gladly have forgotten her life, in sleep, but dared not stay home, dared not be questioned. When she returned from her halfday of work, if he was still there, she would order him to leave or would scream him out of the house.

Coming home from the garage, Nick smelled gas in the hall. He inspected the radiators in his flat, saw they were both lit, then knocked on Frank's door.

After a minute the door opened a crack.*

"Do you smell anything?" Nick said, staring at the eye in the crack.

"Mind your goddamned business."

"Are you nuts?* I smell gas in the house, it's dangerous."

"Gas?" Frank flung open the door. He was in pajamas, haggard.

"What's the matter, you sick?"

"Where do you smell he gas?"

"Don't tell me you can't smell it."

"I got a bad cold," Frank said hoarsely.

"Maybe it's comin' from the cellar," said Nick.

***her sense of elemental self-preservation**:「그녀의 기본적인 자기보존의식」

***the door opened a crack**:「문이 조금 열렸다」 crack「틈」 *e.g.* Open the window a crack.「창문을 조금만 열어 봐라」

***Are you nuts?**:「당신 미쳤소?」 nuts=crazy「미친」 *e.g.* He's nuts.「그는 정신이 이상하다」

They ran down a flight and then the odor hit Frank, an acrid stench thick enough to wade through.*

"It's coming from this floor," Nick said.

Frank pounded on the door. "Helen, there's gas here, let me in. Helen," he cried.

"Shove* it," said Nick.

Frank pushed his shoulder against the door. It was unlocked and he fell in. Nick quickly opened the kitchen window while Frank, in his bare feet, roamed through the house. Helen was not there but he found Morris in bed.

The clerk, coughing, dragged the grocer out of bed and carrying him to the living room, laid him on the floor. Nick closed the stopcock of the bedroom radiator and threw open every window. Frank got down on his knees, bent over Morris, clamped his hands to his sides and pumped.*

Tessie ran in in fright, and Nick shouted to her to call Ida.

Ida came stumbling up the stairs, moaning, "Oh, my God, oh, my God."

Seeing Morris lying on the floor, his underwear soaked, his face the color of a cooked beet,* flecks of foam* in the corners of his mouth, she let out* a piercing shriek.

Helen, coming dully into the hall, heard her mother's cry.

***an acrid stench thick enough to wade through**:「뚫고 지나가야 할 정도로 많이 나는 지독한 악취」 acrid「지독한」 stench「악취」

***shove**=push roughly「난폭하게 밀다」

***clamped his hands to his sides and pumped**:「그의 옆구리에 양손을 대고 상하로 움직였다」 인공호흡을 시켰다는 뜻.

***the color of a cooked beet**:「삶은 사탕무우의 색깔」

***flecks of foam**:「거품이 난 자국」

***let out**=give out「소리를 내다」 *e.g.* let out a groan「신음 소리를 내다」 let out a piercing shriek「찢어지는 듯한 비명을 지르다」

She smelled the gas and ran in terror up the stairs, expecting death.

When she saw Frank in his pajamas bent over her father's back, her throat thickened in disgust. She screamed in fear and hatred.

Frank couldn't look at her, frightened to.

"His eyes just moved," Nick said.

Morris awoke with a massive ache in his chest. His head felt like corroded metal,* his mouth horribly dry, his stomach crawling with pain. He was ashamed to find himself stretched out in his long underwear on the floor.

"Morris," cried Ida.

Frank got up, embarrassed at his bare feet and pajamas.

"Papa, Papa." Helen was on her knees.

"Why did you do it for?" Ida yelled in the grocer's ear.

"What happened?" he gasped.

"Why did you do it for?" she wept.

"Are you crazy?" he muttered. "I forgot to light the gas. A mistake."

Helen broke into sobbing, her lips twisted. Frank had to turn his head.

"The only thing that saved him was he got some air," Nick said. "You're lucky this flat ain't windproof, Morris."*

Tessie shivered. "It's cold. Cover him, he's sweating."

"Put him in bed," Ida said.

Frank and Nick lifted the grocer and carried him in to his

***corroded metal**:「부식된 금속」

***You're lucky this flat ain't windproof, Morris**:「이 집이 방풍장치가 안 되어 천만다행입니다」 lucky 다음에 that가 생략되어 있고 그 이하는 원인을 나타내는 부사절임. *e.g.* I was afraid (that) he might be late.「나는 그가 지각할까봐 걱정했다」

bed. Ida and Helen covered him with blankets and quilt.

"Thanks," Morris said to them. He stared at Frank. Frank looked at the floor.

"Shut the windows," Tessie said. "The smell is gone."

"Wait a little longer," said Frank. He glanced at Helen but her back was to him. She was still crying.

"Why did he do it?" Ida moaned.

Morris gazed long at her, then shut his eyes.

"Leave him rest," Nick advised.

"Don't light any matches for another hour," Frank told Ida.

Tessie closed all but one window and they left. Ida and Helen remained with Morris in the bedroom.

Frank lingered in Helen's room but nothing welcomed him there.

Later he dressed and went down to the store. Business was brisk. Ida came down, and though he begged her not to, shut the store.

That afternoon Morris developed a fever and the doctor said he had to go to the hospital. An ambulance came and took the grocer away, his wife and daughter riding with him. From his window upstairs, Frank watched them go.

Sunday morning the store was still shut tight. Though he feared to, Frank considered knocking on Ida's door and asking for the key. But Helen might open the door, and since he would not know what to say to her over the doorsill, he went instead down the cellar, and mounting the dumb-waiter, wriggled through the little window in the air shaft, into the store toilet.* Once in the back, the clerk shaved and had his

---

***wriggled through the little window in the air shaft, into the store toilet**:「환기통에

coffee. He thought he would stay in the store till somebody told him to scram;* and even if they did, he would try in some way to stay longer. That was his only hope left, if there was any. Turning the front door lock, he carried in the milk and rolls and was ready for business. The register was empty, so he borrowed five dollars in change from Sam Pearl, saying he would pay it back from what he took in. Sam wanted to know how Morris was and Frank said he didn't know.

Shortly after half past eight, the clerk was standing at the front window when Ida and her daughter left the house. Helen looked like last year's flower. Observing her, he felt a pang of loss, shame, regret.* He felt an unbearable deprivation*—that yesterday he had almost had some wonderful thing but today it was gone, all but the misery of remembering it was. Whenever he thought of what he had almost had it made him frantic. He felt like rushing outside, drawing her into a doorway,* and declaring the stupendous value* of his love for her. But he did nothing. He didn't exactly hide but he didn't show himself, and they soon went away to the subway.

Later he thought he would also go and see Morris in the hospital, as soon as he knew which one he was in—after they got home; but they didn't return till midnight. The store was closed and he saw them from his room, two dark figures getting out of a cab. Monday, the day the Norwegians opened

---

있는 작은 창문으로 비집고 빠져 나와, 가게 화장실로 들어갔다」

***till somebody told him to scram**:「누가 그에게 나가라고 말할 때까지」

***pang of loss, shame, regret**:「상실과 수치와 회한의 고통」 *e.g.* the pangs of conscience「양심의 쓰라린 가책」

***deprivation**:「상실, 아까운 손실」

***drawing her into a doorway**:「그녀를 문간으로 들어오게 하여」

***the stupendous value**:「엄청난 가치」

their store, Ida came down at seven A.M. to paste a piece of paper on the door saying Morris Bober was sick and the grocery would be closed till Tuesday or Wednesday. To her amazement, Frank Alpine was standing, in his apron, behind the counter. She entered in anger.

Frank was miserably nervous that Morris or Helen, either or both, had told her all the wrong he had done them, because if they had, he was finished.

"How did you get in here?" Ida asked wrathfully.

He said through the air shaft window. "Thinking of your trouble, I didn't want to bother you about the key, Mrs."

She vigorously forbade him ever to come in that way again. Her face was deeply lined, her eyes weary, mouth bitter, but he could tell that for some miraculous reason she didn't know what he had done.*

Frank pulled a handful of dollar bills out of his pants pocket and a little bag of change, laying it all on the counter.

"I took in forty-one bucks yesterday."

"You were here yesterday?"

"I got in how I explained you.* There was a nice rush around four till about six. We are all out of potato salad."*

Her eyes grew tears. He asked how Morris felt.

She touched her wet lids with a handkerchief. "Morris has pneumonia."

"Ah, too bad. Give him my sorrow if you can. How's he coming along out of it?"

***he could tell that . . . what he had done**:「어떤 불가사의한 이유로 그녀는 아직도 자기가 한 짓을 모르고 있음을 그는 알 수 있었다」

***I got in how I explained you.**=I entered in the way that I previously explained to you.

***We are all out of potato salad**:「감자 샐러드도 다 팔렸읍니다」

"He's a very sick man, he has weak lungs."

"I think I'll go to see him in the hospital."

"Not now," Ida said.

"When he's better. How long do you think he'll be there?"

"I don't know. The doctor will telephone today."

"Look, Mrs," Frank said. "Why don't you stop worrying about the store while Morris is sick and let me take care of it? You know I make no demands."

"My husband told you to go out from the store."

He furtively studied her face but there was no sign of accusation.*

"I won't stay very long," he answered. "You don't have to worry about that. I'll stay here till Morris gets better. You'll need every cent for the hospital bills. I don't ask a thing for myself."

"Did Morris tell you why you must leave?"

His heart galloped.* Did she or didn't she know? If yes, he would say it was a mistake—deny he had touched a red cent in the register.* Wasn't the proof of that in the pile of dough that lay right in front of her eyes on the counter? But he answered, "Sure, he didn't want me to hang around* Helen any more."

"Yes, she is a Jewish girl. You should look for somebody else. But he also found out that Schmitz was sick since December and kept closed his store in the mornings, also

---

***He furtively studied her face but there was no sign of accusation**:「그는 살그머니 그녀의 얼굴을 살펴봤지만 자기를 비난하는 기색은 없었다」

***His heart galloped**:「그의 심장의 고동이 빨라졌다」

***If yes, he would say it . . . the register**:「그녀가 만일 알고 있다면, 그것은 오해에 불과하다고 말하려 했다—금전 등록기 안의 1센트도 만진 일이 없다고 부인하려 했다」

***hang around**:「귀찮게 붙어다니다」

earlier in the night. This was what improved our income, not you."

She then told Frank that the German had sold out and two Norwegians were opening up today.

Frank flushed. "I knew that Schmitz was sick and kept his store closed sometimes, but that isn't what made your business get better. What did that was how hard I worked building up the trade. And I bet I can keep this place in the same shape it is,* even with two Norwegians around the corner or three Greeks. What's more, I bet I can raise the take-in higher."

Though she was half-inclined to believe him, she couldn't.

"Wait, you'll see how smart you are."

"Then let me have a chance to show you. Don't pay me anything, the room and meals are enough."

"What," she asked in desperation, "do you want from us?"

"Just to help out. I have my debt to Morris."*

"You have no debt. He has a debt to you that you saved him from the gas."

"Nick smelled it first. Anyway I feel I have a debt to him for all the things he has done for me. That's my nature, when I'm thankful, I'm thankful."

"Please don't bother Helen. She is not for you."

"I won't."

She let him stay. If you were so poor where was your choice?*

***I bet I can keep this place in the same shape it is**:「나는 이 상점을 현재대로 끌고 가고야 말겠읍니다」

***I have my debt to Morris**:「저는 Morris씨에게 신세를 진 것이 있읍니다」

***If you were so poor where was your choice?**:「가난한 사람에게는 좋고 싫고를 가릴 수조차 없는 것이다」

Taast and Pederson opened up with a horseshoe of spring flowers in their window.* Their pink handbills brought them steady business and Frank had plenty of time on his hands. During the day only a few of the regulars* came into the grocery. At night, after the Norwegians had closed, the grocery had a spurt of activity,* but when Frank pulled the strings of the window lights around eleven, he had only fifteen dollars in the register. He didn't worry too much. Monday was a slow day anyway, and besides, people were entitled to grab off a few specials while they could get them. He figured nobody could tell what difference the Norwegians would make to the business until a couple of weeks had gone by, when the neighborhood was used to them and things settled back to normal. Nobody was going to give specials away that cheap* every day. A store wasn't a charity, and when they stopped giving something for nothing,* he would match them in* service and also prices and get his customers back.

Tuesday was slow, also as usual. Wednesday picked up a little, but Thursday was slow again. Friday was better. Saturday was the best day of the week, although not so good as Saturdays lately. At the end of the week the grocery was close to a hundred short of its recent weekly average.* Expecting some-

---

***with a horseshoe of spring flowers in their window**:「U자형의 봄꽃 화환을 유리창에 장식하고」

***a few of the regulars**:「몇몇 단골손님」

***the grocery had a spurt of activity**:「식료품점은 갑자기 바빠졌다」 *e.g.* a spurt of anger「격노」

***that cheap**:「그렇게 싸게」 that는 지시부사로서 "그렇게" "그만큼"의 뜻임. *e.g.* that far, that much 등

***for nothing**:「공짜로」

***match . . . in~**:「~에서 …와 경쟁하다」

***the grocery was close to . . . average**:「가게의 수입은 최근의 주평균 수입보다 약 백

thing like this, Frank had closed up for a half hour on Thursday and taken the trolley to the bank.* He withdrew twenty-five dollars from his savings account and put the money into the register, five on Thursday, ten on Friday and ten on Saturday, so that when Ida wrote the figures down in her book each night she wouldn't feel too bad. Seventy-five less for the week wasn't as bad as a hundred.

Morris, better after ten days in the hospital, was brought home in a cab by Ida and Helen and laid to bed to convalesce. Frank, gripping his courage,* thought of going up to see him and this time starting out right,* right off. He thought of bringing him some fresh baked goods to eat, maybe a piece of cheese cake that he knew the grocer liked, or some apple strudel;* but the clerk was afraid it was still too soon and Morris might ask him where he had got the money to buy the cake. He might yell, "You thief, you, the only reason you stay here still is because I am sick upstairs." Yet if Morris felt this way he would already have told Ida what Frank had done. The clerk now was sure he hadn't mentioned it, because she wouldn't have waited this long to pitch him out on his ear.* He thought a lot about the way Morris kept things to himself.*

불이나 부족했다」

***had . . . taken the trolley to the bank**:「전차를 타고 은행으로 갔다」

***gripping his courage**:「용기를 내어」

***start out right**:「정직하게 일하기 시작하다」 *e.g.* He started out to reform the society.「그는 사회개혁에 착수했다」

***apple strudel**:「사과를 밀가루 반죽으로 엷게 싸서 구운 과자」

***because she wouldn't have waited this long to pitch him out on his ear**:「그녀는 이토록 오래 기다리지 않고 그를 서둘러 내쫓았을 것이기 때문에」 pitch ~ out on one's ear「~을 신속히 내쫓아 버리다」

***keep ~ to oneself**:「~을 마음에 간직해 두다, ~을 남에게 알리지 않다」

It was a way a person had if he figured he could be wrong about how he sized up* a situation. It could be that he might take a different view of Frank in time. The clerk tried to invent reasons why it might be worth the grocer's while, after he got on his feet again,* to keep him on in the grocery. Frank felt he would promise anything to stay there. "Don't worry that I ever will steal from you or anybody else any more, Morris. If I do, I hope I drop dead on the spot." He hoped that this promise, and the favor he was doing him by keeping the store open, would convince Morris of his sincerity. Yet he thought he would wait a while longer before going up to see him.

Helen hadn't said anything to anybody about him either and it wasn't hard to understand why. The wrong he had done her was never out of his mind. He hadn't intended wrong but he had done it; now he intended right. He would do anything she wanted, and if she wanted nothing he would do something, what he should do; and he would do it all on his own will, nobody pushing him but himself. He would do it with discipline and with love.

All this time he had snatched only glimpses of her, though his heart was heavy with all he hoped to say. He saw her through the plate glass window—she on the undersea side. Through the green glass she looked drowned, yet never, God help him, lovelier.* He felt a tender pity for her, mixed with shame for having made her pitiable. Once, as she came home

---

***size up**=form judgement of「판단하다, 평가하다」

***after he got on his feet again**:「Morris가 병에서 회복된 후에」

***Through the green glass . . . lovelier**:「초록색 유리를 통해 보니 그녀는 물에 빠진 것처럼 보였지만, 그녀는 이전의 어느 때보다도 더 아름답게 보였다」

from work, her eyes happened to look into his and showed disgust. Now I am finished, he thought, she will come in here and tell me to go die some place; but when she looked away she was never there. He was agonized to be so completely apart from her, left apologizing to her shadow, to the floral fragrance she left in the air.* To himself he confessed his deed, but not to her. That was the curse of it, to have it to make but who would listen? At times he felt like crying but it made him feel too much like a kid to cry. He didn't like to, did it badly.*

Once he met her in the hall. She was gone before he could move his lips. He felt for her a rush of love. He felt, after she had left, that hopelessness was his punishment. He had expected that punishment to be drastic, swift; instead it came slowly—it never came, yet was there.

There was no approach to her. What had happened had put her in another world, no way in.*

Early one morning, he stood in the hall till she came down the stairs.

"Helen," he said, snatching off the cloth cap he now wore in the store, "my heart is sorrowful. I want to apologize."

Her lips quivered. "Don't speak to me," she said, in a voice choked with contempt.* "I don't want your apologies. I don't want to see you, and I don't want to know you. As soon as my father is better, please leave. You've helped him and my

---

***to the floral fragrance she left in the air**:「그녀가 주위에 남긴 꽃의 향기에 대하여」

***He didn't like to, did it badly**:「그는 울고 싶지 않았음에도 불구하고 몹시 울고 말았다」

***What had happened had put her in another world, no way in**:「과거에 일어난 일 때문에 그녀는 딴 세계로 가 버린 것이며, 그 세계로 들어갈 통로는 이제 닫혀 있었다」

***in a voice choked with contempt**:「경멸로 가득 찬 음성으로」

mother and I thank you for that, but you're no help to me. You make me sick."

The door banged behind her.

That night he dreamed he was standing in the snow outside her window. His feet were bare yet not cold. He had waited a long time in the falling snow, and some of it lay on his head and had all but frozen his face; but he waited longer until, moved by pity, she opened the window and flung something out. It floated down; he thought it was a piece of paper with writing on it but saw that it was a white flower, surprising to see in wintertime. Frank caught it in his hand. As she had tossed the flower out through the partly opened window he had glimpsed her fingers only, yet he saw the light of her room and even felt the warmth of it. Then when he looked again the window was shut tight, sealed with ice.* Even as he dreamed, he knew it had never been open. There was no such window. He gazed down at his hand for the flower and before he could see it wasn't there, felt himself wake.

The next day he waited for her at the foot of the stairs, bareheaded in the light that fell on his head from the lamp.

She came down, her frozen face averted.

"Helen, nothing can kill the love I feel for you."

"In your mouth it's a dirty word."

"If a guy did wrong, must he suffer forever?"

"I personally don't care what happens to you."

Whenever he waited at the stairs, she passed without a word, as if he didn't exist. He didn't.

***the window was shut tight, sealed with ice**:「창문은 꼭 닫혀 있고 얼음으로 밀폐되어 있었다」

If the store blows away some dark night I might as well be dead, Frank thought. He tried every way to hang on.* Business was terrible. He wasn't sure how long the grocery could last or how long the grocer and his wife would let him try to keep it alive. If the store collapsed everything would be gone.* But if he kept it going there was always the chance that something might change, and if it did, maybe something else might. If he kept the grocery on its feet till Morris came down,* at least he would have a couple of weeks to change how things were. Weeks were nothing but it might as well be nothing because to do what he had to do he needed years.

Taast and Pederson had the specials going week after week. They thought of one come-on* after another to keep the customers buying. Frank's customers were disappearing. Some of them now passed him in the street without saying hello. One or two crossed the trolley tracks and walked on the other side of the street, not to have to see his stricken face* at the window. He withdrew all he had left in the bank and each week padded* the income a little, but Ida saw how bad things were. She was despondent and talked of giving the place over to the auctioneer. This made him frantic. He felt he had to try harder.

***He tried every way to hang on**:「그는 가게에 매달려 살아가려고 온갖 노력을 다 했다」

***If the store collapsed everything would be gone**:「만일 가게가 문닫으면 모든 일이 끝장나는 것이다」

***If he kept the grocery on its feet till Morris came down**:「Morris가 내려올 때까지 그가 가게를 제대로 끌어간다면」

***come-on**=lure「유혹」 decoy「미끼」

***his stricken face**:「괴로와하고 있는 그의 얼굴」

***pad**:「메워넣다」

He tried out all sorts of schemes. He got specials on credit* and sold half the stuff, but then the Norwegians began to sell it cheaper, and the rest remained on his shelves. He stayed open all night for a couple of nights* but did not take in enough to pay for the light. Having nothing much to do, he thought he would fix up* the store. With all but the last five dollars from the bank account, he bought a few gallons of cheap paint. Then removing the goods from one section of the shelves, he scraped away the mildewed paper on the walls* and painted them a nice light yellow. When one section was painted he went to work on the next. After he had finished the walls he borrowed a tall ladder, scraped the ceiling bit by bit and painted it white. He also replaced a few shelves and neatly finished them in dime store varnish.* In the end he had to admit that all his work hadn't brought back a single customer.

Though it seemed impossible the store got worse.*

"What are you telling Morris about the business?" Frank asked Ida.

"He don't ask me so I don't tell him," she said dully.

"How is he now?"

"Weak yet. The doctor says his lungs are like paper. He reads or he sleeps. Sometimes he listens to the radio."

***on credit**:「외상으로」

***He stayed open all night for a couple of nights**:「그는 이틀밤을 밤새도록 가게문을 열어놓았다」

***fix up**:「수리하다」

***the mildewed paper on the walls**:「곰팡이 난 벽지」

***dime store varnish**:「싸구려 가게에서 산 와니스」 dime store=five-and-ten-cent store 「싸구려 백화점」

***Though it seemed impossible the store got worse**:「더 악화될 것 같지 않으면서도, 장사는 점점 더 안 되었다」 it는 사태를 가리킴 *e.g. It* is all over with him.「그는 이제 끝장났다」 *It* seems as if it would snow.「눈이 올 것 같다」

"Let him rest. It's good for him."

She said again, "Why do you work so hard for nothing? What do you stay here for?"

For love, he wanted to say, but hadn't the nerve. "For Morris."

But he didn't fool her. She would even then have told him to pack and go, although he kept them for the moment off the street,* had she not known for a fact that Helen no longer bothered with him. He had probably through some stupidity fallen out of her good graces.* Possibly her father's illness had made her more considerate of them. She had been a fool to worry.* Yet she now worried because Helen, at her age, showed so little interest in men. Nat had called but she wouldn't go near the phone.

Frank scraped down on expenses.* With Ida's permission he had the telephone removed. He hated to do it because he thought Helen might sometime come down to answer it. He also reduced the gas bill by lighting only one of the two radiators downstairs. He kept the one in the front lit so the customers wouldn't feel the cold, but he no longer used the one in the kitchen. He wore a heavy sweater, a vest and a flannel shirt under his apron, and his cap on his head. But Ida, even with her coat on, when she could no longer stand the

---

***although he kept them for the moment off the street**:「그는 당분간 그들을 거리에서 방황하지 않게 했지만」

***He had probably . . . fallen out of her good graces**:「그는 아마도 …그녀의 호의을 잃어 버렸을 것이다」

***She had been a fool to worry**:「그런 근심을 하다니 그녀는 바보였다」 to worry는 이유를 나타내는 부사적 부정사로서 문장전체를 수식함. He must be crazy to talk like that.「그렇게 말하다니 그는 미쳤음에 틀림없다」

***Frank scraped down on expenses**:「Frank는 경비를 깎아내렸다」

emptiness of the front, or the freezing back, escaped upstairs. One day she came into the kitchen, and seeing him salting up a soup plate of boiled potatoes for lunch,* began to cry.

He thought always of Helen. How could she know what was going on in him? If she ever looked at him again she would see the same guy on the outside.* He could see out but nobody could see in.

When Betty Pearl got married Helen didn't go to the wedding. The day before she apologized embarrassedly, said she wasn't feeling too well—blamed her father's illness. Betty said she understood, thinking it had something to do with her brother. "Next time," she remarked with a little laugh, but Helen, seeing she was hurt, felt bad. She reconsidered facing the ceremony, rigmarole, relatives, Nat or no Nat*—maybe she could still go; but couldn't bring herself to.* She was no fixture for a wedding. They might say to her, "With such a face, go better to a funeral." Though she had many a night wept herself out, her memories kept a hard hold in her mind. Crazy woman, how could she have brought herself to love such a man? How could she have considered marrying someone not Jewish? A total, worthless stranger. Only God had

---

***seeing him salting up a soup plate of boiled potatoes for lunch**:「점심으로 먹을 삶은 감자 한 접시에 그가 소금을 뿌리는 것을 보고」 a soup plate「수프 접시」

***If she ever looked at him again she would see the same guy on the outside**:「만약 그녀가 그를 또다시 쳐다본다면 외관으로 변함없는 똑같은 남자를 보았을 것이다」

***She reconsidered facing the ceremony, rigmarole, relatives, Nat or no Nat—**:「그녀는 Nat야 있건 말건, 식에 참석하여 장황한 이야기를 듣고, 친척들을 만나볼까 하고 다시 생각해 봤다」 rigmarole「데데한 긴 이야기」

***but couldn't bring herself to**:「그러나 그녀는 아무리해도 갈 마음이 나지 않았다」
e.g. I could not bring myself to believe it:「나는 아무리해도 그것을 믿을 마음이 나지 않았다」

saved her from a disastrous mistake. With such thoughts she lost all feeling for weddings.

Her sleep suffered. Every day she dreaded every night. From bedtime to dawn she eked out only a few wearisome unconscious hours.* She dreamed she would soon awake and soon awoke. Awake, she felt sorry for herself, and sorrow, no soporific, induced sorrow.* Her mind stamped out endless worries: her father's health, for instance; he showed little interest in recovery.* The store, as ever. Ida wept in whispers in the kitchen. "Don't tell Papa." But they would sometime soon have to. She cursed all grocery stores. And worried at seeing nobody, planning no future. Each morning she crossed off the calendar the sleepless day to be. God forbid such days.

Though Helen turned over all but four dollars of her check to her mother and it went into the register, they were always hard up for cash to meet expenses. One day Frank got an idea about how he might lay hold of* some dough. He thought he would collect an old bill from Carl, the Swedish painter. He knew the painter owed Morris over seventy bucks. He looked for the housepainter every day but Carl did not come in.

One morning Frank was standing at the window when he

***From bedtime to dawn she eked out . . . unconscious hours**:「잠자리에 들어 새벽까지, 그녀는 애써서 겨우 몇 시간 지루한 무의식의 잠의 세계에 들어갔을 뿐이다」 eke out「보충하다」

***sorrow, no soporific, induced sorrow**:「수면제가 아닌 슬픔은 또 다른 슬픔을 불러일으켰다」 soporific「수면제, 마취제」

***he showed little interest in recovery**:「그는 자기의 몸이 회복되는 것에 대하여 거의 관심을 보이지 않았다」

***lay hold of**:「쥐다, 붙잡다」

saw him leave Karp's with a wrapped bottle in his pocket.

Frank ran out and reminded Carl of his old bill. He asked him to pay something on the account.

"This is all fixed up with me and Morris," the painter answered. "Don't stick your dirty nose in."*

"Morris is sick, he needs the dough," Frank said.

Carl shoved the clerk aside and went on his way.

Frank was sore.* "I'll collect from that drunk bastard."

Ida was in the store, so Frank said he would be back soon. He hung up his apron, got his overcoat and followed Carl to his house. After getting the address, he returned to the grocery. He was still angered at the painter for the way he had acted when he had asked him to pay his bill.

That evening he returned to the shabby four-story tenement and climbed the creaking staircase to the top floor. A thin, dark-haired woman came wearily to the door. She was old until his eyes got used to her face,* then he realized she was young but looked old.

"Are you Carl the painter's wife?"

"That's right."

"Could I talk to him?"

"On a job?" she said hopefully.

"No. Something different."

She looked old again. "He hasn't worked for months."

"I just want to talk to him."

She let him into a large room which was a kitchen and

***Don't stick your dirty nose in**:「쓸데없이 참견하지 마」

***Frank was sore**:「Frank는 성이 났다」

***She was old until his eyes got used to her face**:「그녀의 얼굴에 그의 눈이 익숙해질 때까지는, 그녀를 늙은 여자로 알았다」

living room combined, the two halves separated by an undrawn curtain.* In the middle of the living room part stood a kerosene heater that stank. This smell mixed with the sour smell of cabbage cooking. The four kids, a boy about twelve and three younger girls, were in the room, drawing on paper, cutting and pasting. They stared at Frank but silently went on with what they were doing. The clerk didn't feel comfortable. He stood at the window, looking down on the dreary lamplit street. He now figured he would cut the bill in half if the painter would pay up the rest.*

The painter's wife covered the sizzling frying pan* with a pot lid and went into the bedroom. She came back and said her husband was sleeping.

"I'll wait a while," said Frank.

She went back to her frying. The oldest girl set the table, and they all sat down to eat. He noticed they had left a place for their old man. He would soon have to crawl out of his hole.* The mother didn't sit down. Paying no attention to Frank, she poured skim milk out of a container into the kids' glasses, then served each one a frankfurter* fried in dough. She also gave everybody a forkful of hot sauerkraut.*

The kids ate hungrily, not talking. The oldest girl glanced at Frank then stared at her plate when he looked at her.

When the plates were empty she said, "Is there any more,

***by an undrawn curtain**:「열려진 커튼에 의하여」 halves 다음에 being을 넣을 것. undraw「(커튼 등을) 당겨서 열다」

***He now figured he would···the rest**:「만약 칠장이가 현금으로 지불한다면 외상금액을 반감시켜 주겠다고 그는 속으로 생각하고 있었다」

***the sizzling frying pan**:「지글지글 소리내는 후라이팬」

***crawl out of his hole**:「그의 잠자리에서 기어나오다」

***frankfurter**:「쇠고기와 돼지고기를 혼합한 소시지」

***sauerkraut**:「소금에 절인 양배추」

Mama?"

"Go to bed," said the painter's wife.

Frank had a bad headache from the stink of the heater.

"I'll see Carl some other time," he said. His spit tasted like brass.*

"I'm sorry he didn't wake up."

He ran back to the store. Under the mattress of his bed he had his last three bucks hidden. He took the bills and ran back to Carl's house. But on the way he met Ward Minogue. His face was yellow and shrunken, as if he had escaped out of a morgue.*

"I been looking for you," said Ward. He pulled Frank's revolver out of a paper bag. "How much is this worth to you?"

"Shit."

"I'm sick," sobbed Ward.

Frank gave the three bucks to him and later dropped the gun into a sewer.

He read a book about the Jews, a short history. He had many times seen this book on one of the library shelves and had never taken it down, but one day he checked it out to satisfy his curiosity. He read the first part with interest, but after the Crusades and the Inquisition,* when the Jews were having it tough,* he had to force himself to keep reading.* He

---

***His spit tasted like brass**:「그의 침에서 놋쇠맛이 났다」

***morgue**:「시체보관소」

***the Crusades and the Inquisition**:「십자군과 종교재판」

***when the Jews were having it tough**:「유태민족이 고난을 받던 때」 it는 의미가 없고 그저 having의 목적어가 된 것임. *e.g.* If we must fight, we must fight *it* out.「싸워야 한다면 우리는 끝까지 싸워야 한다」

***he had to force himself to keep reading**:「그는 억지로 계속 읽어갔다」

skimmed the bloody chapters but read slowly the ones about their civilization and accomplishments. He also read about the ghettos,* where the half-starved, bearded prisoners spent their lives trying to figure it out why they were the Chosen People. He tried to figure out why but couldn't. He couldn't finish the book and brought it back to the library.

Some nights he spied on the Norwegians. He would go around the corner without his apron and stand on the step of Sam Pearl's hallway, looking across the street at the grocery and fancy delicatessen. The window was loaded with all kinds of shiny cans. Inside, the store was lit as bright as day. The shelves were tightly packed with appetizing goods that made him feel hungry. And there were always customers inside, although his place was generally empty. Sometimes after the partners locked up and went home, Frank crossed to their side of the street and peered through the window into the dark store, as if he might learn from what he saw in it the secret of all good fortune* and so change his luck and his life.

One night after he had closed the store, he took a long walk and stepped into the Coffee Pot, an all-night joint he had been in once or twice.*

Frank asked the owner if he needed a man for night work.

"I need a counterman for coffee, short orders,* and to wash the few dishes," the owner answered.

***ghetto**:「유태인 거주지구」

***the secret of all good fortune**:「모든 번영의 비결」 fortune=prosperity「번영」

***the Coffee Pot, an all-night joint he had been in once or twice**:「그가 전에 한 두 번 왔던, 밤새도록 영업하는 가게 Coffee Pot」

***short order**:「즉석요리」

"I am your boy,"* said Frank.

The work was from ten to six A.M. and paid thirty-five dollars. When he got home in the morning, Frank opened the grocery. At the end of a week's working, wihtout ringing it up, he put the thirty-five into the cash register. This, and Helen's wages, kept them from going under.*

The clerk slept on the couch in the back of the store during the day. He had rigged up a buzzer* that waked him when somebody opened the front door. He did not suffer from lack of sleep.

He lived in his prison in a climate of regret that he had turned a good thing into a bad, and this thought, though ancient, renewed the pain in his heart. His dreams were bad, taking place in the park at night. The garbage smell stank in his nose. He groaned his life away, his mouth crammed with words he couldn't speak.* Mornings, standing at the store window, he watched Helen go off to work. He was there when she came home. She walked, slightly bowlegged,* toward the door, her eyes cast down, blind to his presence. A million things to say, some extraordinary, welled up* in him, choked his throat; daily they died. He thought endlessly of escape, but that would be what he always did last— beat it.* This time he

---

***I am your boy**:「제가 일하겠읍니다」

***go under**:「파산하다, 파멸하다」

***rig up a buzzer**:「버저를 장치하다」

***He groaned his life away, his mouth crammed with words he couldn't speak**:「말할 수 없는 말로 입이 가득 채워진 채, 그는 신음하며 살아갔다」 his mouth 앞에 with를 넣어 해석할 것. cram=stuff「채워넣다」

***bowlegged**:「앙가발이의」

***well up**=spring「샘 솟다」

***that would be what he always did last—beat it**:「도망치는 일은 지금까지 그가 항상 해 오던 짓이다—또 도망쳐야 하나?」 beat it「도망치다, 나가다」

would stay. They would carry him out in a box. When the walls caved in* they could dig for him with shovels.

Once he found a two-by-four pine board* in the cellar, sawed off a hunk, and with his jackknife began to carve it into something. To his surprise it turned into a bird flying. It was shaped off balance* but with a certain beauty. He thought of offering it to Helen but it seemed too rough a thing—the first he had ever made. So he tried his hand at something else. He set out to carve her a flower and it came out a rose starting to bloom. When it was done it was delicate in the way its petals were opening yet firm as a real flower. He thought about painting it red and giving it to her but decided to leave off* the paint. He wrapped the wooden flower in store paper, printed Helen's name on the outside, and a few minutes before she came home from work, taped the package onto the outside of the mailbox in the vestibule.* He saw her enter, then heard her go up the stairs. Looking into the vestibule, he saw she had taken his flower.

The wooden flower reminded Helen of her unhappiness. She lived in hatred of herself for having loved the clerk against her better judgment. She had fallen in love, she thought, to escape her predicament. More than ever she felt

---

***cave in**=collapse sink down「무너지다」

***a two-by-four pine board**:「2×4인치 소나무 목재」

***It was shaped off balance**:「그것은 균형이 잡히지 않은 상태로 되어 있었다」 *e.g.* It threw him off balance.「그것으로 인하여 그는 마음의 균형을 잃었다」

***leave off**:「그만두다」 *e.g.* They left off work earlier than usual.「그들은 평상시보다 일찍 일을 끝냈다」

***taped the package onto the outside of the mailbox in the vestibule**:「현관의 우편함 바깥 쪽에 그 꾸러미를 끈으로 묶었다」 tape「납작한 줄로 묶다」

herself a victim of circumstance—in a bad dream symbolized by the nightmarish store below, and the relentless, scheming presence in it of the clerk,* whom she should have shouted out of the house but had selfishly spared.*

In the morning, as he aimed a pail of garbage into the can at the curb, Frank saw at the bottom of it his wooden flower.

***in a bad dream symbolized by . . . clerk**:「악몽 같은 아래 층의 가게와 그 안에 도사린 잔인하고 교활한 점원의 존재에 의해 상징되는 악몽 속에서」

***had selfishly spared**:「이기심 때문에 그대로 눈감아 주고 있었다」

8

On the day he had returned from the hospital Morris felt the urge to* jump into his pants and run down to the store, but the doctor, after listening to his lungs, then tapping his hairy knuckles across the grocer's chest, said, "You're coming along fine, so what's your big hurry?" To Ida he privately said, "He has to rest, I don't mean maybe," Seeing her fright he explained "Sixty isn't sixteen," Morris, after arguing a bit, lay back in bed and after that didn't care if he ever stepped into the store again.* His recovery was slow.

With reservations, spring was on its way. There was at least more light in the day; it burst through the bedroom windows. But a cold wind roared in the streets, giving him goose pimples in bed; and sometimes, after half a day of pure sunshine, the sky darkened and some rags of snow fell. He was filled with melancholy* and spent hours dreaming of his boyhood. He remembered the green fields. Where a boy runs he never forgets. His father, his mother, his only sister whom he hadn't seen in years, gottenyu. The wailing wind cried to him. . . .

The awning flapping below in the street awoke his dread of

***feel the urge to ~**:「~하고 싶은 강한 충동을 느끼다」
***didn't care if he ever stepped into the store again**:「다시 가게로 내려가는 일에 대해서 그는 신경을 쓰지 않았다」
***He was filled with melancholy**:「그는 우울한 기분이 되었다」

the grocery.* He had not for a long time asked Ida what went on downstairs but he knew without thinking. He knew in his blood.* When he consciously thought of it he remembered that the register rang rarely, so he knew again. He heard heavy silence below. What else can you hear from a graveyard whose noiseless tombstones hold down* the sick earth? The smell of death seeped up through the cracks in the floor. He understood why Ida did not dare go downstairs but sought anything to do here. Who could stay in such a place but a goy whose heart was stone? The fate of his store floated like a black-feathered bird dimly in his mind; but as soon as he began to feel stronger, the thing grew lit eyes, worrying him no end.* One morning as he sat up against a pillow, scanning yesterday's *Forward,* his thoughts grew so wretched that he broke into sweat and his heart beat erratically. Morris heaved aside his covers, strode crookedly out of bed and began hurriedly to dress.

Ida hastened into the bedroom. "What are you doing, Morris—a sick man?"

"I must go down."

"Who needs you? There is nothing there. Go rest some more."

He fought a greedy desire to* get back into bed and live there but could not quiet his anxiety.

***The awning flapping below in the street awoke his dread of the grocery**:「아래 거리에서 차양이 펄럭이는 소리를 듣게 되자 가게에 대한 공포심이 되살아났다」

***He knew in his blood**:「육감으로 그는 알아냈다」

***hold down**=press down「누르다」

***the thing grew lit eyes, worrying him no end**:「그 물건은 빛나는 눈이 되어 그를 끝없이 괴롭혔다」 *e.g.* lit candles「점화된 양초」

***He fought a greedy desire to～**:「～하고 싶은 강한 욕망과 싸웠다」

"I must go."

She begged him not to but he wouldn't listen.

"How much he takes in now?" Morris asked as he belted his trousers.

"Nothing. Maybe seventy-five."

"A week?"

"What else?"

It was terrible but he had feared worse. His head buzzed with schemes for saving the store.* Once he was downstairs he felt he could make things better. His fear came from being here, not where he was needed.*

"He keeps open all day?"

"From morning till night—why I don't know."

"Why he stays here?" he asked with sudden irritation.

"He stays," she shrugged.

"What do you pay him?"

"Nothing—he says he don't want."

"So what he wants—my bitter blood?"

"He says he wants to help you."

He muttered something to himself. "You watch him sometimes?"

"Why should I watch him?" she said, worried. "He took something from you?"

"I don't want him here no more. I don't want him near Helen."

"Helen don't talk to him."

***His head buzzed with schemes for saving the store**:「그의 머리 속은 가게를 구해보려는 계획으로 바빴다」 buzz=move rapidly「바삐 돌아다니다」

***His fear came from being here, not where he was needed**:「그가 있어야 할 곳에 있지 않고 2층에서 쉬고 있기 때문에 공포심이 일어나는 것이었다」

He gazed at Ida. "What happened?"

"Go ask her. What happened with Nat? She's like you, she don't tell me anything."

"He's got to leave today.* I don't want him here."

"Morris," she said hesitantly, "he gave you good help, believe me. Keep him one more week till you feel stronger."

"No." He buttoned his sweater and despite her pleading went shakily down the stairs.

Frank heard him coming and grew cold.

The clerk had for weeks feared the time the grocer would leave his bed, although in a curious way he had also looked forward to it. He had spent many fruitless hours trying to construct a story that would make Morris relent and keep him on.* He had planned to say, "Didn't I starve rather than to spend the money from the holdup, so I could put it back in the register— which I did, though I admit I took a couple of rolls and some milk to keep myself alive?" But he had no confidence in that. He could also proclaim his long service to the grocer, his long patient labor in the store; but the fact that he had stolen from him during all this time spoiled his claim. He might mention that he had saved Morris after he had swallowed a bellyful of gas, but it was Nick who had saved him as much as she. The clerk felt he was without any good appeal to the grocer—that he had used up* all his credit with him, but

---

***He's got to leave today**:「그는 오늘 나가야만 해」 have got to ～=must, have to ～, *e.g.* I've got to write a letter=I must write a letter.

***tying to construct a story . . . keep him on**:「Morris의 마음을 누그러지게 하고 Frank를 계속 가게에 있게 만들 수 있는 거짓말을 꾸미려 하면서」 relent=become less severe

***use up**=consume completely「다 써 버리다」

then he was struck by a strange and exciting idea, a possible if impossible ace in the hole.* He figured that if he finally sincerely revealed his part in the holdup, he might in the telling of it arouse in Morris a true understanding of his nature, and a sympathy for his great struggle to overcome his past. Understanding his clerk's plight—the meaning of his long service to him—might make the grocer keep him on, so he would again have the chance to square everything with all concerned.* As he pondered this idea, Frank realized it was a wild chance that might doom rather than redeem him.* Yet he felt he would try it if Morris insisted he had to leave. What could he lose after that? But when the clerk pictured himself saying what he had done and had been forgiven by the grocer, and he tried to imagine the relief he would feel, he could't, because his overdue confession* wouldn't be complete or satisfying so long as he kept hidden what he had done to his daughter. About that he knew he could never open his mouth, so he felt that no matter what he did manage to say there would always be some disgusting thing left unsaid, some further sin to confess, and this he found utterly depressing.

Frank was standing behind the counter near the cash register, paring his fingernails* with his knife blade when the

---

***he was struck by . . . ace in the hole**:「혹시 불가능할지도 모르지만 가능성 있는 비장의 묘수, 즉 기이하고도 재미있는 생각이 갑자기 그의 머리에 떠올랐다」 ace in the hole「최후의 으뜸패, 비장의 수」

***the chance to square everything with all concerned**:「관련된 모든 사람과 모든 일을 청산할 기회」

***Frank realized it was a wild chance that might doom rather than redeem him**:「그 생각은 그를 구하기보다 단죄할 가능성이 있는 무모한 모험임을 Frank는 깨달았다」 a wild scheme「무모한 계획」

***his overdue confession**:「그의 지연된 고백」

***paring his fingernails**:「손톱을 깎으면서」

grocer, with his face pale, the skin of it loose, his neck swimming in his shirt collar, his dark eyes unfriendly, entered the store through the hall door.

The clerk tipped his cap and edged away from the cash register.

"Glad to see you back again, Morris," he said, regretting he hadn't once gone up to see him in all the days the grocer had been upstairs. Morris nodded coldly and went into the rear. Frank followed him in, fell on one knee, and lit the radiator.

"It's pretty cold here, so I better light this up. I've been keeping it shut off to save on the gas bill."

"Frank," Morris said firmly, "I thank you that you helped me when I took in my lungs so much gas, also that you kept the store open when I was sick, but now you got to go."*

"Morris," answered Frank, heavy-hearted, "I swear I never stole another red cent after that last time, and I hope God will strike me dead right here if it isn't the truth."

"This ain't why I want you to go," Morris answered.

"Then why do you?" asked the clerk, flushing.

"You know," the grocer said, his eyes downcast.

"Morris," Frank said, at agonizing last,* "I have something important I want to tell you. I tried to tell you before only I couldn't work my nerve up. Morris, don't blame me now for what I once did, because I am now a changed man, but I was one of the guys that held you up that night. I swear to God I didn't want to once I got in here, but I couldn't get out of it.*

***you got to go**=you have got to go「너는 나가야 한다」

***at agonizing last**:「잠시 고민한 끝에」 *e.g.* at long last「오랜 시간이 지난 후에 겨우, 마침내」

***I didn't want to once I got in here, but I couldn't get out of it**:「제가 여기에 들어오자마자 강도질을 할 마음은 없어졌읍니다만 저는 빠져 나갈 수 없었읍니다」

I tried to tell you about it— that's why I came back here in the first place,* and the first chance I got I put my share of the money back in the register—but I didn't have the guts* to say it. I couldn't look you in the eye. Even now I feel sick about what I am saying, but I'm telling it to you so you will know how much I suffered on account of what I did, and that I am very sorry you were hurt on your head—even though not by me. The thing you got to understand is I am not the same person I once was. I might look so to you, but if you could see what's been going on in my heart you would know I have changed. You can trust me now, I swear it, and that's why I am asking you to let me stay and help you."

Having said this, the clerk experienced a moment of extraordinary relief—a treeful of birds broke into song;* but the song was silenced when Morris, his eyes heavy, said, "This I already know, you don't tell me nothing new."

The clerk groaned. "How do you know it?"

"I figured out when I was laying upstairs in bed. I had once a bad dream that you hurt me, then I remembered—"

"But I didn't hurt you," the clerk broke in emotionally. "I was the one that gave you the water to drink. Remember?"

"I remember. I remember your hands. I remember your eyes. This day when the detective brought in here the holdupnik that he didn't hold me up I saw in your eyes that you did something wrong. Then when I stayed behind the hall door and you stole from me a dollar and put it in your pocket, I

***in the first place**:「처음에, 우선」

***guts**=courage

***a treeful of birds broke into song**:「나무에 가득 앉은 새들이 갑자기 노래를 부르기 시작했다」

thought I saw you before in some place but I didn't know where. That day you saved me from the gas I almost recognized you; then when I was laying in bed I had nothing to think about, only my worries and how I threw away my life in this store, then I remembered when you first came here, when we sat at this table, you told me you always did the wrong thing in your life; this minute when I remembered this I said to myself, 'Frank is the one that made on me the holdup.'"

"Morris," Frank said hoarsely, "I am sorry."

Morris was too unhappy to speak. Though he pitied the clerk, he did not want a confessed criminal around.* Even if he had reformed, what good would it do to keep him here*—another mouth to feed, another pair of eyes to the death watch?

"Did you tell Helen what I did?" sighed Frank.

"Helen ain't interested in you."

"One last chance, Morris," the clerk pleaded.

"Who was the antisimeet* that he hit me on the head?"

"Ward Minogue," Frank said after a minute. "He's sick now."

"Ah," sighed Morris, "the poor father."

"We meant to hold Karp up, not you. Please let me stay one more month. I'll pay for my own food and also my rent."

"With what will you pay if I don't pay you—with my debts?"

***he did not want a confessed criminal around**:「그는 자백한 범인이 주위에 있는 것을 원하지 않았다」

***Even if he had reformed, what good would it do to keep him here . . . ?**:「비록 그가 개심했다 해도 그를 여기에 두는 게 무슨 소용이 있겠는가？」

***antisimeet**:「반(反)유태주의자」

"I have a little job at night after the store closes. I make a few odd bucks."*

"No," said the grocer.

"Morris, you need my help here. You don't know how bad everything is."

But the grocer had set his heart against his assistant* and would not let him stay.

Frank hung up his apron and left the store. Later, he bought a suitcase and packed his few things. When he returned Nick's radio, he said good-by to Tessie.

"Where are you going now, Frank?"

"I don't know."

"Are you ever coming back?"

"I don't know. Say good-by to Nick."

Before leaving, Frank wrote a note to Helen, once more saying he was sorry for the wrong he had done her. He wrote she was the finest girl he had ever met. He had bitched up* his life. Helen wept over the note but had no thought of answering.

Although Morris liked the improvements Frank had made in the store he saw at once that they had not the least effect on business. Business was terrible. And with Frank's going the income shrank impossibly lower, a loss of ten terrible dollars from the previous week. He thought he had seen the store at

---

***I make a few odd bucks**:「저는 약간 돈을 벌고 있죠」

***the grocer had set his heart against his assistant**:「식료품점 주인은 자기의 점원의 말을 들어주지 않았다」 *e.g.* set one's mind against a person's petition「청원을 들어주지 않다」

***bitch up**:「엉망진창으로 하다」

its worst but this brought him close to fainting.*

"What will we do?" he desperately asked his wife and daughter, huddled in their overcoats one Sunday night in the unheated back of the store.

"What else?" Ida said, "give right away in auction."

"The best thing is to sell even if we have to give away," Morris argued. "If we sell the store we can also make something on the house.* Then I can pay my debts and have maybe a couple thousand dollars. But if we give in auction how can I sell the house?"

"So if we sell who will buy?" Ida snapped.

"Can't we auction off the store without going into bankruptcy?"* Helen asked.

"If we auction we will get nothing. Then when the store is empty and it stays for rent, nobody will buy the house. There are already two places for rent on this block. If the wholesalers hear I went in auction they will force me in bankruptcy and take away the house also. But if we sell the store, then we can get a better price for the house."

"Nobody will buy," Ida said. "I told you when to sell but you wouldn't listen."

"Suppose you did sell the house and store," Helen asked, "what would you do then?"

"Maybe I could find a small place, maybe a candy store. If I could find a partner we could open up a store in a nice neighborhood."

***this brought him close to fainting**:「이 사실을 보고 그는 기절할뻔 했다」

***If we sell the store we can also make something on the house**:「우리가 가게를 판다면 이 집도 얼마쯤은 건질 수 있겠지」

***go into bankruptcy**:「파산하다」

Ida groaned. "Penny candy I won't sell. Also a partner we had already, he should drop dead."*

"Couldn't you look for a job?" Helen said.

"Who will give me at my age a job?" Morris asked.

"You're acquainted with some people in the business,"* she answered. "Maybe somebody could get you a cashier's job in a supermarket."

"You want your father to stand all day on his feet with his varicose veins?"* Ida asked.

"It would be better than sitting in the freezing back of an empty store."

"So what will we do?" Morris asked, but nobody answered.

Upstairs, Ida told Helen that things would be better if she got married.

"Who should I marry, Mama?"

"Louis Karp," said Ida.

The next evening she visited Karp when he was alone in the liquor store and told him their troubles. The liquor dealer whistled through his teeth.

Ida said, "You remember last November you wanted to send us a man by the name Podolsky, a refugee he was interested to go in the grocery business?"

"Yes. He said he would come here but he caught a cold in his chest."

"Did he buy some place a store?"

***Also a partner we had already, he should drop dead**:「우리는 동업자도 갖어 봤죠, 그 동업자는 죽어 마땅한 사람이었어요」

***You're acquainted with some people in the business**:「아빠는 장사하는 사람들과 좀 알고 있겠죠」

***varicose veins**:「정맥노장(靜脈怒張)의 혈관」

"Not yet," Karp said cautiously.

"He still wants to buy?"

"Maybe. But how could I recommend him a store like yours?"

"Don't recommend him the store, recommend him the price. Morris will sell now for two thousand cash. If he wants the house we will give him a good price.* The refugee is young, he can fix up the business and give the goyim a good competition."*

"Maybe I'll call him sometime," Karp remarked. He casually inquired about Helen. Surely she would be getting married soon?

Ida faced the way she hoped the wind was blowing.* "Tell Louis not to be so bashful. Helen is lonely and wants to go out with somebody."

Karp coughed into his fist. "I don't see your clerk any more. How is that?" He spoke offhandedly,* walking carefully, knowing the size of his big feet.

"Frank," Ida said solemnly, "don't work for us any more. Morris told him to leave, so he left last week."

Karp raised bushy brows. "Maybe," he said slowly, "I will call Podolsky and tell him to come tomorrow night. He works in the day."

"In the morning is the best time. Comes in then a few

***we will give him a good price**:「우리는 그에게 싼 값으로 팔겠어요」

***can···give the goyim a good competition**:「이방인들을 상대로 멋지게 경쟁할 수도 있죠」

***Ida faced the way she hoped the wind was blowing**:「자기가 바라던 대로 불기 시작한 바람의 방향으로 얼굴을 돌렸다」 자기가 바라던 화제가 나와 기꺼이 말하기 시작했다는 뜻.

***offhandedly**:「아무렇게나, 허투루」

Morris's old customers."

"I will tell him to take off* Wednesday morning," Karp said.

He later told Louis what Ida had said about Helen, but Louis, looking up from clipping his fingernails, said she wasn't his type.*

"When you got gelt in your pocket any woman is your type," Karp said.

"Not her."

"We will see."

The next afternoon Karp came into Morris's and speaking as if they were the happiest of friends, advised the grocer: "Let Podolsky look around here but not too long. Also keep your mouth shut about the business. Don't try to sell him anything. When he finishes in here he will come to my house and I will explain him what's what."

Morris, hiding his feelings, nodded. He felt he had to get away from the store, from Karp, before he collapsed. Reluctantly he agreed to do as the liquor dealer suggested.

Early Wednesday morning Podolsky arrived, a shy young man in a thick greenish suit that looked as if it had been made out of a horse blanket. He wore a small foreign-looking hat and carried a loose umbrella. His face was innocent and his eyes glistened with good will.

Morris, uneasy at what he was engaged in, invited Podolsky into the back, where Ida nervously awaited him, but the

---

***take off**:「휴가를 얻다」

***said she wasn't his type**:「그녀는 자기에게 맞는 형이 아니라고 말했다」

refugee tipped his hat and said he would stay in the store. He slid into the corner near the door and nothing could drag him out. Luckily, a few customers dribbled in,* and Podolsky watched with interest as Morris professionally handled them.

When the store was empty, the grocer tried to make casual talk from behind the counter, but Podolsky, though constantly clearing his throat, had little to say. Overwhelmed by pity for the poor refugee, at what he had in all probability lived through, a man who had sweated blood to save a few brutal dollars,* Morris, unable to stand the planned dishonesty, came from behind the counter, and taking Podolsky by the coat lapels,* told him earnestly that the store was run-down but that a boy with his health and strength, with modern methods and a little cash, could build it up in a reasonable time and make a decent living out of it.

Ida shrilly called from the kitchen she needed the grocer to help her peel potatoes, but Morris kept on talking till he was swimming in his sea of woes;* then he recalled Karp's warning, and though he felt more than ever that the liquor dealer was thoroughly an ass, abruptly broke off the story he was telling. Yet before he could tear himself away from the refugee, he remarked, "I could sell for two thousand, but for fifteen-sixteen cash, anybody who wants it can take the store.

***a few customers dribbled in**:「몇몇 손님이 들어왔다」 dribble「방울져 떨어지다」 물방울이 똑똑 떨어지듯 손님이 조금 들어왔다는 뜻.

***Overwhelmed by pity for the poor refugee . . . dollars**:「아마도 고달픈 인생을 살아왔으리라고 생각하고, 몇 푼 안 되는 돈을 벌기 위해 피땀 흘린 사람, 즉 가난한 피난민에 대한 연민에 마음이 움직여서」

***taking Podolsky by the coat lapels**:「Podolsky의 코트의 옷깃을 잡고」

***Morris kept on talking till he was swimming in his sea of woes**:「Morris는 계속 이야기를 했으며 드디어 그는 자기도 모르는 사이에 슬픈 감정에 빠져들고 말았다」

The house we will talk about later. Is this reasonable?"

"Why not?" Podolsky murmured, then again clammed up.*

Morris retreated into the kitchen. Ida looked at him as if he had committed murder but did not speak. Two or three more people appeared, then after ten-thirty the dry trickle of customers stopped.* Ida grew fidgety* and tried to think of ways to get Podolsky out of the place but he stayed on. She asked him to come into the back for a glass of tea; he courteously refused. She remarked that Karp must now be anxious to see him; Podolsky bobbed his head and stayed. He tightened the cloth around his umbrella stick. Not knowing what else to say she absently promised to leave him all her recipes for salads.* He thanked her, to her surprise, profusely.

From half past ten to twelve nobody approached the store. Morris went down to the cellar and hid. Ida sat dully in the back. Podolsky waited in his corner. Nobody saw as he eased himself and his black umbrella out of* the grocery and fled.

On Thursday morning Morris spat on his shoebrush and polished his shoes. He was wearing his suit. He rang the hall bell for Ida to come down, then put on his hat and coat, old but neat because he rarely used them. Dressed, he rang up "no sale" and hesitantly pocketed eight quarters.

He was on his way to Charlie Sobeloff, an old partner.

***clam up**=become silent, refuse to speak

***the dry trickle of customers stopped**:「몇몇 안 되는 손님도 이제 오지 않았다」 trickle「실개천, 물방울」

***Ida grew fidgety**:「Ida는 초조해지기 시작했다」 fidgety=restless

***all her recipes for salads**:「그녀가 아는 모든 샐러드 요리법」

***ease . . . out of**～:「살그머니 ～에서 빠져나가다」

Years ago, Charlie, a cross-eyed* but clever conniver,* had come to the grocer with a meager thousand dollars in his pocket, borrowed money, and offered to go into partnership with him*—Morris to furnish four thousand—to buy a grocery Charlie had in mind. The grocer disliked Charlie's nervousness and pale cross-eyes, one avoiding what the other looked at;* but he was persuaded by the man's nagging enthusiasm and they bought the store. It was a good business, Morris thought, and he was satisfied. But Charlie, who had taken accountancy in night school, said he would handle the books,* and Morris, in spite of Ida's warnings, consented, because, the grocer argued, the books were always in front of his eyes for inspection. But Charlie's talented nose had sniffed the right sucker.* Morris never looked at the books until, two years after they had bought the place, the business collapsed.

The grocer, stunned, heartbroken, could not at first understand what had happened, but Charlie had figures to prove that the calamity had been bound to occur. The overhead* was too high—they had paid themselves too high wages—his fault, Charlie admitted; also profits were low, the price of goods increasing. Morris now knew that his partner had, behind his back, cheated, manipulated, stolen whatever lay

---

***cross-eyed**:「사팔뜨기의」
***clever conniver**:「영리한 책략가」
***offered to go into partnership with him**:「자기와 함께 동업하자고 제의했다」
***pale cross-eyes, one avoiding what the other looked at**:「한 쪽 눈이 보는 것을 다른 쪽 눈이 피하는 어슴프레한 사팔뜨기눈」
***handle the books**:「장부를 관리하다」
***Charlie's talented nose had sniffed the right sucker**:「Charlie의 뛰어난 코는 바른 흡반(吸盤)을 냄새맡았다」 잘 속는 사람을 찾아냈다는 뜻. sucker「잘 속는 사람」
***the overhead**:「간접비」

loose. They sold the place for a miserable price, Morris going out dazed, cleaned out,* whereas Charlie in a short time was able to raise the cash to repurchase and restock the store, which he gradually worked into a thriving self-service business. For years the two had not met, but within the last four or five years, the ex-partner, when he returned from his winters in Miami, for reasons unknown to Morris, sought out the grocer and sat with him in the back, his eyes roving,* his ringed fingers drumming on the table as he talked on about old times when they were young. Morris, through the years, had lost his hatred of them an, though Ida still could not stand him, and it was to Charlie Sobeloff that the grocer, with a growing sense of panic,* had decided to run for help, a job —anything.

When Ida came down and saw Morris, in his hat and coat, standing moodily by the door, she said in surprise, "Morris, where you going?"

"I go to my grave," the grocer said.

Seeing he was overwrought,* she cried out, clasping her hands to her bosom, "Where do you go, tell me?"

He had the door open. "I go for a job."

"Come back," she cried in anger. "Who will give you?"

But he knew what she would say and was already in the street.

As he went quickly past Karp's he noticed that Louis had

***Morris going out dazed, cleaned out**:「Morris는 어리벙벙한 채 가게를 떠났고 빈털털이가 되어 버렸다」 *e.g.* I am cleaned out「나는 한푼도 없다」

***his eyes roving**:「눈을 두리번거리면서」 앞에 with를 넣어 해석할 것. rove=look in changing directions「눈을 두리번거리다」

***with a growing sense of panic**:「점점 겁에 질려」

***Seeing he was overwrought**:「그가 너무 과로한 것을 보고」

five customers—drunkards all—lined up at the counter and was doing a thriving business in brown bottles. *He* had sold only two quarts of milk in four hours. Although it shamed him, Morris wished the liquor store would burn to the ground.*

At the corner he paused, overwhelmed by the necessity of choosing a direction. He hadn't remembered that space provided so many ways to go. He chose without joy. The day, though breezy, was not bad—it promised better, but he had little love left for nature. It gave nothing to a Jew.* The March wind hastened him along, prodding the shoulders.* He felt weightless, unmanned,* the victim in motion of whatever blew at his back;* wind, worries, debts, Karp, holdupniks, ruin. He did not go, he was pushed. He had the will of a victim, no will to speak of.

"For what I worked so hard for? Where is my youth, where did it go?"

The years had passed without profit or pity. Who could he blame? What fate didn't do to him he had done to himself. The right thing was to make the right choice but he made the wrong. Even when it was right it was wrong.* To understand why, you needed an education but he had none. All he knew was he wanted better but had not after all these years learned

---

***Although it shamed him, . . . ground**:「부끄러운 일이긴 했지만 Morris는 술가게가 타버렸으면 좋겠다고 생각했다」 it는 Morris . . . ground를 가리킴.

***It gave nothing to a Jew**:「자연은 유태인에게 아무것도 주지 않았다」 it는 nature임.

***prodding the shoulders**:「어깨를 밀면서」 prod=push, urge

***He felt weightless, unmanned**:「그는 자기가 무게가 없고 거세된 남자처럼 느껴졌다」

***the victim in motion of whatever blew at his back**:「그의 등에 불어대는 모든 것 때문에 움직이는 희생자」

***Even when it was right it was wrong**:「선택이 옳았을 때에도 결과는 나빴다」

how to get it. Luck was a gift. Karp had it, a few of his old friends had it, well-to-do men with grandchildren already, while his poor daughter, made in his image, faced—if not actively sought—old-maidhood.* Life was meager, the world changed for the worse. America had become too complicated. One man counted for nothing.* There were too many stores, depressions, anxieties. What had he escaped to here?

The subway was crowded and he had to stand till a pregnant woman, getting off, signaled him to her seat. He was ashamed to take it but nobody else moved, so he sat down. After a while he began to feel at ease, thought he would be satisfied to ride on like this, provided he never got to where he was going.* But he did. At Myrtle Avenue he groaned softly, and left the train.

Arriving at Sobeloff's Self-Service Market, Morris, although he had heard of the growth of the place from Al Marcus, was amazed at its size. Charlie had tripled the original space by buying the building next door and knocking out the wall between the stores, later running an extension three-quarters of the way into the back yards.* The result was a huge market with a large number of stalls and shelved sections loaded with groceries. The supermarket was so crowded with people that

---

***his poor daughter, made in his image, faced—if not actively sought—old-maidhood**:「자기를 꼭 닮은 딸은—일부러 그렇게 한 것은 아니지만—노처녀가 되어가고 있다」 in his image「그의 모양대로」

***One man counted for nothing**:「사람 하나쯤은 아무런 의미도 없다」 count for nothing「대수롭지 않다, 하찮다」

***provided he never got to where he was going**:「만약 그가 가려는 목적지에 절대로 도착할 수 없다면」

***later running an extension three-quarters of the way into the back yards**:「후에 뒷마당 쪽으로 도로의 3/4을 확장시켜서」

to Morris, as he peered half-scared through the window, it looked like a department store. He felt a pang, thinking that part of this might now be his if he had taken care of what he had once owned. He would not envy Charlie Sobeloff his dishonest wealth, but when he thought of what he could do for Helen with a little money his regret deepened that he had nothing.

He spied Charlie standing near the fruit stalls,* the balabos, surveying the busy scene with satisfaction. He wore a gray Homburg and blue serge suit, but under the unbuttoned suit jacket he had tied a folded apron around his silk-shirted paunch,* and wandered around, thus attired, overseeing. The grocer, looking through the window, saw himself opening the door and walking* the long half block to where Charlie was standing.

He tried to speak but was unable to, until after so much silence the boss said he was busy, so say it.

"You got for me, Charlie," muttered the grocer, "a job? Maybe a cashier or something? My business is bad, I am going in auction."

Charlie, still unable to look straight at him, smiled. "I got five steady cashiers but maybe I can use you part time. Hang up your coat in the locker downstairs and I'll give you directions what to do."

Morris saw himself putting on a white duck jacket with "Sobeloff's Self-Service" stitched in red over the region of the

---

***the fruit stalls**:「과일부」

***around his silk-shirted paunch**:「비단와이셔츠를 걸친 올챙이배 둘레에」

***The grocer . . . saw himself opening the door and walking~**:「식료품점 주인은 문을 열고 ~쪽으로 걸어가고 있는 자신을 머리 속으로 상상해 보았다」

heart.* He would stand several hours a day at the checking counter, packing, adding, ringing up the cash into one of Charlie's massive chromium registers. At quitting time, the boss would come over to check his money.

"You're short a dollar, Morris," Charlie said with a little chuckle, "but we will let it go."

"No," the grocer heard himself say. "I am short a dollar, so I will pay a dollar."

He took several quarters out of his pants pocket, counted four, and dropped them into his ex-partner's palm. Then he announced he was through, hung up his starched jacket, slipped on his coat and walked with dignity to the door. He joined the one at the window and soon went away.*

Morris clung to the edge of a silent knot of men* who drifted along Sixth Avenue, stopping at the employment agency doors to read impassively* the list of jobs chalked up on the blackboard signs. There were openings* for cooks, bakers, waiters, porters, handymen. Once in a while one of the men would secretly detach himself from the others and go into the agency. Morris followed along with them to Forty-fourth Street, where he noted a job listed for countermen behind a steam counter in a cafeteria. He went one flight up a narrow

---

***jacket with "Sobeloff's Self-Service" stitched in red over the region of the heart**: 「가슴 부분 위에 "Sobeloff's Self-Service"라고 붉은 실로 수놓은 자켓」

***He joined the one at the window and soon went away**:「(상상 속에서 움직여 온) 그는 창 옆에 있는 자기 자신과 하나가 되어 곧 떠나갔다」

***a silent knot of men**:「말 없는 한 떼의 사람들」 knot=group

***stopping at the employment agency doors to read impassively ~**:「직업소개소의 문간에 서서 ~을 침착하게 읽었다」

***opening**:「일자리」

staircase and into a room that smelled of tobacco smoke.* The grocer stood there, uncomfortable, until the big-faced owner of the agency happened to look up over the rolltop desk* he was sitting at.

"You looking for something, mister?"

"Counterman," Morris said.

"You got experience?"

"Thirty years."

The owner laughed. "You're the champ but they want a kid they can pay twenty a week.

"You got something for a man my experience?"*

"Can you slice sandwich meat nice and thin?"

"The best."

"Come back next week, I might have something for you."

The grocer continued along with the crowd. At Forty-seventh Street he applied for a waiter's job in a kosher restaurant but the agency had filled the job and forgotten to erase it from their sign.

"So what else you got for me?" Morris asked the manager.

"What work do you do?"

"I had my own store, grocery and delicatessen."

"So why do you ask for waiter?"

"I didn't see for counterman anything."*

"How old are you?"

***He went one flight up . . . tobacco smoke**:「좁은 계단을 2층까지 올라가 담배 연기가 나는 방으로 들어갔다」

***rolltop desk**:「셔터식 겉뚜껑이 달린 책상」

***You got something for a man my experience?**:「나와 같은 경험의 사람에 알맞는 일자리는 없소？」

***I didn't see for counterman anything**:「카운터 급사의 일자리를 찾아내지 못했읍니다」

"Fifty-five."

"I should live so long till you see fifty-five again,"* said the manager. As Morris turned to go the man offered him a cigarette but the grocer said his cough kept him from smoking.

At Fiftieth he went up a dark staircase and sat on a wooden bench at the far end of a long room.

The boss of the agency, a man with a broad back and a fat rear,* holding a dead cigar butt between stubby fingers,* had his heavy foot on a chair as he talked in a low voice to two gray-hatted Filipinos.*

Seeing Morris on the bench he called out, "Whaddye want, pop?"*

"Nothing. I sit on account* I am tired."

"Go home," said the boss.

He went downstairs and had coffee at a dish-laden table in the Automat.*

America.

Morris rode the bus to East Thirteenth Street, where Breitbart lived. He hoped the peddler would be home but only his son Hymie was. The boy was sitting in the kitchen, eating cornflakes with milk and reading the comics.*

"What time comes home papa?" Morris asked.

***I should live so long till you see fifty-five again**:「당신이 다시 55세가 될 때까지 내가 살았으면 좋겠군요」

***fat rear**:「살찐 엉덩이」 rear=buttock

***stubby fingers**:「뭉뚝한 손가락」

***gray-hatted Filipinos**:「회색 모자를 쓴 필리핀 사람들」

***Whaddye want, pop?**=What do you want, pop? pop「영감」

***on account**=because

***the Automat**:「자동판매식 음식점」

***the comics**:「(신문 · 잡지 따위의) 연속 만화」

"About seven, maybe eight," Hymie mumbled.

Morris sat down to rest. Hymie ate, and read the comics. He had big restless eyes.

"How old are you?"

"Fourteen."

The grocer got up. He found two quarters in his pocket and left them on the table. "Be a good boy. Your father loves you."

He got into the subway at Union Square and rode to the Bronx, to the apartment house where Al Marcus lived. He felt sure Al would help him find something. He would be satisfied, he thought, with little, maybe a night watchman's job.

When he rang Al's bell, a well-dressed woman with sad eyes came to the door.

"Excuse me," said Morris. "My name is Mr. Bober. I am an old-time customer Al Marcus's. I came to see him."

"I am Mrs. Margolies, his sister-in-law."

"If he ain't home I will wait."

"You'll wait a long time," she said, "they took him to the hospital yesterday."

Though he knew why he couldn't help asking.

"Can you go on living if you're already dead?"*

When the grocer got home in the cold twilight Ida took one look at him and began to cry.

"What did I tell you?"

That night Morris, alone in the store after Ida had gone up to soak her poor feet, felt an uncontrollable craving for* some

---

***Can you go on living if you're already dead?** :「(의사가 말한 대로) 당신이 이미 죽었다면 다시 살아갈 수 있겠소?」

***felt an uncontrollable craving for ~** :「~을 먹고 싶은 참을 수 없는 욕망을 느꼈다」

heavy sweet cream. He remembered the delicious taste of bread dipped in rich milk when he was a boy. He found a half-pint bottle of whipping cream in the refrigerator and took it, guiltily, with a loaf of stale* white bread, into the back. Pouring some cream into a saucer, he soaked it up with bread, greedily wolfing* the cream-laden bread.

A noise in the store startled him. He hid the cream and bread in the gas range.

At the counter stood a skinny* man in an old hat and a dark overcoat down to his ankles. His nose was long, throat gaunt, and he wore a wisp of red beard* on his bony chin.

"A gut shabos,"* said the scarecrow.

"A gut shabos," Morris answered, though shabos was a day away.*

"It smells here,* said the skinny stranger, his small eyes shrewd, "like a open grave."

"Business is bad."

The man wet his lips and whispered, "Insurinks you got —firc insurinks?"*

Morris was frightened. "What is your businecss?"

"How much?"

"How much what?"

***stale**:「말라서 딱딱한」
***wolf**=devour「게걸스레 먹다」
***skinny**=very thin, very lean「아주 마른」
***a wisp of red beard**:「한 다발의 붉은 수염」 *e.g.* a wisp of hair「한 다발의 머리털」
***A gut shabos**:「오순절(五旬節)을 축하합니다」 Shabos=Shabuoth 유월절의 이틀째부터 계산하여 50일이 되는 날을 오순절(五旬節)이라하여 축하함. 이 날은 Moses가 Sinai 산에서 율법을 받은 기념일임.
***shabos was a day away**:「shabos가 되려면 하루가 더 지나야 했다」 *e.g.* Christmas is still three months away.「크리스마스가 되려면 3개월이 더 지나야 한다」
***fire insurinks**:「화재보험」

"A smart man hears one word but he understand two. How much you got insurinks?"

"Two thousand for the store."

"Feh."

"Five thousand for the house."

"A shame. Should be ten."*

"Who needs ten for this house?"

"Nobody knows."

"What do you want here?" Morris asked, irritated.

The man rubbed his skinny, red-haired hands. "What does a macher want?"*

"What kind of a macher? What do you make?"

He shrugged slyly. "I make a living." The macher spoke soundlessly. "I make fires."

Morris drew back.*

The macher waited with downcast eyes. "We are poor people," he murmured.

"What do you want from me?"

"We are poor people," the macher said, apologetically. "God loves the poor people but he helps the rich. The insurinks companies are rich. They take away your money and what they give you? Nothing. Don't feel sorry for the insurinks companies."

He proposed a fire. He would make it swiftly, safely, economically—guaranteed to collect.

From his coat pocket he produced a strip of celluloid. "You

***Should be ten**:「1만불은 들었어야 하는데」

***What does a macher want**:「장인(匠人)이 달리 무엇을 원하겠소?」 der Macher「장인, 제조자」

***Morris drew back**:「Morris는 주춤했다」

know what is this?"

Morris, staring at it, preferred not to say.

"Celluloy," hissed the macher. He struck a large yellow match and lit the celluloid. It flared instantly. He held it a second then let it fall to the counter, where it quickly burned itself out. With a *poof* he blew away nothing.* Only the stench remained, floating in air.

"Magic," he hoarsely announced. "No ashes. This is why we use celluloy, not paper, not rags. You push a piece in a crack, and the fire burns in a minute. Then when comes the fire marshal* and insurinks investigator,* what they find?— nothing. For nothing they pay cash—two thousand for the store, five for the house." A smile crawled over his face.

Morris shivered. "You want me I should burn down my house and my store to collect the insurance?"

"I want," said the macher slyly, "tsu you want?"*

The grocer fell silent.

"Take," said the macher persuasively, "your family and go for a ride to Cunyiland. When you come back is the job finished. Cost—five hundred." He lightly dusted his fingers.

"Upstairs lives two people," muttered the grocer.

"When they go out?"

"Sometimes to the movies, Friday night." He spoke dully, not sure why he was revealing secrets to a total stranger.

"So let be Friday night. I am not kosher."*

***With a *poof* he blew away nothing**:「한 번 훅하고 불어서 그는 아무것도 남지 않게 다 날려 보냈다」

***the fire marshal**:「소방서장」

***insurinks investigator**:「보험회사의 조사원」

***tsu you want?**=do you want?

***I am not kosher**:「나는 유태교의 율법을 지키지 않는 사람이오」

"But who's got five hundred dollars?"

The macher's face fell. He sighed deeply. "I will make for two hundred. I will do a good job. You will get six—seven thousand. After, pay me another three hundred."

But Morris had decided. "Impossible."

"You don't like the price?"

"I don't like fires. I don't like monkey business."*

The macher argued another half hour and departed reluctantly.

The next night a car pulled up* in front of the door, and the grocer watched Nick and Tessie, dressed for a party, get in and drive off. Twenty minutes later Ida and Helen came down to go to a movie. Helen had asked her mother to go with her, and Ida said yes, seeing how restless her daughter was. When he realized that the house was deserted, Morris felt suddenly agitated.*

After ten minutes, he went up the stairs, and searched in a camphor-smelling trunk* in the small room for a celluloid collar he had once worn. Ida saved everything, but he couldn't locate* it. He searched in Helen's bureau drawer and found an envelope full of picture negatives.* Discarding several of her as a school girl, Morris took some of boys in bathing suits, nobody he recognized. Hurrying down, he found matches and went into the cellar. He thought that one of the bins* would

---

***monkey business**=fraud「사기」

***pull up**=stop

***Morris felt suddenly agitated**:「Morris는 갑자기 마음의 동요를 느꼈다」

***a camphor-smelling trunk**:「장뇌(樟腦) 냄새가 나는 트렁크」

***locate**=find out「찾아내다」

***an envelope full of picture negatives**:「사진원판이 가득 찬 봉투」

***bin**:「큰 상자」

be a good place to start the fire but settled instead on the air shaft. The flames would shoot up in an instant, and through the open toilet window into the store. Gooseflesh crept over him. He figured he could start the fire and wait in the hall. Once the flames had got a good start, he would rush into the street and ring the alarm. He could later say he had fallen asleep on the couch and had been awakened by the smoke. By the time the fire engines came, the house would be badly damaged. The hoses and axes would do the rest.*

Morris inserted the celluloid strips into a crack between two boards, on the inside of the dumb-waiter. His hand shook and he whispered to himself as he touched the match to the negatives. Then the flame shot up in a stupefying stench* and at once crawled up the wall of the dumb-waiter. Morris watched, hypnotized, then let out a terrible cry. Slapping frantically at the burning negatives, he knocked them to the cellar floor. As he hunted for something with which to beat out the fire* in the dumb-waiter, he discovered that the bottom of his apron was burning. He smacked* the flames with both hands and then his sweater sleeves began to blaze. He sobbed for God's mercy, and was at once roughly seized from behind and flung to the ground.

Frank Alpine smothered the grocer's burning clothes with his overcoat.* He banged out the fire in the dumb-waiter with

---

***The hoses and axes would do the rest**:「호스와 도끼가 나머지 일을 해 줄 것이다」
***Then the flame shot up in a stupefying stench**:「그러자 불길이 엄청난 악취를 풍기면서 솟아 올랐다」
***beat out the fire**:「불을 끄다」
***smack**=slap「찰싹 때리다」
***smothered the grocer's burning clothes with his overcoat**:「식료품점 주인의 타는 옷을 그의 외투로 덮어서 껐다」

his shoe.

Morris moaned.

"For Christ's sake," Frank pleaded, "take me back here."*

But the grocer ordered him out of the house.

***For Christ's sake, . . . take me back here**:「제발 저를 여기에 돌아오게 해 주세요」

9

Saturday night, about one A.M., Karp's store began to burn.

In the early evening, Ward Minogue had knocked on Frank's door and learned from Tessie that the clerk had moved.

"Where to?"

"I don't know. Ask Mr. Bober," Tessie said, anxious to get rid of him.

Downstairs, Ward peered through the grocery window and seeing Morris, hurriedly withdrew. Though alcohol nauseated him lately, his thirst for a drink was killing him. He thought if he could get a couple of swigs past the nausea* he would feel better. But all he had in his pocket was a dime, so he went into Karp's and begged Louis to trust him to a cheap fifth of anything.*

"I wouldn't trust you for a fifth of sewer water,"* Louis said.

Ward grabbed a bottle of wine from the counter and flung it at Louis' head. He ducked but the wine smashed some bottles on the shelf. As Louis, yelling murder, rushed into the street, Ward snatched a bottle of whiskey and ran out of the

---

***if he could get a couple of swigs past the nausea**:「만약에 구역질을 참고 두 모금을 그가 마신다면」 swig「꿀꺽꿀꺽 들이킴」

***begged Louis to trust him to a cheap fifth of anything**:「무엇이든 좋으니 싼 술 1/5갈론을 외상으로 달라고 Louis에게 간청했다」 fifth「1갈론의 1/5(주류용량의 단위)」

***a fifth of sewer water**:「하수도 물 1/5갈론」

store and up the block. He had gone past the butcher's when the bottle slipped from under his arm and broke on the sidewalk. Ward looked back with anguish but kept on running.

By the time the cops came Ward had disappeared. After supper that night, Detective Minogue, roaming the cold streets, saw his son in Earl's bar, standing over a beer. The detective went in by the side door but Ward saw him in the mirror and bolted out the front.* Although short of breath, driven by great fear, he ran toward the coal yard. Hearing his father behind him, Ward leaped across the rusted chain stretched in front of the loading platform and sped over the cobblestones* toward the back of the yard. He scrambled under one of the trucks in the shed.*

The detective, calling him filthy names, hunted him in the dark for fifteen minutes. Then he took out his pistol and fired a shot into the shed. Ward, thinking he would be killed, crawled out from under the truck and ran into his father's arms.

Though he pleaded with the detective not to hurt him, crying he had diabetes* and would surely get gangrene,* his father beat him mercilessly with his billy* until Ward collapsed.

Bending over him, the detective yelled, "I told you to stay

***bolted out the front**:「앞 문으로 달아났다」 bolt out=run quickly away

***sped over the cobblestones**:「자갈 위를 달렸다」 speed「질주하다, 서두르다」

***He scrambled under one of the trucks in the shed**:「그는 차고에 있는 트럭 밑으로 기어들어갔다」

***diabetes**:「당뇨병」

***get gangrene**:「탈저(脫疽)에 걸리다」

***billy**=truncheon「경찰봉」

the hell out of this neighborhood. This is my last warning to you. If I ever see you again, I'll murder you." He dusted his coat and left the coal yard.

Ward lay on the cobblestones. His nose had been gushing blood but it soon stopped. Getting up, he felt so dizzy he wept. He staggered into the shed and climbed into the cab of one of the coal trucks, thinking he would sleep there. But when he lit a cigarette he was overcome with nausea. Ward threw the butt out and waited for the nausea to leave him. When it did he was thirsty again. If he could climb the coal yard fence, then some of the smaller ones beyond it, he would land up in Karp's back yard.* He knew from having cased* the place once that the liquor store had a barred window in the back, but that the rusty iron bars were old and loose. He thought that if he got his strength back* he could force them apart.

He dragged himself over the coal yard fence, then more slowly over the others until he stood at last in Karp's weedy back yard. The liquor store had been closed since midnight and there were no lights burning in the house. Above the dark grocery one of Bober's windows was lit, so he had to be careful or the Jew might hear him.

Twice, at intervals of ten minutes,* he tried to bend the bars but failed. The third time, straining till he shook, he slowly forced the inside two apart.* The window was unlocked.

***he would land up in Karp's back yard**:「그는 Karp의 뒷마당에 내릴 수 있을 것이다」
***case**:「(범죄의 목적으로) 잘 보아두다」
***if he got his strength back**:「만약 그가 기운만 다시 차린다면」 get back=recover
***at intervals of ten minutes**:「10분 간격을 두고」
***The third time, straining till he shook, he slowly forced the inside two apart**:「세 번째로 온 몸이 떨리도록 힘을 주어 안의 철봉 둘을 서서히 양쪽으로 벌려놓았다」

Ward got his fingertips under it and lifted it with care because it squeaked. When it was open, he squeezed through the bent bars, squirming into the back of the liquor store.* Once in there he laughed a little to himself and moved around freely, knowing Karp was too cheap* to have a burglar alarm.* From the stock in the rear Ward sampled* and spat out three different brands of whiskey. Forcing himself, he gurgled down a third of a bottle of gin. In a couple of minutes he forgot his aches and pains and lost the sorrow he had been feeling for himself. He snickered* when he imagined Louis' comic puss* as he found the empty bottles all over the floor in the morning. Remembering the cash register, Ward staggered out front and rang it open. It was empty. He angrily smashed a whiskey bottle on it. A feeling of nausea gagged him and with a croak he threw up* over Karp's counter. Feeling better, he began by the light of the street lamp to smash the whiskey bottles against the cash register.

Mike Papadopolous, whose bedroom was right above the front part of the liquor store, was awakened by the noise. After five minutes he figured something was wrong so he got up and dressed. Ward had, in the meantime, destroyed a whole shelf of bottles, when he felt a hunger to smoke. It took him two minutes to get a match struck and the light touching his

---

***squirming into the back of the liquor store**:「술가게의 뒷방으로 몸을 뒤틀고 들어갔다」

***cheap**=stingy「인색한」

***burglar alarm**:「자동도난경보기」

***sample**:「시음하다」

***snicker**=giggle「숨 죽여 웃다」

***puss**=face

***with a croak he threw up**:「으악하고 그는 토했다」

butt. He tasted the smoke with pleasure as the flame briefly lit his face, then he shook the match and flipped it over his shoulder. It landed, still burning, in a puddle of alcohol.* The fire flew up with with a zoom. Ward, lit like a flaming tree, flailed at himself.* Screaming, he ran through the back and tried to get out of the window but was caught between the bars and, exhausted, died.

Smelling smoke, Mike came down in a rush* and seeing fire in the store, raced to the drugstore corner to turn in the alarm. As he was running back, the plate glass window of the liquor store exploded and a roaring flame boiled up in the place. After Mike had got his mother and the upstairs tenants out of the house, he ran into Bober's hall, shouting there was a fire next door. They were all up—Helen, who had been reading when the window crashed, had run up to call Nick and Tessie. They left the house, bundled in sweaters and overcoats, and stood across the street, huddled together with some passers-by, watching the fire destroy Karp's once prosperous business, then devour the house. Despite the heavy streams of water the firemen poured into the flames, the fire, fed by the blazing alcohol, rose to the roof,* and when it was at last smothered, all that was left of Karp's property was a gutted, dripping shell.*

***It landed, still burning, in a puddle of alcohol**:「성냥개비는 계속 타면서 알콜 웅덩이에 떨어졌다」

***Ward, lit like a flaming tree, flailed at himself**:「타오르는 나무처럼 봄에 불이 붙어 Ward는 자기 몸을 연거푸 후려쳤다」

***in a rush**:「서둘러」 *e.g.* live in a rush「분주한 생활을 하다」

***the fire, fed by the blazing alcohol, rose to the roof**:「타오르는 듯한 알콜이 공급되어 힘이 난 불길은 지붕까지 솟아 올랐다」 feed「연료(원료)를 공급하다」

***a gutted, dripping shell**:「속은 다 타 버리고 물이 뚝뚝 떨어지는 건물의 뼈대」 *e.g.* The house was gutted by fire.「그 집은 화재로 내부가 다 타 버렸다」

As the firemen began with grappling hooks* to tear out the burned fixtures and heave them onto the sidewalk, everybody fell silent. Ida moaned softly, with shut eyes thinking of Morris's burned sweater that she had found in the cellar, and the singed hair* she had noticed on his hands. Sam Pearl, lost without his bifocals, mumbled to himself. Nat, hatless, an overcoat on over pajamas, edged close to Helen until he stood by her side. Morris was fighting a tormenting emotion.

A car drew up* and parked beyond the drugstore. Karp got out with Louis and they crossed the hose-filled street to their store. Karp took one unbearable look at his former gesheft, and though it was for the most part insured, tottered forward and collapsed.* Louis yelled at him to wake up. Two of the firemen carried the stricken liquor dealer to his car, and Louis frantically drove him home.

Afterward Morris couldn't sleep. He stood at his bedroom window in his long underwear, looking down at the pile of burned and broken fixtures on the sidewalk. With a frozen hand the grocer clawed at a live pain in his breast.* He felt an overwhelming hatred of himself. He had wished it on Karp —just this. His anguish was terrible.

Sunday, the last of March, was overcast at eight A.M., and there were snow flurries* in the air. Winter still spits in my

---

***grappling hook**=grapnel「걸어 잡는 갈고랑쇠」
***the singed hair**:「불에 그슬린 털」
***A car drew up**:「차 한 대가 가까이 와서 섰다」
***tottered forward and collapsed**:「앞으로 비틀비틀 나가더니 쓰러져 버렸다」
***With a frozen hand the grocer clawed at a live pain in his breast**:「언 손으로 식료품점 주인은 심한 고통을 느낄 정도로 자기의 가슴을 쥐어 뜯었다」 *e.g.* a live hatred「심한 증오」
***snow flurry**:「눈보라」

face, thought the weary grocer. He watched the fat wet flakes melt as they touched the ground. It's too warm for snow, he thought, tomorrow will come April. Maybe. He had awakened with a wound, a gap in his side, a hole in the ground he might fall through* if he stepped outside where the liquor store had been. But the earth held him up and the odd feeling wore off. It went as he reflected it was no use mourning Karp's loss; his pocketbook would protect him from too much pain. Pain was for poor people. For Karp's tenants the fire was a tragedy, and for Ward Minogue, dead young; maybe also for the detective, but not for Julius Karp. Morris could have used the fire, so Karp had got it for free. Everything to him who has.*

As the grocer was thinking this, the liquor dealer, apparently the victim of a sleepless night, appeared in the falling snow and entered the grocery. He wore a narrow-brimmed hat with a foolish little feather in the band* and a double-breasted overcoat, but despite his stylish appearance, his eyes, with dark bags under them,* were filled with gloom, his complexion pasty, lips blue. Wherc his forehead had smacked the sidewalk last night he wore a plaster patch—an unhappy figure, the loss of his business the worst that could happen to him. He couldn't stand the vision of dollars he might be taking in, flying daily away.* Karp seemed embarrassed, ill.

***He had awakened with a wound . . . through**:「그는 상처를 입고 옆구리에 구멍이 나고 땅에 그가 빠질지도 모를 구덩이가 나 있는 불길한 공포를 느끼고 잠에서 깨어났다」

***Everything to him who has**:「돈 있는 사람에게 만사는 유리하게 되어 간다」

***a narrow-brimmed hat with a foolish little feather in the band**:「모자의 테에 바보스럽게 깃털을 단 좁은 테의 모자」

***his eyes, with dark bags under them**:「검은 가죽이 밑에 늘어져 있는 그의 눈」

***He couldn't stand the vision of dollars he might be taking in, flying daily away**:「그

The grocer, his shame awakened, invited him into the back for tea. Ida, also up early, made a fuss over him.

Karp took a hot sip or two of tea, but after setting the cup down, hadn't the strength to lift it from the saucer. After a fidgety silence he spoke. "Morris, I want to buy your house. Also the store." He drew a deep, trembly breath.

Ida let out a stifled cry. Morris was stupefied.

"What for? The business is terrible."

"Not so terrible," cried Ida.

"Don't interest me the grocery business," Karp gloomily replied. "Only the location.* Next door," he said, but couldn't go on.

They understood.

He explained it would take months to rebuild his house and place of business. But if he took over Morris's store he could have it refixtured, painted, stocked in a couple of weeks, thus keeping to a minimum his loss of trade.*

Morris couldn't believe his ears. He was filled with excitement and dread that somebody would tell him he had just dreamed a dream, or that Karp, fat fish, would turn into a fat bird and fly away, screeching, "Don't you believe me,"* or in some heartbreaking way change his mind.

So he put his foot on anticipation* and kept his mouth

가 벌어들일 달러가 매일 날아가 버리는 환상 때문에 그는 견딜 수 없었다」

***Only the location**:「단지 장소 때문이야」

***thus keeping to a minimum his loss of trade**:「이렇게 함으로써 장사의 손해를 최소한으로 줄일 수 있을 것이다」

***screeching, "Don't you believe me"**:「"내가 한 말을 믿지 마"라고 새된 소리로 외치면서」 screech=shriek「새된 소리로 외치다, 짹짹거리다」

***So he put his foot on anticipation**:「그래서 그는 부푼 기대를 꾹 눌러 버렸다」 put [set] one's foot on「꾹 누르다」

shut, but when Karp asked him to name his price the grocer had one ready. "Nine thousand for the house—three down, my equity*— and for the store twenty-five hundred cash." After all, bad as it was, the grocery was a going business, and for the refrigerator alone he had paid nine hundred dollars. With trepidation* he figured a fair fifty-five hundred in cash in his hands, enough after he had paid his debts to look for a new business. Seeing Ida's astonished expression, he was surprised at his nerve and thought Karp would surely laugh him in the face and offer less—which he would grab anyway; but the liquor dealer listlessly nodded. "I will give you twenty-five hundred for the store, less the auction price of stock and fixtures."*

"This is your business," Morris replied.

Karp could not bear to discuss the terms any further. "My lawyer will draw the contract."

When he left the grocery, the liquor dealer vanished in the swirling snow. Ida wept joyfully, while Morris, still stunned, reflected that his luck had changed. So had Karp's,* for what Karp had lost he had in a sense gained, as if to make up for* the misery the man had caused him in the past. Yesterday he wouldn't have believed how things would balance out today.*

***three down, my equity**:「담보 등을 빼면 순수 가격은 현금으로 3,000불이지」 down= in cash「현금으로」 equity「(담보・과세 따위를 뺀 재산 물건 등의) 순수 가격」

***With trepidation**:「속으로 떨면서」

***less the auction price of stock and fixtures**:「재고품과 설비의 경매가격은 공제하고」

***So had Karp's**= So had Karp's luck changed

***make up for**:「보상하다, 벌충하다」

***Yesterday he wouldn't have believed how things would balance out today**:「오늘이 되면 사태가 변해 어떻게 균형이 잡히게 될지 어제라면 그는 도저히 믿을 수 없었을 것이다」

The spring snow moved Morris profoundly. He watched it falling, seeing in it scenes of his childhood, remembering things he thought he had forgotten. All morning he watched the shifting snow. He thought of himself, a boy running in it, whooping* at blackbirds as they flew from the snowy trees; he felt an irresistible thirst to be out in the open.

"I think I will shovel the snow," he told Ida at lunchtime.

"Go better to sleep."

"It ain't nice for the customers."

"What customers—who needs them?"

"People can't walk in such high snow," he argued.

"Wait, tomorrow it will be melted."

"It's Sunday, it don't look so nice for the goyim that they go to church."

Her voice had an edge to it.* "You want to catch pneumonia, Morris?"

"It's spring," he murmured.

"It's winter."

"I will wear my hat and coat."

"Your feet will get wet. You have no galoshes."*

"Only five minutes."

"No," she said flatly.

Later, he thought.

All afternoon the snow came softly down and by evening it had reached a depth of six inches. When the snowing stopped, a wind rose and blew clouds of it through the streets. He

---

***whoop**=shout loudly「고함지르다」

***Her voice had an edge to it**:「그녀의 목소리가 날카롭게 변했다」

***galoshes**:「덧신」

watched at the front window.

Ida hung over him all day. He didn't get out till late. After closing he had sat relentlessly over a piece of store paper, writing a long list, until she grew impatient.

"Why do you stay so late?"

"I figure the stock for the auctioneer."*

"This is Karp's business."

"I must help, he don't know the prices."

Talk of the store's sale relieved her. "Come up soon," she yawned.

He waited until he felt she was asleep, then went down to the cellar for the shovel. He put on his hat and a pair of old gloves and stepped out into the street. To his surprise the wind wrapped him in an icy jacket,* his apron flapping noisily. He had expected, the last of March, a milder night. The surprise lingered in his mind but the shoveling warmed him. He kept his back to Karp's burned hole, though with the black turned white it wasn't too hard to look at.*

Scooping up a shovelful of snow he heaved it into the street. It turned to dust in mid-air and whirled whitely away.

He recalled the hard winters when he had first come to America. After about fifteen years they turned mild but now they were hard again. It had been a hard life, but now with God's help he would have an easier time.

***I figure the stock for the auctioneer**:「경매인들을 위해서 나는 재고품을 평가하고 있지」

***the wind wrapped him in an icy jacket**:「바람은 얼음 같은 자켓으로 그의 몸을 덮어버리는 듯했다」

***with the black turned white it wasn't too hard to look at**:「검은 것이 눈으로 희게 변했기 때문에 쳐다 보기에 그렇게 흉하지는 않았다」

He flung another load of snow into the street. "A better life," he muttered.

Nick and Tessie came home from somewhere.

"At least put something warm on, Mr. Bober," advised Tessie.

"I'm almost finished," Morris grunted.

"It's your health," said Nick.

The first floor window shot up.* Ida stood there in her flannel nightgown, her hair down.

"Are you crazy?" she shouted to the grocer.

"Finished," he answered.

"Without a coat—are you crazy?"

"Took me ten minutes."

Nick and Tessie went into the house.

"Come up now," Ida shouted.

"Finished," Morris cried. He heaved a last angry shovelful into the gutter. A little of the sidewalk remained to be cleaned but now that she was nagging he felt too tired to do it.

Morris dragged the wet shovel into the store. The warmth struck him across the head. He felt himself reeling and had a momentary fright* but after a glass of hot tea with lemon felt rested.

As he was drinking the tea it began to snow again. He watched a thousand flakes push at the window, as if they wanted to snow through the glass and in the kitchen. He saw the snow as a moving curtain, and then he saw it in lit single flakes, not touching each other.

***The first floor window shot up**:「2층 창문이 열렸다」

***He felt himself reeling and had a momentary fright**:「그는 현기증이 일어났으며 순간적인 공포심에 사로잡혔다」

Ida banged hard on the floor, so he finally closed and went upstairs.

She was sitting in her bathrobe with Helen in the living room, her eyes dark with anger. "Are you a baby you had to go out in the snow? What's the matter with such a man?"

"I had my hat on. What am I, tissue paper?"*

"You had pneumonia," she shouted.

"Mama, lower your voice," Helen said, "they'll hear upstairs."

"Who asked him to shovel snow, for God's sakes?"

"For twenty-two years stinks in my nose this store. I wanted to smell in my lungs some fresh air."

"Not in the ice cold."

"Tomorrow is April."

"Anyway," Helen said, "don't tempt fate, Papa."*

"What kind of winter can be in April?"

"Come to sleep." Ida marched off to bed.

He sat with Helen on the couch. Since hearing of Karp's visit that morning she had lost her moodiness,* looked again like a happy girl. He thought with sadness how pretty she was. He wanted to give her something—only good.

"How do you feel that I am selling the house and store?" he asked her.

"You know how I feel."

"Tell me anyway."

"Refreshed."

"We will move to a better neighborhood like you like. I will

***What am I, tissue paper?**:「내가 뭐 화장지 같은 존재인가?」

***Anyway, . . . don't tempt fate, Papa**:「어쨌든 운명에 도전하지는 마세요, 아빠」

***moodiness**:「우울」

find a better parnusseh. You will keep your wages."

She smiled at him.

"I remember when you were a little baby," Morris said. She kissed his hand.

"I want the most you should be happy."*

"I will be." Her eyes grew wet." If you only knew all the good things I'd like to give you, Papa."

"You gave me."

"I'll give you better."

"Look how it snows," said Morris.

They watched the snow through the moving windows, then Morris said good night.

"Sleep well," Helen said.

But he lay in bed restless, almost dejected. There was so much to do, so many changes to make and get used to.* Tomorrow was the day Karp would bring the deposit.* Tuesday the auctioneer would come and they would go over* the goods and fixtures. Wednesday they could hold the auction.* Thursday, for the first time in almost a generation, he would be without a place of business. Such a long time. After so many years in one place he hated the thought of having to get used to another.* He disliked leaving the

---

***I want the most you should be happy**:「나는 무엇보다도 네가 행복해지기를 제일 바라고 있지」 the most는 부사. *e.g.* He worked the most.「그가 제일 많이 일했다」 This troubles me the most.「이것이 제일 나를 괴롭힌다」

***There was so much to do, so many changes to make and get used to**:「해야 할 일이 너무 많고, 이룩해야 하고 익숙해져야 할 변화가 너무 많았다」

***the deposit**:「계약금」

***go over**=examine carefully or closely

***hold the auction**:「경매에 부치다」

***he hated the thought of having to get used to another**:「다른 장소에 익숙해져야 한다는 것은 생각하기도 싫었다」

neighborhood though he hadn't liked it. It made him uncomfortable to be in a strange place. He thought uneasily of having to locate, appraise, and buy a new store. He would prefer to live above the store, but Helen wanted them to take a small apartment, so let it be a small apartment. Once he had the store he would let them look for a place to live. But the store he would have to find himself. What he feared most was that he would make another mistake and again settle in a prison. The possibility of this worried him intensely. Why would the owner want to sell? Would he be an honest man or, underneath, a thief? And once he had bought the place, would business keep up or go down? Would times stay good?* Would he make a living? His thoughts exhausted him. He could feel his poor heart running a race against the merciless future.*

He fell heavily asleep but awoke in a couple of hours, drenched in hot sweat. Yet his feet were freezing and he knew that if he kept his thoughts on them he would break into shivering.* Then his right shoulder began to hurt, and when he forced himself to take a deep breath, his left side pained him. He knew he was sick and was miserably disappointed. He lay in the dark, trying not to think how stupid it had been to shovel the snow. He must have caught a chill. He thought he would not. He thought he was entitled, after twenty-two years, to a few minutes of freedom.* Now his plans would

---

***Would times stay good?**:「경기가 잘 지속될까?」

***He could feel . . . future**:「그는 자기의 약한 심장이 무자비한 미래를 상대로 경주를 하고 있음을 느낄 수 있었다」

***he knew that if he kept . . . shivering**:「그가 만약 발에 대해 계속 생각한다면 오한이 나게 될 것을 알 수 있었다」 them은 his feet를 가리킴.

***he was entitled . . . to a few minutes of freedom**:「그에게는 몇 분간의 자유를 누릴

have to wait, although Ida could finish the business with Karp and make arrangements with the auctioneer. Gradually he accepted the thought that he had a cold—maybe flu. He considered waking her to call a doctor but who could they call without a telephone? And if Helen got dressed and used Sam Pearl's phone, what an embarrassment that would be, waking up a whole family when she rang their bell; also arousing a doctor out of his precious sleep, who would say after examining him, "Mister, what's all the excitement? You got the flu, so stay in bed." For such advice he didn't need to call a doctor in his nightshirt. He could wait a few hours till morning. Morris dozed but felt fever shake him in his sleep.* He awoke with his hair stiff.* Maybe he had pneumonia? After a while he grew calmer. He was sick but sickness was nothing new to him. Probably if he hadn't shoveled snow he would have got sick anyway. In the last few days he hadn't felt so well—headachy, weak in the knees. Yet though he tried to resign himself to what had happened, he felt enormously bitter that he had become ill. So he had shoveled snow in the street, but did it have to snow in April? And if it did, did he have to get sick the minute he stepped out into the open air? It frustrated him hopelessly that every move he made seemed to turn into an inevitable thing.

He dreamed of Ephraim. He had recognized him when the

권리가 있었다」

***felt fever shake him in his sleep**:「그는 잠을 자면서 열 때문에 자기가 떨고 있음을 느꼈다」

***He awoke with his hair stiff**:「그는 잠이 깨니 머리털이 뻣뻣했다」

dream began by his brown eyes, clearly his father's.* Ephraim wore a beanie cut from the crown of an old hat of Morris's, covered with buttons and shiny pins,* but the rest of him was in rags. Though he did not for some reason expect otherwise, this and that the boy looked hungry shocked the grocer.

"I gave you to eat three times a day, Ephraim," he explained, "so why did you leave so soon your father?"

Ephraim was too shy to answer, but Morris, in a rush of love for him*— a child was so small at that age—promised him a good start in life.

"Don't worry, I'll give you a fine college education."

Ephraim—a gentleman—averted his face as he snickered.

"I give you my word. . . ."*

The boy disappeared in the wake of laughter.*

"Stay alive," his father cried after him.

When the grocer felt himself awaking, he tried to get back into the dream but it easily evaded him. His eyes were wet. He thought of his life with sadness. For his family he had not provided, the poor man's disgrace. Ida was asleep at his side. He wanted to awaken her and apologize. He thought of Helen. It would be terrible if she became an old maid. He moaned a little, thinking of Frank. His mood was of regret. I gave away my life for nothing. It was the thunderous truth.

***by his brown eyes, clearly his father's**:「분명히 아버지의 눈을 닮은 그의 갈색의 눈에 의하여」

***a beanie cut from the crown···pins**:「Morris의 낡은 모자의 꼭대기에서 잘라내어 만든, 단추와 번쩍이는 핀을 가득히 단 비니모자」 the crown「모자의 꼭대기」

***a rush of love for him**:「그에 대한 격렬한 사랑의 감정」 *e.g.* a rush of anger「격노」

***I give you my word . . .**:「내가 약속하지···」

***in the wake of laughter**:「웃은 다음에」 *e.g.* Miseries follow in the wake of a war.「전쟁 후에는 곤궁이 뒤따른다」

Was the snow still falling?

Morris died in the hospital, three days later, and was buried the day after in an enormous cemetery—it went on for miles—in Queens. He had been a member of a burial society since coming to America and the services took place in the Society's funeral parlor* on the Lower East Side, where the grocer had lived as a young man. At noon in the chapel's antechamber,* Ida, gray-faced and in mourning, every minute on the edge of fainting, sat in a high-backed tapestried chair, rocking her head. At her side, wasted, red-eyed from weeping, sat Helen. Landsleit, old friends, drawn by funeral notices in the Jewish morning papers, lamented aloud as they bent to kiss her, dropping pulpy tears on her hands. They sat on folding chairs facing the bereaved* and talked in whispers. Frank Alpine stood for a moment, his hat uncomfortably on, in a corner of the room. When the place grew crowded he left and seated himself among the handful of mourners already assembled in the long narrow chapel, dimly lit by thick, yellow wall lamps. The rows of benches were dark and heavy. In the front of the chapel, on a metal stand, lay the grocer's plain wooden coffin.

At one P.M., the gray-haired undertaker, breathing heavily, escorted the widow and her daughter to the front row on the left, not far from the coffin. A wailing began among the mourners. The chapel was a little more than half-full of* old

---

***the Society's funeral parlor**:「장례조합의 장례식장」
***the chapel's antechamber**:「교회의 대기실」
***the bereaved**:「유족들」
***The chapel was a little more than half-full of ~**:「교회는 ~에 의해서 반이 조금 넘을 정도로 차 있었다」

friends of the grocer, a few distant relatives, burial society acquaintances, and one or two customers. Breitbart, the bulb peddler, sat, stricken, against the right wall. Charlie Sobeloff, grown heavy-faced and stout, appeared, with Florida tan and sad crossed eye,* together with his stylish* wife, who sat staring at Ida. The entire Pearl family was present, Betty with her new husband, and Nat, sober, concerned for Helen, wearing a black skull cap. A few rows behind them was Louis Karp, alone and ill at ease among strangers. Also Witzig, the baker, who had served Morris bread and rolls for twenty years. And Mr. Giannola, the barber, and Nick and Tessie Fuso, behind whom Frank Alpine sat. When the bearded rabbi entered the chapel through a side door, Frank took off his hat but quickly put it on again.

The secretary of the Society appeared, a soft-voiced man with little hair, his glasses lit with reflections of the wall lamps, and read from a handwritten paper praise for Morris Bober and lamentation for his loss. When he announced the body could be seen, the undertaker and his assistant, a man in a chauffeur's cap, lifted the coffin lid and a few people came forward. Helen wept profusely at her father's waxen, berouged image,* the head wrapped in a prayer shawl, the thin mouth slightly twisted.

Ida flung up both arms, crying in Yiddish at the corpse, "Morris, why didn't you listen to me? You went away and left

---

***appeared, with Florida tan and sad crossed eye**:「Florida에서 햇볕에 그을린 피부색과 슬픔에 찬 사팔뜨기 눈을 하고 나타났다」

***stylish**=refined「멋진」

***at her father's waxen, berouged image**:「왁스와 루즈를 칠한 그녀의 아버지의 모습을 보고」

me with a child, alone in the world. Why did you do it?" She broke into racking sobs* and was gently escorted by Helen and the breathless undertaker to her seat, where she pressed her wet face against her daughter's shoulder. Frank went up last. He could see, where the prayer shawl fell back a little, the scar on the grocer's head, but outside of that it wasn't Morris. He felt a loss but it was an old one.

The rabbi then prayed, a stocky man with a pointed black beard.* He stood on the podium near the coffin,* wearing an old Homburg, a faded black frock coat over brown trousers, and bulbous shoes.* After his prayer in Hebrew, when the mourners were seated, in a voice laden with sorrow* he spoke of the dead man.

"My dear friends, I never had the pleasure to meet this good grocery man that he now lays in his coffin. He lived in a neighborhood where I didn't come in. Still and all* I talked this morning to people that knew him and I am now sorry I didn't know him also. I would enjoy to speak to such a man. I talked to the bereaved widow, who lost her dear husband. I talked to his poor beloved daughter Helen, who is now without a father to guide her. To them I talked, also to landsleit and old friends, and each and all told me the same, that Morris Bober, who passed away so untimely—he caught

---

***She broke into racking sobs**:「그녀는 몹시 괴로운 울음을 터뜨렸다」 *e.g.* a racking pain「심한 고통」

***a stocky man with a pointed black beard**:「끝이 뾰족한 검은 수염을 기른 땅딸막한 남자」 stocky=short and thick

***the podium near the coffin**:「관 옆의 단」

***bulbous shoes**:「구근(球根) 모양의 구두」

***in a voice laden with sorrow**:「슬픔에 찬 목소리로」

***still and all**=nevertheless「그래도」 after all「결국」

double pneumonia from shoveling snow in front of his place of business so people could pass by on the sidewalk—was a man who couldn't be more honest. Such a person I am sorry I didn't meet sometime in my life. If I met him somewhere, maybe when he went to visit in a Jewish neighborhood —maybe at Rosh Hashana* or Pesach*—I would say to him, 'God bless you, Morris Bober.' Helen, his dear daughter, remembers from when she was a small girl that her father ran two blocks in the snow to give back to a poor Italian lady a nickel that she forgot on the counter. Who runs in wintertime without hat or coat, without rubbers to protect his feet, two blocks in the snow to give back five cents that a customer forgot? Couldn't he wait till she comes in tomorrow? Not Morris Bober, let him rest in peace. He didn't want the poor woman to worry, so he ran after her in the snow. This is why the grocer had so many friends who admired him."

The rabbi paused and gazed over the heads of the mourners.

"He was also a very hard worker, a man that never stopped working. How many mornings he got up in the dark and dressed himself in the cold, I can't count. After, he went downstairs to stay all day in the grocery. He worked long long hours. Six o'clock every morning he opened and he closed after ten every night, sometimes later. Fifteen, sixteen hours a day he was in the store, seven days a week, to make a living for his family.* His dear wife Ida told me she will never forget his steps going down the stairs each morning, and also in the night when he came up so tired for his few hours' sleep before

---

***Rosh Hashana**:「유태교의 신년제(新年祭)」
***Pesach**:「유태교의 과월제(過越祭)」
***to make a living for his family**:「가족을 부양하기 위하여」

he will open again the next day the store. This went on for twenty-two years in this store alone, day after day, except the few days when he was too sick. And for this reason that he worked so hard and bitter, in his house, on his table, was always something to eat. So besides honest he was a good provider."*

The rabbi gazed down at his prayer book, then looked up. "When a Jew dies, who asks if he is a Jew? He is a Jew, we don't ask. There are many ways to be a Jew. So if somebody comes to me and say, 'Rabbi, shall we call such a man Jewish who lived and worked among the gentiles and sold them pig meat, trayfe, that we don't eat it, and not once in twenty years comes inside a synagogue, is such a man a Jew, rabbi?' To him I will say, 'Yes, Morris Bober was to me a true Jew because he lived in the Jewish experience, which he remembered, and with the Jewish heart.' Maybe not to our formal tradition—for this I don't excuse him*—but he was true to the spirit of our life—to want for others that which he wants also for himself. He followed the Law which God gave to Moses on Sinai and told him to bring to the people. He suffered, he endured, but with hope. Who told me this? I know. He asked for himself little—nothing, but he wanted his for beloved child a better existence than he had. For such reasons he was a Jew. What more does our sweet God ask his poor people? So let Him now take care of the widow, to comfort and protect her, and give to the fatherless child what her father wanted her to have. 'Yaskadal v'yiskadash shmey, rabo. B'olmo divro. . . .'"

***a good provider**:「가족들에게 풍족한 생활을 하게 하는 자」
***for this I don't excuse him**:「이 점에 대해서는 저는 그를 용서할 수 없읍니다」

The mourners rose and prayed with the rabbi.

Helen, in her grief, grew restless. He's overdone it, she thought.* I said Papa was honest but what was the good of such honesty if he couldn't exist in this world? Yes, he ran after this poor woman to give her back a nickel but he also trusted cheaters who took away what belonged to him. Poor Papa; being naturally honest, he didn't believe that others come by their dishonesty naturally. And he couldn't hold onto those things he had worked so hard to get. He gave away, in a sense, more than he owned. He was no saint; he was in a way weak, his only true strength in his sweet nature and his understanding.* He knew, at least, what was good. And I didn't say he had many friends who admired him. That's the rabbi's invention. People liked him, but who can admire a man passing his life in such a store? He buried himself in it; he didn't have the imagination to know what he was missing.* He made himself a victim. He could, with a little more courage, have been more than he was.

Helen prayed for peace on the soul of her dead father.

Ida, holding a wet handkerchief to her eyes, thought, So what if we had to eat? When you eat you don't want to worry whose money you are eating—yours or the wholesalers'. If he had money he had bills; and when he had more money he had more bills. A person doesn't always want to worry if she will be in the street tomorrow. She wants sometimes a minute's

---

***He's overdone it, she thought**:「그는 좀 과장했다고 그녀는 생각했다」 overdo it (things)「과장하다」

***his only true strength in his sweet nature and his understanding**:「그의 유일한 진정한 힘은 착한 성격과 이해력뿐이었다」 strength 다음에 was가 생략되어 있음.

***he didn't have the imagination to know what he was missing**:「그에게는 자기가 지금 놓치고 있는 것이 무엇인가를 깨달을 만한 상상력이 없었다」

peace. But maybe it's my fault, because I didn't let him be a druggist.

She wept because her judgment of the grocer was harsh although she loved him. Helen, she thought, must marry a professional.*

When the prayer was done the rabbi left the chapel through the side door, and the coffin was lifted by some of the Society members and the undertaker's assistant, carried on their shoulders outside, and placed in the hearse.* The people in the chapel filed out* and went home, except Frank Alpine, who sat alone in the funeral parlor.

Suffering, he thought, is like a piece of goods. I bet the Jews could make a suit of clothes out of it. The other funny thing is that there are more of them around than anybody knows about.*

In the cemetery it was spring. The snow had melted on all but a few graves, the air was warm, fragrant, The small group of mourners following the grocer's coffin were hot in their overcoats. At the Society's plot, crowded with tombstones, two gravediggers had dug a fresh pit in the earth and were standing back, holding their shovels. As the rabbi prayed over the empty grave—from up close his beard was thick with gray*—Helen rested her head against the coffin held by the

---

***professional**:「기술전문가, 지적 직업인」

***hearse**:「영구차」

***The people in the chapel filed out**:「교회 안에 있던 사람들은 줄지어 나갔다」 file in=줄지어 들어가다

***The other funny thing is that . . . about**:「또 하나 이상한 것은 우리가 상상하는 이상으로 우리 주위에는 유태인이 많다는 사실이다」

***from up close his beard was thick with gray**:「바로 가까이에서 쳐다보니 그의 수염

pallbearers.*

"Good-by, Papa."

Then the rabbi prayed aloud over the coffin as the gravediggers lowered it to the bottom of the grave.

"Gently. . .gently."

Ida, supported by Sam Pearl and the secretary of the Society, sobbed uncontrollably. She bent forward, shouting into the grave, "Morris, take care of Helen, you hear me, Morris?"

The rabbi, blessing it, tossed in the first shovelful of earth.

"Gently."

Then the diggers began to push in the loose earth around the grave and as it fell on the coffin the mourners wept aloud.

Helen tossed in a rose.

Frank, standing close to the edge of the grave, leaned forward to see where the flower fell. He lost his balance, and though flailing his arms, landed feet first on the coffin.*

Helen turned her head away.

Ida wailed.

"Get the hell out of there," Nat Pearl said.

Frank scrambled out of the grave, helped by the diggers. I spoiled the funeral, he thought. He felt pity on the world for harboring him.*

은 흰 털이 수북했다」

***pallbearer**:「관에 씌운 천의 구석을 잡고 상여에 따르는 사람」

***though flailing his arms, landed feet first on the coffin**:「두 팔을 마구 흔들었지만 밑으로 떨어져 발로 관을 밟았다」

***He felt pity on the world for harboring him**:「그는 자기 같은 사람도 살게 해 주는 세상에 대해 연민의 정을 느꼈다」 harbor=give shelter to

At last the coffin was covered, the grave full, running over.* The rabbi said a last short Kaddish.* Nat took Helen by the arm and led her away.

She gazed back once, with grief, then went with him.

Louis Karp was waiting for them in the dark hallway when Ida and Helen returned from the cemetery.

"Excuse me for bothering you on this sad occasion," he said, holding his hat in his hand, "but I wanna tell you* why my father couldn't get to the funeral. He's sick and has to lay flat on his back for the next six weeks or so. The other night when he passed out at the fire,* we found out later he had a heart attack. He's lucky he's still alive."

"Vey is mir," muttered Ida.

"The doctor says he's gonna have to retire from here on in," Louis said, with a shrug, "so I don't think he'll wanna buy your house any more. Myself," he added, "I got a job of salesman for a liquor concern."*

He said good-by and left them.

"Your father is better off dead," said Ida.

As they toiled up the stairs they heard the dull cling of the register in the store and knew the grocer was the one who had danced on the grocer's coffin.

***the coffin was covered, the grave full, running over**:「관은 덮히고 묘혈은 채워지고 위로 두둑히 흙이 올라왔다」 running over=more than full

***Kaddish**:「유태교의 예배식 후에 사자(死者)를 위해 외는 기도」

***I wanna tell you**=I want to tell you

***when he passed out at the fire**:「그가 화재 때문에 기절했을 때」

***liquor concern**:「주류판매회사」

10

Frank lived in the back, his clothes hung in a bought closet,* sleeping under his overcoat on the couch. He had used their week of mourning, when mother and daughter were confined upstairs, to get the store going.* Staying open kept it breathing, but beyond that things were rocky.* If not for his thirty-five weekly dollars in the register he would have had to close up. Seeing he paid his little bills, the wholesalers extended credit.* People stopped in to say they were sorry Morris was dead. One man said the grocer was the only storekeeper that had ever trusted him for anything. He paid Frank back eleven dollars that he owed Morris. Frank told anybody who asked that he was keeping the business going for the widow. They approved of that.

He gave Ida twelve dollars a week rent and promised her more when times got better. He said when they did,* he might buy the store from her, but it would have to be on small

---

***bought closet**:「가게에서 사 온 장롱」

***get the store going**:「제대로 장사가 되게끔 힘쓰다」 *e.g.* He got the clock going「그는 시계를 가게 했다」

***Staying open kept it breathing, but beyond that things were rocky**:「가게문을 열어 놓았기 때문에 명맥은 유지되었지만 앞으로의 전망은 아무도 알 수 없었다」 rocky「불안한, 흔들흔들하는」 *e.g.* His business was in a rocky condition.「그의 사업은 불안정한 상태에 있었다」

***extend credit**:「부채의 지불기간을 연기시켜 주다」

***when they did**=when times got better

installments* because he had no money for a down payment.* She didn't answer him. She was worried about the future and feared she might starve. She lived on the rent he paid her, plus Nick's rent, and Helen's salary. Ida now had a little job sewing epaulettes for military uniforms,* a bag of which Abe Rubin, a landsman of Morris's, delivered in his car every Monday morning. That brought in another twenty-eight to thirty a month. She rarely went down to the store. To speak to her, Frank had to go upstairs and knock on her door. Once, through Rubin, someone came to look at the grocery and Frank was worried, but the man soon left.

He lived in the future, to be forgiven.* On the stairs one morning he said to Helen, "Things are changed. I am not the same guy I was."

"Always," she answered, "you remind me of everything I want to forget."

"Those books you once gave me to read," he said, "did you understand them yourself?"

Helen waked from a bad dream. In the dream she had got up to leave the house in the middle of the night to escape Frank waiting on the stairs; but there he stood under the yellow lamp, fondling his lascivious cap.* As she approached, his lips formed, "I love you."

"I'll scream if you say it."

***on small installments**:「소액의 분할불로」

***down payment**:「분할불의 보증금」

***epaulettes for military uniforms**:「군복의 견장(肩章)」

***He lived in the future, to be forgiven**:「앞으로 용서받을 것을 바라고 그는 살아갔다」

***fondling his lascivious cap**:「색정을 이르키게 하는 모자를 만지작거리면서」
lascivious=tending to excite lustful desires

She screamed and woke.

At a quarter to seven she forced herself out of bed, shut off the alarm before it rang* and drew off* her nightgown. The sight of her body mortified her. What a waste, she thought. She wanted to be a virgin again and at the same time a mother.

Ida was still asleep in the half-empty bed that had for a lifetime served two. Helen brushed her hair, washed, and put on coffee. Standing at the kitchen window, she gazed out at the back yards in flower, feeling sorrow for her father lying in his immovable grave. What had she ever given him, ever done to make his poor life better? She wept for Morris, thinking of his compromises and surrenders. She felt she must do something for herself, accomplish some worthwhile thing or suffer his fate. Only by growing in value as a person could she make Morris's life meaningful, in the sense that she was of him.* She must, she thought, in some way eventually earn her degree. It would take years—but was the only way.

Frank stopped waiting for her in the hall. She had cried out one morning, "Why do you force yourself on me?"* and it had struck him that his penitence was a hammer,* so he withdrew. But he watched her when he could, through an opening in the tissue paper backing of the store window.* He watched as if he

---

***she forced herself out of bed, shut off the alarm before it rang**:「그녀는 억지로 잠자리에서 일어나, 시계종이 울리기 전에 단추를 눌러 울리지 않게 했다」

***draw off**:「(잠옷, 장갑, 양말 등을)벗다」

***in the sense that she was of him**:「그녀가 그의 딸이라는 의미에서」

***Why do you force yourself on me?**:「왜 나한테 귀찮게 굴어요?」

***it had struck him that his penitence was a hammer**:「그 말을 듣자 그는 자신의 회개를 돋보이게 한 사실을 알게 되었다」

***through an opening in the tissue paper backing of the store window**:「가게 유리창의 내부에 바른 박엽지의 틈을 통해서」

were seeing for the first time her slender figure, high small breasts, the slim roundness of her hips and the exciting quality of her slightly bowed legs. She always looked lonely. He tried to think what he could ever do for her and all he could think of was to give her something she had no use for, that would end up in the garbage.

The idea of doing something for her seemed as futile as his other thoughts till one day, the tissue paper held a little aside as he watched her impassively entering the house, he had a thought so extraordinary it made the hair on the back of his neck stiffen.* He figured the best thing he could do was help her get the college education she had always wanted. There was nothing she wanted more. But where, if she agreed to let him—he doubted it every minute it was in his mind*—could he get the money unless he stole it? The more he pondered this plan, the more it excited him until he couldn't stand the possibility it might be impossible.

He carried in his wallet the note Helen had once written him, that she would come up to his room if Nick and Tessie went to the movies, and he read it often.

One day he got another idea. He pasted a sign in the window: "Hot Sandwiches And Hot Soups To Go." He figured he could use his short-order cooking experience* to

---

***he had a thought . . . his neck stiffen**:「목뒤의 머리털이 뻣뻣해질 정도의 기막힌 생각을 그는 하게 되었다」

***if she agreed to let him—he doubted it every minute it was in his mind**:「Frank가 그렇게 하도록 설사 그녀가 동의한다 해도—동의해 줄 거라는 생각을 한 때부터 그는 줄곧 그 생각을 의심하고 있었지만」 *e.g.* I am expecting him every minute.「나는 지금 줄곧 그를 기다리고 있소」

***his short-order cooking experience**:「그의 즉석요리에 관한 경험」

advantage in the grocery. He had some handbills printed, advertising these new things and paid a kid half a buck to deliver them to places where there were working men. He followed the boy for a couple of blocks to see that he didn't dump the papers into a sewer. Before the end of the week a few new people were coming in at lunch and suppertime. They said this was the first time you could get any hot food to take out* in the neighborhood. Frank also tried his hand at ravioli* and lasagna* once a week, making them from recipes* he got out of a cookbook in the library. He experimented with baking small pizzas in the gas stove, which he sold for two bits apiece. The pasta* and pizzas sold better than the hot sandwiches. People came in for them. He considered putting a table or two in the grocery but there was no room, so all the food had to go.

He got another little break.* The milkman told him the two Norwegians had taken to yelling at each other in front of their customers. He said they were making less than they had expected. The store was fine for one man but not for two, so they each wanted to buy the other out.* Pederson's nerves couldn't stand the fighting, and Taast bought him out at the end of May and had the place all to himself. But he found that

---

***They said this was the first time you could get any hot food to take out**:「뜨거운 음식을 사 갈 수 있는 것은 이번이 처음이라고 그들은 말했다」

***ravioli**:「간이 밴 얇게 썰은 고기를 넣어 만든 만두」

***lasagna**:「고기, 치즈, 토마토 등을 밀가루로 싸서 구운 요리」

***recipe**=directions for making a dish「요리법」

***pasta**:「macaroni, spaghetti, ravioli 등을 통들어 말함」

***He got another little break**:「그는 또 하나의 작은 행운을 얻었다」

***so they each wanted to buy the other out**:「그래서 그들은 서로 상대방의 투자분을 매입하여 혼자 경영하기를 원했다」 buy out=buy the whole rights of a person in a business

the long hours alone were killing his feet. His wife came in to help out around suppertime; however Taast couldn't stand being away from his family every night, when everyone else was free and at home, so he decided to close at seven-thirty and stop fighting Frank until almost ten. These couple of hours all to himself at night helped Frank.* He got back some of the customers who came home from work late, and also the housewives who at the last minute needed something for breakfast. And Frank noticed, from peering into Taast's window after he was closed, that he was no longer so generous with the specials.

The weather turned hot in July. People cooked less, lived more on delicatessen, canned goods, bottled drinks. He sold a lot of beer. His pastas and pizzas went very well. He heard that Taast had tried making pizzas but they were too doughy.* Also, instead of using canned soups, Frank made a minestrone* of his own that everybody praised; it took time to cook up, but the profit was better. And the new things he was selling pushed other goods along.* He now paid Ida ninety a month for rent and the use of her store. She was earning more money on her epaulettes, and did not think so often that she would starve.

"Why do you give me so much?" she asked him when he raised the money to ninety.

***These couple of hours all to himself at night helped Frank**:「밤의 두 시간을 독점할 수 있게 된 사정이 Frank를 도왔다」

***doughy**=half-baked「설 구운」

***minestrone**:「고기국에 야채, macaroni, 치즈 등을 넣은 진한 수프」

***the new things he was selling pushed other goods along**:「그가 파는 새로운 요리들 때문에 다른 상품도 잘 팔렸다」

"Maybe Helen could keep some of her wages?" he suggested.

"Helen isn't interested any more in you," she said sternly.

He didn't answer her.

But that night after supper—he had treated himself to* ham and eggs and now smoked a cigar—Frank cleared the table and sat down to figure out how much it would cost to support Helen in college if she would quit her job and give all her time to education. When he had figured out the tuition from the college catalogues he had collected, he saw he couldn't do it. His heart was heavy. Later he thought maybe he could work it if she went to a free college * He could give her enough for her daily expenses and also to make up whatever money she now gave her mother. He figured that to do it would be a rocky load on his head,* but he *had* to do it, it was his only hope; he could think of no other. All he asked for himself was the privilege of giving her something she couldn't give back.

The big thing, exciting yet frightening, was to talk to her, say what he hoped to do. He always had it in mind to say but found it very hard. To speak to her, after all that had happened to them, seemed impossible—opening on peril, disgrace, physical pain.* What was the magic word to begin

---

*__he had treated himself to ~__ :「그는 큰 마음먹고 ~을 먹었다」 treat oneself「큰 마음먹고 먹다, (사다, 즐기다)」 *e.g.* He treated himself to a new car.「그는 큰 마음먹고 새 차를 샀다」

*__free college__ :「수업료가 면제되는 대학」

*__a rocky load on his head__ :「머리를 짓누르는 무거운 짐」 *e.g.* the rocky road to accomplishment「~을 달성하기 위한 고난의 길」

*__opening on peril, disgrace, physical pain__ :「(그녀에게 말하는 것은) 위험과 치욕과 고통을 일으킬 것 같았다」

with? He despaired he could ever convince her. She was remote, sinned against, unfeeling, or if she felt, it was disgust of him. He cursed himself for having conceived this mess he couldn't now bring himself to speak of.*

One August night after he had seen her come home from work in the company of Nat Pearl, sick of the misery of unmotion,* Frank made himself move. He was standing behind the counter piling bottles of beer into a woman's market bag when he caught sight of Helen going by with some books on her arm. She was wearing a new summer dress, red trimmed with black,* and the sight of her struck him with renewed hunger. All summer she had wandered at night alone in the neighborhood, trying to outwalk her loneliness.* He had been tempted to close up and follow her, but until he had his new idea he could not think what he dared say that she wouldn't run from. Hurrying the customer out of the store, Frank washed, slicked back his hair and quickly changed into a fresh sport shirt. He locked the store and hurried in the direction Helen had gone. The day had been hot but was cooling now and still. The sky was golden green, though below the light was dark. After running a block he remembered something and trudged back to the store. He sat in the back listening to his heart hammering in his ears. In ten minutes he

---

***He cursed himself . . . to speak of**:「이제 말하고 싶지도 않은 그런 추한 짓을 생각해낸 자기 자신을 그는 저주했다」

***sick of the misery of unmotion**:「꼼짝 못하고 있는 자신의 비참한 상태에 넌더리가 나서」

***a new summer dress, red trimmed with black**:「검은 테두리로 장식한 붉은 색의 새 여름 옷」 trim=furnish with ornaments

***trying to outwalk her loneliness**:「외로움을 쫓아 버리려고 걸으려 하면서」

lit a lamp in the store window. The globe drew a ragged moth.* Knowing how long she lingered among books, he shaved. Then locking the front door again, he went toward the library. He figured he would wait across the street till she came out. He would cross over and catch up with her on her way home. Before she could even see him, he would speak his piece and be done with it.* Yes or no, she could say, and if no, he would shut the joint tomorrow and skiddoo.*

He was nearing the library when he glanced up and saw her. She was about half a block away and walking toward him. He stood there not knowing which way to go, dreading to be met by her as lovely as she looked, standing like a crippled dog as she passed him. He thought of running back the way he had come, but she saw him, turned and went in haste the other way; so, reviving an old habit,* he was after her, and before she could deny him, had touched her arm. They shivered. Giving her no time to focus her contempt, he blurted out what he had so long saved to say but could not now stand to hear himself speak.*

When Helen realized what he was offering her, her heart moved violently. She had known he would follow and speak, but she could never in a thousand years have guessed he would say *this.* Considering the conditions of his existence,

---

***The globe drew a ragged moth**:「초라한 나방 한 마리가 전등을 향해 날라왔다」

***he would speak his piece and be done with it**:「그는 자기의 생각을 말하고 그것으로 끝장을 낼 생각이었다」 speak one's piece「의견을 말하다」

***skiddoo**=go away, depart

***reviving an old habit**:「옛날의 버릇을 되살려」

***could not now stand to hear himself speak**:「자기가 하는 말을 그는 스스로 들을 수 없을 지경이었다」

she was startled by his continuing ability to surprise her, make God-knows-what-next-move.* His staying power mystified and frightened her, because she felt in herself, since the death of Ward Minogue, a waning of outrage.* Although she detested the memory of her experience in the park, lately it had come back to her how she had desired that night to give herself to Frank, and might have if Ward hadn't touched her. She had wanted him. If there had been no Ward Minogue, there would have been no assault. If he had made his starved leap in bed she would have returned passion. She had hated him, she thought, to divert hatred from herself.*

But her response to his offer was an instantaneous no. She said it almost savagely, to escape any possibility of being directly obligated to him, of another entrapment, nausea.*

"I couldn't think of it."

He was astonished to have got this far, to be walking at her side—only it was a night in a different season, and her summer face was gentler than her winter one, her body more womanly; yet it all added up to loss, the more he wanted her the more he had lost.*

"In your father's name," he said. "If not for you, then for him."*

***ability to surprise her, make God-knows-what-next-move**:「그녀를 놀라게 하고 아무도 예측할 수 없는 행동을 하는 능력」

***because she felt in herself . . . a waning of outrage**:「그녀는 마음속에서 분노가 누그러져감을 느끼고 있었기 때문에」 outrage=indignation「분개, 분노」

***to divert hatred from herself**:「증오심을 자신으로부터 다른 곳으로 돌리기 위하여」

***to escape any possibility . . . nausea**:「그에게 직접적으로 신세를 지게 되고 또 다른 함정에 빠져 구역질 나는 일이 다시 일어나지 않게 하기 위해」

***the more he wanted her the more he had lost**:「그녀를 원하면 원할수록 그의 상실감은 깊어져 갔다」

***If not for you, then for him**:「당신을 위해서 안 된다면 당신의 아버지를 위해서라도」

"What has my father got to do with it?"

"It's his store. Let it support you to go to college like he wanted you to."

"It can't without you.* I don't want your help."

"Morris did me a big favor. I can't return it to him but I might to you. Also because I lost myself that night—"

"For God's sake, don't say it."

He didn't, was dumb. They walked dumbly on. To her horror they were coming to the park. Abruptly she went the other way.

He caught up with her. "You could graduate in three years. You wouldn't have any worry about expenses. You could study all you want."

"What would you expect to get from this—virtue?"

"I already said why—I owe something to Morris."

"For what? Taking you into his stinking store and making a prisoner out of you?"

What more could he say? To his misery, what he had done to her father rose in his mind. He had often imagined he would someday tell her, but not now. Yet the wish to say it overwhelmed him. He tried wildly to escape it. His throat hurt, his stomach heaved. He clamped his teeth tight but the words came up in blobs, in a repulsive stream.*

He spoke with pain. "I was the one that held him up that time. Minogue and me. Ward picked on him after Karp ran away, but it was my fault too on account of I went in with

---

***It can't without you**:「당신 없이 가게는 학비를 댈 수. 없죠」

***He clamped his teeth tight but the words came up in blobs, in a repulsive stream**: 「그는 이를 악물었지만 물방울처럼 말이 입에서 새어나왔고, 마침내 메스꺼운 냇물처럼 말이 쏟아져 나왔다」 repulsive=disgusting「불쾌한」

him."

She screamed and might have gone on screaming but strangers were staring.

"Helen, I swear—"

"You criminal. How could you hit such a gentle person? What harm did he ever do you?"

"I didn't hit him, Ward did. I gave him a drink of water. He saw I didn't want to hurt him. After, I came to work for him to square up what I did wrong.* For Christ's sake, Helen, try to understand me."

With contorted face* she ran from him.

"I confessed it to him," he shouted after her.

He had managed well in the summer and fall, but after Christmas business dragged,* and though his night salary had been raised five bucks, he found it impossible to meet all his expenses. Every penny looked as big as the moon. Once he spent an hour searching for a two-bit* piece he had dropped behind the counter. He tore up a loose floor board and was elated to recover more than three dollars in green and grimy coins* that Morris had lost during the years.

For himself he spent only for the barest necessities, though his clothes were falling apart. When he could no longer sew up the holes in his undershirts he threw them away and wore none. He soaked his laundry in the sink and hung it to dry in

---

***to square up what I did wrong**:「내가 저지른 나쁜 짓을 청산하기 위하여」

***With contorted face**:「얼굴을 찡그리고」

***business dragged**:「경기가 악화되어 갔다」 drag「처지다, 질질 끌다」

***two-bit**:「25센트의」 a two-bit piece「25센트 은화 한 개」

***was elated to recover more than three dollars in green and grimy coins**:「녹색으로 녹이 쓸고 더러워진 동전을 3불 이상이나 발견하고 몹시 기분이 좋아졌다」

the kitchen. He was, as a rule, prompt in his payment of jobbers and wholesalers,* but during the winter he kept them waiting. One man he held off his neck by* threatening to go bankrupt. Another he promised tomorrow. He slipped a couple of bucks to his most important salesman, to calm them at the office.* Thus he kept going. But he never missed a payment of rent to Ida. He valued his payments to her because Helen had returned to night college in the fall, and if he didn't give the ninety to Ida, Helen wouldn't have enough for her own needs.

He was always tired. His spine ached as if it had been twisted like a cat's tail. On his night off from the Coffee Pot* he slept without moving, dreaming of sleep. In the dead hours at the Coffee Pot, he sat with his head on his arms at the counter, and during the day in the grocery he took catnaps whenever he could,* trusting the buzzer to rouse him, although other noises did not. When he awoke, his eyes were hot and watery, his head like porous lead.* He grew thin, his neck scrawny,* face bones prominent, his broken nose sharp. He saw life from a continual wet-eyed yawn.* He drank black

---

***jobbers and wholesalers**:「도매상과 도매업자들」

***One man he held off his neck by** ～＝He delayed paying one man by～「그는 ～함으로써 한 사람에 대한 지불을 연기시켰다」

***He slipped a couple of bucks . . . office**:「그는 2불을 가장 중요한 판매원에게 슬쩍 쥐어 주어 회사 사람들을 달래려 했다」

***On his night off from the Coffee Pot**:「Coffee Pot 식당이 비번인 밤에는」

***he took catnaps whenever he could**:「그는 할 수 있을 때마다 선잠을 잤다」 catnap＝doze

***porous lead**:「구멍이 난 납덩어리」

***scrawny**＝lean「여윈」 scraggy「앙상한」

***He saw life from a continual wet-eyed yawn**:「하품 때문에 늘 눈물이 나온 눈으로 그는 세상을 바라보았다」

coffee till his stomach turned sour. In the evening he did nothing—read a little. Or he sat in the back with the lights out, smoking, listening to the blues on the radio.

He had other worries, had noticed Nat was hanging around Helen more. A couple of times a week the law student drove her home from work. Now and then, over the week end, they went for a ride at night. Nat would toot his horn in front of the door and she came out dressed up and smiling, neither of them noticing Frank, in open sight.* And she had had a new telephone put in upstairs, and once or twice a week he heard it ring. The phone made him jumpy, jealous of Nat.* Once on his night off from the Coffee Pot, Frank woke abruptly when Helen and somebody came into the hall. Sneaking into the store and listening at the side door, he could hear them whispering; then they were quiet and he imagined them necking. For hours after, he couldn't get back to sleep, desiring her so. The next week, listening at the door, he discovered the guy she was kissing was Nat. His jealousy ate him good.*

She never entered the store. To see her he had to stand at the front window.

"Jesus," he said, "why am I killing myself so?" He gave himself many unhappy answers, the best being that while he was doing this he was doing nothing worse.*

***in open sight**:「남들이 보는 데서」

***The phone made him jumpy, jealous of Nat**:「전화소리는 그를 안절부절하게 했고 Nat에 대한 질투심을 자극했다」

***His jealousy ate him good**:「질투심이 일어나 그는 몹시 괴로와했다」

***the best being that while he was doing this he was doing nothing worse**:「그러나 가장 좋은 답변은 그가 이 장사를 하는 동안에 다른 나쁜 짓을 하지 않을 거라는 것이었다」 the best being that=but the best answer was that

But then he took to doing things he had promised himself he never would again. He did them with dread of what he would do next. He climbed up the air shaft to spy on Helen in the bathroom. Twice he saw her disrobe.* He ached for her, for the flesh he had lived in a moment.* Yet he hated her for having loved him, for to desire what he had once had, and hadn't now, was torture. He swore to himself that he would never spy on her again, but he did. And in the store he took to* cheating customers. When they weren't watching the scale he short-weighted them. A couple of times he short-changed* an old dame who never knew how much she had in her purse.

Then one day, for no reason he could give, though the reason felt familiar,* he stopped climbing up the air shaft to peek at Helen, and he was honest in the store.

One night in January Helen was waiting at the curb for a trolley. She had been studying with a girl in her class and afterward had listened to some records, so she had left later than she had planned. The trolley was late in coming, and though she was cold, she was considering walking home, when she began to feel she was being watched. Looking into the store before which she was standing, she saw nobody there but the counterman resting his head on his arms. As she

---

***disrobe**=undress「옷을 벗다」

***He ached for her, for the flesh he had lived in a moment**:「그는 그녀를 그가 순간적으로 소유했던 그 육체를 갈망했다」 ache for「갈망하다, 동경하다」 *e.g.* He ached for a sight of her.「그녀를 보고 싶어 견딜 수 없었다」

***take to**=fall into the habit of「빠지기 시작하다, 버릇이 붙다」 *e.g.* He took to drinking.「술 버릇이 붙어 버렸다」

***short-change**:「가스름돈을 덜 주다, 속이다(cheat)」

***for no reason he could give, though the reason felt familiar**:「잘 알고 있는 듯하면서도 말로 표현할 수 없는 이유 때문에」

observed him, trying to figure out why she felt so strange, he raised his sleepy head and she saw in surprise that it was Frank Alpine. He gazed with burning eyes in a bony face, with sad regret, at his refletion in the window, then went drunkenly back to sleep. It took her a minute to realize he hadn't seen her. She felt the momentary return of an old misery, yet the winter night seemed clear and beautiful.

When the trolley came, she took a seat in the rear. Her thoughts were heavy. She remembered Ida saying Frank worked some place at night but the news had meant nothing to her. Now that she had seen him there, groggy from overwork,* thin, unhappy, a burden lay on her, because it was no mystery who he was working for. He had kept them alive. Because of him she had enough to go to school at night.

In bed, half-asleep, she watched the watcher.* It came to her that he had changed. It's true, he's not the same man, she said to herself. I should have known by now. She had despised him for the evil he had done, without understanding the why or aftermath, or admitting there could be an end to the bad and a beginning of good.

It was a strange thing about people—they could look the same but be different.* He had been one thing, low, dirty, but because of something in himself—something she couldn't define, a memory perhaps, an ideal he might have forgotten and then remembered—he had changed into somebody else,

---

***groggy from overwork**:「과로로 휘청거리는」 groggy=shaky, unsteady

***she watched the watcher**:「그녀는 자기를 지켜보는 자를 응시했다」 잠자리에서 눈을 감고 Frank에 대한 생각을 했다는 뜻.

***they could look the same but be different**:「(사람들은) 겉은 똑같지만 속은 달라질 수 있는 것이다」

no longer what he had been. She should have recognized it before. What he did to me he did wrong, she thought, but since he has changed in his heart he owes me nothing.

On her way to work one morning a week later, Helen, carrying her briefcase, entered the grocery and found Frank hidden behind the tissue paper of the window,* watching her. He was embarrassed, and she was curiously moved by the sight of his face.

"I came in to thank you for the help you're giving us," she explained.

"Don't thank me," he said.

"You owe us nothing."

"It's just my way."*

They were silent, then he mentioned his idea of her going to day college. It would be more satisfying to her than at night.

"No, thank you," Helen said, blushing, "I couldn't think of it, especially not with you workings so hard."*

"It's no extra trouble."

"No, please."

"Maybe the store might get better, then I could do it on what we take in here?"

"I'd rather not."

"Think about it," Frank said.

She hesitated, then answered she would.

He wanted to ask her if he still had any chance with her*

***found Frank hidden behind the tissue paper of the window**:「Frank가 창문에 붙은 박엽지 뒤에 숨어있는 것을 발견했다」
***It's just my way**:「이것이 바로 제 타고난 성격입니다」
***especially not with you working so hard**:「더구나 당신이 이렇게 열심히 일하고 있는데 저는 할 수 없어요」
***any chance with her**:「그녀에 대한 사랑이 성취될 희망」

but decided to let that wait till a later time.

Before she left, Helen, balancing the briefcase on her knee,* unsnapped* it and took out a leather-bound book. "I wanted you to know I'm still using your Shakespeare."

He watched her walk to the corner, a good-looking girl, carrying his book in her briefcase. She was wearing flat-heeled shoes, making her legs slightly more bowed, which for some reason he found satisfying.

The next night, listening at the side door, he heard a scuffle in the hall and wanted to break in and assist her but held himself back.* He heard Nat say something harsh, then Helen slapped him and he heard her run upstairs.

"You bitch," Nat called after her.

One morning in the middle of March the grocer was sleeping heavily after a night off from the Coffee Pot, when he was awakened by a pounding on the front door. It was the Polish nut wanting her three-cent roll. She came later these days but still too early. The hell with all that, he thought, I need my sleep.* But after a few minutes he grew restless and began to dress. Business still wasn't so hot. Frank washed his face before the cracked mirror. His thick hair needed cutting but it could wait one more week. He thought of growing himself a beard but was afraid it would scare some of the customers

---

***balancing the briefcase on her knee**:「그녀의 무릎 위에 가방을 균형잡히게 올려놓고」

***unsnap**:「쥠쇠를 풀다」

***wanted to break in and assist her but held himself back**:「개입해서 그녀를 도우려 했지만 자신을 억제했다」

***The hell with all that, he thought, I need my sleep**:「다 귀찮아, 난 더 자야겠어, 하고 그는 생각했다」

away, so he settled for a mustache. He had been letting one grow for two weeks* and was surprised at the amount of red in it. He sometimes wondered if his old lady* had been a redhead.

Unlocking the door, he let her in. The Polish dame complained he had kept her waiting too long in the cold. He sliced a roll for her, wrapped it, and rang up three cents.

At seven, standing by the window, he saw Nick, a new father, come out of the hall and run around the corner. Frank hid behind the paper and soon saw him return, carrying a bag of groceries he had bought in Taast's store. Nick ducked into the hallway* and Frank felt bad.

"I think I will make this joint into a restaurant."

After he had mopped the kitchen floor and swept the store, Breitbart appeared, dragging his heavy boxes. Lowering the cartons of bulbs to the floor, the peddler took off his derby* and wiped his brow with a yellowed handkerchief.

"How's it going?" Frank asked.

"Schwer."*

Breitbart drank the tea and lemon that Frank cooked up for him, meanwhile reading his *Forward.* After about ten minutes he folded the newspaper into a small, thick square and pushed it into his coat pocket. He lifted the bulbs onto his itchy shoulders and left.

***He had been letting one grow for two weeks**:「그는 2주일간 콧수염이 자라게 내버려 두었다」 one=a mustache「콧수염」

***his old lady**:「그의 어머니」

***Nick ducked into the hallway**:「Nick는 슬쩍 몸을 굽혀 현관으로 들어갔다」

***derby**=derby hat「중산모자」

***Schwer**:「힘드는, 괴로운, 무거운」

Frank had only six customers all morning. To keep from getting nervous* he took out a book he was reading. It was the Bible and he sometimes thought there were parts of it he could have written himself.

As he was reading he had this pleasant thought. He saw St. Francis come dancing out of the woods in his brown rags, a couple of scrawny birds flying around over his head. St. F. stopped in front of the grocery, and reaching into the garbage can, plucked the wooden rose out of it. He tossed it into the air and it turned into a real flower that he caught in his hand. With a bow* he gave it to Helen, who had just come out of the house. "Little sister, here is your little sister the rose." From him she took it, although it was with the love and best wishes of Frank Alpine.

One day in April Frank went to the hospital and had himself circumcised.* For a couple of days he dragged himself around with a pain between his legs.* The pain enraged and inspired him. After Passover he became a Jew.

***To keep from getting nervous**:「초조한 기분이 되지 않기 위해」

***With a bow**:「절을 하고」

***had himself circumcised**:「그는 할례수술을 받았다」

***he dragged himself around with a pain between his legs**:「다리 사이에 아픔을 느끼면서 발을 질질 끌고 돌아다녔다」

ESSAYS IN CRITICISM

The Qualified Encounter

by Ihab Hassan

In Bernard Malamud we find further testimony that the urban Jewish writer, like the Southern novelist, has emerged from the tragic underground of culture as a true spokesman of mid-century America. It may be difficult to classify Malamud in the scheme which Fiedler devised for Jewish authors of the last two decades: Bellow (highbrow), Salinger (upper middle-brow), Shaw (middle middlebrow), and Wouk (low middlebrow)[1]. If Malamud does not possess the intellectual vitality of Bellow, his finest work shows an order of excellence no critic—however beetling or elevated his brow—can justly deny. The first and most obvious quality of his fiction is its "goodness." This is a complex quality, compounded of irony, trust, and craft—a touch of Dostoyevsky and Chagall, some-one observed. It is the product of a sensitive yet enduring heart, vulnerable where it counts, and deeply responsible to its feeling of what transforms a man into *mensch*. Behind it is a wry vision of pain, and also of hope. We are not surprised, therefore, to hear Malamud say that "Jews are absolutely the very *stuff* of drama," or that the purpose of the writer is "to keep civilization from destroying itself"; or that much of

1) Leslie Fiedler, "Saul Bellow," *Prairie Schooner* (Summer 1957), p. 107.

current fiction is "underselling Man."[2] But these pronouncements, which may express the natural bent of a man reared virtuously among immigrants in Brooklyn, do not explain the subtleties of his craft. Malamud's vision is preeminently moral, yet his form is sly. It owes something to the wile of Yiddish folklore, the ambiguous irony of the Jewish joke. Pain twisted into humor twists humor back into pain. The starkness of suffering, the leaden weight of ignorance or poverty, the alienation of the Jew in a land of jostling Gentiles —all these become transmuted, in luminous metaphors and strange rhythms, into forms a little quaint or ludicrous, a bittersweet irony of life, into something, finally, elusive.

His first novel, *The Natural,* 1952, is a bizarre, authentic, troubled work about a thirty-three-year-old baseball player who suddenly emerges from painful oblivion into the crazy light of fame and big league corruption. The snappy slang of sport and gloomy language of the soul are fused in an allegorical tale which probes deep into the meaning of personal integrity but fails ultimately to make itself comprehensible. His collection of short stories, *The Magic Barrel,* 1958, includes some of his worst and best fiction. The poorer pieces are usually set abroad; the best deal with native Jewish material and have in common with his second novel, *The Assistant,* 1957, a blazing poetic insight into the daily aches and indignities of man which add up, somehow, to a kind of nobility, a form of aspiration.

The Assistant, presumably, is a love story, domestic

2) *Current Biography Yearbook,* 1958, ed. Margaret Dent Candee (New York, 1958), p. 272.

romance, a grocery store idyll of unwarranted poverty and harsh spiritual deprivation. It is a tale of loneliness, of lifelong frustrations and delicate, budding hopes. It is a "human" story albeit deeply ironic. For irony is indeed the key to Malamud's attitude toward man, to his estimate of him. The irony is not "dry," not scathing; it is best described by Earl Rovit when he says, "The affectionate insult and the wry self-deprecation are parts of the same ironic vision which values one's self and mankind as both less and more than they seem to be worth, at one and the same time."[3] This is the ambivalence of vision which qualifies, sometimes even undercuts, the affirmative power of Malamud's fiction.

The world revealed by *The Assistant* is, materially speaking, bleak; morally, it glows with a faint, constant light. Morris Bober and his wife, Ida, toil sixteen hours a day in a grocery store, barely eking out a living. They are well past middle age, and have given up their lives, their illusions, even the promise of a richer future which comes with education for their single daughter, Helen. The store, as we are told many times, is an open tomb. Twenty-one years are spent in it, and in the end Bober dies of double pneumonia, leaving his family penniless; he has to be buried in one of those huge anonymous cemeteries in Queens. America! "He had hoped for much in America and got little. And because of him Helen and Ida had less. He had defrauded them, he and the blood-sucking store."[4] This is what Bober thinks as one of two men who

3) Earl H. Rovit, "Bernard Malamud and the Jewish Literary Tradition," *Critique* (Winter-Spring 1960), p. 5.

4) Bernard Malamud, *The Assistant* (New York, 1958), p. 25.

hold up his store slugs him on the head, because he is a Jew, and Bober falls to the ground without a cry. An appropriate ending to his weary, profitless day. Others may have luck, like the affluent Karp who owns a liquor store across the street, or the Pearls whose son, Nat, attends law school—and takes Helen's virginity. But the Bobers live on stolidly, honestly, in squalor and sickening destitution. They are, like the grocery "assistant," Frank Alpine, victims of circumstance. What, then, gives these characters the measure of spiritual freedom they still possess?

The nature of the characters themselves holds the answer. Morris Bober, to be sure, is another example of the *eiron,* the humble man. He is more. He has endurance, the power to accept suffering without yielding to the hebetude which years of pain induce. He is acquainted with the tragic qualities of life—"The world suffers. *He* felt every schmerz"—and he defines the Jew as a suffering man with a good heart, one who reconciles himself to agony, not because he wants to be agonized, as Frank suggests, but for the sake of the Law—the Hebraic ideal of virtue.[5)] Yet this is only one source of Bober's strength. His other source is charity, which in his case becomes nearly quixotic. Bober, though close to starvation himself, extends credit to his poor customers. He wakes up every day before dawn so that he may sell a three-cent roll to a Polish woman on her way to work. He takes in Frank Alpine, feeds him, and gives him an opportunity to redeem himself, though Frank begins by stealing the grocer's bread and milk. Nor can he bring himself, in the extremity of despair, to burn down his

5) *Ibid.,* p. 10.

property in order to collect insurance. Inured to failure, Bober still strives to give suffering the dignity of men who may trust one another in their common woe. But Karp calls him a "schlimozel."

The central action of the novel, however, develops from Bober's relation to Frank Alpine, and from the latter's relation to Helen. Frank, as the title suggests, is probably the hero of the book. He, too, is an *eiron,* a collector of injustices —with a difference. The regeneration of Frank—his literal and symbolic conversion to the Jewish faith—is the true theme of the book. His regeneration, at best, is a strange and mixed thing. When Frank first appears, he is a wanderer, an anti-Semite, even a thief. Yet one of his idols is St. Francis, and his hardened face conceals a hungry soul. "With me one wrong thing leads to another and it ends in a trap. I want the moon so all I get is cheese," he tells Bober.[6)] The grocery store, which is Bober's grave, becomes a cave or haven for Alpine. It also becomes the dreary locus of his painful rebirth. Impelled by his gratitude to the grocer, and motivated by his guilt at having robbed him, with the aid of tough Ward Minogue, Frank puts all his energies into the store and ends by pumping some of his own obstinate life into the dying business. Meanwhile, he falls in love with Helen Bober.

From here on, ambiguities prevail. The racial prejudices of Frank are matched by those of Ida Bober, and to some extent, of her daughter Helen, against Gentiles. (The store improves, it is suggested, precisely because Frank is not a Jew.) Frank's gratitude to Morris does not prevent him from continuing to

6) *Ibid.,* p. 32.

steal petty cash from the register—which he keeps account of and intends to return. Yet when Bober is incapacitated by sickness, Frank takes a night job, in addition to his grocery chores, and secretly puts his pay in the cash box. And his gnawing love for Helen, which she is slow to return, finally ends, ironically, with an act of near-rape as he rescues her from the clutches of Ward Minogue, only to force her himself, right there and then in the park, at the very moment in their relationship when she is at last ready to surrender herself freely to him. "Dog," she cries "—uncircumcised dog!"[7] Guilt, gratitude, love—perhaps even the hope of a life he could glimpse but never attain—combine to sustain Frank Alpine, Bober's strange, saintly, pilfering assistant, in his impossible struggle against poverty, against hopelessness itself.

> He wanted her but the facts made a terrible construction. They were Jews and he was not. If he started going out with Helen her mother would throw a double fit and Morris another. And Helen made him feel, from the way she carried herself, even when she seemed most lonely, that she had plans for something big in her life—nobody like F. Alpine. He had nothing, a backbreaking past, had committed a crime against her old man, and in spite of his touchy conscience, was stealing from him too. How complicated could impossible get ?
>
> He saw only one way of squeezing through the stone knot; start by shoveling out the load he was carrying around in his mind. . . .

7) *Ibid.*, p. 133.

> So the confession had to come first—He felt he had known this, in some frightful way, a long time before he went into the store, before he had met Minogue, or even come east; that he had really known all his life he would sometime, through throat blistered with shame, his eyes in the dirt, have to tell some poor son of a bitch that he was the one who had hurt or betrayed him. This thought had lived in him with claws; or like a thirst he could never spit out, a repulsive need to get out of his system all that had happened—for whatever had happened had happened wrong; to clean it out of his self and bring in a little peace, a little order; to change the beginning, beginning with the past that always stupendously stank up the now—to change his life before the smell of it suffocated him.[8)]

Purgation in humility, rebirth through love—this is Frank's inchoate purpose, the reason for his willing acceptance of a backbreaking burden others — Minogue, Karp — find easy to reject. Yet it is in consonance with the character of the novel that purgation and rebirth both should appear ironic, awkward, and inconclusive. Frank tells Bober about his complicity in the robbery only to discover that the latter already knows. Bober catches his assistant rifling his till just when Frank had resolved never to steal again. And Frank's attempt to make a clean breast of it all to Helen merely serves to confirm her revulsion. His dogged and desperate love expresses itself in the form of a physical outrage. The savior of

8) *Ibid.*, p. 72f.

the Bobers is, in a sense, their archenemy. (The symbolic inversion of this relation may be discovered in the burial scene in which Frank topples accidentally into Bober's open grave.) But enemies suffer too, according to their conscience. Frank Alpine, it seems, can only expend the last vestige of his money, energy, or hope in agonized silence, a prey to the ironies which rip and twist his purpose. In the end, the value of confession is to the soul that makes it. And even love is a kind of realized solitude. Like Frank, Helen goes her lonely way, carrying the broken dreams of the Bobers to some distant and uncompromising end.

It is obvious that if the world of *The Assistant* is not drained of values, it is nevertheless saturated with pain, flooded with contradictions. Its two major characters find their identity in humiliation, an extreme and quixotic sense of obligation. They are not tragic heroes but merely heroes of irony. They retreat before the ultimate tragic ordeal; the fullness of tragic awareness itself. This is a fact the form of the novel supports.

Time, we know, leaves the characters suspended in the void which their failures create; the hints of regeneration are barely audible. Morris Bober dies in bankruptcy; Helen continues at her dreary job, dreaming of a better life; Frank slaves at the store, trying to provide for the Bobers, send Helen to college, and win back her love. The fate of each remains less than what it could be in heroic tragedy, less even than what it usually amounts to in realistic fiction. Thus, for instance, does Helen evaluate the life of her father; "People liked him, but who can admire a man passing his life in such a store? He buried himself in it; he didn't have the imagination to know what he was missing. He made himself a victim. He could, with a little more courage, have been more than he was."[9] And thus does Frank reflect upon his incessant labors: " 'Jesus,' he said 'why am I killing myself so ?' He gave himself many unhappy answers, the best being that while he was doing this he was doing nothing worse."[10] Whatever awareness time brings to the characters, whatever qualified dignity it confers upon their failures, every act in the novel is whittled by irony, every motive is mixed with its opposite.

Because time cannot unravel the knotted relations of the characters—what could be more gnarled than the relation of Gentile to Jew, of savior, seducer, and thief to those upon whom he preys, those from whom he gains an identity—the point of view of *The Assistant* dissociates itself from the protagonists, veering toward one then the other in friendly detachment. The characters are simply there, and they criticize each other's behavior; the point of view encourages us to perceive how ludicrous pain can be, and how unhappy virtue. The subtle, incredible twists of the plot, the reversals and accidents which affect the fortunes of the Bobers, are finally envisioned in a moral as well as dramatic perspective which acknowledges no certainties except the fact of suffering. (It is appropriate that Morris Bober should be an unorthodox Jew, and that at his funeral the rabbi should say, "Yes, Morris Bober was to me a true Jew because he lived in the Jewish experience, and with the Jewish heart. . . . He suffered, he endured, but with hope.")[11]

---

9) *Ibid.*, p. 181.
10) *Ibid.*, p. 189.
11) *Ibid.*, p. 180.

The achievement of Malamud's style, which survives his ironic play, lies in the author's capacity to convey both hope and agony in the rhythms of Yiddish speech.

> "I think I will shovel the snow," he told Ida at lunch-time.
> "Go better to sleep."
> "It ain't nice for the customers."
> "What customers—who needs them?"
> "People can't walk in such high snow," he argued.
> "Wait, tomorrow it will be melted."
> "It's Sunday, it don't look so nice for the goyim that they go to church."
> Her voice had an edge in it. "You want to catch pneumonia, Morris?"
> "It's spring," he murmured.[12]

There is a Hemingway cleanness in this dialogue, a kind of humility and courage, but also a softness Hemingway never strove to communicate.

Morris, however, does catch pneumonia and die. Nor can the poetry of the style persuade us to forget that the search of Frank Alpine for an identity ends, in the last, brief paragraph of the novel, with the ritual of circumcision. The act is one of self-purification, of initiation too, in Frank's case, but it is also an act of self-repudiation, if not, as some may be tempted to say, of symbolic castration.

---

12) *Ibid.*, p. 173.

Culture Conflict

by Walter Shear

Although the novel as form is not always restricted to a concern with social milieu, certainly it is a type of literature that is often associated with social awareness. In a given society the writer has available classifications and stratifications which can provide some elements of a literary order and can give an indication, at least, of kinds and qualities of relationships between individuals. Culture, perhaps because of the ambiguity of the term itself, presents materials of a different order, even though it may, in appearance, seem spooned from the same pot. Pervaded with invisible, collective motivations, the novel of culture, as contrasted with the novel of manners, examines more minutely the ambiguities in the relationship between the individual and his values—and thus is both closer to its characters and at the same time attentive to an area beyond them.

Because of the diffused and dynamic society confronting it, the American novel has been inclined toward the broad area of culture rather than toward the national amalgam of behaviors available in its society. This tendency in American literature, a favorite of Eliot-inspired mythseekers, has not only achieved academic respectability but has inevitably been subject to more and more analysis, one result of which has been to make contemporary novelists increasingly aware of their material, its limitations and possibilities. This is not to say that a critical trend has imposed literary methods on current novelists, but by constant reminder of what kind of novel has been written and will probably be written, literary analysis has contributed to the more sophisticated attitude the current novelist has toward his fictional forms.

Perhaps no one better illustrates this kind of sophistication than Bernard Malamud, whose knowledge and manipulation of cultural and literary archetypes has frequently been commented on. Avoiding the analytical preoccupations of other American novelists, Malamud's treatment of his characters is flavored with sympathy, frustration, and exasperation. Knowing that he, as creator, is also contributor to their troubles, he cannot take their situations as seriously as they do. Often he seems to play with his role as "artist" by deliberately blurring the distinction between the archetype, which has universal significance, and the literary cliché, a mode which has exhausted its significance. The result of his peculiar relationship to the characters is that he becomes manipulator of the values they crucify themselves on and in order to remain true to both himself and his characters, two fictional modes—realistic and symbolic—so interact in his fiction as to comment upon each other simultaneously.

In *The Assistant* two cultures, the Jewish tradition and the American heritage (representing the wisdom of the old world and the practical knowledge of the new), collide and to some degree synthesize to provide a texture of social documentation which is manifested in a realistic aesthetic. However, the dichotomy is preserved and in fact given emphasis through an entirely different aesthetic presentation, one which tends to project the characters as types and treats their motivations, environments, and ideas as symbolic threads which link the narrative to the deeper level of personal significance from which the elements of human strength and weakness manage to emerge in the actions which both define and dramatize culture as a phenomenon.

Despite its more overt concern with a Jewish way of life, *The Assistant* deals basically with an implicit conflict between a heritage of ancient wisdom and traditional values and the American atmosphere of practicality and success, a conflict which not merely envelops the characters but—since they are not fully aware of its influence—exists as a constant source of confusion and bewilderment. For the characters these two systems of values become burdens, handicaps, imposers of demands which they cannot meet, most frequently because these demands pull them in opposite directions. Both these value worlds are embodied in all the characters, but the characters also exist in an ironic relationship to the worlds: all are in America, and all are basically secular, thus effectively removed from the traditional religious and social environment in which the old values flourished; in addition all of the major characters are the "have-nots" and blunderers in a country which sanctifies success and efficiency. Thus the characters in a most peculiar way are in the world but not completely in contact with it, a situation Malamud further emphasizes by omitting specific references to time.

On the other hand, the book presents the theme of alienation pushed to the point of an unphilosophic absurdity, and this situation is reiterated in the relationship of the characters, most of whom regard each other with almost premeditated misunderstandings. There is, however, a common meeting ground on the personal level that becomes an important part of the theme: as Solotaroff states, "Malamud's Jews (and his Gentiles) are connected to each other not by religious and social ties but a common fate of error and ill luck and sorrow, of having lost much by their mistakes and recovered little by their virtues."

With montage-like effects, Malamud dramatizes American culture with casual, almost comic allusions, ranging from the popular to the more aesthetic conceptions of American life. Occasionally he even moves beyond national boundaries to treat America as a symbolic pattern for the direction of Western civilization, but for the most part, his social focus is confined to the American dream as nightmare, in particular terms to a poor neighborhood in New York where success, instead of being a goal or source of hope, serves to mock and eventually to envelop everyone like a shroud. Within the realistic bounds of the neighborhood, however, the characters tend, at times, to embody what might be called archetypal images from the level of popular middle-class American culture. The assistant himself, Frank Alpine, is the young man, unencumbered by a past filled with family obligations, who is poor but ambitious, ready to start climbing to the top. In this respect he suggests the typical Horatio Alger hero, but Malamud complements and complicates this portrait with a related stereotype and, with some allusions to *Crime and Punishment* and Raskolnikov's great man theory, pushes Frank toward the journalistic and Hollywood underworld, toward the success dream of the gangster who may become a popular hero by gaining his own kind of fame and fortune.

In presenting such pieces of popular culture Malamud allows the characters to formulate their self-conceptions and speculate on their destinies as those destinies are popularly articulated. For example, Frank's vision of his criminal career is from a pseudoromantic, sensational point of view with equal parts of the tabloids and Hollywood: "At crime he would change his luck, make adventure, live like a prince. He shivered with pleasure as he conceived robberies, assaults —murders if it had to be—each violent act helping to satisfy a craving that somebody suffer as his own fortune improved" (see p. 74; all references are to *The Assistant,* New York: Signet, 1957). Eventually, through the combination of misfortune, conscience, and the influence of a "good" woman, Frank is able to adjust his dreams to a more socially acceptable goal, that of a college education, and he proudly tells his girl, Helen, that he is going to make something of himself.

By juxtaposing such participations in national reveries with Frank's more real experiences, which reveal both incompetence and a deeper moral awareness, Malamud is able to criticize the more romantic tendencies in American culture and the willingness (frequently desperate) of many to prefer an imagined future to a personally unacceptable present.

This willingness to postpone life by a preoccupation with abstract goals is made even more explicit in Malamud's treatment of Helen, a girl who is at once more practical and more idealistic than the confused Frank Alpine whose dreams are big but always dreams. Helen is the person who knows what she wants; she is very much aware of the importance of status and she reads—thereby coming in contact with the "higher things in life" and being intellectually cognizant of other levels of experience than the practical and materialistic.

But with her knowledge and experience (her loss of virginity and innocence is both a realistic and symbolic key to some of her practicality), she still remains determinedly a feminine Jay Gatsby, only slightly more mature. Certainly it is not an accident that some of her comments seem to be heavily colored by the Fitzgerald style: "When a person is young he's privileged with all kinds of possibilities. Wonderful things might happen, and when you get up in the morning you feel they will. That's what youth means, and that's what I've lost. I want a larger and better life. I want the return of my possibilities" (p. 37). "Her constant fear," Malamud informs us, "was that her life would not turn out as she had hoped. . . . she could not part with the substance of her dreams"(p. 107). Dreams, of course, have no substance. Eventually, with the assist of peculiar circumstances, she projects her fantasy into the man least able to bear the kind of ideals associated with success, Frank Alpine; and the dream-world turns to one version of a "practical" outlook, a woman's scorn; "She was filled with loathing at the fantasy she had created, of making him into what he couldn't be—educable, promising, kind and good, when he was no more than a bum" (p. 139). Thus one form of the American dream disintegrates again into the psychological tensions which Malamud seems to prefer, and the cultural tendencies of the characters are reduced to the level of personal relationships.

If we look at Morris Bober as a figure in the American success myth, we find a poor businessman, one who lacks the "get up and go" necessary "to reach the top". The business has not changed with the times—the sign which fell down ten years ago has never been replaced, and the customers are not an occasion for social amenities. Morris does not use the hard sell or the soft sell; he is simply there to serve the customers. (And in this regard Morris contrasts with Frank Alpine's later success as a salesman.) Yet Morris, who can be condemned by his family for failing to be at least the good provider and secure the better things in life for his daughter, strangely echoes an old legend about Abraham Lincoln; the rabbi in his funeral oration mentions that he ran two blocks to give back a nickel. Certainly Morris Bober *is* a part of American history, actually almost a stereotype of those many immigrants seeking to escape tyranny, famine, or persecution, who arrived in the New World with some hopes, some ambitions (at one time *he* had planned to be a pharmacist). To some degree he has not done badly; others have faced worse circumstances and have lived with more misery, but the images and dreams of success —even in his little neighborhood—are continual reminders that something has gone wrong, that Morris Bober, immigrant, has not lived or moved in harmony with the cultural dream. One might say that Morris does not move with the times (the new world constantly becoming newer); this, in fact, occurs to him: "America had become too complicated. One man counted for nothing. . . . What had he escaped to here?" (p. 162). However, his thoughts also accuse him: "He had the will of victim, no will to speak of" *(ibid.)*. At this point he seems to be close to one of those truthful lies Malamud seems to relish —to live faithfully in the aura of the success dream one must believe; a defeatist attitude is fatal. At the end of a day of defeat Morris' unuttered words touch the heart of what sociologists might call the relationship between a man and his environment: "He went downstairs and had coffee at a dish-laden table in the Automat. America" (p. 163). As a final ironic twist of this half truth, Morris in his last thoughts accepts the American verdict upon him, "I gave away my life for nothing."

This is one version of *The Assistant,* but not the final word, for the old world has also figured deeply in the lives and actions of the characters, and in Malamud's treatment of its values, expressed chiefly in more traditional symbols and associations, tells us much more what matters about these people because it alone can explain these values in religious and ethical forms. Since the cultural backgrounds are not exclusive, since they do interact, the old not only explains the lives more fully than the immediate environment; it completes them.

While the characters spend much time thinking of the future and its more promising possibilities, they also at times examine themselves (never with complete insight), and they do want to *be* and *do* good. Thus they are capable of responding, if not morally at least with sympathy, to those around them. This tendency towards introspection and self-analysis is, in fact, what gives much comic and pathetic quality to the characterizations and what brings them closer to Malamud's own ethical perception; they know and think better than they are or can be for long. Malamud widens this discrepancy with what seem superficially to be ridiculous symbolic devices. Frank Alpine, the bungling petty criminal, is almost too heavy handedly associated with St. Francis. When he first appears, he just happens to open a magazine in Sam Pearl's counter and immediately recognizes St. Francis preaching to the birds; it is like a vision out of his childhood. St. Francis, Frank tells Sam, said "poverty was a queen and he loved her like she was a beautiful woman" (p. 28). In his comments here Frank expresses the major motives of his character: Like St. Francis he wants "a new view of things", to slough off the old life and put on garments of true worth. He will, in a stumbling way he has never dreamed, pursue both poverty and a woman; and poverty, love, and the woman will be completely intertwined. At first Frank's character, especially his past, seems to resemble the flitting birds more than St. Francis, but he comes very close to complete embodiment at times, most overtly in a scene in the park where Helen sees him feeding the birds and finally rising from the bench, "the pigeons fluttered up with him, a few landing on his arms and shoulders, one perched on his fingers, pecking peanuts from his cupped palm" (p. 94). Yet this brief identification is shattered in the next sentence: "Another fat bird sat on his hat," and we return to reality.

Because he is almost a composite of fleshly weaknesses, Frank Alpine can never really be Francis of Assisi, but he can struggle under the awareness of the image, approach it at times, turn from it and back again. His Catholic heritage, which for the most part is far in the background, seems to be at least indirectly a source of his pangs of conscience and his compulsion to confess everything to Morris. It is, however, this other compulsion, stealing—also the fruits of his childhood—that first involves Frank with Morris Bober, and this wrong becomes the thin but inseverable cord linking them simply as human beings. These ties of evil which Frank establishes with all the major characters are the strongest bonds Frank has with the human race, and it is only his conscience which forces him to live in terms of such simple elemental obligations and to attempt to correct what he cannot correct, what is already past. For all the unthinking harm he brings to others, he remains somewhat absurdly, "a man of stern morality," whose major problem is "to do good if he wanted." He thereby demonstrates the gap, which for Malamud seems permanent, between the will and the way.

Not simply an incompetent criminal and aspiring saint, Frank is also in love with Helen, the symbol and the person —a role which permits Malamud to explore the mixture and madness in traditional views of love. Frank is a lover with a vast range—from the sensuality of the peeping-tom and the sexual enthusiast to the idealism of a clumsy meeter of minds and unselfish giver of gifts and of himself. Throughout his relationship with Helen he attempts to formulate the proper kind of love, some combination of attitude and action that will be acceptable to both himself and his beloved, but the time and situation are never right. On the physical level his love suffers constant frustration by Helen's "ideals in sex"; from spying on her in the bathroom he progresses to an unsatisfactory meeting in his room and finally to a physical fulfillment in the rape-seduction scene in the park, a culmination on the physical level which is disastrous to the love itself. As the bearer of gifts and the intellectual companion, he also fails. Gifts, which for Helen seem tinged with responsibilities and involvement, are returned or thrown away; and his literary background and appreciation are too limited for the amorphous atmosphere of the intellect. Love in Frank's case is a matter of both receiving—on the physical level—and giving

—in an idealistic sense; both difficulties seem to be reflected in a basically literary methodology, the search for an adequate correlative in actual terms which might allow the love relationship to flourish. As a key symbol for the entire relationship, Malamud uses the traditional rose, a token of his love which Frank carves out of wood, thus giving a form of beauty to natural material. As an emotionally charged object, however, "the flower reminded Helen of her unhappiness," and she drops it into the garbage can. But in Frank's day-dream at the end of the novel it reappears and changes into a real flower, specifically identified here with Helen and presented not by Frank Alpine, but by his idealized vision of himself, St, Francis.

Helen, as her name suggests, comes to represent the beauty and love all the major characters seek, but she herself is too practical to accept this as an accurate description of what she is at the moment. She is a Helen whose better judgment warns her away from the confusion between unrealized potentials and things as they are. Not wanting to exist merely as an object of love, she shies away from involvement even though she feels most acutely the loneliness which may be her fate. For her, love with Frank becomes a resignation to fate, an accepting of the present with all its disappointments as a permanent condition, and therefore love turns to hatred—as she realizes, to divert hatred from herself. Ironically, the more she refuses to acquiesce to circumstances, the more abstract and symbolic she becomes to the others who feel they must be deeply immersed in ordinary life.

Both Morris and Ida seem to think of Helen more in terms of her future, and perhaps inevitably in terms of their future as well, than as an individual. As man of deeper understanding who is aware of a past involving more than simply his own disappointments and of a future which goes beyond his personal goals, Morris sees other people as having a value in themselves but also as a part of a broader fabric of life which incorporates, rather than transcends, the personal psychology of all individuals. Thus, while he is aware of the importance of success to his family obligation, his orientation is not toward the remedying of his failure but toward a form of duty and the acting out of a role, the basis for which he is only dimly aware of. His generosity is evidenced early in such acts as the giving of credit to the little girl whose mother is a drunk and who, Morris knows, will never pay.

He does this not with the conscious pride of doing a good deed—indeed, his conscious thoughts are that this is foolish, bad business—but with the half-awareness that he has done what, for his character, is the easiest course. Morris is the fool of goodness; he does good and helps others because it is his nature, an integral part of the worldview he can only vaguely formulate. Basically, Morris is a product of Jewish thought, perhaps closely connected with the man whose name he echoes, Martin Buber, and this aspect of his character is so insisted upon that the reader is immediately aware of the importance of his comments on the Jew and the funeral message of the Rabbi which claims, perhaps on slim evidence, that Morris "was. . . a true Jew because he lived in the Jewish experience" (p. 180). In the discussions between Morris and Frank on the Jewish experience—and this must be interpreted as both historical and current experience—the characters shift from the contemporary roles of storekeeper and assistant to their purer religious selves, teacher and novitiate. The Jewish Law, Morris explains, "means to do what is right, to be honest, to be good. This means to other people" (p. 99). As Frank points out, these ideas are embodied in other religions, but he gets closer to the particular emphasis of Morris' view by asking about suffering. Do Jews merely suffer because they want to? "If you live, you suffer," Morris says, thereby giving voice to a point of view which sets him apart from the faith in success displayed by most of the people around him. Enlarging the proposition, Morris states that everyone suffers for everyone else. Thematically, such a statement can be illustrated by the lives of all the major characters, who sacrifice themselves for others—with much resentment in most cases, since they do not possess Morris' vision. The statement is, however, hardly as convincing out of context as it is an insight into the way Morris' actions make religious sense and a vision of the lost path in which he walks.

As an outsider, rootless and moving, Frank Alpine is at first attracted by the stability of the store, unaware at the beginning that the Bober family regards it as a tomb from which they wish to escape into the American life. Once he starts to realize what it can really be, he struggles to make it a part of the thriving business community of America, gradually succumbing to its necessity to be what it is. In time he succeeds his teacher and accepts the philosophy of suffering and acquiescence, symbolically represented by his conversion to Judaism and his circumcision, the pain of which both "enraged and inspired him." In Malamud's manipulation of another old story, the wanderer has at last become a Jew.

On the other hand, the ideas about suffering and the

willingness of Frank and Morris to accept such ideas can be accounted for by admitting that only in such a scheme of things could their lives make sense and have purpose. There is, however, imbedded in the novel an ultimate religious perspective that carries the ideas even further than mere apprehensions of roles and duties. Just as Morris is entombed in the store, so all the souls of all the characters are imprisoned in external circumstance, in their culture, and in the very limitations of their senses and the physical demands of their bodies. Norman Leer mentions the social barrier as a symbol of alienation in this novel, but actually all the limitations of the characters serve to set them apart and contradict their best intentions toward one another. Malamud's conception of character is heavily influenced by the naturalistic view of human nature, but his idea of an escape from circumstances in love, and the awareness of the meaning of suffering goes back to an older tradition. The final meaning of such lives, if fiction can ever be final, is in the past, buried in old wisdom of which the characters have only a sketchy knowledge. Perhaps this tendency of Malamud to both give and withdraw his message is also reflected in Marcus Klein's view of his fiction: "The world does not come easily to Malamud, everything is on the verge of not being, and the process of his own holding on, rather than any moralizing he does, is indeed the excitement of his fiction, and its tension."

Oddly enough, a minor character named Breitbart seems to summarize many of the cultural tensions in the novel. As a sufferer, both comic and grotesque, he is the typical victim appearing in sensational tabloid stories—his wife runs away with his brother, leaving him with "a drawerful of bills . . .

and a not too bright five-year-old boy." On his back he lugs around a burden of light bulbs, suggesting many frames of reference from the spark of humanity or conscience to the modern world of progress. Perhaps all these meanings work in the same confused, half-comic, intermittent light which pervades the entire novel. At any rate he appears in the final scene still trapped in his economic journeys, stops briefly for a cup of tea, and gives Frank a last word which may be both advice and description, "Schwer." Moving between existence and nonexistence he has no definite role within either context of meaning and yet a possible place in each. His routine, like those of the other characters, is invested at different times with differing values.

Marcus Klein, paraphrasing some comments by Saul Bellow, writes, "The fat gods of the new materialism are all about us demanding our energies." One might say that in *The Assistant* the same situations exist in regard to meaning, and man, caught between the conflicting claims of cultural values, suffers not only because of his circumstances but because a fragmented abundance of world-views produces uncertainty about intentions, actions, and roles. If Malamud here seems to be on the side of older values, he refuses his characters willed preferences or convictions. They have faith enough to persevere but doubt enough to suspect themselves.

Select Bibliography

Bellman, Samuel, "Women, Children, and Idiots First," *Critique,* VII (Winter, 1964-65), 123-139.

Goldman, Mark, "Bernard Malamud's Comic Vision and the Theme of Identity," *Critique,* VII (Winter, 1964-65), 92-109.

Hicks, Granville, "Generations of the Fifties: Malamud, Gold, and Updike," *The Creative Present* (Garden City, New York: Doubleday, 1963), pp. 217-237.

Klein, Marcus, *After Alienation* (Cleveland: World, 1964), pp. 247-294.

Leer, Norman, "Three American Novels and Contemporary Society: A Search for Commitment," *Wisconsin Studies in Contemporary Literature,* III (Fall, 1962), iii, 67-86.

Solotaroff, Theodore, "Bernard Malamud's Fiction: The Old Life and the New," *Commentary,* XXXIII (March, 1962), 197-204.

The Complex Pattern of Redemption

by Peter L. Hays

I. The Novel

Bernard Malamud's use of the medieval myth of the Grail Quest to inform *The Natural* is by now a critical commonplace,[1] and a broad mythic pattern of rebirth has also been seen by these same critics in both *The Assistant* and *A New Life*. Malamud's protagonists *(schlemiels*, "football[s] of the Gods," Charles A. Hoyt calls them) struggle against a bleak, unfavorable world and their own bad luck and ineptitude; usually the world strips them of material goods and any sense of real accomplishment, but their author endows them with, and communicates to us, their courage, their compassion, their humanity: from hellish depths of human misery they come forth, reborn as secular saints. What is remarkable in *The Assistant*, in addition to the vigor of the individual characters,

1) Leslie Fiedler seems to have been the first to recognize the myth in *The Natural* in his *No! in Thunder* (Boston, 1960). p. 105; among others who refer to or discuss its presence are Jonathan Baumbach, *The Landscape of Nightmare* (New York, 1965). pp. 107-111; Charles Alva Hoyt, "Bernard Malamud and the New Romanticism," *Contemporary American Novelists,* ed. Harry T. Moore (Carbondale, 1964). p. 78; Sidney Richman, *Bernard Malamud* (New York, 1966), pp. 28-49; and Robert Shulman, "Myth, Mr. Eliot, and the Comic Novel," *Modern Fiction Studies,* XII (Winter 1966-1967), 400-403.

is the complexity with which this realistically presented redemptive pattern is reinforced with myth, symbol and a philosophy remarkably like that of Martin Buber.

The protagonist in *The Assistant* is Frank Alpine, a wanderer without home and without values, except for some basic human compassion tempered by prejudice. Desperately poor and hungry and without direction to his life, he helps Ward Minogue, an acquaintance, rob Jewish grocer Morris Bober one November day. Frank is more willing to participate in the robbery because his victim is a Jew, someone for whom he need not feel sympathy. Yet when Ward impatiently pistol whips the old man, Frank gives Bober a cup of water. Alpine is twenty-five and looks much older; of Italian extraction, he was raised in an orphanage as a Catholic, but he no longer believes in that religion or much of anything. He has never known love, success or satisfaction; he is a born loser, a *schlemiel.* As he says:

> "I've been close to some wonderful things—jobs, for instance, education, women, but close is as far as I go. . . . Sooner or later everything I think is worth having gets away from me in some way or other. I work like a mule for what I want, and just when it looks like I am going to get it I make some kind of stupid move, and everything that is nailed down tight blows up in my face.
>
> . . . With me one wrong thing leads to another and it ends in a trap."[2)]

2) Bernard Malamud, *The Assistant* (New York, 1959), p. 36. All subsequent quotations from the novel or its author will refer to this edition and will be paginated in my text.

In this case, the trap is Morris' grocery. Frank, ashamed of his part in the robbery and sorry for Bober, returns to help the old man—to become Bober's assistant in work as he was Ward Minogue's in theft. Like Fitzgerald about the rich, Alpine has conflicting feeling about goodness. In the orphanage where he was raised. Alpine had been taught about St. Francis, of whom he says:

> "He said poverty was a queen and he loved her like she was a beautiful woman. . . . Eeverytime I read about somebody like him I get a feeling inside of me which I have to fight to keep from crying. He was born good, which is a talent of you have it." (p. 31)

But Alpine lacks this talent and neither comprehends St. Francis nor his own feelings about the saint. Yet he sees that Bober's life, like St. Francis', is one of both poverty and goodness, and in his longing for a code to live by, an end to his own aimlessness, he is attracted by Bober's endurance in the face of calamity, by his acceptance of life with all its hardships, by his compassion and by his religion. At the same time, Alpine is repelled by the pain, the suffering and the lack of comfort which Morris' code brings the grocer. He asks Morris what it is to be a Jew. The grocer replies:

> ". . . The important thing is the Torah. This is the Law—a Jew must believe in the Law. . . . This means to do what is right, to be honest, to be good. This means to other people. Our life is hard enough. Why should we hurt somebody else?. . . We ain't animals. . . .This is what

a Jew believes." (p. 124)

Frank is also attracted to Bober's daughter Helen and gradually wins the friendship of father and daughter—only to lose both. Unable to do right, even when he wants to, Frank continuously steals meager sums from the small amounts in the grocery store cash register, causing Morris, when the grocer can finally prove theft, to fire him. The same night Frank goes to the park to meet Helen, who is falling in love with him and has been meeting him in spite of her mother's objections; he arrives at their rendezvous and finds Ward Minogue attempting to rape Helen. But after he drives off Ward, Frank takes her by force himself.

Later when Bober becomes ill, Frank sneaks back into the store, operating it while Morris recuperates. When the grocer is better, he forces Frank to leave. At the end of March, however, Morris catches pneumonia while shoveling snow and dies three days later. At his funeral on a warm, spring-like April day, Frank slips and falls into Morris' grave, landing on the grocer's coffin. Afterwards Frank goes back to the store that had been Bober's tomb-in-life for twenty-two years, assuming the support of Mrs. Bober and Helen, and working at an additional night job as well so that Helen can attend night school. Frank also assumes Morris' values, his honesty and his compassion: his descent into Bober's grave marks Frank's death as an uncommitted wanderer and his rebirth as Bober's spiritual son—one who lives by the Law. The last paragraph in the novel relates the events of the spring a year after Bober's death:

> One day in April Frank went to the hospital and had himself circumcised. For a couple of days he dragged himself around with a pain between his legs. The pain enraged and inspired him. After Passover he became a Jew. (p. 246)

II. Myth and Symbol

That Frank should have himself circumcised and formally convert to Judaism at Passover-Easter time is highly significant: it is the season of Nature's renewal of life in the spring and coincides with the resurrections of Christ, Attis and Adonis. It is also the time of the redemption (resurrection) of the Jewish nation from Egyptian bondage. And that Frank should drag himself around during these holy days is also significant, for *pesach,* the Hebrew word for Passover, is etymologically related not only to *pasahu,* an Assyrian word meaning to propitiate, but also to several Hebrew words meaning lame or hobbling. Thus Malamud has used, consciously or not, religious and mythic allusions, as well as obviously purposeful seasonal changes—the novel moves twice from wintry fall to warm spring—to mark the pattern of death and rebirth. Frank undergoes a rite of initiation, begun at Morris' side in the living death of the grocery store, marked by his descent to the grocer's grave and by his circumcision, and expressed by his conversion from a spiritually empty life: he experiences resurrection, which prepares him for (to borrow from Malamud) a new life, based on the role of the grocer and endowed with Bober's responsibilities, beliefs and values.

Frank's material gains are negligible, or nonexistent, but he does grow in heroic stature and in our admiration. And we can measure Frank's conversion away from his sterile, self-centered life in terms of his relationship with Helen, who is also endowed with mythic characteristics.

Although critics disagree about their relationship at the novel's conclusion,[3] I feel that they probably will marry. At the end of the novel, Helen confesses to herself her feelings for Frank.

> Although she detested the memory of her experience in the park, lately it had come back to her how she had desired that night to give herself to Frank. . . . She had wanted him. . . . If he had made his starved leap in bed she would have returned passion. She had hated him, she thought, to divert hatred from herself. (p. 239)

She learns how hard Frank is working and thinks:

> He had kept them alive. Because of him she had enough to go to school at night. . . . It came to her that he had changed. It's true, he's not the same man, she said to herself. I should have known by now. She had despised him for the evil he had done, without understanding the way or aftermath, or admitting there could be an end to

---

3) Granville Hicks feels that Frank and Helen may marry ("Portraits of the Authors as Men," *Saturday Review,* July 10, 1965, p. 29), but Baumbach (p. 119) and Theodore Solotaroff ("Bernard Malamud's Fiction," *Commentary,* March 1962, p. 198) do not——Baumbach explicitly, Solotaroff implicitly. Nor does Ihab Hassan hold out hope for them in *Radical Innocence* (Princeton, 1961), p. 116. (See Chapter 16 in this collection for Solotaroff essay.)

> the bad and a beginning of good. . . . He had been one thing, low, dirty, but because of something in himself —something she couldn't define, a memory perhaps, an ideal he might have forgotten and then remembered—he had changed into somebody else, no longer what he had been. She should have recognized it before. What he did to me he did wrong, she thought, but since he has changed in his heart, he owes me nothing. (p. 243)

The next week she enters the store and speaks to Frank —only the second time in almost a year since her father's death, and the first time of her own volition—to thank him for all his trouble. She tells him that she will consider his offer to take more money from him so that she can go to college during the day, blushing as she does so, and also tells him that she is still using a volume of Shakespeare he had given her as a present long before. And that night Frank hears her fight with and leave—perhaps permanently—her one boyfriend.

Perhaps Frank and she never become completely reconciled, but most of the barriers that had existed between them have been removed. After Frank's assault on Helen, the one comment from her which Malamud gives us, the one that closes the chapter, is, "Dog—uncircumcised dog!" (p.168). The adjective, at least, is no longer valid.

As Baumbach has noted, "Frank's attraction to Helen is an uneasy fusion of the sensual and the spiritual . . ." (p. 117); also, Frank's "redemption is made possible by his uncompromising love for Helen—which provides the impetus for his commitment to the store."[4] It is undoubtedly part of the

4) Jonathan Baumbach, "The Economy of Love," *Kenyon Review*, XXV (1963),

impetus for his commitment to Judaism, too. Frank was strongly attracted to Judaism and to Helen, and wished to "belong" to both; and he has taken what steps he can, accomplishing the first goal, doing as much as he could to achieve the second. The first brings him a form of rebirth and spiritual peace; the second would bring him sexual fulfillment, a satisfaction of his social needs and probably children, too. The Spartan Moon-goddess was called "Helen," and marriage to her made Menelaus a king. Her name is etymologically related to Helle, bright goddess of death and resurrection. So that to the extent to which Helen has redeemed Frank and brought him to his goals, and could bring him to the others, she is a fertility goddess.

To emphasize this role of hers, Malamud frequently has her described in terms of obvious symbols of fertility: flowers (harbingers of spring's renewal) and birds (roosters; the doves of Noah, Aphrodite and Christian symbolism; the Thanksgiving turkey). Morris thinks Helen "looks like a little bird" (p. 20), and when Frank spies on her in the bathroom he thinks of her a "breasts like small birds in flight, her ass like a flower" (p. 75). And like Aphrodite, Helen leaves a floral fragrance about her in the air (p. 184).

The bird and flower symbols, especially the former, are also significant because of Frank's symbolic relationship to St. Francis of Assissi. There are, of course, their analoguous names; there is also the fact that Frank spent most of his early life in the city of St. Francis, San Francisco (p. 81). Moreover,

456. This article was the basis of Baumbach's chapter on Malamud in *The Landscape of Nightmare.*

Malamud frequently associates the two. There is the initial reference when, in Sam Pearl's candy shop, Frank sees a picture of the saint surrounded by a flock of birds, with a grove of leafy trees in the background (p. 30). At one point in the novel, Helen goes for a walk in a nearby park; as she approaches it, she sees "a man squatting by one of the benches, feeding the birds. . . . When the man rose, the pigeons fluttered up with him, a few landing on his arms and shoulders, one perched on his fingers, pecking peanuts from his cupped palm. Another fat bird sat on his hat" (p. 118). The man, of course, is Frank. At another time, Frank, in his loneliness and desire for Helen, tells her a story he remembers of St. Francis, who, wondering one snowy evening what his life would have been if he had married and had a family, went outside and made a snow wife and several children (p. 95). At the end of the chapter, Helen associates the saint with the thieving assistant: "Who was he making into a wife out of snowy moonlight?" (p. 102). Helen and the moon, again.

The snow that barefoot St. Francis trod upon occurs again in the novel, in a dream of Frank's. After his assault of Helen, he tries again and again to apologize. Then, one night

> he dreamed he was standing in snow outside her window. His feet were bare yet not cold. He had waited a long time in the falling snow, and some of it lay on his head and had all but frozen his face; but he waited longer until, moved by pity, she opened the window and flung something out. It floated down; he thought it was a piece of paper with writing on it but saw that it was a white flower, surprising to see in wintertime. Frank caught it in

> his hand. As she had tossed the flower out through the partly opened window he had glimpsed her fingers only, yet he saw the light of her room and even felt the warmth of it. Then when he looked again the window was shut tight, sealed with ice. Even as he dreamed, he knew it had never been open. There was no such window. He gazed down at his hand for the flower and before he could see it wasn't there, felt himself wake. (p. 185)

Obviously, the rose, the flower Frank desires to receive from Helen, is her love and Helen herself. At her father's funeral, it is a rose which Helen throws onto the coffin and which Frank, intent on observing, follows so blindly that he stumbles into the open grave. But besides these allusions, there are others equally explicit. To pass the time one day, Frank begins to carve a board "into something. To his surprise it turned into a bird. . . . He thought of offering it to Helen but it seemed too rough a thing" (p. 192). Here, the bird may carry its more conventional symbolic weight, the soul, Frank's, which he desires to offer Helen and then refuses in recognition of his unworthiness, of his being "too rough a thing." Next he carves for her, appropriately, "a flower . . . a rose starting to bloom" (p. 192). He gives it to her, to atone in part for his forcing of her, and she, still indignant, throws it in the garbage.

In the penultimate paragraph of the novel, these elements come together for emphasis:

> As he [Frank] was reading [the Bible] he had this pleasant thought. He saw St. Francis come dancing out of the woods in his brown rags, a couple of scrawny birds

> flying around over his head. St. F. [*sic*] stopped in front of the grocery, and reaching into the garbage can, plucked the wooden rose out of it. He tossed it into the air and it turned into a real flower that he caught in his hand. With a bow he gave it to Helen, who had just come out of the house. "Little sister, here is your little sister the rose." From him she took it, although it was with the love and best wishes of Frank Alpine. (pp. 245-246)

By associating Helen with flowers, especially the rose, symbol of love and femininity, and by making her the motive and inspiration for Frank's recurrent redemptive acts and the possible means for his greater personal fulfillment, Malamud has endowed her with characteristics of mythic fertility goddesses. The bird imagery serves the same purposes, and also, through Frank's identification with St. Francis, reinforces my contention that we are meant to believe that Frank and Helen will come together after the novel's close.

There is still another sign which attests to the special nature of Helen's role. In *Symbolic Wounds* (New York, 1962) Bruno Bettelheim discusses the relationship of circumcision to ritual forms of emasculation. Speaking of the self-mutilation of the priests of Cybele, he says, "This example of ritual castration, and many others not mentioned here, indicates that it was exacted by maternal figures as a sign of devotion and submission on the part of their male followers. . . ." (p. 92). If Mrs. Bober objects to Helen's consorting with a non-Jew, if Helen herself loathes Frank because he is "an uncircumcised dog," then Frank is willing to have himself circumcised as a sign of "devotion and submission"—to the Law of Judaism, as

Morris Bober spoke of it, and to Helen. Bettelheim also says, "Loeb is convinced that circumcision was originally performed as a sacrifice to a female goddess. . . . He follows Barton who holds that originally all circumcision was a sacrifice to the goddess of fertility."[5] And Frank's circumcision for love and religion during the Paschal season, the time of propitiation, coincides not only with the death and resurrection of Christ at the time of hobbling, but also with the castration of Attis and Adonis (and their priests) on behalf of their respective lovers and fertility goddesses, Cybele and Aphrodite. To call Helen a fertility figure, though, to compare her, however removed, to Cybele and Aphrodite, is not to say that Malamud has written modern Greek myth, as John Updike has in *The Centaur.* The source of the power which Helen may dispense, the nature of her *mana,* is the same with which the priestess of Isis heals Lawrence's Man Who Died; as Baumbach and Richman have noted, redemption comes to Malamud's protagonists through their ability to give of themselves unselfishly, to love.

III. Philosophy

. . . In a receptive hour of my life a man meets me about whom there is something, which I cannot grasp in any

5) *Symbolic Wounds,* p. 95; B.M. Loeb, "The Blood Sacrifice Complex," "*Memories of the American Anthropological Association,* No. 30 (1933), p. 18. George A. Barton, "Semitic Circumcision," *Encyclopedia of Religion and Ethics* (New York, 1911), p. 680. Cf. Ihab Hassan: "The act is one of self-purification, of initiation too, . . . if not of symbolic castration" (*op cit.,* p. 168).

> objective way at all, that 'says something' to me . . . speaks something that enters my own life. It can be something about this man, for instance that he needs me. But it can also be something about myself.
>
> . . . Perhaps I have to accomplish something about him; but perhaps I have only to learn something, and it is only a matter of my 'accepting'.[6]

The foregoing could well serve as a commentary on the essential relationship in the novel between Frank and Morris, but it was not written for that purpose; instead, it is part of the philosophical canon of Martin Buber. Many readers have stumbled over the similarity in names—Martin Buber, Morris Bober—and there is also a distinct similarity, not only in the beliefs expressed and acted upon by these two men, but in the philosophy one can infer from the novel as a whole.

Bober is not an orthodox Jew, for he does not obey Mosaic dietary laws, nor does he regularly attend religious services. Similarly, ". . . Buber does not regard the Jewish law as essential to the Jewish tradition. . . . He contrasts the false desire for security of the dogmatists of the law with the 'holy insecurity' of the truly religious man who does not divorce his action from his intention."[7] As Buber himself has said in *Between Man and Man,* "I have given up the religious" for "the everyday. . . . I know no fulness but each mortal hour's fulness of claim and responsibility. Though far from being equal to it,

6) Martin Buber, *Between Man and Man,* trans. Ronald Gregor Smith (London, 1947), pp. 9, 10.

7) Maurice S. Friedman, *Martin Buber: The Life of Dialogue* (London, 1955), p. 261.

yet I know that in claim I am claimed and may respond in responsibility. . . ." And for the grocer, too, the key to a moral existence is personal responsibility for others: "A Jew must believe in the Law. . . . This means to do what is right, to be honest, to be good. This means to other people. Our life is hard enough. Why should we hurt somebody else?" (p. 124)

That life is indeed hard, that it is replete with suffering, is part of the view of life expressed by Martin Buber and in *The Assistant.* In the latter, Morris says to Frank, "If you live, you suffer," and Frank asks, "What do you suffer for, Morris?" " 'I suffer for you,' Morris said calmly"(p. 125). In fact, at one point, Malamud says, "The world suffers" (p. 7). Buber also thinks that suffering is an essential part of man's life and is, in fact, what redeems him and gives him stature. Defining a moral man, Buber says he is one "with responsibility for the action of those who act, since he is wholly defined by the tension between being and 'ought to be, and in grotesque and hopeless courage casts his heart piece by piece into the insatiable gulf that lies between them[8)]—a comment which could well describe either Morris or Frank. For Morris' suffering is simply a measure of his endurance and humanity. For Frank, suffering because of what he has done against Morris and then, through relation with Morris, taking over the grocer's very suffering is a path to personal redemption. Frank is indeed defined throughout the course of the novel by the gap he is aware of between what he is and what he ought to be, and so he casts his energy, his endurance, his pride and his

8) Martin Buber, *I and Thou,* trans. Ronald Gregor Smith (New York, 1957), p 108.

heart in "grotesque and hopeless courage"—an apt description of all of Malamud's protagonists from Roy Hobbs to Yakov Bok—into the gap between them. Frank does not become what he thinks he ought to be—rich, powerful, "a big shot" —but his efforts do allow him to become what Buber and Bober would say he ought to be—a man, moral and responsible.

Perhaps the greatest common bond, however, between the philosopher and the grocer's creator, the novelist, is their treatment of "elation" and "dialogue." As I have noted, Baumbach and Richman state that love redeems Frank Alpine. Richman, quoting *I and Thou,* even uses Buber's "Love is responsibility of an *I for a Thou*" as epigraph for his chapter on *The Assistant,* but uses Buber primarily in discussing Malamud's writing that shows the influence of Hasidism (or Chasidism), which Buber invigorated in modern Jewish theology.[9] More important, I feel, is the way in which Malamud has exemplified Buber's precept of the I-Thou relationship, what denying it causes, and what allowing it to exist achieves.

According to Buber, there are two forms of existence: the I-It, which is a subject and object, person and thing, organizing, arranging, advantage-taking relationship; and the I-Thou,

9) Richman says that in *The Assistant,* "as in Martin Buber's famous depiction of the holy men of Chasidism, [there is] the 'hallowing of the everyday,'" *Ibid.,* p. 70, citing Malcolm Diamond, *Martin Buber: Jewish Existentialist* (New York, 1960), pp. 110-137. "Hallowing the *everyday*" is a basic tenet of Buber. Cf. Smith's introduction to *I and Thou:* Buber asserts "the present moment as the real time for faith. . . . His thought is rooted in the concrete situation. . . . The concrete reality . . . is the situation where responsible persons confront one another in living mutual relation" (pp. x-xi).

which is an interpersonal, mutually addressing, mutual exchanging one. Further, Buber states that a man defines himself in his relation with others. And wholeness, integration of personality, depends on eschewing the I-It impersonal for the I-Thou: "Entering into relation is an act of the whole being —it is in fact *the* act by which we constitute ourselves as human . . ." (Friedman, p. 83).

And so it is with Frank, who develops morally in proportion as he sees Helen less as a sexual object, and more as a person to love and be loved by; as he sees Morris less as a Jew, a type of victim for his or anyone's greed, and more as a fellow man, eventually, as a spiritual father. Everyone else in the novel but Bober—Julius Karp, Ward Minogue, Frank (at first), even Helen and Morris' wife Ida—seek to use others, to manipulate them for personal benefit. Only Morris tries constantly to establish I-Thou relationships, even with those who have stolen from him, like his former partner Charlie Sobeloff, or like Frank Alpine. This faith in humanity is what makes Morris the *schlemiel* that he is, like the cartoon character Charlie Brown in "Peanuts," but it is also that which makes him admirable and nearly heroic.

Ultimately, Frank, too, achieves these qualities. Through dialogue—both his conversations with Morris about the Law and with Helen about life and literature, and his turning to the Bobers in his silent observation of the code by which they live—Frank achieves I-Thou instead of I-It, and because of that relation he becomes an assistant for the third time in the novel; first to Ward Minogue, then to Morris, and finally to Helen and her mother. Moreover, Buber defines every approach to another's Thou as an approach to God, the

Eternal Thou; for him relation is essentially triadic, involving self, other and God (*I and Thou,* p. 75). Therefore, Frank's entering into relation with the Bobers is, by Buber's definition, an approach to God, a religious act, and thus prepares for Frank's conversion to Judaism.

In the early part of the novel, Frank fits Buber's definition of evil, for the philosopher considers evil as absence of relation and lack of direction generally—specifically, "lack of direction to ward Good."[10)] Moreover, Buber insists that "man repeatedly experiences the dimension of evil as indecision. . . . These moments merge into a course of indecision, as it were into a fixation in it" (p. 134). Certainly this describes Frank, as does the remedy: "To the extent to which the soul achieves unification it becomes aware of direction. . . . It comes into the service of good or into service for good" (p. 127). At the beginning of the novel, Frank is aimless, without direction. His only desire is generalized materialistic success. But in its place, Morris tells him of the Torah, the Law; as Buber explains: "The intention behind that collection [of psalms] may have been to complete the 'Torah' or 'direction' . . . by means of hymns and songs of a 'directing' kind. Here 'to direct' means to show the way which man should 'choose' (Ps. 25, 12), and that means to teach man to distinguish this way, the right way, from the other, wrong way" (p. 51). By his own life, Morris provides Frank with the example of different, better values; and hope of attaining Helen gives Frank a

10) Friedman, p. 103; Martin Buber, *Good and Evil,* trans. by Ronald Gregor Smith and Michael Bullock (1952, 1953), pp. 87 and 97. The following three quotations, identified only with page references in the text, are also from *Good and Evil.*

distinct purpose, a definite direction.

> "The man with the divided, complicated, contradictory soul is not helpless: the core of his soul, the divine force in its depths, is capable of . . . binding the conflicting forces together. . . ." Again and again temptation overcomes the soul, and "again and again innate grace arises from out of its depths and promises the utterly incredible: you can become whole and one." (Friedman, p. 91)

IV Conclusion

I have not meant to imply in the preceding section that Malamud immersed himself in the philosophy of Martin Buber and then set about embodying it in fiction,[11)] but the striking parallels remain. That love redeems is not an idea original to either Buber or Malamud; neither is the concept that one defines oneself and finds oneself through his relation to others. Maurice Friedman defines Jung's concept of myth, which manifests itself through expressions of archetypes and the collective unconscious, as "an embodiment in different forms and cultures of a perennial reality . . ." (p. 231). The collective unconscious is a difficult concept for many to accept. But perhaps the "perennial reality" is not some Platonic ideal existing independently of man; rather, it might simply be that intelligent, feeling men, especially two with

11) Mr. Malamud was kind enough to reply to a letter and said that he had only a very general acquaintance with Buber's work when he wrote *The Assistant* and did not intend to identify Morris Bober with the renowned philosopher.

similar religious backgrounds and sharing elements of a common tradition, living in the same difficult world and experiencing generally the same crises of despair, misfortune, loss of identity and pain see the problem and answers in roughly the same form: man inevitably suffers; to endure that suffering with as much dignity as possible is a virtue; to continue to strive to do right and to suffer for others is a mark of humanity. When Frank Alpine learns these lessons from Morris Bober, which would have been the same had Martin Buber been his teacher, he redeems himself and approaches a state of secular sainthood where he is indeed worthy of identification with St. Francis of Assisi.

Throughout the novel, Malamud has characterized Alpine by his relation to others, by the extent to which he establishes dialogue. Ward Minogue and he curse at each other and use each other to gain private goals; Frank spies on Helen, possesses her, and is cursed by her. But eventually he speaks, not just of Helen and Morris, but with them. For more than two years he shares their lives, making their needs his responsibilities; by controlling his own impatient, undirected desires he learns to love others, and finds direction, and himself.

Thus Bernard Malamud, with religious allusion, Mediterranean mythology, sacrificial rites and fertility imagery infusing a philosophy of existence very much like Martin Buber's, has created a modern parable in the form of a naturalistic novel, a story of redemption which expresses perennial realities of psychological and philosophical truth.

Selected Bibliography

A. Works by Bernard Malamud

Malamud, Bernard. *The Natural*. New York: Avon Books, 1980.

________________, *The Assistant*. New York: Penguin Books, 1977.

________________, *The Magic Barrel*. New York: Farrar, Straus & Giroux, 1980.

________________, *A New Life*. New York: Avon Books, 1980.

________________, *The Fixer*. New York: Penguin Books, 1977.

________________, *The Tenants*. New York: Avon Books, 1981

________________, *Pictures of Fidelman*. New York: Farrar, Straus & Giroux, 1969.

________________, *Dubin's Lives*. New York: Penguin Books, 1980.

________________, *God's Grace*. New York: Farrar, Straus & Giroux, 1982.

________________, *Idiots First*. New York: Farrar, Straus & Giroux, 1979.

________________, *Rembrandt's Hat*. New York: Farrer, Straus & Giroux, 1973.

B. Works about Bernard Malamud

Alter, Iska, *The Good Man's Dilemma.* AMS Press, 1981.

Astro, Richard and Benson, Jackson J. eds. *The Fiction of Bernard Malamud,* Corvallis: Oregon State Univ. Press, 1977.

Avery, Evelyn Gross, *Rebels and Victims.* New York: Kennikat Press, 1979.

Baumbach, Jonathan, *The Landscape of Nightmare.* New York: New York University Press, 1965.

Cohen, Sandy, *Bernard Malamud and the Trial by Love.* Amsterdam: Rodopi N.V., 1974.

Ducharme, Robert, *Art and Idea in the Novels of Bernard Malamud.* The Hague, Holland: Mouton and Company, 1974.

Field, Leslie A. and Joyce W., eds. *Bernard Malamud and the Critics.* New York: New York University Press, 1970.

________________, *Bernard Malamud: A Collection of Critical Essays.* Englewood Cliffs, N.J.: Prentice-Hall, 1975.

Gunn, Giles B, "Bernard Malamud and the High Cost of Living" in Nathan A. Scott ed. *Adversity and Grace: Studies in Recent American Literature.* Chicago University of Chicago Press, 1968.

Guttmann Allen, *The Jewish writer in America.* New York: Oxford University Press. 1968.

Hays. Peter L., *The Limping Hero: Grotesgues in Literature.* New York. New York University Press, 1971.

Hershinow, Sheldon J. *Bernard Malamud.* New York: Frederick Ungar Publishing Company, 1980.

Hicks, Granville, *Literary Horizons.* New York: New York University Press, 1970.

________________, "His Hopes On the Human Heart" in *Saturday Review,* Oct. 12, 1963.

Hoag, Gerald, "Malamud's Trial: The Fixer and the Critics" in *Western Humanist Review,* vol. XXIV, no.l. Winter, 1970.

Hyman, Stanley E, *Standards: A Chronicle of Books for Our Time.* New York: Horizon Press, 1970.

Klein, Marcus, *After Alienation: American Novels in Mid-Century.* Chicago: The University of Chicago Press. 1978.

Ratner, Marc, "Style and Humanity in Malamud's Fiction" in *Massachusetts Review, V.* 1964.

Richman, Sidney, *Bernard Malamud.* Boston: Twayne Publishers, A Division of G.K. Hall & Co, 1966.

Scholes, Robert, "Malamud's Latest Novel" in *Northwest Review,* vol. 8, no.2. Fall-Winter, 1966–1967.

________________, "Portrait of Artist as Escape-Goat" in Saturday Review, May 10, 1969.

Standley, Fred L., "Bernard Malamud, The Novel of Redemption" in *Southern Humanities Review.* 5, 1971.

Wershba, Joseph, "Close up, An Assessment" in *New York Post,* Sept, 14, 1958.

편저자 : 현광식

고려대 대학원 영문학과 박사과정수료
Georgetown Univ. 교환교수
문학박사(고려대 대학원)
서울대, 원광대 강사
한림대 영문과 교수
• 편저·역서
Mallamud의 『요술통』, 『점 원』

B. Malamud

The Assistant 점원

1판 1쇄 찍음 • 1988년 9월 20일
1판 3쇄 펴냄 • 2006년 3월 5일

편저자 • 현 광 식
발행인 • 정 현 걸
발 행 • 신 아 사
인 쇄 • 현대문화사

출판등록 • 1956년 1월 5일 (제9-52호)
서울특별시 은평구 녹번동 28-36번지 2F
전화 (02)382-6411 • 팩스 (02)382-6401
홈페이지 • www.shinasa.co.kr
E-mail • shinasa@chol.com

ISBN 89-8396-112-0

정가 12,000 원